Persons, Interests, and Justice

Persons, Interests, and Justice

Nils Holtug

OXFORD
UNIVERSITY PRESS

OXFORD
UNIVERSITY PRESS

Great Clarendon Street, Oxford OX2 6DP

Oxford University Press is a department of the University of Oxford.
It furthers the University's objective of excellence in research, scholarship,
and education by publishing worldwide in

Oxford New York

Auckland Cape Town Dar es Salaam Hong Kong Karachi
Kuala Lumpur Madrid Melbourne Mexico City Nairobi
New Delhi Shanghai Taipei Toronto

With offices in

Argentina Austria Brazil Chile Czech Republic France Greece
Guatemala Hungary Italy Japan Poland Portugal Singapore
South Korea Switzerland Thailand Turkey Ukraine Vietnam

Oxford is a registered trade mark of Oxford University Press
in the UK and in certain other countries

Published in the United States
by Oxford University Press Inc., New York

© Nils Holtug 2010

The moral rights of the author have been asserted
Database right Oxford University Press (maker)

First published 2010

British Library Cataloguing in Publication Data
Data available

Library of Congress Cataloging in Publication Data
Data available

Typeset by Laserwords Private Limited, Chennai, India
Printed in Great Britain
on acid free paper by
MPG Books Group, Bodmin and King's Lynn

ISBN 978–0–19–958017–0

10 9 8 7 6 5 4 3 2 1

Acknowledgements

Many people have generously and perceptively commented on parts of this book, including its chapters, articles from which some of the chapters (in part) derive, and presentations. Thus, I would like to thank Richard Arneson, Gustav Arrhenius, Linda Barclay, Nick Bostrom, John Broome, Krister Bykvist, Finn Collin, Roger Crisp, Jan Faye, Marc Fleurbaey, Claus Hansen, David Heyd, Iwao Hirose, Kent Hurtig, Karsten Klint Jensen, Klemens Kappel, Kasper Lippert-Rasmussen, Sune Lægaard, Andrew Mason, Dennis McKerlie, Jeff McMahan, Jonas Olson, Michael Otsuka, Ingmar Persson, Thomas Petersen, Robert Pulvertaft, Wlodek Rabinowicz, Melinda Roberts, David Rodin, Jesper Ryberg, Peter Sandøe, Torbjörn Tännsjö, Larry Temkin, Bertil Tungodden, Peter Vallentyne, Andrew Williams and two anonymous readers for Oxford University Press.

As will transpire, several of the themes and theories I take up in the book have originally been discussed and developed by Derek Parfit or, in some cases, at least been brought to the forefront of contemporary moral and political philosophy by him. Thus, in my discussion of what matters in survival, prioritarianism, and population ethics I have an intellectual debt to Parfit. To my mind, his discussion of these issues is still second to none. This, however, does not mean that I always find myself in agreement with him on these matters and he would be sceptical of some of the views I defend in my discussions thereof.

Parts of the book have been presented at conferences, workshops and lectures and I would like to thank participants at the Copenhagen-Oxford Summit on Ethics, University of Oxford, 1999, the 6th International Conference of the Society for Utilitarian Studies, North Carolina, 1999, the Copenhagen-Lund Workshop on Moral Philosophy, Copenhagen, 2001, the Annual Meeting of the Danish Society for Philosophy, Roskilde University Center, 2002, the 4th European Congress for Analytic Philosophy, Lund University, 2002, the 25th International Wittgenstein Symposium, Kirchberg am Wechsel, 2002, the 7th International Conference of the International Society for Utilitarian Studies, Lisbon, 2003, the International Conference on Egalitarianism, University of Copenhagen, 2004, the Conference on Equality and the Welfare State, University of Århus, 2004, the Scandinavia-Oxford Ethics Summit, University of Oxford, 2005, and the Oxford Moral Philosophy Seminar, University of

Oxford, 2006. Furthermore, I am grateful to Peter Momtchiloff and Catherine Berry at Oxford University Press.

Some of the chapters contain material that has previously been published in books and journals. Thus, Chapters 2–4 include most of my 'Personal Identity, Self-interest and Preferences', in L.V. Siegal (ed.), *Philosophy and Ethics* (Nova Science Publishers, 2007), 57–112. Chapter 3 includes parts of my 'Who Cares About Identity?', in M. A. Roberts and D. T. Wasserman (eds), *Harming Future Persons: Ethics, Genetics and the Nonidentity Problem* (Springer, 2009). Chapter 4 includes parts of my 'The Repugnant Conclusion about Self-interest', *Danish Yearbook of Philosophy*, 36 (Museum Tusculanum Press, 2001): 49–67. Chapter 5 includes most of my 'On the Value of Coming into Existence', *Journal of Ethics*, 5/4 (Kluwer Academic Publishers, 2001): 361–84. Chapter 6 includes parts of my 'Welfarism—the Very Idea', *Utilitas*, 15/2 (Edinburgh University Press, 2003): 151–74. Chapter 7 includes parts of my 'Good for Whom?', *Theoria*, 69/1–2 (Thales, 2003): 4–20, most of my 'Equality, Priority and Levelling Down', in A. G. Parkis (ed.), *Contemporary Ethical Issues* (Nova Publishers, 2005), 97–112, and parts of my 'A Note on Conditional Egalitarianism', *Economics and Philosophy*, 23/1 (Cambridge University Press, 2007): 45–63. Chapter 8 includes most of my 'Prioritarianism', in N. Holtug and K. Lippert-Rasmussen (eds), *Egalitarianism: New Essays on the Nature and Value of Equality* (Clarendon Press, 2006), 125–56, and some of my 'Equality for Animals', in J. Ryberg, T. Petersen and C. Wolf (eds), *New Waves in Applied Ethics* (Palgrave Macmillan, 2007), 1–24. Chapter 9 includes most of my 'Person-affecting Moralities', in J. Ryberg and T. Tännsjö (eds), *The Repugnant Conclusion. Essays on Population Ethics* (Kluwer Academic Publishers, 2004), 129–61, and some of my 'Utility, Priority and Possible People', *Utilitas*, 11/1 (Edinburgh University Press, 1999): 16–36. I am grateful to the editors and publishers concerned for permission to use this material.

Contents

1

Introduction

1.1 Self-interest, Morality, and Justice

If one were trying to identify a universally accepted doctrine in moral philosophy, the following would be a good candidate: self-interest matters morally. To say that something is in an individual's self-interest is, roughly speaking, to say that it will make her life better, that is, it will contribute to her welfare. At least, this is the meaning of 'self-interest' employed in this book. And surely it would be implausible to suggest that, morally speaking, welfare is of no significance whatsoever.

While the claim that self-interest matters morally may be more or less uncontroversial, the claim that welfare is a concern for the particular part of morality known as 'distributive justice' is not. The theories of justice discussed in this book all assume that welfare, or at least something close to it, is the 'currency' of justice. That is, they assume that welfare is the unit, the distribution of which we should ultimately be concerned about. Although this is a controversial claim, I also believe that it is a plausible one.

This book, then, is about self-interest and its importance in regard to morality and, more specifically, distributive justice. What is the nature of self-interest and what does justice require when the self-interests of different individuals conflict? I address the first of these two questions in Part I of the book (Chapters 2–5). In Part II (Chapters 6–10), I then turn to justice. As we shall see, the theory about self-interest developed in Part I has important implications for the scope, shape, and nature of our theory of justice.

More specifically, in the first part of the book (on prudence), a variety of questions are considered. Do self-interests depend on preferences and if so, how? Do self-interests depend on personal identity? Can we benefit possible future individuals by bringing them into existence, such that it may be in their self-interest to come to exist? The answers provided to each of these questions has consequences for how we answer various questions in the sphere of justice.

Among the questions considered in the second part (on justice) are: what is welfarism? Does (welfare) equality have intrinsic value? Should we give priority to the welfare of the worse off? What are our moral obligations to possible future individuals? Does distributive justice depend on personal identity? And what do our answers to these questions imply with respect to various issues in applied ethics, such as the badness of death, abortion, and population policy?

These questions may seem to point in many different directions, but as noted above, there is a particular unifying theme underlying the whole endeavour, namely the importance of self-interest in regards to morality and justice. In particular, I am concerned with the idea that morality—or, more precisely, axiology—ought to take a person-affecting form. The idea that axiology should take a person-affecting form consists in thinking that the moral value of outcomes should be explained in terms of what is good and bad (or better and worse) for individuals. In the first part of the book, I address the issue of what self-interest consists of (and so the nature of that which, according to the person-affecting idea, moral value should be explained in terms of). And in the second part of the book, I develop a particular version of the person-affecting idea and consider its implications for various related moral issues, including welfarism, justice, population ethics, and abortion. As it turns out, the person-affecting idea has a number of interesting and interrelated implications with respect to these issues.

I should stress at the outset that while my focus is on self-interest and the person-affecting idea, I do not attempt to provide a full defence of person-affecting axiological welfarism. Thus, I do not systematically consider the plausibility of various moral ideals that are incompatible with this welfarist doctrine, although I do make some general remarks that suggest we should doubt most of them. Strictly speaking, the theory of justice I develop is not even compatible with welfarism itself, although it is quite close to this nevertheless (it is compatible with what I call 'self-interestism'). More precisely, I claim that outcome value is a function not just of welfare, but also of the physical and psychological relations that unite an individual's consciousness over time. Moreover, even if we wanted to include yet further factors and values in our axiology, the theories I develop here may be relevant in that they may provide *part* of the axiological picture, even if they do not provide the whole picture.

1.2 A More Detailed Overview of the Book

In this first chapter, I provide an overview of the book. I also provide an account of the methodology I employ. More precisely, I show that the types of arguments I use are compatible with a wide variety of more particular epistemic and ontological views about ethics.

In Chapter 2, I start by specifying what I mean, exactly, by 'self-interest'. I then consider various views about what constitutes self-interest. According to what I call the 'Identity View', in order for an individual to have a present self-interest in a future benefit, this individual need only be numerically identical to the future beneficiary. I lay out what I consider to be the main strengths and weaknesses of this view.

Then I consider further conditions that may be imposed on self-interests. In particular, I examine the notion that in order for an individual to have a present self-interest in a future benefit, she must have an appropriate kind of preference with respect to this benefit, such as a present preference, an actual preference, or a necessary preference. As I point out, the reason for requiring such preferences to obtain can—but need not—be that they are necessary in order for the benefit to obtain.

I also consider the view that *particular* kinds of self-interests presuppose such preferences. For instance, I describe a view that has become quite popular, namely that an individual only can have a present self-interest in survival if she presently prefers her own continued existence. Finally, I consider the view that although present self-interests do not presuppose any particular kinds of preferences for the future, they do presuppose that their bearers presently possess consciousness. In the end, I argue that we should not accept any of these alternatives to the Identity View.

In Chapter 3, I turn to the importance of personal identity for self-interests. According to the Identity View, in order for an individual to have a self-interest in a future benefit, she must be identical to the beneficiary. Therefore, the exact implications of the Identity View depend on the particular theory of personal identity assumed. However, I argue that identity is only seen as a plausible condition for self-interests if we assume that identity is what matters in survival; that is, if we assume identity is what gives each of us the basis for special concern for our (own) future. If we do not make this assumption, the Identity View will not have the prudential significance it usually is thought to have and which generates our concern with self-interests in the first place.

Having made this point, I follow Parfit (1984: part 3) in arguing that identity is in fact not what matters in survival. I outline Parfit's argument and then consider and reject a number of objections that have been made to it. I also emphasize that since identity is not what matters, we should reject the Identity View.

In Chapter 4, I then turn to the issue of what *does* matter in survival. I develop a test for assessing our beliefs about what matters and argue that what matters is Relation M: roughly, the continuous physical realization of (appropriate) psychology. In addition, I claim that our theory about self-interest should have Relation M—rather than identity—as its focus. Furthermore, I argue that since what matters is Relation M, and this relation can have different strengths, the value of future benefits should be discounted to the extent that this relation obtains to a reduced degree.

I thus arrive at the Prudential View, according to which a person has a present self-interest in a future benefit if, and only if, she stands in a relation of continuous physical realization of (appropriate) psychology to the beneficiary, where the strength of the self-interest depends both on the size of the benefit and on the strength of this relation.

I also consider a number of objections to this view, including what I call the 'Repugnant Conclusion about Self-interest'. According to this conclusion, it is in a person's present self-interest to die in order to ensure the existence of a number of continuers to whom she stands in the relation that prudentially matters, if only these individuals realize more discounted benefits than she herself would have realized in her future, had she survived. I argue that, on further reflection, this conclusion may in fact be plausible.

In Chapter 5, I address a topic that is of interest in its own right and is furthermore very important for population ethics. This is the issue of whether it can benefit (or harm) an individual to come into existence. If coming into existence can benefit (or harm) an individual, then it would seem that it could be in our self-interest to do so.

I first outline an argument for the Value of Existence View—the view that coming into existence can benefit (or harm). This argument relies on the relational claim that existence can be better (or worse) for an individual than never existing. I then defend the Value of Existence View against a number of objections, including the claim that (a) possible future individuals cannot be identified, and (b) existence cannot be better (or worse) for an individual than never existing, because that would imply that never existing can be worse (or better) than existing.

In Chapter 6, I turn to the importance of self-interest for morality and justice. More precisely, I turn to axiology or, as I mostly call it, 'theories of the moral value of outcomes'. According to my favoured theory about self-interest, the Prudential View, self-interests are functions of both welfare and Relation M. However, in order not to introduce too many complicating factors all at once, I postpone my discussion of the importance of Relation M for outcome value until Chapter 10. Having set aside the issue of Relation M, I develop an account of person-affecting welfarism, according to which outcome value is an increasing person-affecting function only of individual welfare. This function is person-affecting in the sense that, of two outcomes, one can be better (or worse) than the other, only if there is someone for whom it is better (or worse), or someone for whom the other outcome is worse (or better).

I then begin my assessment of various welfarist theories of distributive justice, including (welfare-based versions of) egalitarianism, prioritarianism, sufficientarianism, and leximin. First, in Chapter 7, I provide a critical discussion of (welfare) egalitarianism. I outline what I take to be the core of the egalitarian position. Minimally, to qualify as a (welfare) egalitarian, one must claim that an outcome in which everyone has an equal share of welfare is in one respect intrinsically (non-instrumentally) better than an outcome in which individuals have unequal shares. Any principle that satisfies this condition satisfies what I call the 'Egalitarian Relational Claim'. Furthermore, I clarify egalitarianism in various other respects.

Having thus clarified egalitarianism, I point out that since egalitarianism satisfies the Egalitarian Relational Claim, it invites the Levelling Down Objection. According to the Levelling Down Objection, egalitarianism implausibly implies that we can improve an outcome in at least one respect, by making some individuals worse off and none better off. I consider various replies egalitarians might (and have) come up with, including the claim that this objection relies on an implausible person-affecting account of outcome value. However, relying on my account of person-affecting welfarism, I argue that there is in fact a plausible person-affecting principle that nicely explains why we cannot improve an outcome—in even one respect—by levelling down.

In Chapter 8, I discuss what I consider to be a more promising welfarist theory of outcome value, namely prioritarianism. According to prioritarianism, outcome value is an additive function of weighted individual welfare, where increases in welfare are weighted such that they gain a greater moral value, the worse off the individual is to whom they accrue. This view differs from egalitarianism in that it does not take equality to have intrinsic value. I address some objections to prioritarianism that have been made recently, including the claim that (a) the Levelling Down Objection does not serve to distinguish prioritarianism from egalitarianism, (b) prioritarianism is itself vulnerable to the person-affecting idea that motivates the Levelling Down Objection, (c) prioritarianism fails to account for some firmly held intuitions about relational justice, and (d) prioritarianism does not appropriately reflect the virtue on which it is based, namely that of compassion. I argue that none of these objections is convincing and that prioritarianism remains a plausible theory of justice.

In Chapter 9, I consider the implications of prioritarianism for population ethics. I point out that, in my person-affecting approach to welfarism, the welfare contained in an individual's life contributes to the value of an outcome in which this individual comes into existence, only if, by coming into existence, this individual can benefit (or be harmed). And since I argue (in Chapter 5) that it can in fact benefit (or harm) an individual to come into existence, it would seem that the existence of extra individuals may contribute to outcome value.

However, if we allow prioritarianism to apply to possible future individuals, this principle implies the Repugnant Conclusion, according to which a world populated by individuals, every one of whom has a life barely worth living, would be better than a world populated by ten billion individuals, all of whom have very worthwhile lives—as long as the former population is sufficiently large. In fact, it even implies what I call the 'Super-repugnant Conclusion', according to which the former outcome can be better even if it contains a *lower* sum of welfare than does the latter. I therefore discuss various ways in which a person-affecting prioritarian may attempt to avoid these conclusions.

First, I consider the possibility of replacing the additive function in prioritarianism with a non-additive function. I then consider the possibility of modifying my favoured person-affecting approach by restricting its scope to actual, necessary, or some other modal class of individuals. Finally, I consider the possibility of combining prioritarianism and a non-prioritarian distributive principle. However, as I argue, none of these 'solutions' gives rise to a plausible account of population ethics. In fact, they all fare at least as badly as my favoured person-affecting prioritarian approach. In light of this, I reconsider the repugnance of the Repugnant and the Super-repugnant Conclusion towards the end of the chapter. I suggest that while there are theoretical reasons for accepting these conclusions, they are nevertheless stubbornly counterintuitive. This means that I find myself unable to make a firm commitment to any particular distributive principle in the sphere of populations ethics, but I list what seem to me to be the three main options and explain how they are compatible with prioritarianism.

In Chapter 10, I return to the point that self-interest is a function not just of welfare but also of Relation M. More precisely, I consider its importance for the theory of distributive justice I developed and endorsed in Chapters 8 and 9. I first argue that since Relation M, rather than identity, is what prudentially matters, we should expand the scope of morality. Our moral principles, including prioritarianism, apply even to conflicts of interest *within* a particular life. I then address the claim that if identity is not what matters, we should give less weight to our distribution-sensitive principles, including prioritarianism. I argue that the view that Relation M is what matters is quite compatible with distribution-sensitivity, and therefore is compatible with the prioritarian principle.

I also consider what I call the 'Compensation Argument' for a 'whole lives' approach to distributive justice. According to the Compensation Argument, it is possible for an individual to be compensated for her low welfare at one time by her high welfare at another time. Therefore, what matters for distributive justice is her welfare over her life taken as a whole. Thus, according to Whole Lives Prioritarianism, individuals who are worse off over their lives are entitled to priority. However, I suggest that if we accept the Prudential View, for which I have argued, what the Compensation Argument proposes is not Whole Lives Prioritarianism, but what I call 'Prudential Prioritarianism'. According to Prudential Prioritarianism, the weaker S's self-interest at t in the benefits that occur in the M-relation realized by S (and appropriate predecessors and continuers), the greater the value of a further benefit to S at t and/or an increase in the strength of the M-relation that obtains between S at t and at other times at which positive welfare accrues to S (and appropriate predecessors and continuers), and/or a reduction in the strength of the M-relation that obtains between S at t and at other times at which negative welfare accrues to S (and appropriate predecessors and continuers).

Strictly speaking, Prudential Prioritarianism is not a welfarist theory and it contradicts the person-affecting approach I (provisionally) endorsed in the early chapters. Nevertheless, it is obviously closely related to welfarist theories. More importantly, I develop a revised person-affecting principle that is compatible with Prudential Prioritarianism and which simultaneously explains what is wrong with egalitarianism. Thus, the move from prioritarianism to Prudential Prioritarianism does not compromise my case against egalitarian theories. I also briefly consider the implications of Prudential Prioritarianism for some issues in applied ethics, including the issue of which deaths we have most reason to prevent, and argue that my account thereof is more plausible than is Jeff McMahan's, in some ways, similar account of the ethics of killing (2002).

1.3 Methodology

I now want to comment briefly on the methodology I use in this book. My main aim is not to defend any particular position in metaethics, but rather to point out that my methodology is compatible with a wide variety of such positions. Since my methodology does not differ substantially from that employed by most other contemporary moral and political philosophers in the Anglo-American tradition, I believe that I can afford to be brief. This is not to say, of course, that the methodology employed is uncontroversial, nor that it does not stand in need of further support. Very little is uncontroversial in philosophy and moral methodology is no exception.

I sometimes use *conceptual analysis* to elucidate certain concepts; for instance, the concept of 'welfarism'. This is because different conceptions of welfarism are often conflated and so we need to consider which, if any, is most appropriate (given our particular purposes).[1]

In many instances, I point out that a certain set of judgements is *inconsistent*, so that we cannot hold the entire set. This requirement, according to which sets of moral judgements need to be consistent, is hardly very controversial. Even moral anti-realists, such as Simon Blackburn (1984), Richard Hare (1981), and Crispin Wright (1988), accept it.

I also consider possible rationales for some of the theories I discuss. A rationale may support the moral relevance of a certain distinction by providing an independent (or partly independent) justification for its relevance. Thus, insofar as we are able to provide such a rationale, we can avoid the appeal to what Shelly Kagan has referred to as 'dangling distinctions' (1989: 14). I believe that the degree to which a plausible rationale explains the moral relevance of a certain distinction on which a theory relies, strengthens the case for the theory. But I also believe that even in cases in which we cannot provide such an independent rationale, we may have *some* reason to accept the theory; for instance, because it nicely explains our moral intuitions about particular cases (see below).

Finally, then, I appeal to *moral intuitions* to support (or question) certain claims and theories. This is clearly the most controversial element in my methodology. Thus, several prominent philosophers have argued that moral intuitions cannot be used to support or criticize any moral theory, unless we have independent reason to believe that these intuitions are (likely to be) true or credible (Brandt 1979: 20; Hare 1981: 12; Singer 1974). However, I do not share this scepticism about the justificatory force of moral intuitions. As Saul Kripke (1980: 42) once suggested, 'some philosophers think that something's having intuitive content is very inconclusive evidence in favor of it. I think it is very heavy evidence in favor of anything, myself. I don't really know, in a way, what more conclusive evidence one can have for anything, ultimately

---

[1] For a good defence of conceptual analysis, in ethics as well as in other areas of philosophy, see Jackson (1998).

speaking'. In any case, I find it difficult to believe that substantial moral views can be justified independently of moral intuitions.[2]

Although I cannot provide an adequate defence of the importance of moral intuitions for ethical theory here, I can at least point out that the role I assign to them is compatible with a number of different epistemic and ontological views about ethics. Again, the point is simply that my use of moral intuitions does not presuppose a *particular* stance in metaethics, but is compatible with a range of rather different views.

Often, the claim that moral intuitions have some kind of epistemic weight is associated with coherentist views of justification and, in particular, with Rawls's theory of reflective equilibrium (1971: 17–22, 46–53; see also Brink 1989: ch. 5; Daniels 1979; Tersman 1993). According to Rawls's theory, a particular (set of) principle(s) is justified insofar as it coheres with our considered moral judgements and (possibly) with our background theories (for instance, with our physical, sociological, psychological, and metaphysical theories). The usual criteria for coherence apply here, such as consistency, comprehensiveness, and explanatory power.

Importantly, coherence theories about moral justification are compatible with a number of different accounts of moral ontology. Thus, they may be combined with both reductive and non-reductive moral realisms. However, they may also be construed as anti-realist constructivist doctrines, according to which coherence provides a criterion not only of moral justification, but also of moral truth (or something very like it).

The methodology I use can be fitted easily into a coherentist framework. Obviously, all of the epistemic desiderata I listed above increase coherence. Thus, a moral theory gains coherence as it becomes more consistent, is supported by a rationale, and has intuitively plausible implications. Furthermore, as I pointed out above, support from background theories is an epistemic desideratum in the theory of reflective equilibrium, and in various places I invoke such background theories to support some of my conclusions. For example, my views about personal identity and what matters in survival play a crucial role in the defence of both my favoured theory about self-interest and distributive justice.

While appeals to moral intuitions are often associated with coherentist theories of justification, they play no less of a role in foundationalist theories. According to such theories, moral justification ultimately rests on self-evident moral truths, and I suggest that beliefs in such truths can be described as moral

---

[2] Some, I suspect, will draw the opposite conclusion. They will claim that if substantial moral views cannot be justified independently of moral intuitions, they cannot be justified at all.

intuitions (Audi 1996). Of course, different foundationalists may have different ideas about the sort of moral intuitions that may qualify as candidates for being self-evident moral truths and so there is no guarantee that the moral intuitions I appeal to will qualify in this respect. On the other hand, there is nothing in foundationalism as such that would seem to rule out that they thus qualify.

Furthermore, foundationalists stress the importance of consistency in moral theory and they may very well also stress the importance of providing a rationale for the distinctions one takes to carry moral significance. For all I know, such a rationale may itself qualify as a self-evident moral truth. Note also that, like coherentism, foundationalism is compatible with various moral ontologies.

Of course, some moral theorists hold that theories of justification such as coherentism and foundationalism are too ambitious for the moral 'realm'. That is, they suggest that the sort of justification that is possible in ethics is less robust than what coherentists and foundationalists would have us believe. But even if consistency is all there is to moral justification, appeals to moral intuitions may have a role to play. This is simply because sets of intuitions can be inconsistent. Therefore, when I appeal to a moral intuition to criticize a certain theory, insofar as the reader holds both the theory and the intuition, she will have reason to abandon (at least) one of them.

As I have noted, my purpose in this section has primarily been to elucidate my (by no means original) methodology, and to point out how it is in fact compatible with a number of different epistemic and ontological views about ethics.

1.4 Thought Experiments

In this section and the next, I want to address a few worries some readers may have about my methodology that are less general in nature. Some philosophers, who *in general* are not sceptical about the epistemic worth of moral intuitions, are nevertheless sceptical about the worth of particular intuitions, namely those that rely on (perhaps far-fetched) thought experiments. Let me illustrate this point by giving you an example of a particular thought experiment that I shall employ.

Imagine that you are teletransported to Mars. A computer here on earth records the exact states of all your cells and simultaneously destroys your brain and body. It then transmits the information to another computer on Mars that creates a new brain and body exactly like yours.[3] Now, the question is

---

[3] This case is discussed extensively in Parfit (1984: part 3).

whether you stand in the relation that matters to your replica on Mars. To clarify your views on this, you may consider a so-called pain-avoidance test. Would you be willing to go through a significant amount of pain, just before you are teletransported, if it is the only way of preventing your replica on Mars from suffering a significantly greater amount of pain immediately after the reconstruction takes place? When considering this question, you should set aside any moral views that you may have; for instance, to the effect that it is better if there is less suffering in the universe. Rather, you should be motivated only by what you consider to be in your own self-interest.

If you would be willing to endure the early lesser pain, this may be taken as evidence that you believe that the relation that matters does obtain between you and your replica. Perhaps, then, you believe that what matters is that your present psychology is continuously realized into the future, as it would be by your replica on Mars.

But presumably, like most others, you would not be willing to endure the early pain. This is evidence to the effect that you do not believe that the relation that matters obtains. Nevertheless, it is not decisive evidence. Suppose that when reflecting on what it is that now gives you a reason to care about yourself tomorrow, you cannot find any plausible features that are not also present in your relation to your replica on Mars. You may then become convinced that, despite your initial hesitation, you really should accept the early lesser pain. After all, you have the same reason to care about your replica as you do to care about yourself from one day to the next. And presumably, you would accept a lesser pain today if this were the only way of avoiding a significantly greater amount of pain tomorrow.[4]

As I said, some philosophers are rather sceptical when it comes to the use of thought experiments that involve teletransportation and the like in philosophy (Wilkes 1988: ch. 1). They seem to believe that one cannot have confidence in responses to events that take place in worlds that are very different from our actual world. This is because these responses reflect people's beliefs about the world as it is. So if, for instance, some of our actual scientific beliefs turn out to be false in possible worlds in which teletransportation takes place, we will be led astray if we rely on our responses to teletransportation, at least

---

[4] Similar tests are often employed to determine what people believe about personal identity. If, for instance, you would be willing to go through the early pain, this is taken as evidence that you believe that your replica is not only an exact copy of you, it *is* you. But actually, such tests are better suited to reveal our views on what matters than to reveal our views on identity (Unger 1990: 230). If you would be willing to endure the early pain, this indicates that you take the sort of special interest in what happens to your replica that you usually take in what happens to you. That is, you are prudentially concerned about your replica. We can only interpret this as evidence that your replica is identical to you if we have independent reasons to believe that identity is what matters.

insofar as we have these responses (in part) because we have these beliefs, or would have other responses if we had true scientific beliefs about these possible worlds.

However, I do not think that thought experiments should be avoided for this reason. First, even if some beliefs turn out to be false in the possible world we imagine, presumably, very often, they will be irrelevant concerning our responses. Suppose, for instance, that one of your beliefs about how computers process information must be false in order for teletransportation to be possible. It seems very improbable that this belief is at all relevant for your attitude to the case.[5]

Second, the thought experiment I rely on most heavily in my discussion of what matters in survival is not likely to require that we give up any fundamental beliefs. This experiment involves taking out a person's cerebral hemispheres and inserting one into each of two other people's (appropriately emptied) skulls, resulting in the existence of two people who are psychologically very similar to the brain donor. While it may remain practically impossible for doctors to perform such a brain division, the thought experiment does not seem to require that we imagine away any facts that are likely to be considered important. Of course, it could turn out that even this relatively innocent experiment trades too heavily on insufficient beliefs. But what this shows is merely that the insights we gain from such experiments are fallible, which is something we should acknowledge anyway.

Third, thought experiments are very useful tools when trying to come up with a plausible view on what matters in survival, because, in almost all actual cases, the competing views are extensionally equivalent—they generate the same judgements. In order to uncover the strengths and weaknesses of these views, we must carefully devise fictional cases in which their judgements come apart. So it would be a severe methodological blow if we could not rely on such cases.

1.5 Contrast Arguments and Transitivity

A further word of caution is also in order. In my discussion, I employ what Shelly Kagan (1988) calls contrast arguments. Such arguments consist in comparing two cases that differ only regarding one factor. If it turns out

---

[5] Although, as Quine has pointed out, a revision of a belief may always cause revisions of other beliefs, even ones that are located far from it in our belief-system. See Quine (1961a).

that the two cases diverge evaluatively, this difference is attributed to the varying factor. So, to exemplify again from my discussion of what matters in survival, I shall consider asymmetrical cases of brain division; that is, cases in which two persons each receive a cerebral hemisphere from a donor, where these two hemispheres do not preserve the donor's psychology to the same degree. So, for example, perhaps one person receives a hemisphere that carries the donor's beliefs, preferences, memories, and so on, and the other receives a hemisphere that carries no such psychological traits, but does carry the *ability* to think and prefer. If, from the original person's point of view, the former person matters more than does the latter person, I shall take this as evidence that the preservation of beliefs, preferences, memories, and the like, matters.

However, as Kagan points out, it does not follow from the claim that even though such factors have a particular evaluative significance in some cases, they have this significance in all cases. What this means is that I cannot be said to have argued that some factor generally matters just because I have argued that it matters in a (specific) case of asymmetrical brain division. However, I believe that if I can argue that it matters in such a case, I have provided a presumption in favour of the general significance of the factor. This presumption is of course fallible, but if someone holds that, in other cases, the factor does not matter, they will have to point out why this factor does not always have the significance it sometimes has.

There is also another methodological point I need to make. In various arguments, I rely on the idea that 'betterness' is a transitive relation. More precisely, I rely on the assumption that both 'x is at least as good as y' and 'x is better than y' are transitive. Thus, if A is at least as good as (better than) B, and B is at least as good as (better than) C, then it follows that A is at least as good as (better than) C. This is true as a matter of semantics. For example, take any monadic predicate, such as 'pollute' or 'good'. Out of these, we can form dyadic predicates, or relations —here, 'pollutes more than' or 'is better than'. These dyadic relations are comparatives and as a matter of *semantics*, comparatives are transitive.

However, as John Broome points out, there is not much argument available to support these semantic claims directly (2004: 51). And indeed, these claims have been challenged (Rachels 1998; 2001: 217–19; Temkin 1987; 1996). Nevertheless, like most others in the field, I shall simply take transitivity for granted.[6]

---

[6] But for a defence of transitivity, albeit an 'indirect' defence, see Broome (2004: 50–63).

Like 'x is at least as good as y' and 'x is better than y', I shall also assume the transitivity of 'x is better than y with respect to z' and 'S has a stronger self-interest in x than in y'. Indeed, I also consider the transitivity of these relations a matter of semantics.

This completes my account of moral methodology.

I

Prudence

2

Self-interest

2.1 Self-interest and Morality

The concept of 'self-interest' is of fundamental importance in value theory. It is the cornerstone of theories on prudential value, and it is no less important in morality. In order for a person to live a prudentially good life—that is, a life in which she enjoys a high level of welfare—she must live her life in accordance with what is in her self-interest. And in order for a person to live a morally good life, presumably she must, to some extent, further or at least respect the self-interests of others.

A few examples may illustrate these points. In order to determine why and to what extent death is bad for a person, we need a theory about self-interest. Thus, I shall suggest that death is bad because—and to the extent that—it is in a person's self-interest to survive. Furthermore, a theory about self-interest is also needed to determine the moral status of abortion. Obviously, we need such a theory to determine whether abortion is contrary to the interests of a foetus.

While there may be more to morality than promoting or respecting the self-interests of individuals, surely this is an important part. Rawls (1971: 30) suggests that a moral theory which does not take consequences into account would be crazy. And, we might add, so would a theory that does not take people's self-interests into account.

Nevertheless, self-interest and morality are separate spheres of normativity (Crisp 2006; Nagel 1991; Parfit 1984; Persson 2006; Scheffler 1982a; Sidgwick 1907). To see this, we need only reflect on a case in which a person sacrifices himself for a noble or worthy cause; for example, by throwing himself on a hand grenade and thereby saving the lives of five fellow soldiers. While a morally worthy act, clearly it involves a loss from his particular point of view—indeed, this is why we consider his act heroic. And to fully account for the case we need to invoke both kinds of perspective.

Much of the time, our perspective on the world is that of our own self-interest. We are then concerned with what will make our own lives go well rather than with how we may contribute to other people's lives. Furthermore, while we have deep concerns for others, our concern for ourselves looms large in our overall pattern of concerns. Suppose. for instance, that someone informs you that tomorrow a person is going to be horribly tortured. Presumably, this will sadden you. But now suppose she informs you that that person is *you*. Most likely, this will *terrify* you, and you will now be much more motivated to try to prevent the torture. It matters that the torture is *yours* and the perspective from which this matters is that of your own self-interest.

However, this is not our only normative perspective. Often, we adopt a more impartial perspective on the world, according to which our own self-interest matters no more than the self-interests of others. Perhaps this is the perspective with which we engage when we consider the grossly unequal global distribution of resources unfair, or worry about how global warming will affect future generations.

One aspect of morality is that we must settle the relative weight of these two perspectives. This can be done in various ways, including that of arguing that one perspective simply crowds out the other. Suppose, for simplicity, we claim that what is in an individual's self-interest is to achieve the highest possible sum of welfare in his or her life. Total act–utilitarianism can then be described as the view that each agent should always perform the act, among those available to her, that brings about the highest sum of fulfilled self-interests in the universe. This view implies that the second, impartial perspective exhausts the moral sphere.

At the other end of the moral spectrum, ethical egoism can be described as the view that each agent should always act in accordance with his or her own self-interest. This view comes close to letting the perspective of self-interest or prudence exhaust the moral sphere, although it does not quite do so. There is after all a step from simply being concerned with one's own self-interest to claiming that *each* agent should (only) further his or her self-interest. And this further step is necessary in order to satisfy the requirement of universalizability, which may be considered a minimal requirement for qualifying as a moral view (Hare 1963: 30).

Many moral theorists, however, try to accommodate *both* these perspectives in the moral sphere, emphasizing that each plays an important role in structuring the way we think about the world (Nagel 1991: ch. 2; Scheffler 1982a: ch. 3). There are various ways in which this can be done, including that of combining an impartial theory of outcome value and an (agent-relative) option to, within limits, let one's own self-interests (and perhaps other personal commitments) weigh more than the self-interests (and other commitments) of others.

All the particular accounts of justice I consider in Part II of the book exemplify a completely impartial approach.[1] So why spend time in the first part developing a theory about self-interest? First, as I pointed out in connection with the case of the soldier who throws himself on a hand grenade, we need an account not just of morality but also of self-interest. Second, my concern in Part II is with the distribution of self-interest fulfilment and this requires an account of what self-interest is. As it turns out, my theory about self-interest has important implications for the shape I believe our theory of justice should take. Third, although I do not have the inclination to do so myself, it is in principle possible to combine the theory of justice I develop and (agent-relative) options to give priority to one's own self-interests, since my theory of justice is an account of outcome value only. (I briefly return to this possibility in Chapter 6, Section 6.5.)

My aim in this section has simply been to distinguish self-interest and morality and to suggest why we need an account of both of these normative spheres. When giving such accounts, we may invoke our views about self-interest and morality. And as the case of the soldier who throws himself on the hand grenade brings out, most of us do indeed have views about both self-interest and morality. However, we need (and should) not simply take these views at face value. They may harbour inconsistencies, lack foundation, or lack intuitive support once we work out their wider implications. In short, we should expose our views to the sort of critical thinking I outlined in Chapter 1 when clarifying my methodology, and this is of course what the book is all about.

2.2 On What Self-interest Is

I need to begin by clarifying what, more precisely, I mean by 'self-interest'. Having done so, I critically examine a number of theories about the nature of self-interest—about what self-interest consists of—in the rest of the chapter. But first, to focus my discussion, I need to clarify the concept.

Values

I take theories about self-interest to be theories about (self-interested) value. If someone has a self-interest in something, it is because this something is *valuable*

---

[1] I elaborate further on the kind(s) of impartiality to which my discussion of justice conforms in Chapter 6 (Section 6.6).

for her. In other words, theories about self-interest are theories about what is *good* for people or, more generally, for beings for whom life may go better or worse.

Such theories should not be confused with what Parfit calls the Self-interest Theory, which is a theory about rationality. According to this theory, each person has one ultimate rational aim, namely that his life go as well as possible (1984: 4). Theories about self-interest specify what is involved in life going well, but they do not assign aims to persons. This, of course, is quite compatible with theories about self-interest playing an essential role in theories of rationality, as they would if we were to specify more fully the aim assigned to each of us by the Self-interest Theory.

While values and reasons are obviously related in some way and this relation has received a great deal of attention in recent moral philosophy (Scanlon 1998: ch. 1–2), I shall not attempt to clarify this relation here. Since theories about self-interest are theories about self-interested value, they should be assessed on the basis of how plausible an account they give us of what is *good* for people. Just as the axiological theories of justice I discuss in Part II should be assessed on the basis of how plausibly they account for (moral) outcome value. However, I *shall* make the minimal assumption that if an individual has a self-interest in something, then she has a reason to bring it about, everything else being equal. This means that we may in part assess theories about self-interest in terms of the reasons with which they provide us.

I should emphasize that the self-interests I am concerned with are *intrinsic* (or non-instrumental) self-interests (although, on a few occasions, I do have something to say about self-interests that are not intrinsic). To clarify, an intrinsic self-interest in x is a self-interest in x for its own sake, and not because x is a means to some further goal or value.

Objects

The object of a self-interest, then, is a value (or more precisely, to avoid confusion, a *token* of a value). For instance, I have a self-interest in enjoying myself. This value must be linked to me in the right sort of way. As the name suggests, a self-interest is an interest an individual has regarding her *own* life. It pertains to what will make life (or a slice of life) better for *her*, and not (except maybe indirectly) better for others. Or rather, this is an assumption about self-interest that I shall stick with for now. In Chapters 3 and 4, I argue that due to some metaphysical issues concerning personal identity, a person's self-interest may cover not just her own life, but also the lives of some particularly intimate continuers of hers.

Since my self-interests are interests regarding my own life, not all my interests need be self-interests. I may prefer that the rainforests survive, even though, if they do, this will not benefit me in any way (for instance, because it is not a self-regarding preference, or because I will never experience that it is satisfied). If so, then the value of having the rainforests survive does not give rise to a self-interest.

The objects of self-interests are the objects that make our lives better (or worse) and therefore I call these objects 'benefits' (or 'harms'). Thus, benefits and harms are units of welfare. I shall mostly speak only of benefits, but my discussion is meant to capture harms as well.

Having benefits in her life, then, is what is in an individual's self-interest. As I pointed out above, the self-interests with which I primarily am concerned are intrinsic self-interests, and so when I claim that the object of a self-interest is a benefit, I am assuming that benefits have intrinsic value. While perhaps it is not universally agreed that benefits have such value, it is not a highly controversial view. In any case, it seems to me so plausible that I shall merely assume it.

Since I take an *intrinsic* self-interest in x to be a self-interest in x for its own sake, I take the *intrinsic* value of x to be the value x has for its own sake. The term 'intrinsic value' is not always used in this manner. For example, that which I refer to as 'intrinsic value', Christine Korsgaard (1983: 170) refers to as 'final value', and yet others refer to as 'non-instrumental value'. Korsgaard then reserves the term 'intrinsic value' for the value an object has in virtue of its intrinsic properties. So by 'intrinsic value' I mean what Korsgaard refers to as 'final value'. Furthermore, I remain agnostic on whether that which has intrinsic value (in my sense) has it simply in virtue of its intrinsic properties.

When I say that *benefits* have intrinsic value, I also intend to remain agnostic on the exact nature of the bearers of intrinsic value. Thus, the bearers of such value may be individual objects (a benefit), properties (benefiting), states of affairs (the state of affairs that someone benefits), or fall in some other ontological category.[2]

The concept of 'self-interest' does not presuppose any particular theory of welfare, or any group of such theories. What is in a person's self-interest may be that she has pleasurable mental states, or that her preferences are satisfied, or that items on an objective list are instantiated in her life. Roughly, and

---

[2] For a good discussion of the locus of intrinsic value, see Zimmerman (2001: ch. 3).

without assuming a particular theory of welfare, saying that an outcome is in an individual's self-interest is a way of saying that it would be good for this individual if the outcome occurred.[3]

Although I am not assuming any particular theory of welfare, preferences do play a substantial role in my analysis. There are three reasons for this. First, the idea that preferences, in one way or another, are important for self-interest continues to have significance in much contemporary moral philosophy.[4]

Second, often it is not very clear what kind of preferences philosophers have in mind when giving an account of self-interest. Since the choice of what kind of preferences to focus on makes a great difference concerning the account of self-interest we end up with, it seems worthwhile to try to clarify the options.

And third, it seems to me that preference theory is the most developed value theory to date. Therefore, by considering the importance of preferences for self-interests, we may arrive at conclusions with a degree of sophistication it would have been difficult to reach if we were to consider some other value theory instead. In some cases, these considerations and conclusions may even give us some idea of the directions in which, once equally developed, other value theories will point, or perhaps provide a framework for their further development.

I use the term 'preference' to cover a range of conative attitudes, such as desires, likings, aims, wants, etc. This also allows me to use the same term regardless of whether I am dealing with a one-place or a two-place attitude. Just as I may prefer swimming to reading, I may simply have a preference for swimming. And unless otherwise indicated, what I am concerned with is *intrinsic* preferences; that is, with what is preferred for its own sake.

Further, in Chapters 2–4, I am primarily concerned with self-interests regarding *future* benefits. However, individuals may have self-interests regarding the present and even the past, in addition to the future. And in Chapter 5, I turn to a particular self-interest that at least partly pertains to the past, namely our self-interest in having come into existence. Furthermore, in Chapter 10, I develop a theory of justice according to which the moral value of a benefit to an individual at a particular point in time depends on how strong her self-interest is at that time in the benefits that accrue to her at other times, past and future.

---

[3] I shall sometimes say that we have self-interests in outcomes, or futures, or survival, but these self-interests are, strictly speaking, self-interests in the benefits (whatever the appropriate locus of benefits as bearers of intrinsic value) contained in these.

[4] Thus, the list of philosophers who hold that self-interests depend on preferences includes, among others, Barry (1989b); Feinberg (1980); Glover (1977); Griffin (1986); Hare (1981); Harris (1985); Harsanyi (1982); Heyd (1992); Lockwood (1979); McMahan (1998); Rawls (1971); Singer (1993); Steinbock (1992); Sumner (1996); Tooley (1983); Velleman (1991); and Warren (1997).

Benefits need not fall at particular points in time. Maybe some benefits have temporal extension by their very nature. The point is not that certain benefits last a while, because this is quite compatible with them falling at particular points. For instance, a feeling of joy may last a minute, but each component of joy making up the minute may be located at a particular point in time. Rather, perhaps some benefits cannot be distributed on particular points in time in this way. Consider the benefit that accrues to a person when she writes a first-class novel. It is at least not obvious that this benefit can be reduced to sub-elements that all fall nicely at particular points on a time scale. This is especially true if the benefit depends for its existence on a preference for writing the book. Since the object of this preference has great temporal extension, it would seem that the benefit does as well.

Perhaps there are even benefits that lack temporal location altogether. Some would say that this is true for posthumous benefits. However, I simply assume that all benefits have at least an approximate location in time. This reflects my view that all candidates for non-temporal benefits are not benefits at all, or really do have temporal location. But it is not a position I shall argue for here.

Bearers

Just as a theory about self-interest needs to specify what the relevant objects are, it also needs to specify what sorts of entities can be bearers of self-interests. In fact, one way of assessing such theories is to consider to which kinds of entities they do and, in particular, do not ascribe self-interests. For instance, some theories do not ascribe self-interests to foetuses and we may assess these theories, in part, by considering the plausibility of such claims.

Partly because of my liberal attitude regarding which theories of welfare are compatible with self-interest, I shall not presuppose that an individual has to have preferences or has to possess consciousness at a particular time in order to be a bearer of self-interest at that time. Therefore, I do not presume that, for example, non-conscious foetuses lack self-interests. This is also why I mostly refer to the bearers of self-interests as 'individuals' rather than, for instance, 'persons'. Of course, careful philosophical reflection may reveal that in order to be a bearer of self-interest, an individual must have preferences, but it is not something that can just be assumed or even deduced from the concept.

Nevertheless, some people may think it is awkward to use 'self-interest' in the way I propose; for example, because they think that the present possession of self-interest is somehow conceptually tied to the present possession of preferences. However, it is a terminological decision on my part not to use the concept in this way, and as I shall argue, it is only if 'present bearer of self-interest' and 'present bearer of preferences' are conceptually disassociated that a plausible theory about self-interest can be found, and allowed to play the role in prudential and moral theory it is usually thought to play.

While I am not assuming that an individual has to possess consciousness now to be a present bearer of self-interests, I only consider the self-interests of individuals that possess or may at some time acquire consciousness, and the possible self-interests of possible conscious beings. In part this is because I believe that a being or entity that does not at a particular time possess consciousness cannot at that time benefit. Trees, biotic communities, and classes of things cannot prefer or experience that things go one way or another, and so they cannot have self-interests in things going any particular way (Hare 1991; Holtug 1996a; Singer 1993: ch. 10). Even so, if it turns out that such entities do have self-interests, my theory may not account for them. But this need not imply that my theory is mistaken, as different sorts of beings may have different sorts of self-interests.

Necessary and sufficient conditions

In my discussion, I am concerned with what the necessary and sufficient conditions are for having a self-interest. More precisely, I shall consider various ways of filling out the following scheme:

P_1 has a self-interest at t_1 in P_2 benefiting at $t_2(-t_3)$, if and only if___

By way of illustration, one obvious candidate for a necessary condition is that P_1 and P_2 are numerically identical. Or, to take another example, perhaps it is a necessary condition that P_1 at t_1 has a preference regarding the benefit to P_2 at $t_2(-t_3)$. Now, as I have pointed out, some benefits may have temporal extension. This is why I have added the parenthesis $(-t_3)$. Furthermore, as I pointed out above, just as individuals may have self-interests in benefits that lie in the future, they also may have self interests in benefits that lie in the past and the present. Therefore, while I am most concerned with future benefits in this part of the book, $t_2(-t_3)$ in principle may be prior to or coincide with t_1.

Strengths

Just as the theories I consider specify what the necessary and sufficient conditions for having a self-interest are, they also specify how the strengths of these interests are determined. For instance, according to one view, the strength of a self-interest is simply proportional to the size of the benefit it has as its object. But other views determine its strength differently.

Relativity

In the scheme presented above, I assume that individuals have self-interests at particular times. This may seem strange. If a person now has a self-interest in a particular benefit, accruing to her at a particular time, does she not always have that self-interest? Of course, I may have a self-interest in feeling pleasure an hour from now but not in feeling pleasure tomorrow when, say, I shall be attending a funeral. But that is beside the point. The issue is the following: if I now have a self-interest in feeling pleasure at some future time t, shall I not always have a self-interest in feeling pleasure at t? If so, why have a time-index on self-interests?

It seems natural to say that we have self-interests at times, even if that implies that we have them always. More importantly, some theories about self-interest imply that self-interests vary over time. Consider, for example, the view that an individual only now has a self-interest in surviving if she presently prefers to survive (Harris 1985: 18–19). Since this view links present self-interests to present preferences, it is time-relative. It implies that an individual—for instance, an infant—that does not now have a self-interest in surviving at the age of, say, twenty, because it has no preference for it, may come to have such a self-interest, namely, if it develops such a preference.

Also, self-interests need not be time-relative in order to be relative. In Chapter 4, I argue that self-interests should be discounted due to reductions in certain physical and psychological relations. For example, a person's self-interest in a benefit will typically increase as she approaches the time when the benefit will befall her, because as she approaches, these physical and psychological relations to herself at the time of the benefit will become stronger. Therefore, as I shall argue, self-interests are relative to certain relations, and since these relations vary over time, so do self-interests.

2.3 The Identity View

A theory about self-interest should specify the necessary and sufficient conditions for having a self-interest in a benefit. And as I have pointed out, identity seems to be an obvious candidate for such a necessary condition. It seems that an individual can only have a self-interest in a benefit befalling someone if *she* is that someone. Indeed, it may seem as if this follows from the concept of *self*-interest. Nevertheless, I do question this alleged link between identity and self-interest in Chapters 3 and 4, but for now, I shall assume it, and ask whether there are any other conditions that have to be satisfied in order for an individual to have a self-interest in a benefit. Consider:

> *The Identity View.* (1) P_1 has a self-interest at t_1 in P_2 benefiting at $t_2(-t_3)$, if and only if (a) P_1 exists at t_1, and (b) P_1 and P_2 are numerically identical. (2) The strength of the self-interest depends only on, and is strictly proportional to, the size of the benefit.

According to (1), two conditions have to be satisfied in order for an individual to have a self-interest, at a certain time, regarding a future (or indeed any) benefit. Apart from being identical to the beneficiary, the individual must exist at that time. Why is this? One reason could be that an entity that does not exist at a particular point in time cannot at that time have any properties, including self-interests. I shall return to this point of why properties presuppose the existence of that which they are properties of in Chapter 5 (Section 5.5).

As claimed in (2), the larger the benefit is, the stronger the self-interest in obtaining it is. This seems rather straightforward, since saying that an outcome is in an individual's self-interest is roughly a way of saying that it would be valuable for her if the outcome were to come about. Because a larger benefit is more valuable for an individual, the larger the benefit is, the stronger the self-interest. Of course, obtaining a benefit may prevent this individual from obtaining other benefits, and so obtaining the former benefit need not be in her self-interest, all things considered. But this is just because this individual may have other, competing, self-interests. Furthermore, according to (2), the strength of a self-interest depends on nothing but the size of the benefit. I shall consider and reject various objections to this claim in the present chapter.

Although the Identity View seems intuitively plausible, it is nevertheless highly controversial. One objection that I want to briefly consider and dismiss is that future benefits should be discounted for time. That is, the further into the future a benefit is, the less it presently counts. Now, whatever plausibility such a discount rate has when applied to resources, I believe that it has no plausibility when applied to welfare. Although, for example, it may be better to receive a certain amount of money sooner rather than later, because the money could be profitably invested sooner, there are no similar opportunity costs when it comes to welfare.[5]

---

[5] For valuable critical discussions regarding the idea of discounting welfare for time, see Broome (1992: ch. 3); and Cowen and Parfit (1992).

Another, more fundamental objection implicit in much of contemporary moral philosophy is that it takes more than identity over time in order to have self-interests. Consider foetuses, for example. According to the Identity View, it seems that foetuses have all sorts of self-interests regarding the future, since (usually) there are a great many benefits waiting for them. Of course, this claim rests on the assumption that foetuses are numerically identical to the people who may grow up and obtain all these benefits, but let's make that assumption for now. In Chapter 3, I have more to say about this issue of personal identity. But since many philosophers claim that foetuses do not have a strong, if any, self-interest in obtaining these benefits, and do not base their claims on the issue of personal identity, they must reject the Identity View (Harris 1985: 19; Singer 1993: 127). Similarly, many philosophers claim that most non-human animals do not have strong—if any—self-interests in obtaining future benefits (Harris 1985: 19; Singer 1993: 127). Yet, clearly there may be many benefits waiting in a non-human animal's future, and according to the Identity View, such an animal will thus have numerous future-directed self-interests. But this is exactly what these philosophers deny.

Likewise, the second part of the Identity View, (2), may be challenged. The Identity View does not tell us directly how to aggregate benefits, but let us assume:

> *The Additive Assumption about Benefits.* The value of a life (or a stretch of a life) is an additive function of the benefits it contains.

This assumption is actually stronger than needed to challenge (2), but it is also conveniently simple.[6] On this assumption, the Identity View implies that the self-interest in receiving a future containing a number of benefits is strictly proportional to the sum of these benefits. Let us further assume, plausibly, that an individual's self-interest in her future is her self-interest in surviving. After all, this future is exactly what she stands to lose if she does not survive. This is in accordance with what has been called the 'Future Goods Account' (McMahan 1998: 480) or 'Deprivation Account' (Feldman 1992: 138–42) of the badness of death. Death is bad for an individual to the extent it prevents future goods from accruing to her. Indeed, the Identity View provides a nice explanation of the Deprivation Account. Since the sum of benefits contained in an individual's future is the future value her death deprives her of, this will be a measure not only of her self-interest in her future, but also of the badness of her death.

---

[6] For various objections to this assumption, see Velleman (1991). For a defence, see Broome (2004: ch. 17). In section 2.6, I consider an alternative to the Additive Assumption, namely the view that the value of a life (or a future) is to be assessed on the basis of a global preference.

Consider, then, some of the implications of this account of the self-interest in surviving. Since usually there is more value to be found in the future of a foetus than in the future of, say, a twenty-year-old, as the foetus has more years ahead of it, the foetus generally has the stronger present self-interest in gaining its future. It is then worse for the foetus than for the twenty-year-old to die, since the foetus loses out on more future benefits. And so the Identity View implies that the foetus has a stronger self-interest in surviving than does the twenty-year-old. However, this account of the self-interest in surviving seems dubious. Intuitively, it would seem that the twenty-year-old has the stronger self-interest in surviving.

Furthermore, it may be suggested that this account of self-interest is out of line with certain very common moral views. Most people believe that it is morally worse to kill a twenty-year-old than it is to perform an abortion. And on the assumption that killing is primarily wrong because it is contrary to the self-interest of the victim, this belief does not seem to sit well with the Identity View (McMahan 2002: 232–3).

So perhaps the Identity View needs to be revised. This is not because existence and identity are not necessary conditions for self-interest, but because other conditions need to be added. Further, it is not because the size of a benefit is not relevant for determining the strength of a self-interest, but because other factors are relevant as well. In the rest of the chapter, I consider various views that add such further conditions and factors, consisting mainly of claims about the importance of specific kinds of preferences. However, I shall argue that none presents a plausible alternative to the Identity View. On this basis, I consider and defend a more thorough revision of the Identity View in Chapters 3 and 4. As it turns out, this revision has important implications, not just for prudence but also for justice.

2.4 The Present Preference View

It could be suggested that the problem with the Identity View is that it does not appropriately reflect (or at least does not fully bring to the fore) how self-interests depend on preferences. I shall discuss various ways in which preferences may figure in a theory about self-interest, starting with the suggestion that *present* preferences ground such interests. According to this suggestion, a twenty-year-old has a stronger self-interest in surviving than a foetus does because the former has more and stronger future-directed preferences.

Perhaps Peter Singer appeals to such a view when he claims that:

> If I imagine myself in turn as a self-conscious being and a conscious but not self-conscious being, it is only in the former case that I could have forward-looking desires that extend beyond periods of sleep or temporary unconsciousness, for example a desire to complete my studies, a desire to have children, or simply a desire to go on living, in addition to desires for immediate satisfaction or pleasure, or to get out of painful or distressing situations. Hence it is only in the former case that my death involves a greater loss than just a temporary loss of consciousness. (Singer 1993: 127)

The idea might be this: a being that is conscious but not self-conscious will not presently have preferences that reach beyond a period of unconsciousness, and therefore cannot presently have self-interests that reach beyond it; a being that is self-conscious, on the other hand, will presently have preferences that reach beyond such a period, and so can have present self-interests that reach further into the future. This is why it would suffer the greater loss if it were to die.[7]

In any case, such a view is certainly worth exploring. So consider the following:

> *The Present Preference View.* (1) P_1 has a self-interest at t_1 in P_2 benefiting at $t_2(-t_3)$, if and only if (a) P_1 exists at t_1, (b) P_1 and P_2 are numerically identical, and (c) P_1 at t_1 prefers that the benefit befalls P_2 at $t_2(-t_3)$, or the benefit involves the satisfaction of a preference P_1 has at t_1. (2) The strength of the self-interest depends only on, and is proportional to, the size of the presently preferred benefit, or the strength of the preference, or both.

According to (1), present self-interests depend crucially on present preferences. If I do not now prefer a particular benefit, or the benefit does not involve the satisfaction of one of my present preferences, I do not now have a self-interest in obtaining it. Presumably, some philosophers would want to claim that self-interests are dependent not only on present but also on past preferences. But since such a revision of the Present Preference View raises additional complications, and since the arguments I employ against this view apply equally to a suitably revised version, in the following I can afford to ignore the possibility of including past preferences.

The reason the (c)-clause is a disjunction is because there are different possible theories as to what welfare consists of. This requires a bit of explaining. We need to distinguish between two different views on the sort of value to which

---

[7] There is, however, another possible reading of Singer. On this reading, it is only self-conscious beings who can stand in the relation that prudentially matters to beneficiaries in the further future. Therefore, only such beings have self-interests regarding what happens to such beneficiaries. I return to this interpretation in Chapter 4 (Section 4.3).

preferences give rise (Rabinowicz and Österberg 1996), where the first is known as:

> *The Object Account of Preferences*. The bearer of the intrinsic value to which a (suitable) intrinsic preference gives rise is the object of this preference.

Consider, for example, the state of affairs that the rainforests survive. According to the Object Account, this state of affairs has intrinsic value if it is the object of a (suitable) intrinsic preference; that is, if someone (suitably) prefers that the rainforests survive. What the Object Account does, then, is to locate (at least some of) the bearers of intrinsic value. Note that there are different possible views on what counts as a suitable preference. Perhaps all intrinsic preferences are suitable, or perhaps they must satisfy certain conditions such as being rational, self-regarding, or synchronic with their objects in order to generate intrinsic value.[8]

This account should be contrasted with the following:

> *The Satisfaction Account of Preferences*. The bearer of the intrinsic value to which a (suitable) intrinsic preference gives rise is the state of affairs that consists of the preference and its object.

Thus, if I (suitably) prefer that the rainforests survive, what has intrinsic value is not simply the state of affairs that they survive, but the conjunction of this state of affairs and the state of affairs that my preference takes the former state as an object. So that which has intrinsic value, according to the Satisfaction Account, is the state of affairs *that* an intrinsic preference is satisfied.

Note that these two accounts do not rule out that there might be things that have intrinsic value even if they do not involve any preferences. They merely state that insofar as the intrinsic value is *due* to a preference, it is to be found in a particular place. But of course, both accounts are also compatible with the view that there are no intrinsic values that do not involve preferences. That is, they may be combined with:

> *Preferentialism*. All (intrinsic) value is due to (intrinsic) preferences.

If the Object Account and the Satisfaction Account are combined with Preferentialism, what we get is, respectively, the Object and the Satisfaction Interpretation of Preferentialism. According to the former interpretation, only objects of (intrinsic) preferences are bearers of intrinsic value and, according to the latter, only states of affairs that consist of conjunctions of (intrinsic) preferences and their objects have intrinsic value.

---

[8] For a further list of various possible requirements, see Fehige and Wessels (1998: xxv–vi).

Suppose we accept the Object Interpretation. It then may seem natural to say that in order for something to be a benefit, it must be the object of a (suitable) preference.[9] At least, if we were to deny this, we would have to give up the conventional view that benefits have intrinsic value. So imagine we hold that benefits consist of (some of) the objects preferences take. The Present Preference View then implies that an individual has a present self-interest in a future benefit only if she presently prefers that benefit (the object of the preference).

Things are a little different if we opt for the Satisfaction Interpretation. We would then need to claim that a benefit consists in the state of affairs that a preference is satisfied, in order to preserve the conventional view that benefits have intrinsic value. Thus, it would seem awkward to say that an individual prefers a future benefit (unless we are referring to a second-order preference—a preference for preference-satisfaction). Rather, the preference is part of the benefit. Better then to say that an individual only has a present self-interest in a benefit if that benefit involves (or at least partially consists of) the satisfaction of a present preference. Hence, the (c)-clause needs to be a disjunction.

Note that we need not hold a preference theory of welfare in order to hold the Present Preference View. Suppose, for instance, that benefits consist in pleasurable mental states, as the hedonist would have it. The Present Preference View would then imply that an individual has a present self-interest in a future benefit only if she presently prefers the pleasurable mental state of which the benefit consists. Let us call versions that combine different types of value theory 'impure' versions of the Present Preference View, and versions that rely only on preferences 'pure' versions. While impure versions are 'messier', they are not obviously mistaken. Nor is it clear to me that they have no 'takers' in contemporary moral philosophy.

Claim (2) accommodates both different theories of welfare and different views on the weight of present preferences when assessing the strengths of self-interests. For a pure version of the Present Preference View, the strength of a present self-interest in a future benefit may depend only on the strength of the present preference it relies on. Alternatively, the strength of a self-interest may depend also, or even exclusively, on the strength of future preferences. These future preferences may affect the strength of the self-interest by affecting the size of the future benefit.

---

[9] By a 'suitable' preference, I mean a preference that fulfils one or more requirements that preferences must satisfy in order to give rise to benefits. Unless otherwise stated, I simply assume that the preferences we are dealing with are of the suitable kind.

Suppose, then, that I presently prefer to go on a holiday next year and that doing so will in fact benefit me. Imagine also that next year when I am on holiday, my preference will be even stronger. As long as I presently prefer going on the holiday, I have a self-interest in doing so, and we could assess its strength either on the basis of my present preference, my future preference, or both.[10] However, since a pure version of the Present Preference View is simpler if it focuses only on my present preference, and since the points I shall make apply quite generally, this is the version I shall assume.

Similarly, for an impure version of the Present Preference View, the strength of a present self-interest may depend only on the size of the benefit it has as an object (say, a pleasurable mental state), or the strength of the present preference for this object, or both. In any case, since the pure and the impure versions have certain structures in common, and it is these structures I assess, I will not distinguish between them in the following.

Before I begin to assess the Present Preference View, it is worth pointing out in greater detail how it differs from the Identity View. The difference is not that the Identity View cannot accommodate preferences. In fact, the Identity View allows that self-interests may be explained entirely in terms of them. This is because all benefits may be due to preferences. The Identity View even allows that self-interests are to be explained entirely in terms of present preferences, namely if we adopt a present preference theory of welfare. Assuming such a theory, the Identity View actually coincides with the Present Preference View.

However, the difference between these two views is that in some versions of the Identity View, an individual has self-interests in certain things that she does not presently prefer, possibly because she will prefer them in the future. Thus, the Identity View, unlike the Present Preference View, allows that future preferences may ground present self-interests.

Note also that the Present Preference View is time-relative. For instance, my self-interest in having pleasurable mental states tomorrow may change over time. If, for example, today I prefer to have such states tomorrow, but do not prefer this when tomorrow arrives, my self-interest in having such states will have vanished when tomorrow comes. This need not be so for the Identity View, since the benefit of feeling pleasure tomorrow may depend only on the feelings or preferences I will have then.

One final introductory remark is in order: we should distinguish between global and local preferences. Global preferences have entire lives or at least large

---

[10] The idea that an individual has a stronger present self-interest in a future benefit to the extent she presently prefers it is endorsed by Jeff McMahan (1998: 489).

chunks of them as their objects, whereas local preferences are directed towards rather smaller portions of lives (Griffin 1986: 34–5; Parfit 1984: 497–9). I shall assume that when assessing a self-interest in a larger stretch of a life, the Present Preference View does so in terms of local preferences rather than a global preference for the entire stretch. For most of my criticism of the Present Preference View, this assumption will make no difference. However, in a later section, I consider the importance of global preferences for the self-interest in surviving. This is because much has been made of the connection between global preferences and such self-interests in recent moral philosophy.

Consider now the first part of the Present Preference View. Why claim that present preferences are necessary conditions for present self-interests? The following rationale could be suggested. In order for me to have a *present* self-interest, this interest must be rooted in me as I am now. And this is exactly what the Present Preference View does, by rooting my present self-interests in my present preferences. Of course, this rationale may be appealed to by proponents of both pure and impure versions.

However, even if my present self-interests must be rooted in me as I am now, it does not follow that they should be rooted in my present preferences. In fact, there is a sense in which a proponent of the Identity View who attaches no special significance to present preferences may concede that my present self-interests must have such a present rooting. After all, I exist now and am identical to someone who will exist in the future and enjoy various benefits then. And in order for this to be the case, my present states have to stand in the right sort of relation to the future states of this future person. Thus, my present self-interests are rooted in my present states.

Furthermore, rooting present self-interests in present preferences seems implausible in its own right. Suppose that I do not now prefer to read Hume's *Treatise* because I have no appreciation of philosophy, but that if I do read him, I will enjoy it and form a strong preference to do so. It seems that it is in my present self-interest to read *Treatise*. After all, even if I do not presently prefer to read it, reading it will benefit me. And it seems that this benefit should count for something from my present evaluative perspective. But the claim that it is in my present self-interest to read *Treatise* is exactly what the Present Preference View denies.

Let me briefly consider (and reject) some responses the proponent of the Present Preference View may come up with at this point. She may argue that while I do not have a present self-interest in reading *Treatise*, I may nevertheless have reason to do so. However, first, it seems to me that the claim that it is in my present self-interest to read *Treatise* is plausible in its own right, quite independently of what we say about my reasons for action. Second, if we followed the Present Preference View in claiming that I do not have a present self-interest in reading Hume, on what basis can we then hold that I nevertheless have a present (self-regarding) reason to read him? Indeed, while some philosophers claim that I may have a self-interest in something and yet no reason to bring it about (for example, because I do not have the required present preferences), I know of none who claims that I can have a present (self-regarding) reason to do something I have no present self-interest in doing.

Instead, it may be argued that if I now have a self-interest in reading Hume, it is because I will enjoy it, and surely I now have a preference for enjoyable experiences. But perhaps I simply do not now have a preference for intellectual experiences, because I believe that they are a waste of time, and so no preference for enjoying Hume. Of course, if I were to read him, I would also prefer to do so, seeing the error of my ways. But still, I do not now have a self-interest in reading him, according to the Present Preference View, and so apparently no (self-regarding) reason to do so.

Finally, the proponent of the Present Preference View may argue that while I may not now prefer to read Hume, I would prefer to do so if I were rational. She may then add that it is not just any old preference, but rational preferences that ground self-interests; that is, the preferences people would have if they were fully rational.[11] For present purposes, the most important feature of rational preferences is that they are based on full information about their objects (and perhaps about other things as well).[12] Thus, the point is that if I knew what reading Hume would amount to, I would in fact want to read him, and so it would be in my present self-interest to do so, even according to the Present Preference View. However, I doubt that present rational preferences need to conform to future (rational) preferences in this manner. And if they did, the requirement that present self-interests must be grounded on *present* preferences, in effect, would be abandoned. What we would have would simply be a rational preference view.

Maybe the inadequacy of the Present Preference View is yet more apparent if we consider *harms* that are not linked to present preferences. Suppose a

---

[11] Actually, while this is a possible account of rational preferences, it is not the only one. According to this account, an individual's rational preferences are those she would have in a possible world in which she is fully rational (Harsanyi 1982: 55; Brandt 1979: 113; Rawls 1971: 421). However, an alternative account suggests that an individual's rational preferences are those of her *actual* preferences that satisfy certain rational requirements (Griffin 1986: 11; Sumner 1996: 130). Obviously, this second account cannot be invoked to explain why it is in my present self-interest to read Hume (since I may not actually prefer to read him). Incidentally, for a critical discussion of the second account, see Holtug (2003b: 172, n. 40).

[12] For an account of how preferences can be criticized for not being rational, see Brandt (1979: ch. 6).

young Buddhist spends all of his time trying to get rid of his preferences for earthly goods. In order not to be tempted, he gives away all of his money. However, a month from now he will starve and no longer be thinking so highly of his Buddhist persuasions, suffering much. Even though the Buddhist knows that a month from now he will want not to suffer, he does not now care about it (perhaps he even thinks that in his future depraved condition he will deserve to starve). Thus, he has no present preference not to be miserable then and so, according to the Present Preference View, no present self-interest in not being so. But surely this cannot be right. Surely the Buddhist's future suffering should be taken into account when assessing his self-interest in his future.

Consider also the implications of the Present Preference View regarding foetuses and infants. Suppose a woman takes thalidomide during her pregnancy and thus causes her offspring to have a disability. According to the Present Preference View, she does not act against the self-interest of the foetus, as it has no preferences regarding the condition of the child that will be born. However, assuming that the foetus is identical to the child, this is implausible. Surely it is in the self-interest of the foetus not to suffer from a severe disability some time in the future.

It may be objected that even if a foetus has no present self-interest in not being subjected to thalidomide, there are nevertheless other reasons why it would be wrong for a pregnant woman to take this drug. One particularly important reason, it may be argued, is that it will be contrary to the future self-interest of the child. It may then be added that, with respect to our moral reasons, we should be impartial between self-interests that are held at different times (or at least assign some significant weight to future self-interests).

However, even if this suggestion were to enable us to preserve the Present Preference View, it would also rob it of its teeth. For example, when Singer argues that it is (normally) worse for a self-conscious than for a non-self-conscious individual to die, he takes this to be an argument for why we (normally) have a much stronger moral reason not to kill the former kind of individual than not to kill the latter kind. But if we are to be impartial between present and future self-interests, why don't the future self-interests of, for instance, a foetus ensure that we have as strong a reason not to kill it as we have not to kill a self-conscious individual?[13] And even if we do not require

---

[13] Of course, if we kill the foetus, it will not have future preferences on the basis of which it can have a future self-interest. It may be suggested that for this reason, these possible future preferences cannot contribute to the wrongness of killing it. But what this line of argument supports is really an alternative to the Present Preference View, namely the Actual Preference View—a view that I consider in the

impartiality, but still assign significant weight to future self-interests, our reason not to kill a foetus will be stronger than Singer allows. In other words, if we take this view on reasons, the Present Preference View does not help us solve the moral problems it was designed to solve.

In fact, once we realize that proponents of the Present Preference View cannot assign in this way significant weight to future self-interests, a similar problem arises with respect to future individuals. If the future preferences of present individuals do not give rise to significant (present) moral reasons, then surely future preferences of future individuals do not give rise to such reasons either. But then what sort of reason do we have not to pollute to such an extent that future generations will be seriously harmed, assuming that not polluting in this way will slightly decrease our own welfare?

Furthermore, the Present Preference View is no more plausible with respect to infants than it is with respect to foetuses. Suppose a doctor administers a drug to an infant that causes her to experience excruciating pain from her twentieth birthday and for the rest of her life. The infant will have no preferences regarding what happens to her at age twenty and so, according to the Present Preference View, the doctor has not acted against the infant's present self-interest.

It seems to me that the second part of the Present Preference View fares no better than does the first. Again, the problems derive from the fact that future benefits that are not presently preferred (or do not involve present preferences) have no weight. Consider the following case. A child—call her Mary—suffers from a brain disorder that causes her to have only a few, relatively weak preferences, say, for sleeping, eating, not being in pain, and for some mild enjoyments. Perhaps her mental development has simply stopped at an early age. However, her disease can be treated, and if it is, as she grows up she will form many new and strong preferences—while retaining her old ones—such as for writing poetry, living a rich and fulfilling family life, and for travelling all over the world. Regardless of whether or not she is treated, all her preferences will be satisfied. So there are two possible outcomes for her, and it certainly seems that she has a stronger self-interest in the outcome in which she is treated. In fact, this seems to be the main reason she should receive the treatment.

I have made the assumption that, according to the Present Preference View, an individual's present self-interest in her future is a function of all the individual's local present preferences regarding future benefits and perhaps the

___

next section. This is because what the killing of the foetus ensures is that its possible future preferences will not be actual preferences.

size of these presently preferred goods. And on this assumption, Mary has an equal present self-interest in the two possible futures. After all, they contain an equal satisfaction of her *present* preferences. But surely Mary has a stronger present self-interest in the future in which she is treated.[14]

The second part of the Present Preference View has another implausible implication. Let us assume that beings that do not have present global preferences should have their self-interests in their futures assessed in terms of present local preferences. The Present Preference View then implies that infants and many non-human animals have roughly equal present self-interests in their futures (McMahan 1998: 477). After all, the preferences of a one-year-old infant may not differ much in complexity and intensity from the preferences of, for example, a dog.

To summarize, the problem with the Present Preference View is in fact its distinctive feature; it does not assign any significance to benefits that are not presently preferred or that do not involve present preferences. Therefore, the Present Preference View does not represent an improvement as compared to the Identity View.

Nevertheless, it may be suggested that while the Present Preference View is implausible in its own right, it would make sense to combine the Identity View, with the claim that present preferences have a special significance with respect to present self-interests. Such a combined view would claim that while an individual need only be identical to a future beneficiary to have a present self-interest in the benefits of the latter, the strength of this self-interest is boosted to the extent she presently prefers these benefits (or they involve her present preferences). In fact, this revision of the Identity View would enable us to reject the implication that, usually, a foetus has a stronger present self-interest in surviving than a twenty-year-old.

However, this combined view inherits some of the problems associated with the Present Preference View. In particular, present preferences must be a very weighty factor in order for this view to imply that the foetus does not have the stronger self-interest in surviving. After all, the foetus has twenty years extra to 'look forward to'. But this implies that, quite generally, the self-interests of foetuses are downplayed in comparison to the self-interests of, for example, twenty-year-olds. Therefore, the self-interest of a foetus in not experiencing a great amount of excruciating pain in the further future may be outweighed by a twenty-year-old's self-interest in not experiencing a much smaller amount of future pain, because the twenty-year-old will have a present preference for not

---

[14] Note also that we cannot explain this self-interest by focusing on global preferences instead, because Mary *has* no global preference with respect to her two possible futures.

experiencing it. And so this combined view does not seem to be the solution to the problems to which the Identity View gives rise.

2.5 The Actual Preference View

While the Present Preference View denies that self-interests can be grounded on future preferences, there are other preference-based views that do not. One such view focuses on actual preferences rather than on present preferences. Actual preferences are the preferences that exist in the actual world, whether they are past, present, or future. These preferences should be contrasted with merely possible preferences, which are the preferences that might have existed, but will in fact never exist.

The shift from present to actual preferences seems well motivated. Consider a preference I do not yet have but will in fact have in the future. It seems that since I will *in fact* have this preference, it is relevant even for my present self-interest. Thus, by rooting self-interests in actual rather than present preferences, we allow ourselves to avoid some of the problems encountered by the Present Preference View. Suppose, for example, that I do not presently prefer to read Hume, but will do so when, some time in the future, I do read him. If present self-interests are rooted in actual preferences, then I do have a present self-interest in reading Hume, because I actually prefer to do so. The point is that by focusing on actual rather than present preferences, we bring more future benefits within the range of present self-interests.

Perhaps Joel Feinberg is implicitly rooting self-interests in actual preferences when he claims that:

> for foetuses, lacking actual wants and beliefs, have no actual interest in being born, and it is difficult to think of any other reason for ascribing any rights to them other than on the assumption that they will in fact be born.   (Feinberg 1980: 180)

First, note that what Feinberg here refers to as 'actual wants' is what I refer to as 'present preferences'. Feinberg is prepared to ascribe rights to foetuses on the assumption that they will in fact be born. Why is this? He claims that having interests is a precondition for having rights, and that having preferences is a precondition for having interests (1980: 165–6). So, it seems that interests are in some sense rooted in preferences. Furthermore, returning to the passage quoted above, it appears that foetuses have interests on the assumption that they are born. Further, if these interests are to be explained in terms of preferences, they may well be explained in terms of actual preferences, because what the birth of the child ensures is that the foetus has such preferences.[15]

Consider, then:

> *The Actual Preference View.* (1) P_1 has a self-interest at t_1 in P_2 benefiting at $t_2(-t_3)$, if and only if (a) P_1 exists at t_1, (b) P_1 and P_2 are numerically identical, and (c) P_1 actually prefers that the benefit befalls P_2 at $t_2(-t_3)$, or the benefit involves the satisfaction of an actual preference P_1 has. (2) The strength of the self-interest depends only on, and is proportional to, the size of the actually preferred benefit, or the strength of the preference, or both.

I have already explained part of the difference between this view and the Present Preference View. Here is a further difference. Whereas the Present Preference View implies that self-interests are time-relative, the Actual Preference View implies that they are time-neutral. Whereas a person need not have the same preferences today as she will tomorrow, her actual preferences remain constant. Even if she will prefer something tomorrow that she does not prefer today, it is still an actual preference, because it is a preference that is part of the actual history of the world.

Since the Actual Preference View does not rule out that self-interests may be grounded on future preferences, it has certain advantages as compared to the Present Preference View. Consider again the self-interests of foetuses and infants. The Actual Preference View implies that if a foetus or an infant is now caused to develop some disability in the future, this may be contrary to its present self-interest, since it may later come to prefer not to suffer from such a condition. Furthermore, the Actual Preference View implies that infants will (usually) have stronger self-interests in their futures than will non-human animals, since they will (usually) have more and stronger actual preferences. Again, this seems plausible.

---

[15] Alternatively, Feinberg's point may be that only the preferences of actual people—people who in fact exist at some point in time—can ground self-interests. Thus, what the birth of the child ensures, besides the actual existence of her preferences, is, of course, the actual existence of *her*.

   However, whether we accept one or the other interpretation, it is difficult to reconcile with certain other remarks Feinberg makes. Thus, he also claims that foetuses do not have a right to be born, presumably because it is not in their interest. And if in fact they will be born, they are actual and have actual preferences, and so it may be difficult to explain why being born is not in their interest, at least if interests are to be rooted in actual preferences (or the preferences of actual people).

   For similar defences of the view that self-interests are rooted in actual preferences, see Steinbock (1992: 40–1); and Barry (1989b: 281). But as with Feinberg, it is not entirely clear whether Steinbock's focus is on actual preferences or actual people. For an insightful criticism of Barry, see Goodin (1991b). Finally, Rabinowicz suggests that if we hold the Object Interpretation of Preferentialism, we should claim that only *actual* preferences give rise to intrinsic value; see Rabinowicz and Österberg (1996: 10). If we further hold that benefits have intrinsic value (and so are objects of [suitable] actual preferences), again, self-interests will be rooted in actual preferences.

Why accept the Actual Preference View? The following rationale could be suggested. If self-interests are to be based on preferences, it may seem reasonable to focus only on actual preferences. After all, why should we care about preferences that no one will actually have? What matters must be what is actually preferred, and the Actual Preference View accommodates this intuition nicely.

Nevertheless, as I shall now argue, the Actual Preference View should be rejected *precisely* because it restricts self-interests to actual preferences. Consider part (1). Suppose our young Buddhist has succeeded in getting rid of his preferences for the future, and that all of his previous preferences were rather short term, such that their objects are all in the past. Enraged by the Buddhist's beliefs, someone now kills him. Imagine also that had he not been killed, the Buddhist would have changed his ways and had a very happy future indeed, because, perhaps, he would have formed many new preferences and had the good fortune of seeing them all satisfied. But because he is killed, these new preferences are not actual. Hence, according to the Actual Preference View, he has no present (or, for that matter, future) self-interest in having a future, and so no self-interest in surviving. But this is absurd. Surely the killer cannot legitimately claim that he did not act contrary to the Buddhist's self-interest. And what this suggests is that we cannot restrict self-interests to actual preferences.

This suggestion is further confirmed when we consider part (2). Remember Mary, who has a serious brain-disorder and so can only form a few weak preferences for the future. If she is treated, she will be able to form many new (much stronger) preferences—while retaining her old ones—and whether she is treated or not, all her preferences will be satisfied. But, in fact, she is not treated. So these new preferences are not actual. Therefore, according to the Actual Preference View, these preferences are irrelevant when determining her self-interest in the (merely) possible outcome in which she is treated, and so she has an equal self-interest in this outcome and the actual outcome in which she is not treated. But this seems wrong. Her self-interest in the outcome with more satisfied preferences is stronger.

Furthermore, this case exposes the following puzzling general feature of the Actual Preference View: an individual's self-interest in an outcome may depend upon whether or not the outcome comes about.[16] Whether or not Mary is treated will determine her self-interest in being treated. But this seems perplexing. While an individual may certainly have a self-interest in an outcome being actual, how can the actuality of an outcome affect her self-interest in it being so?

---

[16] For an analogous point regarding the moral status of choices and actions, see Bykvist (1998: 103).

Finally, the Actual Preference View shares with the Identity View the problem of accounting for the claim that a twenty-year-old will usually have a stronger self-interest in her future than will a foetus. This is because, usually, the foetus' future will include more actually preferred benefits (or satisfied actual preferences) than will the twenty-year-old's future. Of course, if a foetus is killed, its future preferences will not be actual and so, on the assumption that it is aborted, it will have only a relatively weak self-interest in not being so. Nevertheless, the claim that a foetus usually has a stronger self-interest in its future than a twenty-year-old may seem counterintuitive in its own right, even on the assumption that both will have an average-length life. Thus, since the Actual Preference View shares this problem with the Identity View, and faces various other difficulties as well, it does not seem a plausible alternative.

2.6 The Necessary Preference View

The Actual Preference View is a modal view, since it claims that only preferences that exist in a particular world—the actual world—may ground self-interests. But it is not the only modal preference-based view. We may ground self-interests on *necessary* preferences instead. Suppose we want to compare different outcomes or worlds with respect to an individual's self-interests. This individual's necessary preferences, then, are the preferences that exist in all the outcomes or worlds compared. Necessary preferences should be contrasted with contingent preferences, which are preferences that exist in some but not all the outcomes compared. Note that the fact—if it is a fact—that one of the worlds compared is the actual world is irrelevant for the question of which preferences are necessary.[17]

Consider the following:

> *The Necessary Preference View.* (1) P_1 has a self-interest at t_1 in P_2 benefiting at $t_2(-t_3)$, if and only if (a) P_1 exists at t_1, (b) P_1 and P_2 are numerically identical, and (c) P_1 necessarily prefers that the benefit befalls P_2 at $t_2(-t_3)$, or the benefit involves the satisfaction of a necessary preference P_1 has. (2) The strength of the self-interest depends only on, and is proportional to, the size of the necessarily preferred benefit, or the strength of the preference, or both.

Note that the Necessary Preference View always presupposes a particular comparison of outcomes when assessing self-interests. This is because the claim

---

[17] For an excellent account of present, actual and necessary preferences and their moral importance, see Bykvist (1998).

that a preference is necessary only makes sense relative to such a comparison.[18] Thus, suppose we want to know whether my present preference for going to the movies gives rise to a present self-interest of mine. For simplicity, let us assume a preference theory of welfare. We must then compare the outcome in which I prefer and, indeed, go to the movies, with an outcome in which I prefer to go, but do not go. That is, we must compare the outcome in which I have the preference and it is satisfied, and the outcome in which I have the preference and it is not satisfied. And since, relative to this comparison, my preference is necessary, I have a self-interest in going.

One issue concerns how to construe the relevant outcomes. Imagine, as in the case just presented, I have a present preference for going to the movies. I assumed that since I presently have this preference it should be included in both the outcome where it is satisfied and in the outcome where it is not, when assessing my self-interest. That is, this preference should be included even if I am about to lose it. After all, if not, individuals cannot have a self-interest in surviving. When I die, my preferences die with me. Therefore, if my self-interests are to be based on necessary preferences, we had better include my present preferences in the outcome in which I die. Only then will these preferences be necessary.

When we go from present preferences to possible future preferences, things get more complicated. We may wonder whether I have a self-interest in acquiring and satisfying a preference I do not already have. For example, we may wonder whether I should study philosophy in order to acquire and satisfy a preference for reading Hume's *Treatise*. There are now three available outcomes to consider. In outcome A, I acquire the preference and read Hume. In outcome B, I acquire the preference but do not read him. And in outcome C, I do not acquire the preference. Relative to a comparison between A and B, I have a self-interest in reading Hume. But, relative to a comparison between A and C, I have no such self-interest, because my preference is not necessary. Therefore, everything else being equal, and as far as my self-interests are concerned, I should rather acquire the preference and satisfy it than acquire it and yet not satisfy it. However, I might as well not acquire the preference as acquire and satisfy it.

The Necessary Preference View faces problems that are quite similar to those facing the Actual Preference View. Thus, the restriction to necessary

---

[18] Therefore, we might say that whereas the Present Preference View is time-relative, the Necessary Preference View is comparison-relative.

preferences does not seem plausible either. Consider (1) in the Necessary Preference View. And remember once again the young Buddhist who does not care about his future, but who would have cared, and indeed been happy, had he not been killed. Now compare the outcome in which he is killed and the outcome in which he is not. The preferences he would have had in the future are not necessary (relative to the comparison), since they do not exist in the outcome in which he is killed. Therefore, implausibly, he has no self-interest in surviving.

Claim (1) also has another implausible implication. Suppose a person may either acquire a preference or not acquire it. If we compare an outcome in which he acquires the preference and satisfies it, and an outcome in which he acquires it but does not satisfy it, he may well have a self-interest in the former outcome. In fact, let us assume a preference theory of welfare and so that he has such a self-interest.[19] But now suppose that the former outcome is not available. In other words, either he acquires a preference that will be frustrated or he does not acquire it. When comparing these two outcomes, his preference is contingent. Therefore, relative to this comparison, he does not have a self-interest in avoiding the outcome in which he acquires the (frustrated) preference. Surely, this is extremely implausible.

Then consider (2), and remember Mary, who has a serious brain-disorder. Compare the outcome in which she is treated and the outcome in which she is not. Since the only preferences that exist in both these outcomes are of the sort she presently has, and since they will be equally satisfied in the two outcomes, implausibly, she does not have a stronger self-interest in the outcome in which she is treated.

Finally, there is a further problem with (2), namely that it generates an intransitive ordering of self-interests. Again, for simplicity, let us assume a preference theory of welfare. Now consider Table 2.1.

Table 2.1.

D	E	F
pβ (1) pπ (2)	pπ (1) pμ (2)	pβ (2) pμ (1)

[19] Besides a preference theory of welfare, we must also assume that it has positive value for an individual when one of her preferences is satisfied. There is a particular theory of the value of preference satisfaction that denies this, namely frustrationism. According to frustrationists, preference satisfaction merely has zero value, whereas preference frustration has negative value. I consider frustrationism in greater detail in Chapter 5 (Section 5.7) and argue that we should reject it.

D, E, and F are possible outcomes, and pß, pπ, and pμ are preferences of mine that, respectively, take ß, π, and μ as their objects. The numbers represent the strengths of these preferences. Finally, assume that the preferences are satisfied in the outcomes in which they exist.

How do D and E compare with respect to my self-interests? Since only pπ exists in both these outcomes and thus is necessary relative to the comparison of the two, and since it is stronger in D than it is in E, I have a stronger self-interest in D. Now compare E and F. Since only pμ exists in both, and since it is stronger in E than it is in F, I have a stronger self-interest in E. Assuming that the relation 'S has a stronger self-interest in x than in y' is transitive, it then follows that I have a stronger self-interest in D than I do in F. However, when comparing these two outcomes, the only preference that is necessary is pß. And since this preference is stronger in F than it is in D, I have a stronger self-interest in F. Thus, the Necessary Preference View violates the transitivity of the 'S has a stronger self-interest in x than in y' relation.

There are two ways in which this objection can be answered, but both raise problems of their own.[20] The proponent of the Necessary Preference View may argue that since this view is comparison-relative, the self-interest relation is always relative to a comparison of particular outcomes. Thus, the relevant relation is: 'Relative to comparison C, S has a stronger self-interest in x than in y'. And since the ranking of D and E involved a different comparison than did the ranking of E and F, transitivity does not imply anything about the ranking of the first and the last outcome.

The problem with this suggestion is that it makes it impossible to rank all three outcomes. Since we are dealing with different Cs, there is no common scale on which to rank them. Therefore, the Necessary Preference View offers no guidance on what prudence requires when facing such possible outcomes.

The second answer to the intransitivity objection solves this problem. It suggests that when comparing more than two outcomes that differ in the preferences they include, only preferences that exist in *all* the outcomes compared are necessary. Thus, when comparing D, E, and F, there are no necessary preferences. Therefore, with respect to my self-interests, these outcomes are equally good (or, alternatively, they are incomparable). However, this suggestion has the rather strange implication that whether or not I have a self-interest in D coming about, rather than E, depends upon whether we

---

[20] Actually there is also a third possible answer, namely simply to deny that the relevant relation is transitive. I shall not consider this option here. But I do briefly suggest in Chapter 1 (Section 1.5) that comparatives are transitive in virtue of their semantics.

include a *third* outcome, F, in the comparison. This violates the plausible claim that the ranking of two outcomes can depend only on facts about these two outcomes and the relation between them.[21] Also, this solution implies that even if we assume that pπ has a strength of 100 in D and hold everything else constant, I still do not have a stronger self-interest in D than I do in E and F.

All in all, then, we had better reject the Necessary Preference View.

2.7 The Present Preference for Survival View

One of the reasons why we need a theory about self-interest is that we want to be able to assess self-interests in surviving. For example, as I have suggested above, surely our moral views about abortion should depend, at least in part, on whether a foetus has a self-interest in continuing to exist. In previous sections, I have considered the implications of various general views, including their implications regarding the self-interest in surviving. I now want to address a view that is less general; in fact, it only makes claims about self-interests of this latter sort. According to this view, having a self-interest in surviving depends crucially on having a *global* preference for surviving.

Consider the following passage from John Harris:

> In order to value its own life a being would have to be *aware* that it has a life to value. This would at the very least require something like Locke's conception of *self-consciousness*, which involves a person's being able to 'consider itself as itself in different times and places'. Self-consciousness is not simple awareness, rather it is awareness of awareness. To value its own life, a being would have to be aware of itself as an independent centre of consciousness existing over time with a future it was capable of envisaging and wishing to experience. Only if it could envisage the future could a being want life to go on, and so value its continued existence. (Harris 1985: 18)

While Harris does not explicitly state this, apparently he believes that in order for a future to be valuable to an individual, this individual must value its future. And an individual can only value its future if it has a global preference for having it. Furthermore, an individual can only prefer to have a future if it is aware of what having a future is. And finally, it can only be aware of what having a future is if it possesses self-consciousness.[22]

---

[21] For a general discussion of the separability issue here, albeit in the context of betterness rather than of self-interest, see Broome (1991: ch. 4).

[22] For other versions of the idea that an individual cannot have a self-interest in (and/or right to) life unless it possesses self-consciousness, see e.g., Engelhardt (1986: ch. 6); Kuhse (1987: ch. 5); Singer

However, this is hardly self-explanatory. Suppose we grant Harris that a future can only be valuable to an individual if it values it. Still, why can an individual only value its future if it prefers to have the future? After all, an individual may have preferences for all sorts of things that obtain in its future, even if it does not prefer to continue to exist. I think that the best explanation would appeal to the Object Interpretation of Preferentialism.[23] According to the Object Interpretation, an entity has to be the object of an (intrinsic) preference in order to be a bearer of intrinsic value. According to the Object Interpretation, then, a future has intrinsic value only if it is (intrinsically) preferred. Of course, an individual may prefer all sorts of other things, including things in its future that will then come to have intrinsic value; but in order for a *future* to have such value, it must be (intrinsically) preferred.[24]

Next, we must ask why it is only possible for an individual to prefer to have a future if it is aware of what having a future is, and why it has to be self-conscious to be so aware. This seems more straightforward. An individual cannot prefer something it does not understand, and it cannot understand something unless is possesses the relevant concepts. Therefore, if an individual does not possess the concept of an independent centre of consciousness existing over time and is not aware that it is such a centre, it cannot prefer its continued existence. Furthermore, the possession of the concept of an independent centre of consciousness existing over time, and the awareness of being such a centre, are what having self-consciousness amounts to (or at least part of what it amounts to). Therefore, an individual cannot prefer her future unless she possesses self-consciousness (Tooley 1983: 104–5).

Harris then claims that the reason it is (normally) wrong to kill individuals who have self-consciousness is that they are thereby deprived of something they value (if, of course, they value their lives), whereas individuals who cannot value their lives cannot be wronged in this way. I take it that this is because only beings that prefer to survive have a self-interest in surviving, whereas beings that do not—for instance, because they do not possess self-consciousness—have no such self-interest. Nevertheless, there are things that

---

(1993, chs 4–7); Tooley (1983); and Velleman (1991). Velleman (1991: 70–1) seems to endorse an argument very similar to Harris's, in that only individuals who possess self-consciousness can have self-interests in surviving.

[23] This was pointed out to me by Klemens Kappel. Alternatively, the explanation may appeal merely to the Object Account of Preferences; but since the argument I shall employ against the former suggestion applies just as much to the latter, I need not distinguish between them here.

[24] An individual's future may also have intrinsic value in virtue of being the object of someone *else's* (intrinsic) preference. However, in the present context, where we are considering an individual's *self-interest* in her future, this is hardly relevant.

are wrong to do to individuals who lack self-consciousness; for example, it is wrong to cause them to be in pain, everything else being equal.[25]

Partly relying on this argument, we may propose:

> *The Present Preference for Survival View.* (1) P_1 has a self-interest at t_1 in P_2 existing at $t_2(-t_3)$, if and only if (a) P_1 exists at t_1, (b) P_1 and P_2 are numerically identical, and (c) P_1 prefers at t_1 that P_2 exists at $t_2(-t_3)$. (2) The strength of the self-interest depends only on, and is proportional to, the present (or future) strength of the preference (or both).[26]

The reason I ground self-interests on *present* preferences here is that Harris implicitly rejects the idea that an individual can have a present self-interest in surviving on the basis of a future preference for doing so. If she could, then some beings that do not yet possess self-consciousness (for instance, foetuses and infants) would have self-interests in surviving and, as I have pointed out, Harris denies this. However, perhaps a view at least similar to Harris's could be arrived at by focusing on actual or necessary preferences for survival instead. I briefly return to these possibilities at the end of this section.

By saying that P_1 has a self-interest in P_2 existing at $t_2(-t_3)$, I do not mean to imply that P_1 has an intrinsic self-interest in future existence *as such*. Presumably, what she will have a self-interest in is P_2's particular future life (not just the abstract fact *that* she exists).

According to (2), the strength of a present self-interest in surviving depends only on a global preference for doing so. Why is this? The argument employed to set up the Present Preference for Survival View relied on Preferentialism, and so on the view that what gives value to an individual's life is *preferences*. And it relied on the Object Interpretation, according to which it is an individual's *global* preference for its future as a whole that gives this future value. Therefore, presumably, a self-interest in survival will depend only on such a preference. However, even if a present preference for survival is a necessary condition for having a self-interest in surviving, perhaps the strength of the self-interest may rely partly, or even entirely, on the future strength of this preference.

Before I consider the Present Preference for Survival View on its own merits, as it is formulated above, I want to suggest that it may not make sense to allow this view to have such a narrow scope, where it applies only to a particular sort of self-interest, namely the self-interest in surviving. Consider the underlying

---

[25] Harris (1985: 18–19). Along similar lines, Peter Singer argues that 'the fetus has no right to, nor strictly speaking even an interest in, life. But . . . in the case of animals, to say that a being has no right to life does not mean that the being has no rights or interests at all. If the fetus is capable of feeling pain, then, like animals, the fetus has an interest in not suffering pain . . . ' (Singer 1993: 164).

[26] As is the Present Preference View, and for the same reason, the Present Preference for Survival View is time-relative.

rationale: the Object Interpretation and the requirement that preferences be present in order to ground present self-interests. The Object Interpretation implies quite generally that what makes something a bearer of intrinsic value is that it is the object of an (intrinsic) preference. Thus, we may have self-interests in all sorts of things, as long as these things are the objects of such preferences. It would be arbitrary to claim that a present self-interest in surviving has to be grounded on a present preference, but that other self-interests need not be grounded on present preferences. What this suggests is that, quite generally, an individual has a present self-interest in something only if she presently prefers it.

Thus, the Present Preference for Survival View is in danger of evolving into a version of the Present Preference View, and so of encountering at least some of the problems that bedevil this latter view.[27] However, in the following, I consider the Present Preference for Survival View, as formulated above, on its own merits.

What, then, should we think of the Present Preference for Survival View? Suppose we accept the Object Interpretation and the requirement that preferences have to be present in order to ground a present self-interest. It still seems to me that we can ascribe a self-interest in surviving to an individual, even if it has no preference for—or is even incapable of preferring—survival. Perhaps this individual has other preferences for the future; for instance, for various pleasures it may experience. Experiencing these pleasures then will have intrinsic value, according to the Object Interpretation. So even if this future does not have, as a whole, intrinsic value (because it is not preferred), specific components of it will.

In other words, what the Object Interpretation and the requirement that preferences be present do, of course, is rule out that a specific object—this future—(now) has intrinsic value, but they are quite compatible with the claim that *parts* of this future (now) have such value. Why is this not enough to ground a present self-interest in surviving? If it is in an individual's self-interest to enjoy various (presently preferred) future pleasures, how can we deny that it is in her self-interest to survive, when surviving is a necessary condition for enjoying them? Of course, the self-interest in surviving is conditional on her intrinsic self-interest in enjoying the pleasures.[28] But even such a conditional

---

[27] Perhaps it is such a version of the Present Preference View that Harris is appealing to in the argument presented above. I have already pointed out that perhaps Peter Singer can be interpreted along these lines.

[28] Therefore, it is surprising when Singer claims that 'As long as sentient beings are conscious, they have an interest in experiencing as much pleasure and as little pain as possible. Sentience suffices to place a being within the sphere of equal consideration of interests; but it does not mean that the being has a personal interest in continuing to live' (Singer 1993: 131). If a being has an (intrinsic) self-interest

self-interest is a self-interest and, indeed, it may provide a weighty reason to preserve the life of a conscious being.

Furthermore, when discussing the Present Preference View, I pointed out that the requirement that preferences be present is not plausible as a general requirement for self-interests. I have also noted that it would be arbitrary to limit this requirement to preferences for surviving. Without this requirement, however, there is nothing to prevent us from ascribing self-interests in surviving to individuals on the basis of their future preferences, including future preferences for continued existence. Therefore, even if we were to accept the Object Interpretation *and* the claim that an individual only has a self-interest in surviving if it has a global preference to survive, we could ascribe a self-interest in surviving to, for example, a foetus, on the basis of a future preference for survival.

Having raised these somewhat general and theoretical objections, I now want to consider the intuitive plausibility of the two parts of the Present Preference for Survival View. According to (1), an individual only has a present self-interest in surviving if she presently prefers to survive. This means that most non-human animals, foetuses, and even infants, have no self-interest in continued existence. Perhaps the view that non-human animals or even foetuses have no such self-interests seems intuitively plausible to many people, but when it comes to infants, most of us will protest vigorously. Of course, the fact that a view is counterintuitive is hardly a decisive objection, because there may be philo-sophical or theoretical reasons for accepting it nevertheless. However, I have argued that the Present Preference for Survival View does not seem to have this sort of support. Therefore, I do find its lack of intuitive plausibility troubling.[29]

Claim (1) also seems rather counterintuitive when we apply it to cases in which futures look very bleak indeed; for example, because they contain nothing but suffering. Suppose that due to some terrible disease an infant is destined to die before she reaches her fifteenth birthday and to experience continuous intense pain until then. Intuitively, it would seem to be in this infant's self-interest not to survive. However, on the assumption that self-interests in futures are to be assessed in terms of present global preferences, the infant has no present self-interest in dying. Of course, this is compatible with

---

in future pleasure and can only satisfy this interest by continuing to live, it has a conditional self-interest in surviving. For a similar objection to Singer, see McMahan (1998: 493).

[29] It may be objected that any view that attempts to cover the self-interests of beings that possess self-consciousness, infants, foetuses, and non-human animals, is bound to be counter-intuitive on some point or other. But I argue in Chapter 4 that once we realize that self-interests should be discounted for reductions in certain physical and psychological relations, an intuitively appealing view can be developed.

her having a present self-interest in not experiencing the (immediate) pain. But if we claim that this self-interest establishes a strong reason for allowing the infant to die, we are left wondering why self-interests in (immediate) pleasures do not establish a strong reason for allowing an infant to live (which is something that, as we have seen, Harris denies). Therefore, in the following, I assume that according to proponents of the Present Preference for Survival View, such *other* self-interests, even if related to survival or death, do not generate a strong reason for ensuring survival or death.

Now consider (2). Suppose first that we assess the strength of self-interests in surviving solely on the basis of the *present* strength of global preferences. Consider Ali and Venus, who both prefer to survive and do so to an equal extent. Neither has very strong preferences for anything, but whereas Ali's life will never change, Venus will develop all sorts of new strong preferences in the future and will have the good fortune of seeing them all satisfied. Despite the fact that Venus' future is much brighter than is Ali's, according to the Present Preference for Survival View, they have an equal self-interest in surviving. But this seems wrong; Venus has the stronger self-interest.

Perhaps, then, it would be better to claim that the strength of self-interests in surviving may depend (at least in part) on the *future* strength of global preferences. Insofar as Venus' preference for surviving will increase in the future, her present self-interest in surviving thus increases as well. This, of course, is as it should be. However, let us now slightly change the example. Neither Ali nor Venus has a present global preference for surviving. And while they will both gain such a preference in the future, Venus' preference will be much stronger than will Ali's. Nevertheless, the Present Preference for Survival View implies that Venus does not have a stronger self-interest in surviving than Ali does. In fact, neither has *any* self-interest in so doing.

Thus, because the Present Preference for Survival View is both theoretically and intuitively dubious, there are good reasons for rejecting it. We must search for a plausible account of the self-interest in survival elsewhere. Now, as I pointed out above, a global preference for survival view may be based on actual or necessary such preferences instead of present ones. However, just as the Present Preference for Survival View suffers from problems similar to those of the Present Preference View, such alternative global preference for survival views will suffer from problems similar to those of the Actual and the Necessary Preference View. Furthermore, they will also suffer from problems with respect to justification similar to those we have encountered when considering the Present Preference for

Survival View. Therefore, I shall not consider these options any further here.

2.8 Preferences, Goals, and Futility

I have now considered various views that add further conditions to the Identity View, which have to be satisfied in order to generate self-interests. These alternative views all claim that certain kinds of preferences are the basis of such interests. However, none of these views is particularly plausible. Nevertheless, perhaps preferences do have a role to play in a theory about self-interest—a role, that is, other than that they may play according to the Identity View (because benefits may be based on preferences).

Consider the following passages from Jeff McMahan:

> When a person has a long-standing desire for a certain long-term good, he or she is motivated, where possible, to take action to realize that good. Often this involves a considerable investment of time and effort. When death intervenes to prevent the satisfaction of a desire that has governed and structured a person's activities in these ways, it thereby retroactively condemns to futility certain significant dimensions of a person's past.   (McMahan 1998: 490)

> If a life lasts from t_1 to t_2, the death at t_2 may not only affect the value of the life as a whole by preventing it from containing more value than that which existed from t_1 to t_2, but may also affect the amount of value the life had between t_1 and t_2. That is, if the life had lasted to t_3, the value of the period from t_1 to t_2 might have been greater than it was given that the life ended at t_2.   (McMahan 1998: 490)

Imagine I have spent ten years of my life writing a book on moral philosophy, and that a couple of months before I am able to complete it, unfortunately I die. It seems that we may then consider my work on the book, to some extent at least, futile. I had set myself the goal of writing a book, and although I worked hard for many years, I never achieved it. My death seems to have rendered my strivings (to a certain degree) vain and pointless (McMahan 1988: 57; see also Lockwood 1979: 167).

To accommodate this point about futility, McMahan (1998: 490) suggests that an individual's self-interest in surviving depends not only on the benefits she may obtain in the future, but also on whether and to what extent activities in the individual's past were dependent for their meaning or value on their relation to these benefits. This is why (or part of the reason why), if I die before I finish my book, my death will be worse for me. So McMahan claims that past activities are relevant for assessing self-interests in surviving, not because they are necessary conditions for such interests, but because they affect their strengths.[30]

Note that McMahan rejects the Identity View, since he makes self-interest in survival dependent on things other than future benefits. Of course, a proponent of the Identity View may acknowledge that the past may be relevant for assessing self-interests in surviving. For instance, past and present preferences may be relevant since these preferences may contribute to the value of future benefits. If I have long preferred to finish my book, finishing it may involve a greater benefit to me than if my preference had had a shorter history. But what McMahan claims, if I understand him correctly, is that, apart from this future benefit, my self-interest in surviving may also depend on the value of my past. That is, it may also depend on the (alleged) fact that if I survive, my past will have been more valuable since my strivings to finish the book have not been in vain. That the value is to be located in the past becomes clear from the second passage quoted above.

While intuitively McMahan seems to have a point about futility, I am not convinced that we need to reject the Identity View in order to accommodate it. As I have just pointed out, a proponent of the Identity View can let the value of future benefits depend upon the strength and temporal extension of past and present preferences. So the fact that I have long preferred to finish my book may make its completion all the more valuable to me. Furthermore, futility may be explained by pointing out that my strivings to write a book gain their meaning from my (long-term) preference to do so, and that if it is satisfied, my strivings will not have been in vain. If so, my past and present preferences boost my self-interest in surviving, since my survival enables me to satisfy these preferences. And, it may be argued, if my self-interest is stronger, my death will be worse for me, just as McMahan would claim.

However, McMahan may insist that the disvalue of futility is to be located at the time of the pointless striving; that is, at the time when I am working on the book. After all, it is my work *then* that is futile. So if I work on my book from t_1 till I die at t_2, before I am able to complete it, my life from t_1 to t_2 will be less valuable than it would have been had I lived from t_1 to t_3 and so had seen my book finished. The explanation I have just offered, on the other hand, locates the value of (avoiding) futility at the time when I complete the book.

---

[30] Presumably, McMahan would claim that it is not just the self-interest in survival, but self-interests quite generally, that rely on past activities. As an example, suppose that I have worked on my book for the past nine years. Probably McMahan would say that my self-interest in finishing the book rather than abandoning the project is increased by the fact that, if I do finish my book, my strivings will not have been in vain.

It seems to me that there are no conclusive arguments for preferring either of these temporal locations of value. McMahan is surely right to point out that if I die at t_2, it is the period from t_1 to t_2 that is futile. On the other hand, we may stress that if I live until t_3, it is the completion of the book that prevents the futility of my work. So why not hold that this is where the value is located? Furthermore, if I am correct in suggesting that we may accept either of these locations, the issue concerning futility offers us no reason to reject the Identity View.

2.9 The Consciousness View

There is one more view that I would like to consider before ending this chapter. According to this view, the possession of consciousness is a necessary condition for having self-interests. For example, Bonnie Steinbock claims that:

> The restriction of interests to beings capable of conscious awareness stems from a certain conception of what it is to have interests. . . . If we think of interests as stakes in things, and understand what we have a stake in as defined by our concerns, by what matters to us, then the connection between interests and the capacity for conscious awareness becomes clear. Without conscious awareness, beings cannot care about anything.   (Steinbock 1992: 14)

The claim that self-interests presuppose consciousness adds to the Identity View a further condition that must be satisfied in order for us to ascribe self-interests to an individual. However, unlike the other alternative views I have considered, this condition is not coined (entirely) in terms of preferences. At the same time, it is not independent of preferences, since clearly an individual may possess consciousness (at least partly) in virtue of the preferences she may hold.

Thus consider the following:

> *The Consciousness View*. (1) P_1 has a self-interest at t_1 in P_2 benefiting at $t_2(-t_3)$, if and only if (a) P_1 exists at t_1, (b) P_1 and P_2 are numerically identical, and (c) P_1 possesses consciousness at t_1. (2) The strength of the self-interest depends only on, and is strictly proportional to, the size of the benefit.

Consciousness may involve feelings or qualia (such as pleasure or pain), preferences, and thoughts. Of course, an individual need not actually feel, prefer, or think at a particular time in order to possess consciousness at that time; rather, all that is required is that she has the capacity to do so in some appropriate dispositional sense.

Also, the different components of consciousness need not all be at the same level of importance, so to speak. For example, it may be claimed that the reason an individual has to have feelings and thoughts in order to have self-interests is that, otherwise, she cannot form preferences.[31] Therefore, according to the Consciousness View, it may well be preferences that ground self-interests after all. However, in order for the Consciousness View to be a *distinctive* view, and not just a version of the Present Preference View, it should not require that an individual presently prefers a benefit, or that the benefit involves a present preference, in order for the individual to have a self-interest in the benefit. Rather, it should at most require that the individual has preferences of some kind.[32]

The second part of the Consciousness View is identical to that of the Identity View, and so it requires no further discussion. Clearly, many other accounts are compatible with the first part, but presumably, they would proceed along lines similar to those of the preference-based views I have already considered. Moreover, at a minimum, the account presented here is commendable for its simplicity.

The Consciousness View may seem intuitively plausible in many cases. Unlike the Present Preference View, it does not require an individual presently to prefer something in order for her to have a present self-interest in having that something come about. For instance, an infant may have a self-interest in not having a drug administered to her that will later cause her to experience excruciating pain, although she does not presently have preferences regarding what should happen to her then. And unlike (some versions of) the Present Preference for Survival View, it does not require an individual to possess self-consciousness in order to have a self-interest in surviving. Finally, unlike (some versions of) the Identity View, it does not imply that a non-conscious foetus has a self-interest in surviving, which may come as a relief to many pro-abortionists.

However, the Consciousness View does imply that a non-conscious foetus does not have its self-interests thwarted by being exposed to thalidomide or similar drugs that may cause severe disabilities.[33] Nevertheless, proponents of

---

[31] Thus, Bonnie Steinbock (1992: 14) emphasizes that 'Conscious awareness is a prerequisite to desires, preferences, hopes, aims, and goals.'

[32] Despite their differences, however, the Consciousness View shares with the Present Preference View the feature of being time-relative.

[33] Although Steinbock claims that embryos and early foetuses do not have interests since they do not possess consciousness, she rejects the Consciousness View. This becomes clear when she points out that 'their future interests can be damaged by events that occur while they are still in the womb . . . ' (Steinbock 1992: 41). Applied to my example of thalidomide, her point seems to be that, if a non-conscious foetus is exposed to this drug, it will be contrary to its future actual preferences. Thus,

the Consciousness View may claim—with some plausibility—that a non-conscious foetus is not numerically identical to the child who later develops, and so that even though it would be wrong to expose the foetus to thalidomide, this has nothing to do with the self-interests of the *foetus*. But then, of course, a new difficulty emerges, namely that of accounting for the self-interest of the future child (who is obviously not presently conscious).

Additionally, the Consciousness View is in desperate need of a rationale. Why claim that the possession of consciousness is a necessary condition for having a self-interest in a future benefit? First, note that we cannot appeal to the view that when a being develops consciousness, it begins to have a special sort of importance or value (moral standing). The reasoning is that if it begins to have a special value, presumably it is because it begins to have interests. So interests explain moral standing, not the other way around.

Second, note that we can benefit or harm an individual without affecting her present conscious states. In the example considered above, an infant has a self-interest in not having a drug administered to her that will later cause her to experience excruciating pain. However, while the Consciousness View accommodates this claim, it does nothing to explain it. Since the present conscious states of the infant are not affected (or so we may assume), why is it required that the infant have such present states in order to have a present self-interest in not experiencing the pain?

Finally, note that the conscious states of an individual in no way need to refer to or represent the benefits she will later enjoy. At least according to the Present Preference View, we could explain why an individual's present preferences might be relevant for her present self-interest in a benefit. These preferences are relevant insofar as they have the benefit as their object, or the benefit involves their satisfaction. But no similar account seems available to the proponent of the Consciousness View. According to this latter view, even if an individual has to possess consciousness in order to have self-interest in a future benefit, and to have preferences in order to be conscious, these preferences need not have the benefit as their object, or involve the benefit. It seems, then, that there is nothing that links present consciousness to future benefits, on the basis of which we could explain the need for the former in order to have a self-interest in the latter.

Nevertheless, proponents of the Consciousness View may plausibly claim that there is in fact one dimension in which the present possession of consciousness links an individual to her future benefits. As I have already pointed out, perhaps an individual cannot be numerically identical to the individual to whom future benefits accrue unless she possesses consciousness. In other words, perhaps the pre-conscious foetus is not identical to the beneficiary, precisely because it does not (yet) possess consciousness. When consciousness develops, a new entity begins to exist and, since it is conscious, it is capable of benefiting. But whatever benefits accrue to it, they are not benefits of the pre-conscious foetus, for that would require identity. This, then, seems a reasonable explanation of why non-conscious individuals have no self-interests.

While this explanation may seem reasonable, however, it is of no help to the proponent of the Consciousness View who wants her view to remain a *distinctive* view. This is because, in effect, it turns the Consciousness View into a version of the Identity View. What the (c)-clause does, according to this explanation, is to render it possible that P_1 and P_2 are numerically identical. But the identity of P_1 and P_2 is already ensured by the (b)-clause. Thus, the (c)-clause is entirely superfluous. A version of the Consciousness View, then, that relies on consciousness to ensure identity, is just a version of the Identity View coupled with a particular theory of what personal identity consists of (presumably, some sort of psychological continuity).

Yet, as I argue in the next two chapters, we should reject the claim that identity is a necessary condition for self-interest. Therefore, we should reject the Identity View, including the version in which identity over time consists in psychological relations. However, I also argue that consciousness is nevertheless a necessary condition for self-interest. This part of the Consciousness View, then, is preserved.

2.10 Summary and a Look Ahead

According to the Identity View, all that is required for an individual to have a self-interest in a future benefit is that it exists and is identical to the beneficiary. Furthermore, the strength of such a self-interest depends only on, and is strictly proportional to, the size of the benefit. I have considered various alternatives to this view, most of which attach special significance to specific preferences—preferences that are present, actual, or necessary, and possibly have continued existence as their object. But none of these alternatives is very compelling. I have also considered the importance of futility, and argued that a reasonable explanation of this phenomenon can be provided within the limits of the Identity View. Finally, I have considered a view that focuses more broadly on consciousness, but have argued that it, too, fails to establish a plausible alternative.

Thus, it seems that we are back where we started—back to the Identity View. Nevertheless, we have made some progress, because we have considered various ways not to develop this view. For instance, it should not rely on a present preference, actual preference, or necessary preference theory of welfare. This also means that benefits are not time-relative. Rather, the value of a benefit is its value as assessed at the time of the benefit.

However, as I have also argued, the Identity View has problems of its own. It implies that a foetus (or an infant) has a stronger self-interest in surviving than does a twenty-year-old, and this strikes most of us as wrong. In the next two chapters, I argue that this problem can be solved once we realize that it is not identity that matters in survival, but some specific physical and psychological relations. These relations may obtain in different degrees, and the weaker they obtain, the weaker the self-interest is. Since a foetus is not as strongly related to itself at the age of thirty, for example, as the twenty-year-old is to herself at a similar age, the self-interest of the foetus in benefits at the age of thirty is diminished as compared to the twenty-year-old. This is why the twenty-year-old may have the stronger self-interest in surviving.

In Chapter 3, I introduce the issue of personal identity, which has been lurking in the background in the present chapter. All the views considered until now have relied on the assumption that (part of) what gives an individual a self-interest in a future benefit is that it is identical to the beneficiary. However, I shall argue that this assumption is wrong because identity is not what matters in survival. In Chapter 4, I then argue that what matters is certain physical and psychological relations, and that an individual's self-interest in a future benefit should be discounted for reductions in these relations.

3

Personal Identity

3.1 Personal Identity, Self-interest, and Morality

How is it possible for persons to survive the vast physical and psychological changes they undergo over their lives? This is the question of what personal identity over time consists in. It is the question of what makes a person at one time *numerically identical* to a person at another time. By 'numerically identical' I mean 'is one and the same entity'. This concept should not be confused with qualitative identity. We can imagine that two cars are qualitatively identical, that is, exactly similar. That, however, does not make them numerically identical; it does not make them one and the same car. Likewise, two people may be qualitatively identical and yet numerically different.

In the present chapter, I consider the importance of personal identity for our theory about self-interest. Remember that all the views considered in Chapter 2 rely on the assumption that identity is a necessary condition for such interests. Therefore, in order to clarify these views more fully, we would have to explain what personal identity consists in. Once this explanation is clear, at least in theory, we will be able to determine on the basis of each view whether an individual (for example, a foetus) has a self-interest in a future benefit. It seems, then, that there is a great need to clarify personal identity.

Whereas in Chapter 2 I mostly refer to the bearers of self-interests as 'individuals', in this chapter and the next I mostly refer to them as 'persons'. This is partly because the issues I address in these chapters are usually referred to as issues of 'personal identity', and partly because I primarily am concerned with the self-interests of beings such as ourselves, who are clearly persons. By 'persons', I mean individuals who have (or are) minds (that is, conscious beings). Thus, an individual does not have to exhibit a great deal of psychological complexity in order to be a person. For instance, she does not have to possess self-consciousness. All that is required is that she has a psychology. However, I do not assume that in order for an individual to have self-interests, it must be a person. Rather, one of the points of the exercise is to determine whether or not having a psychology is required.

The issue of personal identity seems not only relevant for our theory about self-interest, but also for morality. After all, as I point out in Chapter 2, the concern for self-interests is an important part of our moral concern. Consider again abortion. And suppose that our theory of personal identity implies that a foetus is not identical to the child who might be born and enjoy various benefits in life. It appears, then, that it is not in the foetus's self-interest to survive, because it is not the foetus that may enjoy these benefits. If so, at least one serious moral objection to abortion can be rebutted.

However, while personal identity certainly *seems* relevant for our theories about self-interest and morality, as I shall argue, it is not, or at least not to the extent it is usually thought. This is because personal identity is not what matters in survival. In Section 3.3, I elaborate on the meaning of the concept 'what matters in survival'. But for now, let me just give the following brief characterization: the question of 'what matters in survival' is that of what it is about a person's survival that makes the future him a particularly natural object of his present concern. The obvious answer seems to be that personal identity is what matters. It is the fact that the future him is the future *him*—is identical to him—that makes this future person especially interesting from his present perspective. However, following Parfit, I argue that this answer is wrong. And because it is wrong, the Identity View should be rejected, right along with the other views considered in Chapter 2. Furthermore, as I argue in Chapter 10, we need to rethink our theories of justice to accommodate the claim that identity is not what matters.

3.2 Two Concepts of Identity

In this section I want to consider two distinct concepts of identity and their relevance for some of the identity issues that were lurking in the background in Chapter 2. The first concept is that of personal identity over time. I have already explained this concept, but let me emphasize again that a person's (numerical) identity over time is the sort of identity associated with survival. To say that a person survives into the future is to say that there is a future individual who is numerically identical to him.

Here, we need to be careful; criteria of personal identity over time are often formulated along the following lines (Garrett 1998: 45; Noonan 1989: 3; Parfit 1984: 204; Unger 1990: 109):

Person P_1 at t_1 is numerically identical to person P_2 at t_2 if and only if_____

However, such criteria only fully account for survival on the assumption that we cannot survive as—and never were—non-persons (Olson 1997: 22–7). And this assumption is controversial. For example, some philosophers hold that our continued existence consists in the continued existence of the animals that we are. On this account, we were not always persons, because we were once non-conscious foetuses, and we may not always be persons in the future, because we may suffer brain damage that permanently erases our psychology but does not kill us. This is why I claim that to say a person survives into the future is to say there is a future *individual* who is numerically identical to him.

Instead of asking what personal identity over time consists in, we might ask what sort of beings we essentially are. That is, which of our properties (if any) are such that we could not exist without them? More technically, something is essentially a Φ (for instance, a person or a human being) if, and only if, in all possible worlds in which it exists, it is a Φ throughout its existence. Clearly, there are many properties that can be ruled out in advance. For example, although Barack Obama is president of the United States in 2009, he is not essentially the president of the United States, since he was not always a president and he might never have become one.

But perhaps he and the rest of us are essentially persons. If so, we could not have been entities without minds (for instance, rocks or oysters). Furthermore, we cannot survive having our minds destroyed, say, by a stroke, even if our bodies are kept artificially alive. And we did not come into existence before the foetuses from which we originated developed brains with the complexity necessary for sustaining consciousness.[1] Alternatively, perhaps we are essentially animals (of the species *Homo Sapiens*). If so, we could have been entities without minds (for example, anencephalic infants, missing their

---

[1] The question of what we essentially are should not be confused with another question sometimes raised in discussions of personal identity, namely the question of whether 'person' is a substance sortal. A concept C is a substance sortal if and only if an entity that falls under C at any time in its existence must fall under C throughout its entire existence. Now, even if some concept is a substance sortal, it does not follow that it refers to an essential property (Kripke 1980: 114, n. 57). This is because, even if an entity that *at some time* falls under C must do so throughout its existence, it does not follow that it could not have been such that it had never fallen under C. (For a criticism of various attempts to bridge the gap between substance sortals and what she calls essential sortals, see Mackie 1994).

cerebral hemispheres); we can survive having our minds destroyed (as long as the animal that we are continues to exist, for example, in a persistent vegetative state); and we did exist before our brains developed the complexity necessary for consciousness.

Although importantly different, these two concepts of identity are related. More precisely, our account of what sort of beings we essentially are provides valuable information about what our identity over time consists in, and vice versa. If, for instance, we are essentially persons, we will be persons throughout our existence, and we will have persistence conditions *qua* persons. Our account of what constitutes personal identity over time will then imply that we have never been and cannot become non-persons.

Furthermore, just like our account of what sort of beings we essentially are, our account of personal identity has implications for when we begin and cease to exist. A theory of personal identity over time identifies the relation that makes a person at one time numerically identical to an individual at a different time. Therefore, we can trace a person's existence back in time by determining how far back this relation obtains. We will then be able to answer the question of when the person came into existence (Lockwood 1985: 14). Likewise, at the other end of life, we can determine when a person ceases to exist by tracing the relation in the opposite direction.

These concepts of identity are commonly thought to be of great significance for both self-interests and morality (Carter 1982; Green and Wickler 1980; Lockwood 1985; 1994; McMahan 1995; Quinn 1993). For example, since they are relevant for when we begin and cease to exist, they are considered relevant for whether a foetus has a self-interest in the benefits of the child that may later emerge and whether a person now has a self-interest in what happens to 'her' in a future persistent vegetative state. Furthermore, what we say about self-interest in such cases may be relevant for our moral assessments of abortion and letting people with severe brain damage die (McMahan 1995: 126).

How are these concepts of identity relevant for the identity issues I pretty much neglect in Chapter 2? I objected to the Identity View, because it implies that a foetus (usually) has a stronger self-interest in surviving than does a twenty-year-old, since (usually) there are more benefits to be found in the future of the foetus. However, a proponent of the Identity View might argue that we are essentially persons and that the foetus is not, or that the relation of personal identity over time does not obtain between the foetus and the person who will later emerge to enjoy the various benefits of life. If so, then, according to the Identity View, the foetus has no self-interest in surviving (or perhaps only a very weak self-interest, insofar as it might develop consciousness before the sort of being we essentially are emerges, such that benefits may befall it at this early stage).

Nevertheless, I believe that the objection would still be powerful if, instead of a foetus, we consider the self-interests of an infant. Assuming that an infant is the sort of being we essentially are, according to the Identity View, the infant will (usually) have a much stronger self-interest in surviving than will a twenty-year-old. And this strikes me as almost as implausible as the claim that a foetus has such a strong self-interest in survival.

The proponent of the Identity View might of course deny that an infant can be the sort of being we essentially are. For instance, she may believe that we are essentially persons, and that in order to be a person, an individual has to possess self-consciousness.[2] But I rather doubt that we are essentially persons in this rather loaded sense of the term. Consider the implications. If we are essentially beings that possess self-consciousness, then parents care for two numerically distinct individuals during the childhood of their child(ren). They care for the infant, and they care for the person who later emerges. This may in itself seem counterintuitive. But it is rendered even more counterintuitive by the fact that both these individuals are conscious beings and so are clearly beings for whom things can go better and worse. The claim that there are two such distinct individuals for whom parents care is wildly out of line with some of our firm intuitions, as any parent will confirm.

We might also wonder how such a two-individual childhood should be construed, metaphysically. One possibility is that a conscious being comes into existence when the brain of the foetus begins to realize consciousness, and that a different conscious being comes into existence when that brain begins to realize self-consciousness. However, this suggestion seems seriously to overpopulate the world. There are then three distinct entities to keep track of: the animal (or organism); the first conscious being; and the second conscious being. Furthermore, what happens to the first conscious being when the second comes into existence? Since presumably all psychological states from then on should be ascribed to the second conscious being, it would seem gratuitous to claim that the first conscious being continues to exist. But if it goes out of existence, it would seem that the parents would be justified in

---

[2] Along such lines, Tooley suggests that although full self-consciousness perhaps is not a necessary condition for being a person, the possession (and possibly exercise) of the concept of a continuing mental substance is (Tooley 1983: 146). And along what seem to be similar lines, Kuhse and Singer write: 'We must recall, however, that when we kill a new-born infant there is no *person* whose life has begun. When I think of myself as the person I now am, I realize that I did not come into existence until some time after my birth. At birth I had no sense of the future, and no experiences which I can now remember as "mine" ' (Kuhse and Singer 1985: 134).

mourning the loss of this being, for whom they have cared greatly. After all, assuming the Identity View, the self-interests of the first conscious being do not extend to the second conscious being. In other words, the existence of the second conscious being is of no comfort from the egoistic perspective of the first such being.

Thus, it would seem better instead to claim that there are only two distinct entities for whom the parents care: the animal, and the self-conscious being who later emerges. This implies that the psychological states that surface before the self-conscious being emerges are states of the animal. Such an account may seem innocent enough since any proponent of the view that we are essentially persons will have to acknowledge that the person is distinct from the animal. However, we still need to know what the relation is between the psychology of the animal and of the self-conscious being. When the self-conscious being comes into existence, presumably it possesses all the psychological states from then on. But, what about the animal? Suppose it ceases to have psychological states. Surely, the parents would then be justified in mourning, since this being for whom they have cared greatly has turned into an insentient 'vegetable'. After all, assuming the Identity View, the animal has no self-interests regarding what happens to the self-conscious being.

Suppose instead that the animal and the self-conscious being 'co-possess' all the psychological states that exist after the latter being comes into existence. It would then seem that the parents care for two distinct beings who coexist throughout the entire duration of the self-conscious being's life. Again, this is wildly out of line with our intuitions. Therefore, it would seem that the proponent of the Identity View cannot render her view more plausible by claiming that we are essentially self-conscious beings and so we were never infants.

Another objection I raised, this time concerning the Present Preference View, is that a foetus appears to have a self-interest in not being subjected to thalidomide. The problem is that since the foetus does not have a present preference regarding the condition of the child who will be born, according to this view, it cannot have a self-interest in avoiding that the child is disabled. The proponent of the Present Preference View might now reply that the foetus and the person who emerges are not identical, and the reason thalidomide should not be used is that the person who will come into existence has a self-interest in not suffering from a disability.

However, there are three problems with this answer. First, as I point out in Chapter 2, a similar problem may occur in the case of an infant. She too seems to have self-interests regarding benefits (or harms) to which her present preferences do not apply. Second, suppose that the foetus is conscious. To claim that the person does not yet exist, and thus there are (at least) two conscious beings, will get us into the sort of trouble I have just highlighted in connection with the Identity View. And third, if an individual cannot have any present self-interests if she does not have any present preferences, then how can a future person have present self-interests? Of course, a future person can have future self-interests, but if we allow the future self-interests of future persons to ground present moral reasons (such as the strong reason a pregnant woman has not to take thalidomide), then why can't the future self-interest of a child in obtaining various benefits give rise to a strong moral reason not to kill a foetus from which this child may later emerge?

3.3 Two Senses of What Matters in Survival

According to the Identity View, it is in a person's self-interest that his future contains benefits, in fact, as many as possible. These benefits are what makes his future—and so his surviving into the future—valuable for him. This is a claim regarding what Peter Unger (1990: 92–7) calls the *desirability sense* of what matters in survival, namely that which makes survival desirable; that is, the benefits it involves. This, of course, is not to say that survival is intrinsically valuable. It may or may not be. But, at least usually, when a person survives, certain benefits befall him.

However, a theory about self-interest needs more than an account of what matters in the desirability sense. It needs a focus, a specification of to *whom* it is desirable that future benefits accrue. According to the Identity View, future benefits must fall in a person's *own* future in order for them to be in his self-interest. And indeed, this condition seems quite natural. As the name 'a theory about self-interest' suggests, the focus of such a theory is simply the person whose self-interest we are considering.

Nevertheless, there is more to self-interest than what is suggested by the name. Thus, a person is usually much more concerned about his own self-interest than about the interests of other people. In other words, his self-interests feature more predominantly in his total pattern of concerns than do the self-interests of others. As I pointed out in the last chapter: if he is informed that some person will be tortured in the near future, he may be saddened. But if he is informed that this person is him, he will probably be terrified. This, it seems, is exactly because the pain will be *his*.

Furthermore, a person's self-interest is often thought to provide him with reasons of a particularly strong sort and, again, this has to do with the fact that his self-interest pertains to his *own* benefits. In fact, some philosophers believe that, ultimately, no one has a reason to do anything unless it is in his self-interest to do so.

What, then, is it about a person's own future life that makes it so important that benefits fall in *his* rather than in someone else's future life? In other words, what is it that is involved in a person's survival that makes the future him a natural focus of special interest? Posing this question is to ask what matters in survival in what Unger calls the *prudential sense*. In the prudential sense, what matters in survival—if anything—is that which gives a person special concern regarding the person he will be in the future.

I should emphasize that I am not assuming we should be more concerned about our own self-interests than about the self-interests of others, or even that it is permissible for us to be so. Indeed, the theory of justice I develop in the second part of the book is fully impartial between the self-interests of different individuals. So when I say that what matters in the prudential sense is what gives a person *special* concern regarding the person he will be in the future, I am characterizing our prudential perspective rather than making a claim about what our overall pattern of concern should be. I am enquiring about the relation in virtue of which, for example, we find it natural to fear our own future pain more than the future pain of others; look more forward to our own pleasures than the pleasures of others etc.

I need to be more precise here. I am not looking for our more or less unreflective answers to questions about the nature of this relation. The question of what matters prudentially is a normative question and what I have said about method in Chapter 1 applies as much to this question as to the other normative questions I attempt to answer in this book. Thus, we need to consider what sort of rationale (if any) can be provided for the various candidates for being the relevant relation; what these candidates imply with respect to our self-interests in actual and hypothetical cases; the extent to which these implications match our considered judgements or intuitions; and we need to apply the usual criteria of theory-choice such as consistency, comprehensiveness, and explanatory power. This also means that if a certain theory can be shown to be implausible as a criterion of personal identity, we should reject the claim that identity *in this sense* is what matters prudentially.

Note that what matters in the prudential sense need not be something that matters in the desirability sense; that is, makes survival good. Consider a case in which a person's future holds neither benefits nor harms. Nevertheless, her future may hold all of what matters in the prudential sense. After all, she may be very concerned about her future looking so bleak, which suggests that the future her is the focus of a special interest on her part.

What, then, does prudentially matter in survival? All of us start off believing that it is, simply, survival. What prudentially matters for a person is that he survives; that is, that there will exist a future being who is *him*. Since his survival just consists in the obtaining of an identity relation between him and a future person, most philosophers refer to this as the view that identity is what prudentially matters. And, indeed, this view fits nicely with the Identity View and with other views that take numerical identity to be a necessary condition for self-interest. It fits nicely in the sense that, if it is true, we can explain why the Identity View (and these other views) hold the prudential significance they are usually taken to have. Since these views assume that identity is a necessary condition for self-interest, and since identity is what prudentially matters, clearly these views have prudential significance.

But suppose that it turned out that it was not identity, but some different relation that prudentially matters; for instance, a relation that a person can stand in to two numerically different people. Then this relation, rather than identity, would define the scope of our prudential concern. Thus, identity would not be a natural focus in a theory about the sort of special concern we usually have for ourselves.

We could respond to such an insight in either of two ways. We could claim that the Identity View and, more generally, self-interest do not hold the prudential significance we usually assign to them. Or we could revise the Identity View such that it had a different scope; that is, had the relation that matters rather than identity as its focus. This revised view would then claim that what is in a person's self-interest is that benefits befall individuals to whom she stands in the relation that matters. Since this would ensure that our theory about self-interest would have the prudential significance that is usually assigned to it, I suggest that we should opt for the revisionist alternative. After all, what motivates our special interest in self-interest is primarily the prudential significance it is thought to have.

Of course, it may be objected that for semantic reasons, a theory about *self*-interest must have the identity of the self—that is, personal identity—as its focus. However, this is a merely verbal point. We might decide to use the term 'self-interest' differently if we have a reason to do so. Secondly, in the literature on personal identity it is standard to refer to the future individuals to whom one stands in the relation that prudentially matters as one's future selves, whether or not one is identical to them. Thus, we can say that it is in a person's self-interest that his future selves fare well, without implying identity.

I submit that if identity is not what prudentially matters in survival, then we should change the scope of our theory about self-interest. And, as I shall argue, we should also change the component that has to do with the strength of a person's self-interest.

Thus, if it is not identity that prudentially matters, what does? One suggestion is that it is psychological continuity and connectedness, and I discuss this suggestion at some length in the next chapter. However, it may be worth briefly commenting on an objection to this suggestion here, while the distinction between what matters in the prudential and in the desirability sense is still fresh. According to the objection—which is raised by Peter Unger—David Lewis and other proponents of the view that what matters in survival is psychological continuity and connectedness are making claims about what matters in the desirability sense, rather than the prudential sense.

Before I discuss Unger's objection, these psychological relations need to be explained. There is a direct psychological connection between a person—call her Wendy—today and the person ten years ago, if today she can remember some of the experiences she had then, or if today she carries out an intention she had then. Likewise, there is a direct psychological connection if Wendy continues to have some of the preferences, beliefs, or character traits she had then. If such direct psychological relations hold between Wendy now and Wendy then, she is now *psychologically connected* to herself ten years ago.

Psychological continuity is the holding of overlapping chains of psychological connectedness. Therefore, if Wendy today remembers some of her experiences from yesterday, and yesterday she remembered some of her experiences from the day before, and so on, twenty years back, then she is presently *psychologically continuous* with herself twenty years ago, even if she does not remember a single experience she had then.

Lewis believes that these psychological relations are what matter in survival. As he says:

> When I consider various cases in between commonplace survival and common-place death, I find that what I mostly want in wanting survival is that my mental life should flow on. My present experiences, thoughts, beliefs, desires, and traits of character should have appropriate future continuers.   (Lewis 1976: 17)

One might think that this suggestion does not really amount to an alternative to the view that what prudentially matters is identity, because these psychological relations may be what personal identity consists of. However, it is possible for a person to stand in these psychological relations to two numerically distinct people. And since one person cannot be identical to two (who are not identical), the suggestion that these psychological relations are what matter does not coincide with the suggestion that identity is what matters.[3] In fact, I discuss such a case of multiple psychological continuers in Section 3.5.

After these preliminary remarks, I can return to Unger's objection. When Unger claims that psychological continuity and connectedness matter only in the desirability sense, apparently it is because he thinks that the concern for these relations flows from one's present projects (1990: 94–5). And since these projects (or their fulfilment) are part of what makes life worth living, their importance is found in the fact that they make survival desirable. For example, if a person currently wants to create a work of art, it will be imperative for her that she continues to have this wish (along with a number of her other present psychological features). This, she thinks, will make her future more valuable.

Is Unger's objection plausible? If Unger takes the passage cited from Lewis to mean that Lewis wants psychological continuity and connectedness because this will make his life more worth living, then, of course, Lewis is making a claim about what matters in the desirability sense. In fact, I do think that to some extent the existence of such psychological relations bestows future benefits on people. For instance, I think that it will normally add to the value of a person's future if, in the future, she can remember her present life.

But Lewis might be making a different claim instead, or as well. He might be claiming that psychological continuity and connectedness are what make his future prudentially matter to him, rather than what makes it good for him. These relations make his future benefits matter especially from his perspective. If some psychological relations matter in both the desirability and the prudential sense, then sometimes they go together. But then there are two different explanations of why these relations matter. They matter because, when they hold, this involves future benefits; and because, when they hold, this gives the person a special reason to care about his or her future, and so especially about these future benefits.

Of course, Lewis does say that he *wants* certain psychological relations to hold between himself now and in the future. But this need not indicate that he believes that these psychological relations matter (only) in the desirability sense. After all, if psychological relations are what prudentially matter, it is hardly surprising that we want them to obtain. This need not be a claim that

---

[3] It should be noted, however, that according to Lewis himself, these two views really do coincide. But, in order to defend this claim, he has to accept (and does accept) a rather peculiar view on personal identity, which includes the so-called multiple occupancy thesis. According to this, two persons can occupy one and the same body and mind at the same time. See Lewis (1976).

we unconditionally prefer that they obtain, but, perhaps, that we prefer this conditionally on the fact that our futures hold a net surplus of good over bad. In other words, we want these relations to obtain (at least partly), because it is a precondition for something we intrinsically prefer, namely future benefits to beings to whom we stand in the relation that prudentially matters. (For brevity, from now on, I shall refer to the prudential sense of what matters merely by the term 'what matters'.)

Therefore, I think that Unger's objection does not rule out the view that what matters are certain psychological relations. In fact, later on, I defend a modified version of this view.

3.4 Theories of Personal Identity Over Time

People who believe that what matters in survival is identity, do not all believe the same thing. This, of course, is because they accept different theories of what personal identity consists in.

According to non-reductionists, facts about persons and their existence over time are facts over and above physical and psychological facts. Thus, according to one leading proponent of non-reductionism, Richard Swinburne, we are essentially souls; that is, indivisible immaterial beings, and our psychological properties are properties of the souls that we are (1984: section 2; 1987: 33–4). Our continued existence, then, consists in the continued existence of these immaterial beings. Furthermore, questions about whether two persons are identical always have determinate answers; either they are or they are not.

This view, I believe, does not have much to be said for it. In fact, there are good reasons for believing that it is false. Let me briefly mention two. Consider first the following thought experiment. Gradually, one cell at a time, a person is taken apart. At one point, when a large number of cells have been removed, a very sophisticated life support system is hooked up to the person, to keep him alive. It secures his blood circulation, respiratory function, etc. At some point, when (enough of) his brain cells have been removed, he will start to lose some of his memories, desires, and character traits. And at some (perhaps later) point, his ability to reason, form preferences, and so on will be weakened. Furthermore, because of the gradualness of the surgical removals, these psychological changes themselves will be very gradual. So much so, in fact, that one might hardly be able to detect any psychological changes from the removal of one cell to the removal of the next.

At the far end of this spectrum, when only a small group of cells remain, his brain (or what's left of it) will no longer realize any psychology, nor animal functions such as metabolism etc. It would be gratuitous, then, to claim that the person still exists. Rather, he has ceased to exist. Furthermore, given the gradualness of the physical and psychological changes, it is difficult to believe that there is a single cell of which it is true that before it is removed, the person exists, and after it is removed, he has ceased to exist. Rather, there is a range in which it is neither true that the person ceases to exist, nor true that he does not cease to exist. In other words, it is hard to accept that questions of personal identity always have determinate answers. And since Swinburne claims that they do, it is difficult to believe in his non-reductionism.[4]

My second objection to non-reductionism is this. If we are souls and souls are immaterial beings, then how do we succeed in interacting with our bodies? In other words, how is mental causality possible? We seem to need some sort of explanation of how that which is not physical can causally engage that which is physical (and the other way round for that matter), and it is difficult to imagine what such an explanation might look like, even in an outline form (Kim 1996: 130–2).

Instead, let us consider reductionism, or, more precisely, three versions of this view. According to animalism, we are essentially animals (of the species *Homo Sapiens*), and our continued existence consists simply in the continued existence of the animals that we are (Carter 1982; Johansson 2005; Oderberg 1997; Olson 1997; Snowdon 1990). However, not all parts of an animal are equally important for its survival. Thus, animalists tend to focus on (what controls our) vital animal functions, such as metabolism, circulation, respiration, temperature regulation, etc. (Olson 1997: ch. 6). Consider:

> *The Animalist Criterion of Personal Identity over Time.* If P_1 is an animal at t_1, then P_1 at t_1 is numerically identical to P_2 at t_2 if and only if (a) the vital animal functions P_1 has at t_1 are sufficiently causally continuous with the vital animal functions P_2 has at t_2, and (b) this causal continuity does not take a branching form.[5]

Since our vital animal functions are located in our lower brains, some animalists are prepared to say that we could survive as mere heads (Olson 1997: 133), or as mere brains (van Inwagen 1990: 172), if only our heads or brains were secured a suitable environment for survival. In fact, such animalists should be

---

[4] Essentially the same objection is also made in Parfit (1984: 236–43), and Unger (1990: 191–7). For a criticism of the objection, as formulated by Parfit, see Madell (1985).

[5] Strictly speaking, it is a bit misleading to refer to this as a criterion of *personal* (rather than animal) identity, but since it is standard in the literature, and convenient (because I can then refer to the different criteria as criteria of personal identity), I shall do so nonetheless. Also, the point of the (b)-clause, which rules out branching, will become clear in the next section.

prepared to say that if, for example, only the lower brain were transplanted from one body to another (in which the skull had been suitably emptied), the resulting individual would be the donor of the lower brain.[6]

Nevertheless, many theorists find animalism implausible because it implies that identity may be disassociated with psychology. Consider two persons, *a* and *b*, who are identical twins. Suppose that while the lower brain of *a* is destroyed, her cerebral hemispheres are transplanted into the head of *b* (from which *b*'s cerebral hemispheres have been removed). While a person's vital animal functions are located in her lower brain, her psychology is located in her cerebral hemispheres. Therefore, the resulting person will be psychologically continuous with *a* and, according to these theorists, it is therefore plausible to claim that they identical. After all, the resulting person will seem to remember *a*'s life, and share her thoughts, commitments, and plans. This means that a person can survive having her lower brain destroyed, which again implies the rejection of animalism.[7]

A number of philosophers have suggested a criterion that preserves an essential link between identity and psychology and yet does not give up the idea of accounting for personal identity in physical (or material) terms:

> *The Physical Criterion of Personal Identity over Time.* If P_1 is a person at t_1, then P_1 at t_1 is numerically identical to P_2 at t_2 if and only if (a) there is sufficiently continuous physical realization of a core psychology between the physical realizer of P_1's core psychology at t_1 and the physical realizer of P_2's core psychology at t_2, and (b) this continuous physical realization does not take a branching form.[8]

This criterion needs to be clarified further. The continuous physical realization of psychology refers to the continuous physical realization of *dispositional* psychology. Thus, a being can realize the ability to think at a particular time, without actually thinking at that time. It is enough that, provided with suitable stimulation, she would think.

Also, it needs to be specified that 'core psychology' refers to the capabilities that are generally shared by human beings; for instance, the capacity to remember, form intentions, reason, and, I would add, the capacity to have certain sensations, such as pleasure and pain. This sort of psychology should be distinguished from the sort involved in psychological continuity and connectedness, which is distinctive psychology; that is, the particular memories,

---

[6] Cases of brain transplants were first discussed, I believe, in Shoemaker (1963: 22–5).

[7] Note that this is also an argument against bodily approaches to personal identity (Thomson 1997) that, strictly speaking, are not versions of animalism.

[8] In formulating the Physical Criterion like this, I am heavily indebted to Unger (1990: 109).

intentions, preferences, and character traits that make each of us psychologically different from other people.

Notice that the Physical Criterion implies that if *a*'s cerebral hemispheres are inserted into *b*'s body, the resulting person will be *a*, since *a*'s core psychology is continuously realized physically by *a*'s cerebral hemispheres, from *a*'s body into *b*'s body. And, indeed, this is a result that many identity theorists will welcome.

Note also that, according to this criterion, a person's psychology need not be realized in the brain to ensure his survival. In fact, he could survive having his brain replaced with some other medium that could realize his psychology (for instance, a complex bionic circuitry), if only there was sufficiently continuous physical realization of core psychology between his brain and this new medium.[9]

The final main contender is:

> *The Psychological Criterion of Personal Identity over Time.* If P_1 is a person at t_1, then P_1 at t_1 is numerically identical to P_2 at t_2 if and only if (a) between P_1 at t_1 and P_2 at t_2 there is sufficient psychological continuity, (b) this continuity has the right kind of cause, and (c) does not take a branching form.   (Parfit 1984: pt 3; Shoemaker 1984)[10]

Note that the sort of psychology referred to here is distinctive (dispositional) psychology. To many identity theorists, this is an advantage. After all, we may ask ourselves why people tend to believe that in the case in which the cerebral hemispheres are transplanted, the resulting person is *a*. At least part of the reason seems to be that the resulting person can remember *a*'s experiences, and has similar preferences, projects, character traits, etc. That is, it is (at least partly) because the resulting person has *a*'s distinctive psychology.

The (b)-clause in the Psychological Criterion may be interpreted in different ways. On one reading, the right kind of cause is the normal cause; that is, the continued existence and functioning of the brain. This will turn the

---

[9] In this respect, the Physical Criterion differs from the brain-based criterion, according to which we are essentially psychology-realizing brains, and our continued existence consists (roughly) in the continued existence of our brains (Nagel 1986: 37–43; Mackie 1976: 199–203; Lockwood 1985; McMahan 2002: 66–94). However, the reason for focusing on the brain seems to be that it is the carrier of our psychologies. But if psychological features really are doing the work, then why insist that they are realized in a brain?

[10] Actually, to avoid the so-called circularity objection (which is sometimes ascribed to Butler), this criterion must be formulated in terms of quasi-memory rather than memory. A person P quasi-remembers the experience E if and only if (i) P is in a state as of remembering E, (ii) the content of this state corresponds to the content of E, and (iii) P's apparent memory is causally related to E in the right sort of way. The point is that the fact that P quasi-remembers E does not imply that it was in fact she who had E, and so quasi-remembering does not presuppose identity. Likewise, the criterion should be formulated in terms of quasi-intention rather than intention etc. In the following, when I talk about psychological continuity and connectedness, I have these quasi-relations in mind.

Psychological Criterion into a version of the brain-based criterion. However, on a different reading, the right kind of cause can be any cause. To illustrate the difference between these two readings, remember the case of teletransportation to which I referred in Chapter 1. A computer records the states of all your cells and sends the information to another computer on Mars, where an exact copy of you is made out of new material. At the same time, your entire body is destroyed here on earth. On the second reading, unlike on the first reading, you are identical to your replica on Mars (Parfit 1984: 207–8).

There are, then, three main versions of the claim that identity is what matters, where each has some initial plausibility. They are based on the Animalist, the Physical, and the Psychological Criterion, respectively. However, as I shall now argue, they are all ultimately implausible—identity is not what matters.

3.5 Why Identity is Not What Matters in Survival

If we are animalists, I believe we should deny that identity is what prudentially matters (Olson 1997: ch. 3). Consider again the two cases of brain transplantation outlined above. In the case in which the lower brain is transplanted, it seems implausible that the donor should be prudentially concerned about the resulting person. How can the causal continuity of animal functions such as metabolism etc. have such significance? But this is exactly what we must assume that such continuity does have, if we are to maintain the claim that animalist identity is what prudentially matters.

Then consider the case in which a person's cerebral hemispheres are transplanted. In this case, it seems plausible to claim that the relation that prudentially matters *does* obtain between donor and the resulting person. After all, while the resulting person will not have the donor's body, she will know all about her, share her memories, character traits, and plans for the future, and be in every other psychological respect exactly similar to her. But since, according to animalism, the resulting person is not identical to the donor, the claim that the prudentially significant relation obtains between them is incompatible with the view that animalist identity is what prudentially matters. Therefore, if we are animalists, we should claim that identity is not what matters. Therefore, in the rest of the chapter, I shall only consider the Physical and the Psychological Criterion in relation to our prudential concerns.

Let us consider a new case of brain transplantation, where *a* is one of three identical triplets. His brain is removed from his head, and one of his cerebral hemispheres is inserted into each of his brothers' skulls, from which their cerebral hemispheres have been removed. Since, as it is believed to be the case in some people, a's two hemispheres are equally good realizers of psychological continuity, both the resulting people, b and c, are psychologically continuous with a, and, we may assume, to the same degree. Furthermore, idealizing somewhat, let us assume that both of a's hemispheres realize all of a's psychology. So b and c both seem to remember a's life, and have emotional attachments, projects, and character traits that are exactly similar to his. This case is represented in Figure 3.1 as World 1.

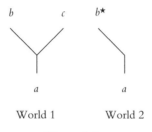

World 1   World 2

Figure 3.1.

As it has been famously argued by Parfit (1971; 1984: ch. 12), we can use this case to show why identity is not what matters in survival, even on the assumption that our identity is to be explained by the Physical or the Psychological Criterion.[11] However, in order to show this, we need to contrast World 1 with World 2. In World 2, a's brain is divided by destroying one hemisphere, and the other hemisphere is then inserted into one brother's skull.

The Physical and the Psychological Criterion imply that if the resulting person had both of a's cerebral hemispheres, then he would clearly be a. Furthermore, people have survived having one cerebral hemisphere destroyed—for instance, by a stroke—with only one functioning hemisphere remaining. This judgement is supported by the fact that there may be massive psychological continuity between the pre-stroke and the post-stroke person, and the fact that most of his core psychology may be intact. Combining these beliefs, it is plausible to claim that even when only one of a's hemispheres is transplanted, the resulting person is a. So in World 2, $a = b\star$. And, indeed, this is what we should claim according to both the Physical and the Psychological Criterion.

---

[11] For a more recent account of why identity is not what matters, and an attempt to deal with various objections, see Parfit (1995).

What, then, about the case in which both of *a*'s brothers receive a brain hemisphere from *a*; that is, World 1? It seems that both *b* and *c* are equally good candidates for being *a* as *b*★ is in World 2. But since *b* and *c* are not the same person, they cannot both be *a*. Furthermore, it would be arbitrary to say that *a* is one rather than the other. Therefore, *a* is neither. He has simply ceased to exist. To accommodate this judgement, of course, is why both the Physical Criterion and the Psychological Criterion have a clause to rule out branching.[12]

How do we get from the claims about identity in Worlds 1 and 2 to the conclusion that identity is not what matters? Consider World 2 again. Even though what *a*'s survival amounts to is having one of his hemispheres destroyed and the other transplanted, presumably his relation to the future him—that is, *b*★—contains what matters. This is because *a* is related to *b*★ by *b*★ having one of *a*'s hemispheres that continuously realizes a core and distinctive psychology, which, of course, is also why *b*★ *is a*.

In World 1, *a* stands in exactly the same physical and psychological relations to each of *b* and *c*, as he does to *b*★ in World 2. And since *a*'s relation to *b*★ contains what matters, so will his relations to both *b* and *c*. Therefore, *a*'s relations to *b* and *c* can contain what matters without *a* being identical to (either of) them, and so identity cannot be what matters. This argument to the effect that identity is not what matters I shall call the Anti-identity Argument.

Apart from being supported by the Anti-identity Argument, it seems to me that the conclusion that identity is not what matters is supported by our intuitions about what matters in such cases of division. Consider World 2 again. Assume that *a* is informed that *b*★ is going to be tortured terribly immediately after the brain transplant has been completed. Naturally, he is devastated. In fact, putting myself in *a*'s shoes, I am inclined to be just as concerned about this torture as I would be if I were to learn that tomorrow it would be me who would be tortured. So, regarding what matters, there appears to be no difference between ordinary survival and the sort of survival that *a* experiences in World 2.

But suppose now that *a* learns that, as it turns out, both of his brain hemispheres are going to receive a new body; that is, that the actual world is World 1. Nevertheless, the person on the left branch is still going to be tortured terribly. Putting myself in *a*'s shoes, I am inclined to care just as much about *b*'s torture in World 1 as I would about *b*★'s torture in World 2 (and as I

---

[12] The Animalist Criterion implies that just as *a* is not identical to *b* or *c*, he is not identical to *b*★ either. Yet, there are other cases of division that require this criterion to have a similar clause.

would in an ordinary case of survival). In other words, the existence of c (for example in some other wing of the hospital) does not change my attitude to the torture. Of course, c's existence may make a difference in the sense that World 1 is better from a's perspective, because here, the benefits that c may enjoy can be held to *compensate* for b's suffering. But that is beside the point. The point is that the attitude concerning the *torture* does not depend on which world a occupies. And this suggests that the relation that matters is preserved equally well in both worlds, despite the fact that a only survives in one of them. Thus, it suggests that identity is not what matters.

3.6 Survival, Existence, and the Only X and Y Principle

One concern regarding the Anti-identity Argument should be addressed immediately. It may appear to violate the following principle:

> *The Only X and Y Principle.* Whether y is identical to x can depend only on facts about x and y and the relations between them.

In particular, this principle implies that whether a person P_1 is identical to a person P_2 cannot depend upon facts about persons other than P_1 and P_2. The problem is that I claimed that, in World 1, $a \neq b$ and it seems that all that prevents b from being identical to a is the existence of someone else, namely c (after all, in World 2, there is no competition, and so a is identical to the recipient of his brain hemisphere). But, in fact, we can deny this. Assuming that $a \neq b$, and assuming that $a = b^\star$, and since identity is transitive and necessary, it follows that $b \neq b^\star$. Therefore, whether or not c exists, $a \neq b$, and so the Only X and Y Principle is not violated (Garrett 1990: 31–2).

However, although the Only X and Y Principle is not violated, the Anti-identity Argument has other metaphysical implications that may seem disturbing. Whether a continues to exist depends upon whether someone else, c, comes into existence. After all, in World 2, where c does not come into existence, a survives the transplant, whereas he does not survive in World 1. Furthermore, whether b comes into existence also depends upon whether c comes into existence. After all, b only comes into existence in World 1 because here, c does so as well. And these judgements may seem quite absurd. After all, c's existence does not causally affect b.

Nevertheless, I shall not assess these metaphysical implications any further here. I believe that we should give up the idea that events cannot determine the existence of entities to which they stand in no causal relations, whether these entities are persons or mere objects.[13] Yet, it is worth pointing out that (at least part of) our hesitation with respect to giving up this idea in the case of persons may have more to do with our views about prudence than with our views about metaphysics. Thus, except maybe for legal reasons, identity judgements about mere objects do not seem to be of much significance. But when it comes to persons, such judgements seem crucial. If one was in a's shoes, it would seem to be of the utmost importance whether someone else, namely c, came into existence, because one would cease to exist if he did.

What this line of reasoning suggests, however, is not that existence and survival cannot depend on causally unrelated events, but that what matters cannot. This is because the difference between mere things and persons is held to be a difference in significance. And the significance that a person's survival has is that it provides her with the relation that matters; that is, the relation that gives her a special interest in the person she will be in the future. Plausibly, then, it may be claimed that the relation that matters does not depend on causally unrelated events. And this claim is accommodated by the Anti-identity Argument, since it involves the suggestion that what matters to a is simply his intrinsic relation to b, $b^\star$, and c.

Consider again, then, the two alleged absurdities in the Anti-identity Argument. Although a will cease to exist if c comes into existence, this sort of death may not matter from his perspective. Neither of a's continuers will be him, but his relation to them will contain what matters. Therefore, the special sort of badness that is associated with the death of a person (but not with the death of a mere thing), and which may motivate the thought that the Anti-identity Argument is absurd, does not even come into play.

When one considers the second alleged absurdity—that whether b comes into existence depends upon whether c comes into existence—one realizes that there are in fact two distinct ways in which identity is not what matters. It does not matter whether a's future continuer(s) are identical to him. This is a claim about the significance of personal identity over time. But the second absurdity does not concern the significance of identity over time, but rather concerns the significance of *transworld* identity, or of coming into existence in the first place.

Why, exactly, is the second absurdity thought to be absurd? According to Harold Noonan (1989: 160), we could say to b: 'You should consider yourself fortunate that the other fellow's brain transplant [that is, c's brain transplant]

---

[13] There are, however, other ways of dealing with identity that do not force us to give up this idea. But they seem to me less plausible. For one such account, which involves a commitment to the multiple occupancy thesis mentioned earlier, see Noonan (1989: ch. 7).

went so well—if it hadn't, you would never have existed.' But why claim that *b* is *fortunate*? Just as it does not matter from *a*'s point of view whether his future continuers are identical to him, as long as the relevant relations hold between him and them, it may be claimed that it does not matter from *b*'s perspective whether the person who comes into existence in the *b*-body is *b*. After all, if all the non-existence of *b* would really amount to would be the non-existence of *c*, then why should non-existence matter from *b*'s perspective? So *b* might answer Noonan by saying, 'Although I would not have existed if the doctors hadn't done such a good job on the other fellow, why should I care about *that*?' This, I think, takes the sting out of the second absurdity as well.

Let me briefly elaborate on this point. When I say that 'all the non-existence of *b* would really amount to would be the non-existence of *c*', I of course do not mean to imply that the state of affairs that *b* does not exist and the state of affairs that *c* does not exist are one and the same state of affairs.[14] Obviously, they are distinct. Rather, all that *prevents* the existence of *b* in World 2 is the fact that *c* does not exist there.

Noonan holds World 1 to be better than World 2 from what we may call *b*'s prudential point of view. This is because *b* exists in the former world but not in the latter. But the existence of *b* depends in a very intimate way on the existence of *c*. This is clear when we consider that World 2 contains everything that is needed for the existence of *b* *except* the existence of *c*. Furthermore, while *c* enables the existence of *b* in World 1, this is not in virtue of any causal relations between them. Rather, it is the *mere* existence of *c* that brings *b* into existence here.

In light of these connections between the existence of *b* and the existence of *c*, can we maintain that since *b* exists in World 1 but not in World 2, World 1 is better from *b*'s prudential point of view? Such a claim would not be incoherent. Nevertheless, it seems to me very hard to believe. The difference between World 1 and World 2, in virtue of which *b* exists in the former but not in the latter, is simply that (the causally isolated) *c* exists in the former but not in the latter. And why should the existence of *c* make a difference from *b*'s prudential perspective?

Some readers may be worried about these claims regarding the value of World 1 and World 2 from *b*'s prudential point of view. After all, *b* does not exist in World 2 and so does not have a prudential point of view there. So

---

[14] Here and elsewhere, I speak of negative states of affairs. Yet, I do not want to commit myself to the claim that there are any such states. Thus, depending on what sort of an ontology we assume, claims about negative states of affairs may have to be reinterpreted in terms of positive states of affairs, which may serve as truth-makers for claims about the non-existence of entities. But since it is convenient to speak of negative states of affairs, I shall continue to do so.

how can this world be prudentially better or worse for him than World 1 is? Note first that if we were to deny that World 1 and 2 can be compared from b's prudential point of view, what this would mean is that the objection I have ascribed to Noonan would collapse. It would no longer make any sense to say to b that he is *fortunate* that c's transplant went so well.

Second, it seems to me that it is in fact possible to compare World 1 and 2 from b's prudential point of view. Furthermore, from this evaluative standpoint, they have equal value. We can compare these two worlds from b's prudential point of view in World 1. In this world, the state of affairs that b exists is equal in prudential value for b to the state of affairs that $b\star$ exists (and so the lack of transworld identity between b and $b\star$ is prudentially insignificant). Perhaps you find this claim rather obscure. If so, I must ask for your patience until Chapter 5 (Section 5.5), where I defend the value-theoretic and metaphysical assumptions on which it relies. And if my argument is sound, we have a second reason why Noonan's objection does not pull through.

In conclusion, the lesson of the Anti-identity Argument is not just that identity over time is not what matters, but also that transworld identity does not matter. It is not in itself important from a person's prudential perspective whether or not he comes into existence.

Incidentally, these points about the prudential insignificance of identity are not just important because they can be invoked in defence of the Anti-identity Argument; they also have implications for various issues in applied ethics. Let me give an example. It has been argued that if the performance of gene therapy on a conceptus, embryo, or foetus causes a numerically different person to come into existence than if this intervention had not taken place, there cannot be a person-affecting reason to perform such therapy, or at least none that derives from the interests of the conceptus or embryo, or from the person who is thus caused to exist (Zohar 1991; for critical discussions, see Elliot 1993; Holtug 2009; Holtug and Sandøe 1996; Persson 1995).

There are various reasons why this argument seems to me mistaken. First, as I argue in Chapter 5, a person can benefit from coming into existence, and for this reason alone there can be a person-affecting reason to perform the relevant kind of gene therapy; a reason that derives from the self-interest of the person who will then exist (and may benefit more from coming into existence than the child who would otherwise have existed and had a severe genetically determined disease).

Second, and more importantly in the present context, a conscious foetus may have a self-interest in the welfare of the child who later emerges, even if the therapy causes a change of identity such that the foetus and the child are numerically distinct. What this requires is just that some of the physical and/or psychological relations that *do* matter in survival exist between them (where these are insufficient to ensure identity).

Third, there is a sense in which a person may have a self-interest in having therapy performed on a conceptus even if, because of the therapy, she will never come into existence. This is because, from her prudential point of view (in the possible world in which she exists), it may be better if someone else exists and has a much better life, as long as enough of her relevant physical and/or psychological states overlap with the states of this other person to generate a prudential concern on her part (where such an overlap is insufficient to ensure identity). Thus, the prudential insignificance of both identity over time and transworld identity has important implications in applied ethics (a point I argue at much greater length in Holtug 2009).

3.7 Division and Indeterminacy

I now want to consider a different objection to the Anti-identity Argument. According to this objection, which is raised by Mark Johnston and Peter Unger, the case of division does not support the claim that identity is not what matters, even on the assumption that we hold the Physical or the Psychological Criterion. The objection relies on the view that, in World 1, it is not determinately true that *a* ceases to exist. This is because it is neither determinately true that *a* is identical to (for example) *b*, nor determinately true that they are not identical. Indeed, *almost* all of what ordinary survival consists in is present in World 1—all that prevents *a*'s survival is that he stands in the relevant relation to both *b* and *c*. Therefore, *a*'s prudential concern for *b* (and *c*) is a reasonable extension of his concern for himself. So while identity is what matters, a person's concern for himself (and so for identity) in certain rather bizarre situations may be extended to people to whom he is not (determinately) identical (Johnston 1997: 169–70; Unger 1990: 255–9).

However, I am inclined to hold that, in fact, it is determinately true that *a* is not identical to *b* (or *c* for that matter). This is not because I believe that statements about identity always have determinate answers. Actually, when considering the spectrum of gradual physical and psychological changes illustrated in the example in Section 3.4, where a person is dismantled one cell at the time, I claimed that there is a range in this spectrum in which it is neither true that the person ceases to exist, nor true that he does not cease to exist. Nonetheless, it seems to me that the case of division is relevantly different. Here, we have a clear reason to claim that *a* is not identical to *b* or *c*.

He cannot be, since neither *b* nor *c* has the stronger claim to being identical to *a*. In the spectrum of gradual physical and psychological changes, on the other hand, there appears to be no clear reason to claim that there is a particular cell of which it is true that before it is removed, the person exists, and after it is removed, he has ceased to exist.

Furthermore, the view that it is not determinately true that *a* is not identical to *b*, and not determinately true that *a* is not identical to *c*, has counterintuitive implications. Intuitively, there is one and only one person inhabiting the *a*-body before division takes place. However, if it is not determinately true that *a* is not identical to *b*, and not identical to *c*, then there is no determinate answer to the question of how many persons there are in the *a*-body at this stage. Therefore, it is not determinately true that there is only one person inhabiting the *a*-body prior to division (Garrett 1998: 64).[15]

Finally, I believe that it is uneconomical to claim that what matters is identity, but that the concern for oneself can be extended to some beings it is not determinately true that one is identical to. Suppose we correctly believe that a particular criterion of personal identity is true; say, the Physical Criterion. And suppose we hold that what matters is the continuous physical realization of core psychology referred to in this criterion, regardless of whether it branches or not. The difference between our view of what matters and the view that identity is what matters will then consist merely in the fact that the latter view has a clause to rule out branching. Which view should we accept?

After presenting the Anti-identity Argument, I noted that my attitude regarding the torture of *b* would be no different than would my attitude towards the torture of *b*★. The existence or non-existence of a further continuer, besides the one who will be tortured, will not make a difference. However, this means that the fact that the continuous physical realization of core psychology takes a *non-branching* form in World 2 is irrelevant to my attitude towards the torture.

In other words, the fact that the relevant relation holds uniquely does not seem to make a difference. Thus, it appears that we can account for our value judgements merely by invoking the view that what matters is continuous physical realization of core psychology *whether or not branching occurs*.

Why, then, claim that uniqueness matters? We do not need to claim this in order to explain our judgements. And since the only difference between our view of what matters and the view that identity is what matters is that the latter includes a clause to rule out branching, it seems that the former view is

[15] We might say that the view under consideration involves a weaker version of the multiple occupancy thesis.

superior. In particular, it is uneconomical to claim that what matters is identity and that in cases of indeterminacy the concern for oneself is extended to one's continuer(s). At best, this would be to assign a role to uniqueness in which it makes no difference.

3.8 Other Values

There is one final objection to the Anti-identity Argument I want to consider. Brian Garrett (1998: 92–3) has contended that even if we do not consider division as bad as ordinary death, this does not support the claim that identity is not what matters. Rather, this merely means that given the choice between ordinary death and division, we would choose division. And there may be reasons for preferring division that do not rely on the judgement that identity is not what matters. Garrett suggests the following: if a divides, b and c can complete his public projects (those of his projects that others can complete). That is, b and c can, for example, finish his book, look after his family, etc.

I agree with Garrett that even if we prefer division to ordinary death, this does not prove that identity does not matter. However, I have made a stronger claim than that division is preferable to ordinary death. In Section 3.5, I argue that a's attitude to future torture is not likely to change just because he is informed that it will be b rather than $b^\star$ who is tortured. True, if it is b who it is tortured, this means that c will exist as well, but why should the existence of c make a difference to a's attitude concerning the torture? If this is correct, then a's attitude toward the torture will not depend on whether he is identical to the recipient or not. And this suggests that identity does not matter.

This, of course, is compatible with the other claim Garrett makes, namely that the completion of public projects matters. Both b and $b^\star$ could complete a's public projects, and this fact may indicate part of the reason why they matter to a. However, even if it is important to a that someone completes his public projects, this need not be because this someone prudentially matters to a. It may be because the completion of these projects matters in the desirability sense. Or it may even be because they matter in what we might call an 'impersonal' or 'other-regarding' sense. Perhaps it is important to a that someone takes care of his family, not because it either benefits him or someone else to whom he stands in the relation that prudentially matters, but simply because it makes his *family* better off.

3.9 Summary and a Look Ahead

According to the Identity View, identity is a necessary condition for self-interest. So in order for the Identity View to be a complete theory about self-interest, one would have to specify what personal identity over time consists in. I have suggested that the Animalist Criterion, the Physical Criterion, and the Psychological Criterion are the most plausible theories of our identities, and so provide the most plausible explanations of what, according to the Identity View, gives a person a self-interest in a future benefit.

However, while it seems natural for a theory about self-interest to claim that benefits have to fall in a person's *own* future in order for her to have a self-interest in them, there is more to self-interest than what is suggested by its name. The reason we are particularly interested in self-interest is because of the prudential significance associated with such an interest. Thus, we may ask what it is about a person's survival that gives her special concern for the person she will be in the future. If it turns out that it is not identity that matters in this prudential sense, I have suggested that we should revise our theory about self-interest such that it has the relation that matters as its focus, rather than identity. We may then attribute the sort of prudential significance to our theory that is usually associated with self-interests.

In fact, it turns out that it is not identity that matters, or so I have argued. The argument for this is simplest if we assume the Animalist Criterion. However, even assuming the Physical or the Psychological Criterion, I have argued we should consider identity prudentially insignificant. Thus, I have invoked the Anti–identity Argument, according to which the relation that matters may obtain between two people even if they are not identical. Since, then, identity is not what matters, we should reject the Identity View. And our theory about self-interest should claim that what is in a person's self-interest is that benefits befall persons to whom she stands in the relation that *does* matter.

In itself, it may not seem particularly interesting that identity is not what matters, at least not if, in all actual cases, the relation that matters only obtains when the identity relation does so as well. But, as I argue in Chapter 4 (Section 4.5), once we have realized that identity is not what matters, we have opened the door for the view that future benefits should be discounted when the relation that does matter holds to a reduced degree. This is because, while identity does not admit of degrees, the relation that matters does.[16] And when this relation is reduced, so is a person's self-interest in future benefits. Furthermore, as I have briefly suggested in Section 3.6, there may be actual cases in which the relation that prudentially matters obtains even if the identity relation does not.

[16] Even if identity does not admit of degrees, as I have pointed out, there may be cases in which questions of identity do not have determinate answers. In that sense, then, identity may admit of degrees. But whereas, if it is determinately true that two people are identical, there is no further issue of to what degree they are so, the relation that matters may hold to different degrees between them.

4

What Matters

4.1 Survival, Division, and What Matters

According to the argument presented in the last chapter, identity is not what matters in survival. Thus, what makes the person I shall be in the future prudentially important to me now is not the fact that I am identical to him. Furthermore, as I have argued, what makes it in my self-interest that, in the future, I shall receive various benefits, is not that I am identical to the beneficiary. Rather, it must be some other relation that obtains between me now and me then that gives me a present self-interest in future benefits.

What might this relation be? As emerged from my discussion in the last chapter, it will have to satisfy two requirements. Presumably, it must obtain in ordinary cases of survival. That is, at least in normal cases in which a person survives from one day to the next, the relation that matters must obtain. After all, if we were to suggest a relation that does not obtain in such ordinary cases of survival, we could hardly claim that this is the relation that matters in survival.

The other requirement that the relation that matters will have to satisfy is that, in the case of division, it should obtain between the original person and each of his continuers. I argued that in this case, although *a* is identical to neither *b* nor *c*, the relation that matters obtains between *a* and each of them. So our theory of what matters had better imply that it does indeed obtain.

In the following, I defend the view that what matters in survival is the continuous physical realization of core and/or distinctive psychology. I then argue that this relation admits of degrees, and that a future benefit should be discounted when—and to the extent that—this relation is reduced, when assessing one's self-interest in this benefit. Therefore, my present self-interest in a benefit that will befall me, for example, ten years from now, is reduced to the extent that, between me now and me then, the relation of continuous physical realization of core and/or distinctive psychology obtains to a reduced degree.

I then present my favoured view about self-interest—a view that differs from the Identity View in two respects. First, it claims that what is in a person's self-interest is that benefits befall persons to whom she stands in a relation of continuous physical realization of core and/or distinctive psychology. And, secondly, it claims that the strength of a person's self-interest in a future benefit is proportional to the size of the benefit—appropriately discounted for reductions in the continuous physical realization of such psychology. Furthermore, I consider some of the implications of this view, including those for the badness of death, and for abortion.

Finally, I consider what may seem a considerable challenge to my favoured view, namely that it implies it is in a person's self-interest to cease to exist, if only she will have multiple future continuers (to whom she is not identical but stands in the relation that matters), who will enjoy a larger sum of appropriately discounted benefits than she herself would have, had she survived. I argue that although this implication may indeed seem troubling, it is not as troubling as it initially seems. In fact, I think it is believable. Thus, I am able to propose my favoured view on self-interest, both as an account of prudence in its own right, and as a basis for developing a theory of the just distribution of self-interest fulfilment.

4.2 The Asymmetrical Division Test

Until now, I have just assumed that something does matter in survival. That is, I have assumed that there is some relation that gives a person a reason for special concern for the person he will be in the future. However, perhaps nothing matters in this sense. If so, there would be no reason, even from his *own* present perspective, why a person should have a stronger interest in future benefits to himself than in similar benefits to others.

I consider this view briefly in Section 4.3, but for now I will set it aside. After all, we do believe that something matters in survival and so from your perspective, for example, it is worse if you are tortured horribly some time in the future than if some complete stranger is. Furthermore, most people who reflect on the question of what matters in connection with cases of division seem to firmly believe that this relation obtains between *a* and each of *b* and *c*. Let us now try to explore and systematize these beliefs further.

To test the various possible views, I present some asymmetrical variations on the case of division. These cases are asymmetrical in the sense that one of *a*'s continuers preserves more of *a*'s properties than does the other. In each case, *a* is informed that one of his continuers—*b* or *c*—will be horribly tortured for an hour, while the other will receive a large benefit, say, of one hour of intense pleasure, and in all other respects they will be equally well off. But being a lucky fellow, *a* gets to decide who should have the torture and who should have the benefit.[1] The point is that if putting ourselves in *a*'s shoes, we believe that, for example, *b* should have the hour of pleasure and *c* the hour of torture, it suggests we (also) believe that the respect in which *b* differs from *c* matters.

One reason for making use of the case of division is that because there are two continuers, we are less likely to attach any significance to identity. A note of warning should be made here, though. Since the cases I present are asymmetrical in the sense that one continuer preserves more of the properties of the original person than does the other, according to some theories of personal identity, such as Robert Nozick's closest continuer theory, one continuer may be identical to the original person (1981: ch. 1). Nevertheless, since there are two continuers, we are reminded not to focus on identity.

Furthermore, in these cases our attention is removed from various other irrelevant factors, such as whether there is bodily continuity or, rather, whether there is continuity of other parts of the body than that which is the carrier of psychology (the brain).[2] After all, neither *b* nor *c* are, regarding these other parts, continuous with *a*, and so if we say that *b* should have the pleasure and *c* the torture, it cannot be because we are influenced by such an irrelevant factor. Of course, alternatively, I could have made *b* and *c* further (but equally) bodily continuous with *a*, but it is better to leave out the irrelevant factor entirely. However, *b* and *c* are supplied with bodies exactly similar to that of *a*, and so we will not be influenced by irrelevant considerations of how desirable it would be to live either without a body or with a qualitatively different one.

There is a further reason for my using cases of asymmetrical division to test our beliefs about what matters. Consider the following alternative test. We ask the test person how much pain she would be willing to go through now to ensure that after she has gone through certain physical and/or psychological changes, she will not be horribly tortured. The more pain she would be willing to go through, the better the relation that matters is preserved through these changes. However, this test is not ideal for our purposes. This is because

---

[1] Bernard Williams introduces a combined harm/benefit test in Williams (1973a: 48). For an excellent discussion and application of a (pure) harm test that in many ways resembles the use I make of a combined harm/benefit test here, see Unger (1990: 27–34).

[2] The continuity of these other parts is irrelevant, because if such continuities mattered, the relation that matters would not (fully) obtain between a pre-brain-transplant person and a post-brain-transplant person; see the case of World 2 in Figure 3.1 of Chapter 3 (Section 3.5).

we need to consider cases in which the torture of the future person is in the further future. And if a test person is not willing to go through much pain now to prevent the torture of her temporally distant continuer, this may reveal something about her attitude to time rather than about whether she believes that the changes that have been made have preserved what matters. In other words, she may be inclined to employ a discount rate with respect to time.

When considering cases of asymmetrical division, on the other hand, whenever one continuer is placed in the further future, so is the other. So if we believe that, say, *b* should have the pleasure and *c* the torture, presumably this is not because we employ such a discount rate. After all, we would need to employ it to *both* the welfare of *b* and of *c*, and so the effects of discounting would cancel each other out. If *c*'s welfare is less significant, so is *b*'s, and so a discount rate with respect to time is no reason to prefer that *c* is tortured rather than *b*.

It may be objected that my proposed test is not sufficiently revealing of the test-person's deepest beliefs. After all, it may be claimed that even if one does not have any firm beliefs about who should be tortured, someone has to be, and so there is a temptation to voice even a weak belief. And, indeed, I submit that only judgements that are somewhat confidently held should be taken into consideration.

To accommodate this point about the depth of our beliefs, I ask whether, putting ourselves in *a*'s shoes, we would be willing to go through some significant, but not intolerable, amount of pain to ensure that (for example) *b* receives the hour of pleasure and *c* the hour of torture. The reason the pain should not be too great is that we may believe the respect in which *b* differs from *c* matters, but does not matter too much. If so, even though the difference matters, we could hardly expect *a* to be willing to endure great pain to ensure that *c* rather than *b* is tortured. So let us say that by having a fairly intense headache induced for ten minutes, before the division takes place, *a* can ensure that the pleasure goes to his favoured continuer, while the torture goes to his less-favoured continuer. If, putting ourselves in *a*'s shoes, we are willing to make this trade, presumably it is because we somewhat confidently believe that the respect in which *b* differs from *c* matters.

4.3 The Psycho-physical View of What Matters

I shall now use my proposed test to try to determine what matters. Since it seems that what matters is present in *a*'s relation to both *b* and *c*, it is obvious to suggest that what matters is either continuous physical realization of relevant psychology, or just continuity and/or connectedness of relevant psychology. Let us first focus on clarifying the relevant sort of psychology, and then return to the question of whether it needs to be continually realized physically. We should ask whether both core and distinctive psychology matter. And if distinctive psychology matters, do both psychological continuity and connectedness matter?

Suppose that because of the structure of a's brain hemispheres, b will have all of a's distinctive psychology, as well as his core psychology, while c will have only his core psychology.[3] Some people may be inclined to think that since c's psychology is so minimally developed—perhaps it is less sophisticated than that of a cat—it does not matter as much whether he is tortured as whether b is. Beings such as him simply do not count as much. However, this sort of consideration must not affect a's choice, because his choice would then reveal something about what matters not only in the prudential sense, but also in a moral sense. Let us therefore assume that before he awakes after the transplant, c has a new distinctive psychology wired into his brain, while his capacity to realize psychology is not interfered with and so he continually realizes core psychology throughout the procedure. Let us further assume that although this new distinctive psychology is not the same as b's, it is equally desirable.

When imagining yourself in a's shoes, presumably you are inclined to want b to have the pleasure and c to have the torture. After all, b is strongly psychologically connected to a—he prefers, believes and loves the same things a does—whereas c bears no such resemblance in terms of distinctive psychology. And presumably, you would be willing to endure ten minutes worth of a fairly intense headache in order to secure this distribution of pleasure and torture. What this suggests is that distinctive psychology matters.[4]

Does this mean that only distinctive psychology matters? No, it does not. Suppose that while b will realize only a's core psychology, c will not even do that. So the hemisphere that c receives will carry no psychology at all. However, before c wakes up, the hemisphere that he has received will be rewired such that it comes to realize a new core psychology. Since only b continues to realize a's core psychology, putting yourself in a's shoes, in all likelihood you would want b to have the pleasure and c the torture, and even be willing to endure a ten-minute headache in order to secure this distribution.

---

[3] Perhaps, for reasons that will be made clearer later, I should rather stipulate that b and c will have core psychologies exactly *similar* to a's, but let us leave that out for now.

[4] For a roughly similar example that supports a similar conclusion, see McMahan (2002: 77).

So it seems that, apart from distinctive psychology, core psychology matters as well.[5]

However, it does not follow from our judgements about these two cases of division that if a future being will have both one's core and distinctive psychology, then this being matters more than if it only has one's core psychology. In the first case considered, *a* has two continuers and only one of them has his distinctive psychology. And it may be suggested that it is because *a* has a future continuer, *b*, who has both his core and distinctive psychology, that *c*, who only has his core psychology, matters less. In other words, perhaps a continuer matters less in the presence of another, more qualified continuer, but not in the absence of such a continuer. So perhaps a particular continuer does not matter less if he just has the original person's core psychology than if he also has his distinctive psychology, as long as he faces no (superior) competition.

Here, it is important to distinguish between two different issues. One issue is whether a particular continuer matters less when there are other (numerically distinct) continuers; that is, the issue of whether the total of prudential concern is distributed such that each continuer receives a reduced share when division occurs. I already considered this issue in Chapter 3, and shall discuss it at greater length at the end of the present chapter. The other issue, which is the one I want to focus on now, is whether one's prudential concern for a particular continuer varies with the presence or absence of a more qualified continuer. On further reflection, this does not seem to be the case. Suppose that, unlike in the first case described above, the brain hemisphere *b* has received from *a* carries only core psychology, and that a new distinctive psychology similar to *c*'s is wired into it, such that *b* and *c* are now equally qualified continuers. Imagining yourself in *a*'s shoes, would you then become more concerned about the torture *c* will suffer, now that he does not face superior competition? Presumably not.

Therefore, prudential concern for a particular continuer does not seem to vary with the presence or absence of a better continuer, in accordance with a claim made in Chapter 3, namely that the relation that matters between two persons can depend only on these two persons and the relations between them (Section 3.6). Plausibly, then, in the first case of asymmetrical division

---

[5] This judgement is also supported by our reactions to some real-life type cases. Suppose you learn that you have a disease—maybe Alzheimer's—that will gradually reduce your psychology to a level where your brain continually realizes core but not distinctive psychology. Would you be willing to go through some significant amount of pain now to prevent this future impoverished being from being horribly tortured? Presumably, even focusing only on prudential considerations, you would. Again, this supports the judgement that core psychology matters.

presented above, what makes *b* matter more than *c* is that a future person matters more if, besides one's core psychology, she also has one's distinctive psychology.

Since it seems that distinctive psychology matters, we must further ask whether psychological continuity or connectedness, or both, matter. Consider, then, a case in which there obtains many direct relations of distinctive psychology between *a* just before division and *b* five years later, whereas there obtains no such relations between *a* just before division and *c* five years later, although there does obtain relations of continuity.

In this case, it is important to keep in mind the distinction between what matters in the prudential sense and in the desirability sense. This is because it may seem that *c*'s life cannot possibly be very good since it lacks overall unity. However, we must be careful not to think that because it is not very good, it prudentially matters less. So to even things out, let us assume that *b*'s life is equally bad. Perhaps it is not at all going the way in which he wanted it to go.

Now, imagining yourself in *a*'s shoes, in all likelihood you are inclined to prefer that five years after the division, *b* gets an hour of pleasure and *c* an hour of torture, and you are even inclined to endure ten minutes of a fairly intense headache in order to secure this favoured distribution. This is because, apart from being psychologically continuous with *a*, *b* continues to prefer, believe, and love the same things *a* does. However, again imagining yourself in *a*'s shoes, presumably you would care a great deal about the torture *c* is going to receive. In fact, you would care more about the welfare of *c* than about the welfare of a person who shares with *a* only his core psychology. What this suggests is that both continuity and connectedness matter.

Furthermore, if one stands in a relation of both psychological continuity and connectedness to a future being, then this being matters more than if only the continuity relation obtains. This claim does not immediately follow, but it can be supported by invoking an argument similar to that I used to show that a future person matters more if he has both one's core and distinctive psychology, than if he only has the former.

Here, it may be worth reconsidering one of Peter Singer's views, to which I referred in Chapter 2 (Section 2.4). Singer (1993: 127) claims that only self-conscious beings have self-interests that reach beyond periods of sleep or temporary unconsciousness. I suggested that this claim may be based on the Present Preference View, according to which only benefits that are appropriately captured by present preferences give rise to present self-interests. But there is also another possible interpretation of Singer's claim, namely that it is only in beings that possess self-consciousness that the relation that matters can survive a period of sleep or unconsciousness. Consider the following passage, in which Singer talks about beings who are conscious but not self-conscious:

> They will not have desires that project their images of their own existence into the future. Their conscious states are not internally linked over time. We can presume that if fish become unconscious, then before the loss of consciousness they would have no expectations or desires for anything that might happen to them subsequently, and if they regain consciousness, they have no awareness of having previously existed. . . . For a non-self-conscious being death is the cessation of experiences, in much the same way that birth is the beginning of experiences. Death cannot be contrary to an interest in continued life. . . .   (Singer 1993: 126)

Singer's point may be that beings who do not possess self-consciousness, do not exhibit the sort of overall psychological coherence over time that is necessary for prudential concern for the beings they shall be in the (further) future. After all, he emphasizes that 'their conscious states are not internally linked over time', that 'they would have no expectations or desires for anything that might happen to them subsequently', and 'if they regain consciousness, they have no awareness of having previously existed'. Thus, they seem to lack psychological continuity and connectedness. This may be why they do not have a self-interest in continued life.

However, as my discussion in this section reveals, it seems that both distinctive and core psychology matter. Thus, a being who does not possess self-consciousness may stand in the relation that matters over time in virtue of continuity of core psychology. Furthermore, I doubt that it is impossible for such beings to maintain relations of psychological continuity and connectedness over time. What periods of sleep or unconsciousness may prevent is that distinctive psychological states are manifested in these periods. But in order for there to be psychological continuity and connectedness over a period of time, the relevant psychological states need not be manifested at all times in this period. It is sufficient if they are dispositionally realized. Thus, if a dog has a preference for eating the bone in front of it and, after a period of sleep, again has a preference for eating the bone, I see no reason to deny that it is the same preference that is manifested at different times.

What is true, of course, is that beings who do not possess self-consciousness do not have beliefs and global preferences that involve their conception of themselves as existing over time; for example, preferences for their own continued existence. This is true by definition. Yet, although such beliefs and global preferences can certainly contribute to psychological continuity and connectedness, so can many other beliefs and preferences. Therefore, an individual need not possess self-consciousness in order to stand in the relation that matters to its future self.

Let us now turn to the question of what sort of physical realization is needed to make psychological relations matter. Note that in the cases of division we have considered, these relations are continuously realized physically by the cerebral hemispheres. But is this sort of physical continuity a necessary condition for prudential concern?

Consider first core psychology. What makes a particular future core psychology matter (especially) from your point of view? As we have seen, the answer is not that it is yours; that is, that you are identical to the bearer of that future psychology. But then consider this suggestion. What makes a particular future core psychology matter from your perspective is the fact that it is numerically identical to your present core psychology. So what matters is not personal identity, but the identity of core psychologies (although, in some theories of personal identity, these two relations coincide).

We must then ask, what makes it the case that the core psychology that is realized by you now is the numerically same core psychology as that which will be realized by you later? Presumably, it is the fact that it is continuously realized by your brain, or, in a science fiction scenario, by an appropriate succession of physical entities, where perhaps your brain is gradually replaced by a bionic circuitry (Unger 1990: 116).[6]

However, when we consider the case of symmetrical division, we see that what matters cannot be the identity of core psychologies. After all, while c does have a core psychology, it is not numerically identical to a's. It cannot be, since b and c both have core psychologies that have an equal claim to being identical to that of a. Nevertheless, a's relation to b and c contains what matters and, at least in part, this is because they are bearers of appropriate continuers of his core psychology. So, more plausibly, a particular future person will matter from a's perspective if there is continuous physical realization of core psychology between the physical basis of a's psychology and the physical basis of this future person's psychology. And this is one reason why b and c matter to a in a way that you do not, for example, even though your core psychology is similar to b's and c's.

Now, it may be objected that a has two core psychologies, not one, and thus, in fact, we may reasonably claim that it is the identity over time of a

---

[6] McMahan suggests that if the replacement of your brain parts by a bionic circuitry is gradual and has extensive temporal overlap, the resulting realizer of core psychology would in fact be your brain (personal communication). But nothing in my argument hinges on whether we take the two realizers to be identical or not.

core psychology that matters. Since we are assuming that a's hemispheres are equipollent, we may claim that each realizes a core psychology, and thus b and c each receive a core psychology that is identical to one of a's. Yet, I think it would be rather strange to claim that a has not one, but two such psychologies. After all, since they work together, the claim that there are two would have no behavioural manifestations, or at least so we assume. Rather, a has one core psychology that is jointly realized by his two hemispheres. Furthermore, if we were to claim that a has two separate psychologies, on what grounds could we deny that there are two persons who inhabit his body? We would be in danger of committing ourselves to the counterintuitive multiple occupancy thesis.

We should now ask how much physical continuity is needed to make a future bearer of core psychology matter. In the case of division, there is massive physical continuity, since there is massive physical continuity between a's brain hemispheres and those of b and c. So clearly they matter. But consider instead the case of teletransportation. Perhaps there is some degree of physical continuity between your core psychology and that of your replica on Mars, but nowhere near as much as that which obtains between a and each of b and c. After all, in teletransportation, your brain is destroyed and a new brain is constructed out of new matter. And, besides, there is a time-interval in which no core psychology is realized (unless one is willing to say that it is realized by an entity consisting of a sequence of information moving through space, a computer on Mars, and a bunch of organic molecules waiting to be brought together).

Presumably, like most of us, focusing only on prudential considerations, you would not be willing to go through much pain to prevent your replica from being horribly tortured. What this suggests is that, unlike in the case of division, there is not enough continuous physical realization of core (and, as we shall see, other) psychology to make your replica matter, or at least not enough to make it matter much.

In terms of psychological continuity and connectedness, what sort of continuous physical realization do they need in order to matter? As in the case of core psychology, a person's distinctive psychology is only realized through time if there is continuous physical realization of it into the future by her brain or an appropriate succession of physical entities. For example, a future preference is only a manifestation of a present preference if there is appropriate continuity between the physical realizers of the two.

On this basis, we may claim that a particular future person will matter to you now if there is continuous physical realization of distinctive psychology between the physical basis of your present psychology and the physical basis of her psychology (which amounts to psychological connectedness, with an appropriate physical foundation). Of course, in order for there to be continuous physical realization of distinctive psychology, it is not enough that at each point in time, some distinctive psychological traits are realized. Rather, similar traits must be realized over time, and the reason they are so realized must be that their physical foundation is continuous.

Furthermore, a particular future person will matter to you now if there is a succession of people, starting with you now and ending with this future person, such that a relation of continuous physical realization of distinctive psychology obtains from each to the next (which amounts to psychological continuity, also with an appropriate physical foundation). Alternatively, this latter relation can be characterized as a continuous physical realization of a chain of distinctive psychology. Thus, both these relations are part of what makes the future you matter in a way that a future person who just happens to have a distinctive psychology exactly like yours does not.

Additionally, as in the case of core psychology and for the same reason, the physical continuity that carries distinctive psychology into the future must have a certain strength for it to matter, or at least for it to matter much.

Bringing the different results in this section together, I can now present:

> *The Psycho-physical View of What Matters.* Person P_1 at t_1 stands in the relation that prudentially matters to person P_2 at t_2, if and only if there is continuous physical realization of core psychology, and/or distinctive psychology, and/or a chain of distinctive psychology, between the physical realizer of P_1's psychology at t_1 and the physical realizer of P_2's psychology at t_2.

4.4 Justifying a View of What Matters

I now want to examine an objection to my argument for the Psycho-physical View. Consider the suggestion that although it seems intuitively plausible that the relevant psychological relations must be continuously realized *physically* in order to prudentially matter, we cannot provide an explanation of the importance of such physical continuity. This objection can (but need not) be seen as a particular application of the view considered in Chapter 1 (Section 1.3), according to which normative views cannot be justified by appeal to intuitions. In order for our intuitions to support a normative view, these intuitions would have to have some kind of independent plausibility.

I shall not repeat my discussion of the role of intuitions in normative theory. Rather, I will consider a particular version of the objection that there is no credible explanation of why continuous physical realization of relevant psychology prudentially matters, namely one which is due to Parfit. In order to describe the objection, let us first have a look at Parfit's preferred view of what matters.

According to Parfit, what matters is simply psychological continuity and connectedness. However, when *arguing* that connectedness matters, it is not entirely clear if he is concerned with the prudential sense or the desirability sense. He writes:

> If our lives have been worth living, most of us value highly our ability to remember many of our past experiences. . . . More generally, I want my life to have certain kinds of overall unity . . . most of us value some aspects of our character. We will want these not to change.   (Parfit 1984: 301)

These claims may suggest that it is desirable for a person that there will exist a future person who is connected to her, rather than that connectedness prudentially matters. But perhaps Parfit's point is that we value and prefer these relations at least in part because if they obtain, our prudential concerns are extended into the future, such that future benefits may fall within the scope of them. In any case, I believe this is what we should claim. Not only may overall psychological unity make a life more valuable, it is also a sort of unity that, if it obtains between a present and a future person, will give the former a special interest in future benefits to the latter. It is a sort of unity that raises our prudential concern.

While Parfit believes that psychological continuity and connectedness matter, he rejects the view that they must have a basis of continuous physical realization. Rather, he holds:

> *The Psychological View of What Matters.* Person P_1 at t_1 stands in the relation that prudentially matters to person P_2 at t_2, if and only if there obtains psychological continuity and/or connectedness, with any cause, between P_1 at t_1 and P_2 at t_2. (Parfit 1984: sect. 13)

When defending this view, Parfit argues that it cannot matter whether the cause carrying the relevant psychological relations into the future is abnormal. Or, as he puts it, it is *irrational* to claim that it matters (or at least to claim that it matters to any great degree). For example, it cannot matter whether there is much continuous physical realization or not. What matters must be the *effect*, which is psychological continuity and connectedness (Parfit 1984: 286). For the same reason, it cannot matter whether the cause is reliable. So what matters is psychological continuity and connectedness, with any cause. One implication of this view, of course, is that you stand in the relation that matters to your replica on Mars.

It is not clear to me why Parfit thinks it is *irrational* to claim that what matters is continuous physical realization of relevant psychology. Perhaps it is because the reason we might want to focus on such physical continuity is precisely because it is the continuous physical realization of *psychology*. Then it may seem that the psychological relations are really doing the work, rather than their physical basis. However, even if we focus only on physical continuity insofar as it gives rise to the relevant sort of psychological relations, this does not in itself imply that the physical relations cannot be part of what matters. All it implies is that physical relations matter only conditionally—they matter only insofar as they give rise to the relevant psychological relations.

Furthermore, it seems to me that Parfit's line of argument has drawbacks of its own. Let us try to assess his claim that what matters must be the effect, by seeing where it leads us. Psychological continuity and connectedness include two elements: causality and psychological similarity. In order for you to be psychologically connected to some future person, he or she must be psychologically similar to you and his or her psychological features must stand in a causal relation to your psychological features. But if it does not matter what the causal relation *is*, then why claim that it matters *whether* a causal relation obtains?[7]

Of course, one reason for making such a claim is that it yields intuitively plausible judgements; but if we are concerned about intuitive plausibility, we should rather accept the Psycho-physical View. Among other things, this view implies that the relation that matters does not obtain between you and your replica on Mars, or at least does not obtain to any great degree. Furthermore, I cannot think of a different explanation of why it should matter whether a causal relation obtains, if it does not matter what the cause is. So, following Parfit's line of argument, perhaps we should rather accept:

> *The Psychological Similarity View of What Matters.* Person P_1 at t_1 stands in the relation that prudentially matters to person P_2 at t_2, if and only if P_1 at t_1 is psychologically similar to P_2 at t_2.[8]

However, it is not really clear that we can stop here. After all, why should it matter whether one is psychologically *similar* to some future person? Perhaps,

---

[7] Compare the case of teletransportation with a case in which you are destroyed here on earth but, by mere coincidence, and with no causal relation to you, an exact copy of you is created on Mars. According to the Psychological View, the difference between these two cases makes all the difference in the world. In the former case, the relation that matters is fully preserved, whereas in the latter case, it is fully destroyed. But what is missing in the latter case is simply the recording of information about you, its travel through space, and its reception by a computer on Mars that then uses it to make a copy of you. Why should this difference matter?

[8] For a defence of a somewhat similar view, see Persson (1985: 150–5).

somewhere in Cairo, there exists a person who is psychologically very similar to you, but it is by no means clear that you should have greater prudential concern for this person than for some other complete stranger, who is psychologically less like you. So if we are not willing to invoke our intuitive judgements about what matters in various cases, perhaps we should rather accept:

> *The Eliminative View of What Matters.* For beings like us, there is no relation that person P_1 at t_1 can stand in to person P_2 at t_2 that will make P_2 at t_2 prudentially matter to P_1 at t_1.[9]

The Eliminative View, it should be noted, does not rule out that some beings maintain a relation that prudentially matters; for example, God or angels. Nor does it rule out that if 'we' had been souls or some other kind of spiritual substances, something would have prudentially mattered for us.

However, the Eliminative View is wildly out of line with some of the firmest beliefs most of us have. Presumably, you believe, from your prudential perspective and everything else being equal, it is worse if you (or appropriate continuers of yours) are to be tortured horribly in the future than if some complete stranger will be tortured. Furthermore, this prudential concern of yours is reflected in a vast number of interrelated beliefs you have and indeed in many of the choices you make every day. Therefore, if you were to accept the Eliminative View, you would have to revise fundamentally your system of beliefs. Surely, everything else being equal, this speaks against the Eliminative View.

What this suggests to me is that we cannot settle the issue of what matters without invoking intuitions about actual and possible cases. In this respect, it seems to me that the Psycho-physical View is more plausible than is the Psychological View, for example. This does not mean that we cannot do *anything* to show the attraction of the Psycho-physical View, except appeal to such intuitions. For instance, we can point out that when the relations referred to in this view obtain in a life, this life will have a particular kind of overall psychological and physical unity. Nevertheless, by saying this perhaps we do little more than point out in more colourful terms that the relevant relations obtain.

---

[9] John Perry seems to accept this view; see Perry (1976). He does claim that a future person must have (distinctive) psychological features exactly similar to his in order to be, from his perspective, an acceptable replacement, which might indicate that he holds the Psychological Similarity View. However, he does not think, in itself, it matters whether this similar replacement or some less similar person suffers great pain in the future. Rather, this only matters because it is less likely that his present non-private projects (projects that do not essentially involve him being in a certain state) will be carried out if his similar replacement suffers the pain. So, for Perry, psychological similarity seems to matter in the desirability sense, or perhaps in a moral sense, rather than in the prudential sense.

Before I end this section, I want to briefly comment on an assumption I (and most others who engage in this discussion) make, namely that it is the *same* relation that prudentially matters for all of us. Consider instead the suggestion that an individual's prudential concern for a future individual is settled on the basis of his or her preferences for whom future benefits should go to, where these preferences pick out different relations in the case of different people. The suggestion raises various questions about the nature of reasons that I cannot adequately deal with here. For example, do our prudential responses with respect to the cases of division considered above simply express brute preferences, or do they reflect independent prudential reasons pertaining to the relations *a* stands in to *b* and *c*?

Nevertheless, I believe that even if we were to claim that prudential relations rely on (brute) preferences, the methodological constraints I have imposed in Chapter 1, and exposure to the sort of cases of division I considered in the last section, do tend to restrict individual differences with respect to prudential concern. Furthermore, it is worth emphasizing that while I am indeed assuming a common prudential relation, this assumption may be relaxed in various ways and yet be compatible with at least most of the claims I make later on about the nature of self-interest and justice.

Thus, these claims are compatible with the existence of individual variations in the relative importance of core and distinctive psychology and of psychological continuity and connectedness. For example, when I suggest in Chapter 10 that the (moral) value of an additional unit of welfare to an individual depends in part on the prudential relations he or she realizes, this is compatible with the claim that there are individual variations in the way this dependence works. In addition, the principle of justice I propose there may be adjusted to accommodate individual differences in what matters and yet still have roughly the implications I outline.

However, there are of course important aspects of my account of the relation that matters prudentially that cannot be relaxed in this way. For instance, my theories of self-interest and justice depend crucially on a claim I shall be defending in the next section, namely that an individual's present self-interest in a future benefit is weakened, to the extent the relation that matters obtains to a reduced degree between the individual now and at the time of the benefit.

This completes my defence of the Psycho-physical View. Since it is convenient to have a name for the relation that matters according to this view, let me introduce:

Relation M. The continuous physical realization of a core psychology, and/or a distinctive psychology, and/or a chain of distinctive psychology.

According to the Psycho-physical View, then, what prudentially matters in survival is Relation M. Since Relation M is what matters, the Identity View should be revised. It should have this relation, rather than identity, as its focus. Before I make such a revision, though, I shall argue that there is also another revision that needs to be made.

4.5 The Argument for Discounting

According to Parfit (1984: 313), it is not irrational to be less prudentially concerned about one's future when the relation that matters obtains to a lesser degree. And since Parfit believes that psychological connectedness matters, he believes that it is not irrational to care less about one's further future, because (normally) relations of psychological connectedness weaken over time. For example, you will have far more of your present preferences, memories, and beliefs tomorrow than you will in ten years.

However, as I pointed out in Chapter 2 (Section 2.2), my concern with theories about self-interest focuses on value rather than on rationality. Nevertheless, the question of whether future benefits matter less when there is less connectedness is just as relevant for value as it is for rationality. That is, if future benefits matter less, then their value should be discounted in an adequate theory about self-interest.

Parfit does not argue that future benefits matter less when there is less connectedness, only that we make no mistake if we assign them less weight. However, I want to contend that according to some plausible basic beliefs, such benefits matter less. In my argument, I shall make use of the test employed to show that Relation M is what matters; that is, the asymmetrical division test. In fact, this test is equally well suited to show that when Relation M is reduced, so is a person's prudential concern.

Consider again the case in which there obtains many direct psychological relations between *a* just before division and *b* five years later, whereas there are no such relations between *a* then and *c* five years later, although a relation of psychological continuity does obtain. I suggested that if you were in *a*'s shoes, presumably you would be more concerned for *b* than for *c* and that you would even be willing to endure a ten-minute fairly intense headache in order to ensure that *b* received the hour of pleasure and *c* the hour of torture (five years later).

Suppose now that the degree of connectedness between *a* and *b* is gradually reduced. First we imagine that, say, 99 per cent of the connectedness obtains, then 98 per cent, and so on. As we move down this spectrum, if you were in *a*'s shoes, presumably you would gradually start to become less concerned about *b*'s welfare five years after the division. It is not as if there is some cut-off point, where there is a sudden dramatic decline of concern. In light of the gradualness of the underlying realities—the psychological changes—such a cut-off point would indeed be strange. Rather, your concern decreases gradually until it reaches the same strength as your concern for *c*. At this point, you would be indifferent regarding who gets the hour of torture and who gets the hour of pleasure and you would not be willing to endure any pain at all in order to secure a particular distribution. What this suggests is that future benefits (or harms) gradually matter less when, gradually, there is less psychological connectedness.

Parfit does not consider whether future benefits matter less when there is less psychological continuity. This is because he defines 'psychological continuity' as 'the holding of overlapping chains of strong connectedness', where 'strong connectedness' is the holding over any day of at least half the number of direct psychological connections that hold over every day, in the lives of nearly every actual person (1984: 206). This relation either holds or it does not; it does not admit of degrees. I, on the other hand, have not made any claims about how strong the chain of connectedness has to be in order to establish psychological continuity. Let us then say that there is less psychological continuity when the chain of psychological connectedness is less strong. The chain can be less strong in either of two ways. It is less strong if the psychological connections that make up the chain (on average) last less time. And it is less strong if (on average) the links of the chain consist of fewer such connections.

Let us now consider whether future benefits matter less in cases with less psychological continuity. Consider, then, the following case. Between *a* just before the division and *b* five years later, there obtains no psychological connectedness, but fairly strong continuity. On average, *b*'s distinctive traits last four years. Nor does there obtain any connectedness between *a* just before the division and *c* five years later but, again, continuity obtains. However, this continuity is much less strong; in fact, on average, *c*'s distinctive traits last only four days.

Once more it is important to keep in mind the distinction between what matters in the prudential sense and the desirability sense; *c*'s life may not seem very good, since it fundamentally lacks overall psychological unity. But this does not indicate that it prudentially matters less. Again, to even things out, we should assume that *b*'s life is equally bad.

Presumably, if you were in *a*'s shoes, you would want *b* to have the hour of pleasure and *c* to have the hour of torture, and even be willing to endure the ten-minute headache to secure this distribution. This, of course, suggests what we already suspect, namely that overall (psychological) unity matters not just in the desirability sense, but also in the prudential sense. More importantly, if the degree of continuity between *a* and *b* were slowly reduced, presumably you would gradually start to care less about *b*. At the point where *b*'s distinctive psychology lasts, on average, four days, you would be indifferent between who gets the torture and who the pleasure. What this suggests is that future benefits gradually matter less when, by degrees, there is less psychological continuity.

What about core psychology, then? If your psychological capacities start to deteriorate, will this make the future you (or your continuer) matter less to the present you? Let us say that when these capacities deteriorate, there is less continuity of core psychology. Normally, when this happens—for instance, because of a severe disease such as Alzheimer's, or because of old age—a great deal of distinctive psychology will disappear as well. This is so, at least in part, because certain distinctive beliefs and preferences can be held only on the basis of a rather developed ability to reason. Nevertheless, there is a separate issue of whether, independently of the fact that distinctive psychology is lost, the deterioration of capacities makes future benefits matter less. I believe that it does; but to avoid a tedious further psychological version of my favourite case of division at this point, I shall merely state that it does. In other words, future benefits gradually matter less when, little by little, there is less continuity of core psychology.

Finally, we come to the question of whether future benefits matter less when there is less continuous physical realization of the relevant kinds of psychology. Previously, I pointed out that in the case of teletransportation, there does not seem to be sufficiently continuous physical realization to make your replica matter to you, or at least not sufficient to make him or her matter much. I am now in a position to explain this claim more fully. Perhaps gradually, when there is less continuous physical realization, future benefits matter less. If so, perhaps your relation to your replica contains some (but not much) of what matters.

Consider the following case: *b* receives one of *a*'s cerebral hemispheres, whereas *c* receives a hemisphere that consists of 1 per cent of *a*'s other hemisphere, and 99 per cent of an exact copy of it. There does not seem to be much difference between *c* and someone who just happens to be psychologically very similar to *a*. So presumably, imagining yourself in *a*'s shoes, you will want *b* to have the pleasure and *c* the torture and even be willing to endure ten minutes worth of a fairly intense headache to secure this distribution. Furthermore, if the physical continuity between *a* and *b* were slowly decreased (such that *b* gradually receives less than 100 per cent of *a*'s hemisphere, but also receives an appropriate replacement), in all likelihood you would steadily start to care less about *b*. What this suggests is that future benefits gradually matter less when, by degrees, there is less continuous physical realization of relevant psychology.

However, note that in the case of symmetrical division, the relation that matters fully obtains between *a* and each of *b* and *c*, even if they each only have half of *a*'s cerebrum. This is because, while there is a great reduction in brain continuity, there is the usual amount of continuous physical realization of relevant psychology. This is because the relevant psychological relations fully obtain to both continuers and, on the physical side, there is the usual physical continuity of each cerebral hemisphere, which realizes *all* the relevant psychology.

Of course, it may be argued that since each continuer only receives a reduced share of *a*'s brain (or of the relevant parts of it), *a*'s prudential concern for each of them is reduced. Yet, since both continuers receive a hemisphere that realizes all the psychology that *a* realizes, it is unclear why it should matter that they only receive a reduced share of the relevant parts of his brain. The reason continuity of the brain matters in the first place is that it is the physical realizer of psychology. Therefore, if a certain section of the brain continuously realizes all the relevant psychology, it seems reasonable to say that the relation that matters is fully preserved. Furthermore, as I suggested in Chapter 3 (Section 3.5), it intuitively seems that a benefit (or harm) to one of *a*'s continuers does not prudentially matter less than a benefit (or harm) that falls in his own future, where his brain remains 'untouched'.

To sum up, all the particular relations that make up Relation M admit of degrees. And when they are reduced, future benefits matter less. Let us express this by saying that future benefits should be discounted for reductions in continuity and connectedness in Relation M.[10]

4.6 The Prudential View

I am now finally in a position to revise the Identity View. First, as I have argued, our theory about self-interest should have Relation M as its focus,

[10] For a roughly like account of what matters, including the claim that future benefits should be discounted, see McMahan (2002: 66–94). However, McMahan's account differs from mine in at least two respects. He seems to hold that in order for a future person to matter to me, there must be *continuity of the brain* rather than merely *physical continuity* between what realizes his psychology and what realizes mine. And he does not rule out the view that in order for a future person to matter to me, that person must have *enough* of my brain such that it can support consciousness, presumably even in the absence of other brain parts that support consciousness (2002: 85). I, on the other hand, do rule out this claim; not only because brain continuity is not required, but also because I claim that *any* degree of continuous physical realization of relevant psychology matters.

rather than identity. This is because Relation M is what prudentially matters and so gives us a special concern for the people we shall be in the future (or for our continuers). Thus, what gives a person a present self-interest in a future benefit is that this relation obtains between her and the beneficiary. Second, since Relation M is what matters, and since future benefits matter less when it holds to a reduced degree, a person's present self-interest in a future benefit is reduced when this relation is reduced between her and the beneficiary. Therefore, the strength of a person's present self-interest in a future benefit is not just a function of the size of the benefit; rather, it is a function of the size of the benefit, appropriately discounted for reductions in continuity and connectedness in Relation M.

Thus, we arrive at:

> The Prudential View. (1) P_1 has a self-interest at t_1 in P_2 benefiting at $t_2(-t_3)$, if and only if (a) P_1 exists at t_1, and (b) P_1 at t_1 is M-related to P_2 at $t_2(-t_3)$. (2) The strength of P_1's self-interest at t_1 depends only on the size of the benefit befalling P_2 at $t_2(-t_3)$ and on the continuity and connectedness in the M-relation between them at these times; the larger the benefit—appropriately discounted for reductions in continuity and connectedness—the stronger the self-interest.[11]

One implication of this view is that, in general, our self-interest in a future benefit weakens the further into the future this benefit lies. After all, the strength of the M-relation between oneself now and in the future gradually weakens the further into the future we go. Preferences, beliefs, and character traits change, and the physical basis of these psychological features is slowly replaced. This has a number of important real-life implications. For example, our present self-interest in saving for our retirement may be weaker than we tend to think. Likewise, our present self-interest in not smoking may be weaker. This is because, although one may develop cancer some time in the further future, the harm one will suffer at this time should be discounted from one's present perspective.

---

[11] It may be instructive to point out how this view differs from Parfit's. The Prudential View is a theory *about* self-interest, and so a theory about value, whereas Parfit's discussion is in terms of theories of rationality. Also, Parfit claims that what matters is psychological continuity and/or connectedness (relation R), whereas the Prudential View claims that what matters is Relation M, which includes more than relation R does. Furthermore, Parfit holds that it is *not irrational* to discount future benefits for lack of psychological connectedness, whereas the Prudential View claims that future benefits *should* be discounted for lack of continuity and connectedness *in all the particular relations that make up Relation M*. Finally, Parfit claims that, because it is not irrational to discount future benefits, the self-interest theory—which assigns to each of us one rational aim, i.e., to maximize value in our own life—is false. I, on the other hand, revise the theory about self-interest to accommodate discounting. (For a suggestion as to how the Self-interest Theory (a theory about rationality) can be revised to accommodate discounting, see Bodanszky 1987.)

Following up on this last claim, the Prudential View has important implications for what we should say about the badness of death. This view implies that we should reject the Deprivation Account of the badness of death to which I referred in Chapter 2 (Section 2.3). First, we should replace the concern with survival and death with a concern for Relation M. After all, according to the Prudential View, an individual may have a self-interest in benefits that occur after her death. Consider again the case of symmetrical brain division. Even though a is identical to neither b nor c, benefits to them clearly fall within the scope of her prudential concern. Therefore, the Prudential View suggests that we should replace our concern with death with a concern for the termination of Relation M. However, for *most* practical purposes, it may not make much of a difference whether we focus on death or the termination of Relation M. This is because, in most cases, death will roughly coincide with the termination of this relation (at least if we assume an appropriate criterion of brain death).

Note that the termination of Relation M may be a very gradual affair. Consider, for example, a person with Alzheimer's disease, before the disease breaks out. Due to the deterioration of her memory, cognitive capacities, etc. that her disease will cause, her present prudential concern for her future benefits is significantly reduced. And the final termination of the M–relation that she realizes may be considered the limiting case of such reductions in this relation.

Incidentally, the case of Alzheimer's disease may be a case in which it *does* make a difference whether we focus on death or the termination of Relation M. Suppose we hold a version of the Psychological Criterion of Personal Identity over Time, according to which identity requires rather strong psychological connectedness. Now consider a person who is going through the final stages of Alzheimer's. According to the Psychological Criterion under consideration, this person may cease to exist even before 'her' brain ceases to realize mental states, including pleasant and painful ones.[12] Thus, even after she dies, the M–relation that she has realized continues and benefits occur in it. And prior to her death, she had a self-interest in these benefits, even though they do not accrue to her.

Furthermore, as I suggested in Chapter 3 (Section 3.6), there may also be cases at the other end of life in which it makes a difference whether we focus on death or on the termination of Relation M. Thus, for example, I suggested that perhaps a conscious foetus can have a self-interest in the welfare of a

---

[12] For a view on personal identity and (brain) death that would seem to imply this, see Green and Wickler (1980: 125–7).

future person to whom it is not identical, where this future person comes into existence as a result of gene therapy performed on the foetus.

A second reason why the Prudential View implies that we should reject the Deprivation Account is that an individual's present self-interest in having the M-relation that she realizes extended into the future is determined not simply on the basis of the benefits that fall in this M-relation in the future, but rather on the basis of these benefits *appropriately discounted*. The higher the sum of discounted benefits, as assessed from her present perspective, the worse it would presently be for her if the M-relation she realizes is now terminated. Thus, instead of the Deprivation Account, we arrive at what may be called the 'Prudential Account' of the badness of death (although, strictly speaking, it is not an account of the badness of death but of the termination of Relation M). Like the Deprivation Account, the Prudential Account will assess badness in terms of what an individual is deprived of, but it will do so in a different manner.

It seems to me that the Prudential Account has several advantages compared to the Deprivation Account. First, according to the Deprivation Account, we need to be able, temporally, to locate an individual's death in order to determine the badness of that death. After all, the temporal location is relevant for determining the amount of value in the counterfactual outcome in which this individual does not die (then). If this individual dies at t, the relevant value will be the benefits that would have accrued to her from t onwards, had she not died at t. Furthermore, as we have seen, we need a theory of personal identity to determine this temporal location. However, with the Prudential Account, we can entirely sidestep the notoriously complicated issue of what personal identity consists in. This is because what matters is not when the individual dies, but when the M-relation that she realizes is terminated. And it is terminated when there ceases to be continuous physical realization of core and distinctive psychology into the future.

This leads me to the second advantage of the Prudential Account. Consider again the implications of the Deprivation Account with respect to the importance of the temporal location of an individual's death. Suppose again that we hold a version of the Psychological Criterion, according to which identity requires rather strong psychological connectedness. And consider again a person who is going through the final stages of Alzheimer's, or for that matter has massive amnesia as a result of a stroke that destroys significant parts of the cerebral hemispheres. It may be difficult to say exactly when this person ceases to exist. Not because we do not know enough about her mental states (although this will also be true), but because of the indeterminacy to which the theory itself will give rise. This means that, according to the Identity

View, it is neither determinately true, nor determinately false, that a benefit in the indeterminacy range is in this person's self-interest. And so nor will the Deprivation Account provide us with a determinate answer to whether her death deprives her of benefits that fall in this range.

In the Prudential Account, on the other hand, there seems to be less scope for indeterminacy. An individual's M-relation is terminated when she ceases to realize any distinctive and core psychology. Suppose, surely too simplistically, that an individual has only one belief left, and no other distinctive psychology. Imagine now that she loses this belief as well as the capacity to realize any psychology again. Thus, her M-relation is now terminated. Of course, there may be no determinately true answer to precisely when an individual loses the capacity to ever realize any psychology again. But, apart from this indeterminacy, the Deprivation Account also faces the indeterminacy of just how strongly the relevant relation must be realized over time to preserve identity.

Third, as I pointed out in Chapter 2 (Section 2.3), the Identity View implies that it is normally worse to die young than to die old, and the Deprivation Account 'inherits' this implication. After all, usually, a young person has more benefits in his future than does an old person. And in general, the claim that it is worse to die young seems plausible enough. However, the Identity View and the Deprivation Account also imply that, as a rule, it is worse for a foetus or an infant to die than it is for, say, a twenty-year-old person. But this seems wrong. The twenty-year-old has a stronger self-interest in surviving.

In the following, for simplicity, I shall assume that an individual's death coincides with the termination of the M-relation that she realizes. Unlike the Deprivation Account, then, the Prudential Account suggests that it need not usually be worse to die as a foetus or an infant than to die as a twenty-year-old. More precisely, the twenty-year-old may well have a stronger present self-interest in surviving than does a foetus or an infant, even if the foetus and the infant have more benefits waiting in their futures. This is because the twenty-year-old is more strongly M-related to his future and so his future benefits are discounted at a lower rate.

Let me elaborate a little bit on this idea. In particular, it is with respect to distinctive psychology that a foetus or an infant will have weak relations to its future (in fact, it may be argued that it does not have all that strong relations in terms of core psychology either). Thus, it will not have many enduring preferences, beliefs, and the like. On the other hand, as we have seen, it will usually have more (undiscounted) benefits waiting in its future than a twenty-year-old person has. So who has the stronger self-interest in his future will depend on the discount rate due to reductions in Relation

M. If this rate is sufficiently high, the twenty-year-old will have a stronger self-interest in surviving. And if so, there is a clear sense in which the death of the twenty-year-old is worse for him.

Fourth, the Prudential Account explains why humans normally have a stronger self-interest in surviving than do non-human animals. Usually, humans have futures with more benefits and this tends to give them a stronger self-interest in their futures. Of course, the Deprivation Account has a similar implication. But the Prudential Account implies that even if a human and a non-human animal have equally good futures, the human will generally have the stronger present self-interest in surviving. This is because, usually, her M-relation will be stronger and so her future benefits tend to matter more from her present prudential point of view. And again, this seems plausible enough.

It is worth pausing to also consider the implications of the Prudential Account for the issue of abortion. This is because much of the discussion of this issue has been premised implicitly on the Deprivation Account. Thus, some have argued that abortion is *prima facie* immoral because it deprives the foetus of the welfare it would otherwise have had (Marquis 1989: 189–94). This argument is based on a combination of the Deprivation Account and the view that killing is primarily wrong because of the harm it inflicts on its victim. As several have stressed, the crucial question then becomes whether the foetus and the person who later emerges are identical, because if they are not identical, the *foetus* cannot be said to be deprived of the benefits that would later accrue to the person (Lockwood 1994: 68; McMahan 2002: 3; Quinn 1993: 51). Accordingly, various ethicists have vigorously argued that non-conscious foetuses are identical to the persons who later emerge from them (Oderberg 1997; Quinn 1993), just as other ethicists have argued that they are not (Kuhse and Singer 1990; Lockwood 1994; McMahan 2002; Tooley 1983). While these theorists therefore differ with respect to the permissibility of abortion, they nevertheless share the assumption that the foetus is harmed by being aborted only if it is identical to the person who may later emerge.

The Prudential Account, on the other hand, allows us to sidestep the identity issue or more precisely, the question of *when* we come into existence. What matters is rather how far back in time we can trace Relation M. And this, in turn, depends on when the foetus begins to realize the relevant kinds of mental states. Of course, this is in itself a difficult question to answer, but the difficulty is an empirical, not a metaphysical one. And the empirical difficulty is one we would have to face even if we were to endorse the Deprivation Account, because, assuming a reductionist criterion of personal identity, we would have to determine when the physical or psychological relation which is constitutive of personal identity begins to obtain.

Since Relation M consists in the continuous physical realization of core psychology, and/or distinctive psychology, and/or a chain of distinctive psychology, it seems plausible to suggest that Relation M begins to hold whenever the foetus becomes capable of having simple sensations such as pleasure and pain. As I pointed out in Chapter 3 (Section 3.4), I take 'core psychology' to refer to capabilities such as the capacity to remember, form intentions, reason, and to have certain sensations such as pleasure and pain. And within these, it seems plausible that the capacity to have simple sensations is among the first to 'break out'. With respect to more complex psychological relations such as psychological continuity (chains of distinctive psychology), perhaps these develop considerably later. McMahan (2002: 269) even suggests that they do not begin to exist until some time after the child is born. However, a case might also be made that a sufficiently developed foetus is capable of realizing psychological continuity; for example, simple preferences such as a continued preference that a certain pain should go away.

In any case, at some time in its development, and arguably between the twentieth and the twenty-eighth week of gestation (McMahan 2002: 267–8), consciousness breaks out in a (normal) foetus and Relation M is realized. Let us assume for simplicity that, besides the existence of Relation M, there then exists a person who is identical to the person to whom various benefits may accrue in childhood and adult life (although this does not really matter according to the Prudential Account). This means that an individual exists who has a present self-interest in its future and may be deprived of this future if it is aborted. And, of course, according to the Prudential View, the strength of the self-interest will equal the present discounted value of the benefits that may occur in its future (or in the M-relation that it realizes). Furthermore, according to the assumptions about the discount rate that I made earlier in this section, the foetus will have a relatively weak self-interest in its future. And so, insofar as it is aborted, it is only a relatively weak present self-interest that is thwarted.

However, as the psychology of the foetus, infant, and child gradually develops and becomes more complex, its self-interest in survival gradually increases. Unlike the Deprivation Account, then, the Prudential Account accommodates the intuitively plausible view that it is worse for, say, an infant to die than it is for a foetus that has just acquired consciousness.

My account of the self-interests involved in abortion is in various ways similar to McMahan's account in *The Ethics of Killing*. McMahan relies on his view on the badness of death, which again in part relies on what he calls the 'Time-relative Interest Account' (McMahan 2002: 165–74). The Time-relative Interest Account is relevantly similar to the Prudential Account in that it implies that the future benefits death deprives an individual of should be discounted for reductions in relevant psychological relations when assessing the badness of her death.[13] With respect to killing foetuses and other beings that do not have a psychology comprehensive enough to be worthy of respect—where such worth is based on the capacity for autonomy—McMahan claims that the wrongness of killing them consists in the frustration of time-relative interests. An individual's time-relative interest in not being killed is her self-interest, at the time of her death, in the appropriately discounted benefits that would otherwise have occurred in her future. Thus, the self-interest that is relevant for the wrongness of killing is the individual's self-interest in her future *at the time of her death*. This is the sense in which the Time-relative Interest Account is time-relative.

Nevertheless, turning from self-interest to morality and briefly acknowledging some points that will be further developed in Part II of the book, there are also important respects in which my conclusions differ from those of McMahan. First, McMahan *does* consider the identity issue important and argues that an abortion that occurs before the foetus develops the capacity for consciousness is permissible, because it 'does not kill anyone; it merely prevents someone from coming into existence' (McMahan 2002: 267; see also Stretton 2004: 174). This is because his favoured theory of personal identity implies that we are essentially persons (that is, conscious beings).

Second, McMahan's account of the ethics of killing relies only on *actual* self-interests. Thus, if a foetus is aborted, the moral badness of killing it relies only on the self-interests it has at the time of the abortion. And even in the case of a conscious foetus, these interests will be relatively weak. Therefore, McMahan concludes that aborting even a conscious foetus cannot be seriously wrong, everything else being equal (McMahan 2002: 277). I, however, shall argue that we should reject McMahan's actualist account of the badness of killing. An individual's future self-interests are relevant, even if they are merely possible. This means that when assessing an abortion, we should take into consideration the future self-interests the foetus (or the resulting person) would

---

[13] Although the Time-relative Interest Account and the Prudential Account do differ with respect to the precise nature of these relations; see note 10.

have had, had the foetus not been aborted. I argue this point in Chapter 10 (Section 10.10) on the basis of my account of justice.

Note that the claim that we should also take into account the future self-interests of the foetus is a claim about the morality of abortion, not about prudence. So in including the foetus's future self-interests I am not contradicting anything I have said so far, since I have only been concerned with developing a theory about self-interest. But when we move from self-interest to morality, we should be impartial between the self-interests an individual has at different times, or at least so I shall argue.

I should also emphasize that since the Prudential View is an account of prudence (only), it need not be the full story about the concerns we may have for people, even for their own sake. Consider, for example, a case in which there is a conflict between what is in a person's self-interest and what he prefers to happen. Even if we hold the Prudential View, this does not imply that we should violate this person's autonomy, because autonomy is after all a different kind of value than self-interest. Rather, to settle the question, we would need to weigh these values against each other. Just as, in cases in which the self-interests of different individuals conflict, we will have to weigh their interests.

4.7 Who Are the Bearers of Self-interest?

The Prudential View specifies the conditions and the extent to which an individual has self-interests regarding the future. But who, according to the Prudential View, are the bearers of self-interest? In other words, to what sort of beings does it ascribe such interests? As a first approximation, we can answer this question by saying that it ascribes self-interests to all beings that exist, are capable of sustaining Relation M, and at the relevant time experiencing what, according to the most plausible theory of welfare, amounts to a benefit (or harm). Therefore, presumably, it applies to almost all human beings (non-conscious foetuses and people that have had their cerebral hemispheres destroyed excluded). It also ascribes self-interests to very many other animals.

To answer fully the question of who the bearers of self-interest are, we need to consider their temporal boundaries. So far, I have been assuming a basic ontology of persons in the sense that persons are the bearers of self-interest. But the temporal extension of a person is determined by a criterion of personal identity over time, and, as I have argued, identity is not what matters. Therefore, it may be suggested, when determining the temporal extension of the bearers of self-interest, we should focus on what matters rather than on identity. Along this line of argument, the bearers of self-interest could be held to be person-stages. A person-stage (or segment) is a temporal part of the life of a person and is characterized by more continuity and connectedness in Relation M than that which we find stretching over the person's whole life, from beginning to end.

Nevertheless, it would be premature to suggest that we should adopt an ontology of person-stages. In fact, there is no apparent good reason to abandon a basic ontology of persons. Clearly, there may be some reason to shift from persons to person-stages when considering to whom one wants future benefits to go. This is because it is in your present self-interest that a future benefit falls in your present person-stage rather than in some future person-stage, everything else being equal. But I am not asking to whom, according to your self-interest, this future benefit should go, but rather who it is that, presently, has the self-interest in it going to anyone. And, when answering *that* question, there appears to be no advantage in shifting to an ontology of person-stages.

It might be objected that you, the *person*, do not have a self-interest in receiving a benefit sooner rather than later. This is because you, the person, consist not just of a present stage but of all the stages in your life, and it is not in the self-interest of the later stages that the benefit arrives sooner. There is a question here as to whether persons are such four dimensional beings and so are not present in their entirety at any particular time, but I shall not go into that discussion here (see Brennan 1988; Lewis 1976; Lowe 2002: ch. 3; Quine 1961b; Mellor 1981). Rather, let me just point out that, according to the Prudential View, self-interests have a time-index. And even though, at some future time, it will be in your self-interest that a benefit arrives later rather than sooner, this is not in your *present* self-interest. Instead, what determines your present self-interest is how strongly you are presently M-related to the beneficiary.[14]

I have now argued that there appears to be no good reason to go from an ontology of persons to a different ontology. And, as it turns out, there are good reasons not to adopt any of these alternative ontologies. Consider the person-stages illustrated in Figure 4.1.

---

[14] Observe that by indexing self-interests rather than persons, I avoid committing myself to an ontology of person-stages. See also Brennan (1988: 135).

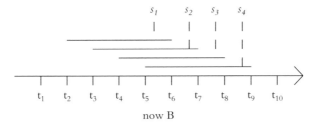

Figure 4.1.

As this figure illustrates, at any particular point in time, there will be numerous stages of a particular person present. Thus, now (that is, at t_5) there are four person-stages, s_1–s_4, that have present self-interests in a benefit, B, that falls at t_6. But the claim that there are four beings that have present self-interests in B provides us with three self-interested beings too many. It would seem unduly extravagant to multiply self-interested beings in this manner.

Therefore, we are under pressure to move from person-stages either to persons or to person-slices. Person-slices are person-stages with the shortest possible duration; that is, persons at particular points in time. Since no two (distinct) person-slices will overlap, a basic ontology of person-slices will not encounter the problem of multiplying bearers of present self-interests. Are person-slices, then, plausible candidates for being bearers of self-interest?

David Brink (1997: 112) suggests that they are not, because, in any plausible theory of welfare, they cannot be benefited. He does admit that, perhaps, in a simple version of hedonism, person-slices can be benefited, because a pleasurable mental state can fall at a particular point in time. But in more plausible versions of hedonism, pleasurable mental states are such that a being that has them will want them to continue and, everything else being equal, will act on that preference. The point is that benefits of this kind require the existence of a temporally extended being. Furthermore, preference theories and objective list theories also imply that only temporally extended beings can be benefited.

However, this argument conflates bearers of self-interest and beneficiaries. We have already seen that in order for P_1 to have a self-interest at t_1 in P_2 being benefited at t_2, P_1 and P_2 need not be identical. So even if a beneficiary has to be temporally extended, this does not imply that the bearer of self-interest has to be so.

Nevertheless, although it is not incoherent, it does seem awkward to be committed to two ontologies, one of person-slices, who are the bearers of self-interests, and one of persons or person-stages, who are beneficiaries.

Moreover, there is the issue of the temporal extension of agents. Presumably, person-slices cannot act and so they cannot be agents (Brink 1997: 112; see also Korsgaard 1989; Scheffler 1982b). Therefore, if we were to claim that person-slices are the bearers of self-interests, we would again be stuck with an awkward commitment to two ontologies.

Also, if person-slices were the bearers of self-interest, this would obscure how agents can have reasons for furthering their own good. Since agents are not person-slices, they are not bearers of self-interests, and without any self-interests, how can they have such reasons? Note that it will not suffice to claim that since agents are persons (or person-stages), and since persons (or person-stages) consist of person-slices who have self-interests, agents have self-interests. This is because, if we claim that persons (or person-stages) have self-interests, the claim that person-slices have self-interests becomes superfluous.

Therefore, since it appears that there is no good reason to abandon a basic ontology of persons, and good reason not to, I shall stick with persons. In other words, it is as persons we are the bearers of the self-interests referred to in the Prudential View.

4.8 M-relativity

According to the Prudential View, self-interests are relative and will vary over time. A person's self-interest at t_1 in obtaining a certain benefit at t_3 need not coincide with her self-interest at t_2 in obtaining this benefit at t_3. However, while self-interests are relative, they are not time-relative. It is not the passing of time as such that causes variations in self-interests, but rather the changes in the M-relation that accompanies it. Therefore, like the Present Preference View considered in Chapter 2 (Section 2.4), the Prudential View is relative, but it involves a different kind of relativity. Rather than being time-relative, it is M-relative.

One implication of such relativity is that what is in a person's self-interest at one point in time need not be in her self-interest at another point in time. For instance, from her perspective at age twenty, it may not be in her self-interest to invest her money at t such that she can take care of herself in her old age, but nevertheless be so from her perspective at age forty, when her old age matters more.

It may be tempting to say that a person's self-interest cannot vary in this way; that is, that there must be a unique answer to the question of what is in her self-interest. By way of illustration, consider the following case. Nick and

Jennifer both suffer from a serious disease that will kill them at the age of thirty, unless, that is, they are offered a very expensive treatment. This treatment is so expensive that it can only be offered to one of them. Nick and Jennifer stand to gain equally from receiving the treatment, namely fifty (equally) good years. But whereas Nick is now twenty, Jennifer is now ten. Figure 4.2 illustrates this case:

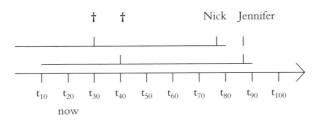

Figure 4.2.

Who has the stronger self-interest in receiving the treatment? This, it turns out, depends on the temporal location from which we assess their self-interests. Let us assume that the M-relation fades equally over time in the lives of Nick and Jennifer. Therefore, at t_{20}, Nick has a stronger self-interest in being treated than Jennifer does, because between him now and in the extra fifty years he can gain, there is more continuity and connectedness than there is between Jennifer now and in the extra fifty years she can gain. However, if instead we assess their self-interests at the point in time where they are just about to die—at t_{30} and t_{40}, respectively—their self-interests are of equal strength. So what would be the adequate temporal position from which to assess their self-interests?

The answer to this question, I believe, depends on the context in which it is asked. When Nick and Jennifer assess their futures for prudential reasons, the appropriate perspectives are their present perspectives. However, if, on the basis of their self-interests we are trying to make a moral decision about who should have the treatment, it is far from obvious that the self-interests we should focus on are their present self-interests. Rather, perhaps we should be impartial between the self-interests Nick and Jennifer have at different times and so claim that Nick and Jennifer's present self-interests do not have a privileged status. In fact, in Chapter 10, I argue that this is exactly what we should do and suggest a particular distributive principle that allows us to deal with such trans-personal and trans-temporal issues of self-interests in a plausible manner. But for now, the point is merely that according to the Prudential View, self-interests are M-relative, and that different temporal perspectives may be appropriate in different contexts.

Nevertheless, it may be argued that since the Prudential View does not give us a unique answer to how bad an individual's death (or the termination of an M-relation) is, this view suffers from a serious drawback. However, I believe that I have provided a compelling reason why self-interests do in fact vary over time. Variations in self-interests simply reflect changes in the relation that underlies our prudential concern. To the extent that we find it intuitively disturbing that self-interests vary over time, this may just show that we are assuming that identity is what prudentially matters. But, in fact, identity is not what matters, or at least so I have argued.

4.9 On the Value of Having Multiple Continuers

Having considered some of the implications of the Prudential View, I now want to consider, at some length, what I call the 'Multiple Continuer Objection'. This is an objection to views that hold that the relation that matters is one a person can stand in to several (at least two) distinct people. Roughly, the objection consists in claiming that such views, including the Prudential View, may (absurdly) imply that it is in a person's self-interest to divide.

Ernest Sosa identifies such views as pointing at 'the intrinsic merit to be found in such a notion of extending one's causal influence into the future' (1990: 309). Presumably, this description is meant also to capture the view that what prudentially matters is Relation M, since this view holds that what matters is the (right sort of) causal extension into the future of psychological features. Sosa then poses the following challenge:

> Suppose a 'replicator' machine which produces as many replicas as may be desired with the right causal relation to one's psychology. Would there be great demand for that machine? Suppose the practical problems could all be solved: e.g., all repli-cas might be sent immediately to distant galaxies. Even so, is such mere multipli-cation of one's own causal influence an obvious desideratum?   (Sosa 1990: 309)

Sosa believes that if we accept that what matters is extending one's causal influence into the future, we are committed to the claim that it is in our self-interest to multiply. He does not actually state this as an objection, but merely as an implication. However, as we shall see shortly, Sosa's point can easily be turned into what seems to be a rather forceful objection, when suitably revised.

Sosa goes on to consider the claim that what matters is 'extending the causal influence of our psychology into the future *at least once*' (1990: 309), in which case it would not be in one's self-interest to have multiple continuers. But he argues that this claim can only be defended if we have an explanation of *why* it is not in a person's self-interest to have more than one continuer. After all, if it is good to have one continuer, why is it not good to have more than one? In order to explain this, we need a defeating reason.

What, then, might be a defeating reason? Sosa provides the following analogy: someone may prefer to have at least one spouse, and yet not prefer to have many or even more than one. The defeating reason here is that having more spouses will cause a loss in terms of closeness. But, says Sosa, regarding the case of multiple continuers, 'I for one have no inkling of what important values would be endangered by the existence of more than one effluent' (1990: 311).

Here, and elsewhere, Sosa speaks as if the view he is up against is the view that a person's causal influence on the future (exemplified by *a*'s relation to *b* and *c* in the case of symmetrical division) is intrinsically *valuable* to him; that is, matters intrinsically in the desirability sense. Thus, he speaks of: 'the value of extending the causal influence of our psychology into the future' (1990: 309), which his opponent claims to be 'what we really do or should seek for its own intrinsic worth' (309); 'the good contained in the causal extension of our psychology *per se*' (310); and 'the supposed value intrinsic to such causal influence' (311).

However, Sosa here conflates the desirability and the prudential sense of what matters. If we claim that Relation M is what prudentially matters, we do not thereby claim that it is *good* for a person to stand in this relation to a continuer. It may or may not be, depending on what sort of life the continuer will have. Rather, what we claim is that she has a special interest in future persons to whom she is M-related. Therefore, Sosa is also wrong to suggest that his opponent is committed to the claim that mere multiplication is a desideratum. If, for instance, one's multiple continuers would have lives worth not living, it would be in one's self-interest *not* to multiply, everything else being equal.

Nevertheless, Sosa's challenge can be rephrased so as to give rise to a more plausible version of the Multiple Continuer Objection. Consider again the case of symmetrical division: *a* stands in the relation that matters to both *b* and *c*. Now suppose that one of two things may happen to *a*: either (a) he survives himself and enjoys another fifty years that contain a certain (high) sum of welfare, or (b) he divides, and *b* and *c* each live fifty years and each enjoy the same (high) sum of welfare in their lives. Furthermore, let us assume that the M-relation would weaken gradually and to the same extent in the future of *a* and the lives of *b* and *c*.

According to the Prudential View, what is in a person's self-interest is that (appropriately discounted) benefits befall individuals to whom he is M-related.

Furthermore, if *a* were to divide rather than survive, twice the amount of (appropriately discounted) benefits would accrue to his M-related continuers. So it seems that, according to the Prudential View, it is in *a*'s self-interest to divide. If he does, more (appropriately discounted) benefits will fall within the scope of his prudential concern. (Consistently with this, Richard Hare once said that he had often wished he could divide, such that he could write more books.)

Of course, even if the lives of *b* and *c* and *a*'s future contain the same sum of welfare, it does not follow that they are equally good. And if they are not equally good, perhaps *a*'s future is better than the lives of *b* and *c*, such that we are not entitled to claim that it is in *a*'s self-interest to divide. However, for simplicity, I make the Additive Assumption about Benefits, according to which the value of a life (or a stretch of a life) is an additive function of the benefits it contains. This assumption makes my argument simpler, but it is in fact a stronger assumption than I need. In any case, according to this assumption the value of *b*'s life equals the value of *c*'s life, and they are both equal in value to the future *a* would have, were he to survive.

Strictly speaking, it still does not follow from the Prudential View that it is in *a*'s self-interest to divide. This is because the Prudential View only makes claims about *a*'s self-interest in having a benefit befall one future person, not about how benefits to two (or more) future persons should be represented in his self-interest. However, if we accept the Additive Assumption and the line of reasoning that led to the acceptance of the Prudential View, we should also accept the following:

> *The Additive Prudential View.* A person's self-interest is an additive function of the (appropriately discounted) benefits that befall persons to whom she is M-related.

In terms of the Additive Assumption, it would seem natural to claim that a person's self-interest in her future is an additive function of the benefits it contains. This, in effect, is what the Identity View implies, when appropriately combined with the Additive Assumption. But, as we have seen, this view should be revised in two respects. First, the benefits do not need to fall in a person's own future in order for them to be in her self-interest. They need only befall persons to whom she is M-related. Second, they should be appropriately discounted. By taking these two revisions into account, what we get is the view that a person's self-interest is an additive function of the (appropriately discounted) benefits that befall persons to whom she is M-related. And this, of course, is the Additive Prudential View.

Therefore, if we accept the Additive Assumption and the Prudential View, we should also accept the Additive Prudential View. And according to the

Additive Prudential View, clearly it is in *a*'s self-interest to divide, because he will then double the sum of appropriately discounted benefits that befall his M-related continuers. Hence, we encounter the Multiple Continuer Objection.

There may be yet worse to come for the proponent of the Additive Prudential View. Might we not imagine that *a* stands in the relation that matters to one hundred people, for example, who will all have lives like *b* and *c*? And would we not have to say that, everything else being equal, *a* has a much stronger self-interest in having a hundred continuers than in surviving or even than dividing in two?

In order to fully appreciate these implications of the Additive Prudential View, it may be fruitful to consider what burdens it would be worthwhile for *a* to endure to realize some of these outcomes. Apparently, it would be in *a*'s self-interest to endure a significant amount of pain in order to ensure that he divides and has, say, two continuers. After all, on the assumptions listed above, this will double the amount of appropriately discounted benefits that fall within the scope of his prudential concern. So if his continuers (altogether) get fifty good years more than he himself would have had, had he survived, would it not be in his self-interest to endure, for example, at least a month of having a fairly intense headache? And, if he could bring about a hundred continuers, would it not be in his self-interest to endure at least a year with such a headache?

There is, however, a question of how many continuers a person can have to whom he stands in the relation that matters. Suppose we hold the Psychological View of What Matters, according to which what matters is psychological continuity and connectedness with any cause. Then there is no limit as to how many continuers a person can have. After all, as we have seen, this relation would obtain between you and your replica on Mars. And instead of constructing one replica, we could make a hundred, or a thousand. Furthermore, between you immediately before the teletransportation and each of these replicas immediately after, there would be very strong psychological connectedness. Therefore, much, if not all, of what matters would obtain between you and each of them. And so, you could vastly increase the sum of appropriately discounted benefits that fall within the scope of your prudential concern by opting for such a multiple teletransportation.

If, instead, we hold that Relation M is what matters, we reach a more conservative judgement regarding the number of possible continuers you can have. To see this, consider the fact that between you and your hundred replicas there would be little, if any, continuous physical realization of relevant psychology. So, from your prudential point of view, benefits to each of them would not matter much. In fact, the only multiple continuer case that fully preserves the relation that matters is the case of symmetrical (brain-)division.

It may thus seem that if we are worried about the Multiple Continuer Objection, we have a further reason to accept the Psycho-physical View rather than the Psychological View of What Matters. This is because Relation M is a less generous generator of continuers. However, even if we hold the Psycho-physical View or, rather, its ally the Additive Prudential View, we still have to admit that it may be in a person's self-interest to have two continuers.

Nevertheless, on further reflection, it is not so clear that the fact that the Psycho-physical View is a less generous generator of continuers than is the Psychological View is a good reason to prefer the former. This is because there could be persons who could divide into many more continuers to whom Relation M would fully obtain, for instance, persons who had many more equipollent cerebral hemispheres. According to the Additive Prudential View, such persons would have a much stronger self-interest in dividing into many continuers than we have in dividing into two.

Yet, perhaps it could be argued that our theory about self-interest need not account for the self-interests of persons who are, in the relevant sense, different from us. In other words, perhaps it need not be a theory about self-interest for persons in all possible worlds.[15] But I will not try to settle this issue here. Even if we claim that our theory about self-interest needs to account only for *our* self-interests, there is a further problem of multiple continuers that we must deal with, in order to defend the Prudential View and the Additive Prudential View.

4.10 The Repugnant Conclusion about Self-interest

While the one method of duplication that fully preserves what matters (Relation M) allows a person (or rather, persons like us) to have only two continuers, there may be other, more generous methods of duplication that preserve *some* of what matters. Consider the following Ungerian method (1990: 289–90; I slightly modify Unger's method to suit my own purposes). A person's cerebral hemispheres are gradually separated. A few nerves are cut at the time and immediately radio communicators are inserted that allow the hemispheres to create in each other the usual neural impulses. After this procedure has been completed, a similar procedure is employed at the interface of the

---

[15] For a discussion of which possible worlds our philosophical theories must 'fit', see Kirkham (1997: ch. 1). Kirkham considers theories of truth, but his discussion is relevant for other theories as well.

cerebral hemispheres and the rest of the brain. The two hemispheres are then removed and placed in different vats, where they continue to communicate with each other and with the rest of the brain and body. Since the usual sort of communication takes place, the person causes her body to move about and performs her usual tasks.

In the next phase, a hundred exact copies are made of each cerebral hemisphere, with appropriate radio communicators. Each left hemisphere is then caused to communicate with each right hemisphere, including the original right hemisphere, and vice versa for the right hemispheres. Since each left hemisphere is qualitatively identical, they will send the same signals to each right hemisphere, and vice versa. This process is allowed to go on for, say, a year. Then the two original hemispheres and the rest of the original person are destroyed, and each remaining left hemisphere is paired with a remaining right hemisphere and inserted into an exact duplicate of the original body (along with a duplicate of the remaining part of the brain), resulting in a hundred new people, who are all very similar to the original person. From then on, each hemisphere only sends impulses to the particular other hemisphere with which it is paired.

Now, the most important feature in this process is the fact that there is a great deal of communication going on between the new cerebral hemispheres and the original ones for a year. This means that the new hemispheres are 'assimilated' (Unger 1990: 147–52).

To understand more clearly what is meant by 'assimilation', consider a case in which a quarter of a person's brain is replaced with an exact copy every fifteen minutes. An hour later, all of the brain has been replaced and almost nothing of what matters has been preserved. But now consider a case in which a brain quarter is replaced once a year. In this case, the first new brain quarter is allowed to communicate extensively with the rest of the brain before the second new brain quarter is inserted. Because there is this extensive communication, there is extensive assimilation. Therefore, although all of the original brain will be gone after four years, more of what matters has been preserved.

Not to make things unnecessarily complicated, I consider assimilation an element in physical continuity. So, just as the preservation of physical parts is an element in physical continuity, so is assimilation.[16] Therefore, in the case in which a hundred continuers are produced, there is a fair amount of assimilation, and so some continuous physical realization of relevant psychology. However,

---

[16] Unger, on the other hand, seems to consider assimilation a further factor, besides physical continuity, that may contribute to a person's survival (which, according to Unger, is what matters).

there is not *a lot of* continuous realization, because the original parts are destroyed after a year. On the other hand, since a hundred merry continuers are produced, many benefits come about and, from the point of view of the original person's self-interest, the sheer amount of these benefits may compensate for the reduced degree of continuity.[17]

More generally, the Additive Prudential View implies:

> *The Repugnant Conclusion about Self-interest.* Since a person's future has a finite value, there must be some imaginable number of possible continuers who are all weakly M-related to this person and who all live lives that are equal in value to her future, such that she has a stronger self-interest in having these continuers come about than in surviving herself.[18]

The point is illustrated graphically in Figure 4.3.

Figure 4.3. The Repugnant Conclusion About Self-interest

If a person—call her Ann—survives, she will enjoy a certain (large) amount of benefits. The present discounted value of these benefits is represented by the size of her column in the diagram. However, she is not nearly as strongly M-related to her continuers—c_1–c_n—as she is to her own future. Therefore, although her continuers would all have lives that were as good as her future, from her present prudential point of view, the discounted value of each of their lives is much smaller. Nonetheless, if there are a sufficient number of them, together they will produce a larger sum of discounted value than that contained in Ann's own future. And so, according to the Additive Prudential View, it is in Ann's self-interest to have these continuers come about, even if it involves dying herself. However, this judgement may seem rather counterintuitive.

---

[17] Another method of duplication is the following: a person's brain hemispheres are divided into a number of parts, and each part is coupled with an exact copy of the rest of the brain and of the person's body. However, the problem with this method, at least for present purposes, is that it generates a limited (although large) number of possible continuers.

[18] The name is, of course, derived from Parfit's (structurally somewhat similar) repugnant conclusion; see Parfit (1984: 388), and my discussion of this conclusion in Chapter 9 (Section 9.3).

4.11 The Additive Function

How might we avoid the Repugnant Conclusion about Self-interest, without giving up the view that what matters is Relation M? According to the Additive Prudential View, self-interest is an additive function of discounted benefits. And, it may be argued, it is exactly the additive function that gets us into trouble when applied to multiple continuers. After all, if we were not entitled to add up the discounted benefits of c_1-c_n to reach an assessment of Ann's self-interest in their coming about, why should we conclude that she has a stronger self-interest in their coming about than in surviving herself? Thus, if we claim that Relation M is what matters, perhaps we should not construe self-interest as an additive function.

As I pointed out in Chapter 2 (Section 2.7), some philosophers suggest that when assessing the value of a person's life, we should do so in terms of the person's global preferences; that is, preferences for her entire life or at least large chunks of it. Along these lines, it may be suggested that when assessing whether Ann's self-interest in having c_1-c_n come about is stronger than her self-interest in surviving, we should ask whether she globally prefers the former outcome to the latter. And if she does not prefer the former outcome, as she may well not, it is not in her self-interest to bring it about.

However, while perhaps there may be something to be said in favour of assessing value in terms of global preferences, I am reluctant to use this as an argument for why it is not in Ann's self-interest to divide. Consider the fact that Ann is M-related to both her own future and to c_1-c_n. If, then, she prefers surviving to having any number of such continuers, this might very well be because she prefers surviving to other ways of extending Relation M into the future. If so, she will be relying on the view that survival is at least part of what matters. And clearly, we cannot defend the view that Relation M is what matters by relying on the view that identity matters. Let me, therefore, turn to the question of just how repugnant the Repugnant Conclusion about Self-interest is.

4.12 Disturbing Irrelevant Factors

On further reflection, perhaps the Repugnant Conclusion about Self-interest is less counterintuitive than it initially seems. One reason why it may appear counterintuitive is that it is difficult to fully fathom (except maybe abstractly) how much value would be realized by an appropriately large number of continuers. Consider this analogy: if you are told that today 35,000 children died in developing nations from malnutrition and related health problems, you are likely to be sad. But if, instead, you are told that 40,000 children died, are you likely to be sadder? Probably not. When such large numbers are at stake, it is difficult to get an intuitive feel of them. And perhaps, for that reason, you are likely to underestimate your self-interest in having many continuers. Let us call this irrelevant factor that disturbs our intuitions the 'Inadequate Comprehension Factor'.

Of course, there is a question here of how many continuers would be enough to outweigh Ann's survival. I shall not make any attempt to answer this question. Nevertheless, it may be worth pointing out that how many it would take is in part a question that must be resolved by considering intuitions about the very sort of situation Ann is in. In order to determine how many continuers it takes, we would need to know how weighty a factor assimilation is in Relation M. And, in order to answer that question, we shall have to consider cases in which assimilation takes place, such as the case presently considered. Thus, if one is inclined to believe that a large number of continuers is necessary in order to counterbalance Ann's future, this may suggest that the sort of assimilation that takes place when the hundred continuers are created is not very weighty.

More importantly, another reason why the Repugnant Conclusion about Self-interest may seem counterintuitive is that it may be difficult to believe that Ann's continuers *can* have lives that are as good as her future. This is because they cannot (all) have her singular goods. One's spouse is a good example of such a singular good. If you were to divide in two, at least one of your continuers would not enjoy the sort of closeness with your spouse that you now enjoy. Therefore, he or she is likely to be frustrated, and so in at least one respect, his or her life is likely to be worse. Something similar goes for his or her relations with the rest of your family and with your close friends. There would be a loss. And, of course, if you were to have, say, a hundred continuers, these continuers would find it more than difficult to establish close relations with your spouse, family, and friends.

However, this is not a good reason to find the Repugnant Conclusion about Self-interest repugnant. Rather, an assumption made in this conclusion is that the lives of the continuers have the same (undiscounted) value as Ann's future. Therefore, if one is inclined to think that the lives of the continuers cannot be very good, one must also assume that Ann's future is not very good. And then it becomes less counterintuitive that it would be in Ann's self-interest to resign and let her continuers take over. Let us call this further disturbing factor the 'Singular Goods Factor' (Unger 1990: 275–82).

Someone may want to object that the solution to the problem of singular goods is to create as many continuers of these favoured people as of Ann, such that each of Ann's continuers can be appropriately matched to these other continuers. However, just as Ann's continuers matter less to her because she is not as strongly related to them, the continuers of her spouse, family, and friends would matter less to her since they would not be as strongly related to the people she loves. So this is no solution to the problem that value would be lost.

A further (related) factor that may be important for our intuitions regarding the Repugnant Conclusion about Self-interest is the following: perhaps we are inclined to weight future benefits according to how much they are presently preferred, when assessing self-interest. This factor—let us call it the 'Appeal to Present Values Factor'—requires some discussion.

Let us say we are in fact inclined to weight future benefits according to how much they are presently preferred, when determining what is in our present self-interest.[19] This will affect our intuitions about Ann's self-interest in the benefits that befall her continuers. Since there are many of her present projects that only one or a few of these continuers can take up—close relations with her family and friends, her job, etc.—they will have to form new preferences and values for their lives. But these new preferences and values, and the benefits to which they give rise, may not be very important when assessed from Ann's present preferences. Therefore, if these benefits are discounted according to her present preferences, her self-interest in bringing them about is reduced. And so we may be inclined to believe that her self-interest in bringing these continuers into existence is not very great, and thus that the Repugnant Conclusion about Self-interest is counterintuitive.

There are, in fact, two distinct ways in which present preferences may be thought to affect Ann's self-interest in a way relevant to the discussion here. It may be claimed that, because of her present preferences, her own future holds more welfare than do the lives of each of c_1–c_n. Or it may be claimed that, for some different reason, her self-interest in c_1–c_n is less strong. Let us consider these alternatives in turn.

The claim that her multiple continuers have less welfare than she would have in her future because of her present preferences is, of course, similar to the claim that they have less welfare because they cannot have her singular goods. However, the difference is this. The Singular Goods Factor concerns the claim that when her multiple continuers come into existence, they will

---

[19] As I pointed out in Chapter 2 (Section 2.8), McMahan believes that we *should* employ such a weight when assessing self-interests; see McMahan (1998: 489).

have preferences that are frustrated (or will experience frustration) and will be burdened by having to adopt new projects. The Appeal to Present Values Factor, on the other hand, concerns the claim that their lives are worse than Ann's own future because her future includes, to a larger extent than their lives, the satisfaction of her present preferences. Here, her present preferences are claimed to be relevant regardless of whether her continuers share them or not.

However, we need not go further into the issue of whether Ann's future is better than the lives of her continuers, because in the Repugnant Conclusion about Self-interest, it is assumed that the value of Ann's future equals the value of each of her continuer's lives. So if we are inclined to think that Ann's future is better, we must boost the value of her continuers' lives, such that they are equal in value. And, more importantly, to the extent that we consider the Repugnant Conclusion about Self-interest repugnant, because we believe that Ann's future holds more welfare than do the lives of each of her continuers, these intuitions are unreliable.

We now need to consider the other way in which present preferences may be thought to affect Ann's self-interest. This involves the claim that although Ann's present preferences do not affect the welfare contained in her future and in the lives of c_1-c_n, they do affect her self-interest in bringing her future and c_1-c_n about. Yet, if future welfare is not affected, why claim that her self-interest is? The only plausible explanation I can think of is the following: although future welfare is not affected by Ann's present preferences, Ann's prudential concern for the people who will experience this welfare is. Since the sort of psychology that Relation M is the continuous physical realization of (at least partly) consists of distinctive psychology, changes in preferences will weaken Relation M. And so when c_1-c_n are forced to alter their preferences to accommodate shortages in singular goods, this weakens the M–relation between them and Ann. Therefore, her self-interest in benefits to them is also weakened.

Of course, what this means, according to the Additive Prudential View, is that it will take more continuers to counterbalance Ann's self-interest in her own future than we will initially expect if we are not influenced by the Appeal to Present Values Factor. In other words, when we consider the Repugnant Conclusion about Self-interest, we may underestimate the number of continuers involved. And while this realization may not immediately increase our confidence in the Additive Prudential View, it may be argued that this is because we are under the disturbing influence of the Inadequate Comprehension Factor.

The upshot of my discussion regarding the Appeal to Present Values Factor, then, is this. Suppose that when we find the Repugnant Conclusion about

Self-interest counterintuitive, we are influenced by the thought that, because of Ann's present values, her future contains more welfare than do the lives of c_1–c_n. To the extent that this thought influences us, we should consider our intuitions unreliable. Imagine instead we are influenced by the thought that c_1–c_n are likely to ditch Ann's present values, such that Relation M obtains to a reduced degree between them and her, causing a loss in her self-interest in them. This will increase the likelihood that we have a correct assessment of how many continuers it takes to outweigh Ann's own future. If, on the other hand, we are not influenced by this thought, we are more likely to underestimate the number of necessary continuers, in which case our intuitions about the repugnancy of the Repugnant Conclusion about Self-interest are again unreliable.

I submit, then, that factors such as inadequate comprehension, singular goods, and the (unwarranted version of) the appeal to present values make the Repugnant Conclusion about Self-interest seem more damaging to the Additive Prudential View than it really is.

4.13 Summary and a Look Ahead

I have argued that if we accept the view that identity is not what matters, we should claim that Relation M is. I have also argued that if we accept this claim, we should take self-interest to have Relation M as its focus and discount the value of benefits when the M-relation holds to a reduced degree. Therefore, we should reject the Identity View and accept the Prudential View instead. According to this view, what is in a person's self-interest is that (appropriately discounted) benefits befall persons to whom she is M-related.

Furthermore, in the Prudential View, we may reasonably claim that persons (rather than person-stages or person-slices) are the bearers of self-interests, and that it may be appropriate to assess a person's self-interest from different temporal locations in different normative contexts.

I have also discussed a particular objection to the Prudential View, namely the Multiple Continuer Objection. I have argued that once we take into consideration how certain irrelevant factors may disturb our intuitions, this objection is not as damaging as it initially seems. In fact, I think it may be in our self-interest to divide. Nevertheless, I realize that many people will think, for example, the Repugnant Conclusion about Self-interest is too incredible to believe.

Until now, I have focused on self-interests in future benefits. However, in the next chapter, I consider some self-interests that are not temporally restricted in this manner. More precisely, I consider our self-interest in having come into existence. If it can be argued that it is in our self-interest to have done so, this may have important moral implications. In order for it to be in our self-interest to have come into existence, presumably our coming into existence must have benefited us. And, as I shall argue, in fact it has (or at least most of us).

5

On the Value of Coming into Existence

5.1 The Value of Existence View

In previous chapters, I have considered our self-interests in the benefits that may occur in our lives. I have also considered our self-interests in our entire futures; that is, in surviving. We can now further ask: if we can have a self-interest in surviving, and so receiving the rest of our lives, can we not also have a self-interest in receiving our lives *tout court*? That is, may we not also have a self-interest in coming into existence? Our answer to this question has important implications for the issue of what justice requires with respect to future generations. Thus, I argue in the next chapter (Section 6.3) that our theory of justice should take a person-affecting form, and this implies that we can only assign weight to the welfare of future individuals on the assumption that they benefit from coming into existence.

Consider again the Prudential View. It implies that in order for a person to presently have a self-interest, she must presently exist. Thus, the (a)-condition states that P_1 can only have a self-interest at t_1 if she exists at t_1. Therefore, the Prudential View suggests that possible future people cannot now have self-interests in coming into existence. But why, we might enquire, should the Prudential View include the (a)-condition in the first place?

Here is one suggestion, which I mentioned in Chapter 2 when presenting the Identity View (Section 2.3). A person who does not (yet) exist cannot (yet) have any properties, and so cannot (yet) have the property of having a self-interest. Furthermore, my account of what matters implies that possible future people are not presently M-related to themselves at the time when they may experience (and benefit from) life. Clearly, since they do not presently have any physical and psychological properties, they cannot be. Therefore, they cannot satisfy the (b)-condition in the Prudential View, according to which P_1

at t_1 only has a self-interest in a benefit to P_2 at t_2 if P_1 at t_1 is M–related to P_2 at t_2. And, as we can now see, the (b)-condition implies the (a)-condition. People cannot have present self-interests unless they presently exist.

However, although we cannot say that a person who does not (yet) exist has present self-interests, once this person exists, she will have interests, and so, perhaps, a self-interest in having come into existence. In fact, on the assumption that it has benefited her to come into existence, on what grounds could we deny that it is in her self-interest to have done so? The crucial question, then, seems to be whether coming into existence can benefit a person. This is the question I am primarily concerned with in the present chapter. Towards the end of the chapter, I shall return to the connection between whether existence can benefit an individual and whether it can be in her self-interest.

Thomas Nagel writes: 'All of us, I believe, are fortunate to have been born' (1979a: 7). I believe that Nagel is right in holding that we (at least, most of us) were fortunate to have come into existence; and in the following I shall defend:

The Value of Existence View. Coming into existence can benefit (or harm) a person.

A few words of clarification are in order. The Value of Existence View does not claim that existence *as such* (or the state *that an individual exists*) is intrinsically valuable for the individual who exists. It is compatible with the more plausible claim that the benefit of coming into existence consists in the welfare enjoyed in life (where mere existence is not an element in welfare). The idea is that a person is benefited by coming into existence if, on balance, his life is worth living, and harmed if, on balance, it is worth not living. Thus, the benefit of coming into existence accrues to a person *while* living that life.

One issue is to determine to whom the Value of Existence View applies. My claim is that it can benefit (or harm) *persons* to come into existence, and this reflects a conviction of mine I mentioned in Chapter 2 (Section 2.2), namely that only individuals who are conscious at some time can at that time benefit. Since I have defined 'persons' as individuals who possess consciousness, it follows that only persons can benefit from anything, including existence. Furthermore, since only a conscious being can realize Relation M, only a conscious being can have a self-interest in a benefit that accrues to a person, according to the Prudential View.

Although the Value of Existence View applies to very many non-human animals (namely conscious ones), I am only concerned with humans in the present chapter. However, I have something to say about the moral implications of the view that it can benefit non-human animals to come into existence in Chapter 9 (Section 9.10).

There is a further issue of to whom the Value of Existence View applies. Let us call people who exist in the actual history of the world—whether in the past, the present or the future—*actual* people. These are the people who are benefited or harmed by coming into existence (although, of course, some might fall into neither category, having lives that are neither worth living, nor worth not living).

There is, however, also a sense in which the Value of Existence View applies to merely possible people, that is, people who could have existed but will in fact not. The view tells us that although such people will never exist, it is still the case that had they been caused to do so, they may have benefited (or been harmed) thereby. In that sense, then, the Value of Existence View applies to merely possible people as well.

Another relevant distinction—which is sometimes confused with the distinction between actual and possible persons—is that between necessary and contingent persons. A person is necessary relative to a particular comparison of outcomes if she exists in all those outcomes. If, on the other hand, she exists in some but not all, she is contingent. To see that these distinctions are distinct, note that a person may be both actual and contingent at the same time. She will be both actual and contingent if we are comparing an outcome in which she exists with one in which she does not and the former outcome is actual.

We often compare different outcomes because we want to make a choice between them. For instance, if we are deciding whether or not to bring a child into existence, this child is a contingent person. The Value of Existence View applies to this contingent child since it informs us that, if she is caused to exist, she may thereby benefit (or be harmed).

In the following, I first present my argument for the Value of Existence View. Then I consider (and reject) a number of semantic, logical, metaphysical, and value-theoretical objections that have been raised. I also consider an alternative defence of the Value of Existence View, and argue that it is inferior to mine. Finally, I contend that we (most of us) have a self-interest in having come into existence. What this implies regarding our moral obligations to possible future people, however, is an issue that I shall not consider until Chapter 9.

5.2 The Argument for the Value of Existence View

I shall argue that existence can be intrinsically better for an individual than never existing. Note, again, that it is not the mere state *that an individual exists*, but rather the state *that an individual exists and has such and such a life* that I claim can be better (or worse) for her than non-existence. Furthermore, the value I am concerned with is intrinsic (rather than merely instrumental) value. I need to be a bit more specific here. The intrinsic value of an existence need not be a value that attaches to that existence or life in its entirety; it may attach only to specific parts (say, to the pleasurable mental states contained in it). Thus, when I say that existence is intrinsically better (or worse) for an individual than non-existence, what this means is that existence either has, or contains, more intrinsic value for her than non-existence.

Since I argue that existence can be better (or worse) for an individual than non-existence, my argument for the Value of Existence View is based on a *comparative* judgement. Some philosophers defend the Value of Existence View in a different way. They believe that in order to claim that it can benefit (or harm) a person to come into existence, one need only claim that coming into existence can be good (or bad) for her. These judgements are not comparative. However, as I argue later, such judgements cannot support the Value of Existence View.

Let us consider a particular person who, we shall assume, exists—call him Jeremy. What is needed in order to defend the Value of Existence View is an evaluative comparison of his existence and his non-existence; or, more precisely, an evaluative ranking of them in terms of their value for him. It is essential that they are assessed in terms of their value *for* Jeremy, rather than, for example, in terms of their aesthetic value or value for others. What we are interested in is the effect in terms of benefits and harms on the person whose existence is at stake.

Since the sort of value we are interested in when comparing existence and non-existence is welfare, the details of the comparison will depend on the particular theory of welfare assumed. I shall begin by considering the implications of a preference theory, and then, much more briefly, consider hedonism, and an objective list theory.

The simplest comparison will appeal to the Object Account of Preferences. This account claims that insofar as an (intrinsic) preference gives rise to intrinsic value, it is the state of affairs that is the object of this preference that has such value. If, then, Jeremy intrinsically prefers reading Rimbaud at t, what has intrinsic value is the state of affairs that he reads Rimbaud at t. Or suppose that Jeremy intrinsically prefers reading Rimbaud at t to skiing at t. The state that he reads Rimbaud at t then has greater intrinsic value than does the state that he skis at t. Furthermore, since we are assuming that this account is to serve as an account of welfare, these values are values *for him*.

The Object Account allows for an assessment of Jeremy's existence and his non-existence on the basis of a global preference. Suppose Jeremy intrinsically prefers existing (with all that his particular life includes in terms of achievements, enjoyments, sorrows, disappointments, and so on) to never existing. We then have a ranking of the two objects, the state of affairs that Jeremy exists (and has such and such a life), and the state of affairs that he does not. The former state is better for him.

In order to conclude that the former state is better *for Jeremy*, maybe Jeremy's preference must satisfy certain requirements. Perhaps, for instance, it must be self-regarding and rational. Jeremy's preference for existing, it seems to me, qualifies as self-regarding and it may very well be rational. For present purposes, the most important feature of a rational preference is that it would survive full (or ideal) information about its objects. Importantly, this condition does not require Jeremy *actually* to possess full information about his life and about what non-existence would amount to in order to rationally prefer existence.

As I pointed out in Chapter 2 (Section 2.5), Wlodek Rabinowicz suggests that if we hold the Object Interpretation of Preferentialism, we should claim that only actual preferences give rise to intrinsic value. This implies that it is only if Jeremy actually exists (and has the relevant preference) that his existence is intrinsically better for him. However, in the same section, I argued that we should reject the claim that only actual preferences can ground self-interests. Therefore, I believe that, insofar as we hold the Object Account, we are entitled to invoke a person's non-actual preferences in a world in which he exists when comparing his existence in this world to his non-existence in the actual world. So if, contrary to what I am assuming here, Jeremy did not actually exist, I might have based the comparison on a preference of his in some other possible world.

The Object Account does not imply that the value of Jeremy's existence and non-existence should be assessed on the basis of a single global preference. But since this provides the simplest comparison, I shall assume such a global version of this account. Since Jeremy prefers existing to never existing, he has benefited from coming into existence. Had he preferred never to exist, he would have been harmed instead.

Alternatively, suppose that we accept the Satisfaction Account of Preferences. According to that account, insofar as an (intrinsic) preference gives rise to intrinsic value, it is the compound state of affairs that consists of the preference *and* the object that satisfies it that is the bearer of this value. It seems that we should then compare the state of affairs that Jeremy exists and the state of affairs that he does not on the basis of the preference-satisfactions generated by each of these states. The value of each state for Jeremy will thus be determined on the basis of the preferences he has in that state and the extent to which they are satisfied.[1] And the argument for the Value of Existence View will then advance as a two-step procedure. First, the value of each state must be assessed, and then a comparison must be made.

Moreover, one may want to compare existence and non-existence using a hedonistic theory or an objective list theory of welfare. Since I do not want to presuppose the superiority of any particular theory, let me just briefly suggest how the Value of Existence View can be accommodated by those who accept the Satisfaction Account, hedonism, or an objective list theory.

Let us suppose that Jeremy's life contains a net surplus of positive values (preference-satisfactions, positive mental states, or items on an objective list). What can we say about the value of his non-existence, then? If Jeremy never exists, no positive or negative values accrue to him, and so his non-existence has no value for him. On the basis of these value assessments, existence seems to be better. After all, it seems to be more desirable for a person to have a surplus of positive value than to have no value accrue to him (such an absence of value may of course be realized in either of two ways; by non-existence or a life with no values). Therefore, once again, Jeremy has benefited from coming into existence.

This concludes my argument for the Value of Existence View. I now need to consider a number of objections.

5.3 The Identifiability Objection

In my argument for the Value of Existence View, I compared the existence and non-existence of a person who exists. The identification of this person therefore posed no problem. But the Value of Existence View also applies to people who might exist in the future (that is, possible future people, whether they be actual or merely possible). It has been argued that possible future people are not identifiable, because they cannot be picked out by rigid designators (Bayles 1975–6: 299–300; McKie 2001). (A rigid designator is a referring term that denotes one and the same individual in all possible worlds in which it has denotation.) This argument forces us to reconsider whether the Value of Existence View makes any sense: when it is said that one can benefit (or harm)

---

[1] Again, the assessment may be based on either global or local preferences. If local preferences are employed, we can assume (for simplicity) that the value of a state for Jeremy will be the sum of preference-satisfactions contained in it. Furthermore, again, perhaps the relevant preferences must satisfy certain conditions; e.g., perhaps they must be self-regarding and rational.

a person by bringing her into existence, what is the reference of 'a person' supposed to be?[2]

To clarify the point about identifiability, consider the following case. James and Sharon are planning to have a child. They refer to this child as 'our future child'. However, 'our future child' does not refer uniquely, but possibly to a class of individuals, namely all those children they might have, depending on which sperm fertilizes which egg (Bayles 1975–6: 299–300). In other words, 'our future child' is not a rigid designator, even when uttered by James or Sharon. So who is it that they may benefit (or harm)?

The problem of identifiability can be interpreted in three distinct ways. In one interpretation, the problem is claimed to be that there are no rigid designators available to us by which to refer to possible future people. However, at least sometimes, we do in fact have access to such designators. Suppose that a doctor is about to micro-inject a sperm into an egg to perform IVF. Arguably, in such a case, the term 'the person who will result if this sperm fertilizes this egg, and the fertilized egg is inserted into a woman, and twinning does not occur, and the foetus is carried to term, and develops a psychology (of a certain complexity)' is a rigid designator. It uniquely picks out a particular person.

Here, I am of course assuming that only one person *could* come into existence in the organism that results if the sperm fertilizes the egg, twinning does not occur, and so on. This might be denied. It might be held that different psychological features (traits, memories, etc.) could be instantiated in this organism, and that a numerically distinct person would emerge if a sufficiently different psychology was instantiated.

However, it is not obvious that distinct persons could emerge in this way. Suppose Tony Blair had been adopted at birth, taken to Brazil to work in a coffee plantation and so had grown up in an environment very different from that in which he in fact grew up. His memories, beliefs, and habits of mind would then have been quite different from what they actually are. But surely this is something that could have happened to *Tony Blair*. In other words, surely Tony Blair—the very man we watch on television—is numerically identical to the person who is adopted and grows up in Brazil in our imagined possible world.[3] It seems, then, that where there is no question of there being more than one organism, significant psychological variation can be accommodated by one and the same person (Persson 1995).

---

[2] For a critical discussion of the identifiability objection, see also Hare (1988: 219–21) and Persson (1997: 48).

[3] Or, if we do not believe in transworld identity, surely the person who grows up in Brazil is a *counterpart* of Tony Blair.

In any case, even if one of several persons could develop in an organism, this need not make it impossible to provide rigid designators for possible future people. We would then just have to make the reference more specific than suggested above. We could refer to a person along the lines of 'the person who will result if this sperm fertilizes this egg (etc.) . . . *and the fertilized egg* (or the organism that results from it) *develops such and such distinctive psychological traits*'.

To return to the case of James and Sharon, then, we could in principle provide rigid designators for all the children they could have nine months from now by itemizing possible combinations of gametes and perhaps specifying certain further conditions. For any one of these children, we can claim that *it* would benefit (or be harmed) by coming into existence, in accordance with the Value of Existence View. Note, also, that we can refer to these possible future children whether or not they actually come into existence.

However, the problem of identifiability can be interpreted differently. Perhaps the problem is that of identifying, not possible future people, but actual future people—those who will *in fact* exist in the future. We can identify children James and Sharon might have in nine months, it might be conceded, but this is inadequate: we cannot identify the child they *will* have (if any).

What prevents the identification of actual future children? The problem can take one of two forms. In an epistemic version, it is claimed that there are no rigid designators available to us which can be *known* to refer to future people. For example, we do not know, in the case of James and Sharon, which sperm will fertilize which egg, and thus we have no way of uniquely referring to their future child. In a stronger, ontological version, the problem is claimed to be that the identities of future people are not *fixed* by present states of affairs and therefore there are no rigid designators available to us by which to refer to them. Notice that neither version excludes the possibility of our possessing rigid designators that refer to possible future people. The epistemic version merely rules out our knowing whether they also refer to actual future people. The ontological version rejects it being presently fixed that they refer to such people.

In fact, an inclination to accept the epistemic version puts one under pressure to accept the ontological version as well. An obvious basis on which to deny that we can know whether a person will come into existence, at least, is that the issue is not fixed by present states of affairs. Equally, if the future existence or non-existence of this person were fixed by present states of affairs then, at least ideally, it seems that we could know about it.

As it turns out, however, these epistemic and ontological versions of the problem of identifiability fail to undermine the Value of Existence View.

Suppose *s* is a rigid designator that picks out a possible future person. All that the Value of Existence View claims is that *if s* comes into existence, he may thereby benefit or be harmed. The fact (if it is a fact) that we do not *know whether* he will come into existence, and so whether *s* refers to an actual future person, does not impugn this claim. Nor does the fact (if it is a fact) that it is not *presently fixed* whether or not he will come into existence (and so whether or not *s* refers to an actual future person).

Having now established the possibility of identifying possible future people, it is worth pointing out that the Value of Existence View does not really depend on this possibility, even when applied to possible future persons. That is, the view can be taken to mean that if one brings a person into existence, then *whoever she is*, she may thereby be benefited (or harmed). Imagine we cannot provide rigid designators for the children James and Sharon may have. We can still claim that if they have a child, then, whoever it is, this child may thereby be benefited (or harmed). While we cannot pick out the candidates for being their child (or rather, so we are falsely assuming), we can employ a description—'their child'—and claim that if, in the future, anything satisfies it, this individual might be benefited (or harmed) by coming into existence.[4]

Some might object that this claim does not make any sense, because one cannot benefit (or harm) non-identifiable people. Arguably, benefits and harms accrue only to particular people. But if James and Sharon have a child, they will have a particular child, and so there will be a particular person to whom the value (or disvalue) of having come into existence accrues. The fact that, at some time, this child may not have been identifiable does not change the fact that once it exists, values can accrue to it. In short, then, even if possible future people are not identifiable (a dubious assumption), it seems that we can make sense of the Value of Existence View.

5.4 On the Logic of Betterness

I have argued for the Value of Existence View by making the comparative claim that existence can be better (or worse) for a person than non-existence. However, some philosophers suggest that it is incoherent to defend the Value

---

[4] Perhaps, to ensure that only one thing can satisfy the description, we should opt for 'their firstborn child'.

of Existence View in this way. Here are representative observations, made by
Parfit and Broome respectively:

> Causing someone to exist is a special case because the alternative would not have
> been worse for this person. We may admit that, for this reason, causing someone
> to exist cannot be *better* for this person.   (Parfit 1984: 489)

> At least, it cannot ever be true that it is better for a person that she lives than
> that she should never have lived at all. If it were better for a person that she lives
> than that she should never have lived at all, then if she had never lived at all, that
> would have been worse for her than if she had lived. But if she had never lived
> at all, there would have been no her for it to be worse for, so it could not have
> been worse for her.   (Broome 1993: 77)

The argument set out by Parfit and Broome has two premises. According to
the first, the judgement that it is better (or worse) to exist than never to exist
entails that it is worse (or better) never to exist than to exist. According to the
second, it cannot be worse (or better) never to exist.

Presumably, the first premise is based on a claim about the logic of the
'betterness' relation; and presumably, the second premise is based on the
following metaphysical principle:

> *The No Properties of the Non-existent Principle.* An individual cannot have any
> properties in world W if it does not exist in W.

It is because a person who does not exist in a world cannot have any properties
there that she cannot be worse (or better) off.

The claim that Parfit and Broome are committed to the No Properties of the
Non-existent Principle can be disputed, but their argument is best explained
by invoking this principle, or so it seems to me. After all, what reason could
there be for denying that it is worse (or better) never to exist, if not because,
in general, a person cannot have properties in a possible world in which she
does not exist? This interpretation it also suggested by Broome's remark that
'if she had never lived at all, there would have been no *her* for it to be worse
for, so it could not have been worse for her' (my emphasis). Broome's point
would seem to be that, in a possible world in which a person does not exist,
her absence makes it impossible for properties to 'stick' to her.

Let us call this argument against the view that existence can be better (or
worse) than non-existence the 'Metaphysical Argument' (due to its metaphysical second premise).[5] In this section, I briefly comment on the logic of the

---

[5] Besides being pressed into service by Broome and Parfit, it also seems to be endorsed by David
Heyd; see Heyd (1992: 122; see also 30–1).

betterness relation. In the following section, I shall attempt to show how both premises of the Metaphysical Argument are in fact compatible with my defence of the Value of Existence View.

What logical property, or properties, of the betterness relation ensure that the proposition that existence is better (or worse) than non-existence implies that non-existence is worse (or better) than existence? Such an entailment must be based on the way 'better than' and 'worse than' are defined. So consider the following definition:

(1) y is worse for S than x, if and only if x is better for S than y.

Claim (1) implies that if existence is better (or worse) for a person than non-existence, non-existence is worse (or better) for her. And the claim that non-existence is worse (or better) for her seems to violate the No Properties of the Non-existent Principle. It seems to ascribe to her the property of being worse (or better) off in a possible world in which she does not exist. So (1) seems to be just what Broome and Parfit need.

5.5 Metaphysics

Let us now examine more closely the other premise in the Metaphysical Argument—the No Properties of the Non-existent Principle. What exactly is it that this principle rules out regarding the properties of non-existent entities? Consider what we may call a positive property such as *having black hair*. This property is instantiated in any object that has black hair. Certainly, the No Properties of the Non-existent Principle rules out that entities can have positive properties in possible worlds in which they do not exist.

According to the Metaphysical Argument, we cannot claim that existence is better (or worse) for a person than non-existence, because this implies that non-existence is worse (or better) for him than existence, and this is ruled out by the No Properties of the Non-existent Principle. Let us now reassess this argument. Consider the following (allegedly dubious) proposition:

P: Non-existence is worse for Jeremy than existence.

The question is whether the truth of P can be established without ascribing positive properties to Jeremy in a possible world in which he does not exist.

In my argument, I described different theories of welfare on the basis of which the Value of Existence View can be defended. Each of these theories involves distinctive ontological commitments. Invoking the Object Account of Preferences, I argued that existence is better for Jeremy because he prefers existence to non-existence. And it may now be argued that, for the same reason, non-existence is worse for him. Here, the truth of P is established merely by appeal to a preference Jeremy has in a possible world—the actual world—in which he exists. In this world, then, he has the positive property of having a particular preference. More importantly, the truth of P is established without ascribing any positive properties to Jeremy in a possible world in which he does not exist.

The three other theories of welfare that I used to argue for the Value of Existence View involved a two-step procedure. First, it was pointed out that Jeremy's life includes a surplus of positive value (preference-satisfactions, positive mental states, or items on an objective list), and that his non-existence involves no such values. Both of these claims, of course, are compatible with the No Properties of the Non-existent Principle. It was then pointed out that it seems to be better to have a surplus of positive value than to have no value. Contrariwise, it seems to be worse to have no value than it is to have a surplus of value. Thus, assuming any of these other theories of welfare, once again, the truth of P is established without presupposing any dubious ontology.

It may be objected that I have not yet shown that P is metaphysically innocent. It may be argued that if P is true, it follows that Jeremy must have a relational property in a possible world in which he does not exist—in this world, he is worse off.[6]

However, we may claim that P is in fact true in virtue of a relation that obtains without ascribing any properties to Jeremy in a world in which he does not exist. The relevant (triadic) relation—x is worse for S than y—obtains between the state of affairs *Jeremy does not exist*, *Jeremy*, and the state of affairs *Jeremy exists*. Now, in the actual world, the second relata, *Jeremy*, exists and thus the third relata, *Jeremy exists*, obtains. The first relata, *Jeremy does not exist*, therefore does not obtain. However, it seems clear that a state need not actually obtain in order to be an object in a betterness relation. Consider, for example, the following relation: the state of affairs that *the allies win the war* is better than the state of affairs that *the Nazis win the war*.

A more plausible requirement, then, is that in order for a relation to obtain, its relata must *exist*. And while the state of affairs *Jeremy does not exist* does not obtain in the actual world, it can be sensibly claimed that it exists there (as an

---

[6] Strictly speaking, it does not follow from the claim that a many-place predicate applies that it does so in virtue of a genuine relation holding between the objects to which it applies. See Armstrong (1978: 28). But nothing in what follows hinges on this.

abstract entity).[7] Since all three relata thus exist, we can claim that the triadic relation, *non-existence* is worse for *Jeremy* than *existence*, obtains.[8] Therefore, assuming that this relation is indeed the truth-maker for P, P is true. And since according to the Metaphysical Argument, P cannot be true, the Metaphysical Argument should be rejected.[9]

This rebuttal of the Metaphysical Argument also brings to the fore how I can answer a second, related objection to my defence of the Value of Existence View. Above, I consider three theories of welfare on the basis of which the comparison of existence and non-existence is a two-step procedure. And I suggest it is better to have a surplus of positive value than to have no value, and therefore that existence can be better than non-existence. However, it may be objected that we cannot compare positive value to no value, only to zero value. And the No Properties of the Non-existent Principle precludes the ascription of zero value to non-existence. Along such lines David Heyd writes:

> First, there is no way to compare the amount of suffering of states of actual people and the state of nonexistence of these people. We should resist the temptation of assigning a zero-value to nonexistence, thus making it quantitatively commensurable with either the positive or the negative net value of the lives of actual people.   (Heyd 1992: 113)

According to Heyd, then, a miserable life cannot be worse than non-existence, because we cannot assign a value, even zero value, to non-existence. Heyd does not explicitly state why he thinks that we have to be able to assign zero value (rather than no value) to non-existence in order evaluatively to compare it to existence. But presumably it is because he holds that 'no value'

---

[7] Thus, it is common for modal actualists (i.e., proponents of the view that everything that exists actually exists) to distinguish between existence and obtaining. A merely possible entity is one that exists but does not obtain (is not instantiated). See Stalnaker (1979) and Plantinga (1979).

[8] Wlodek Rabinowicz has suggested this account of the relevant relation (personal communication). With respect to ontological modesty, it is located between two alternative accounts of the relation. In the more modest account, statements about possible (but non-actual) states have actual states as their truth-makers—i.e., what renders them true, when true is the way things actually are (Armstrong 1997: ch. 10). The relevant relation can then be claimed to obtain between the state of affairs *Jeremy exists, Jeremy,* and (appropriate) states of affairs serving as truth-makers for claims about Jeremy's non-existence. This account is ontologically less extravagant in the sense that it does not claim the existence of non-obtaining states of affairs. More extravagant than both this account and that offered in the main text is one according to which the relevant relation obtains between *Jeremy* and the state of affairs *Jeremy exists* in one world, and the state of affairs *Jeremy does not exist* in another world. This account relies on a highly controversial modal realism; but for discussion and defence of such a realism, see Lewis (1986).

[9] Incidentally, Broome now believes that according to some (coherent) theories of value, the relevant relation may obtain. He believes that P therefore cannot be shown to be false on logical grounds (personal communication); see also Broome (2004: 63−4).

cannot figure on a value-scale and so cannot be compared to either positive or negative value.

Yet, on the basis of the metaphysical and value-theoretical assumptions I made above, we can in fact assign zero value to non-existence. I argued that the following relation obtains in the actual world where Jeremy exists: the state that *Jeremy exists* is intrinsically better for *Jeremy* than the state that *Jeremy does not exist*. And we can further say that in *this* world, the latter state, *Jeremy does not exist*, has zero value for Jeremy. We are then not ascribing a property, or even a predicate, to Jeremy in a world in which he does not exist. And so obviously, we are not violating the No Properties of the Non-existent Principle. Since Jeremy's non-existence has zero value for him, then, we can compare the zero value of his non-existence to the positive value of his existence and reach the verdict that his non-existence is worse for him.

Nevertheless, perhaps Broome, Heyd, and Parfit's point is not that P cannot be true. Perhaps their point is that it cannot be true if Jeremy does not come into existence. Indeed, this (counterfactual) situation seems to be what Broome aims at in the passage quoted above: 'if it were better for a person that she lives than that she should never have lived at all, then *if she had never lived at all*, that would have been worse for her than if she had lived' (my emphasis). However, claim (1) does not suggest that if existence is better for Jeremy than non-existence, then if Jeremy does not exist, non-existence is worse for him than existence. In order for this to follow, we would have to accept something like:

> (2) If x is better (or worse) for S than y, then x is better (or worse) for S than y, even if x obtains.

How does claim (2) challenge my argument for the Value of Existence View? I have argued that existence is better for Jeremy than non-existence. Claim (1) then implies that non-existence is worse for Jeremy than existence. And given this implication, (2) implies that even if Jeremy had not existed, non-existence would be worse for him. But the No Properties of the Non-existent Principle rules out that Jeremy can have any positive properties, including relational ones, if he does not exist. So it would seem that my claim that existence is better for Jeremy than non-existence leads to a contradiction.

But, nothing forces us to accept (2). In fact, assuming the account of the truth-making relation suggested above, we have reason to reject (2), at least in cases in which x implies the non-existence of S. Consider again P. Since Jeremy exists, P is true in virtue of the obtaining of the truth-making relation. But in a world in which Jeremy does not exist, P does not preserve this truth-value for the simple reason that one of the relata, Jeremy, does not exist.

Thus, we have a perfectly natural explanation of why (2) does not hold in such cases. The metaphysical basis for P is not preserved.

5.6 Actual, Possible, and Contingent People

Sometimes it is suggested that only actual people, or, alternatively, only necessary people, can be benefited or harmed (Steinbock 1992: 71). I now want to consider the compatibility of these claims with my defence of the Value of Existence View.

Consider first the distinction between actual and merely possible people. Since I have assumed that Jeremy actually exists, obviously my claim that he has benefited from coming into existence is in tune with the claim that only actual people can benefit or be harmed. Likewise, my defence is compatible with a claim I considered (and rejected) in Chapter 2 (Section 2.5), namely that only actual preferences can ground self-interests. Since Jeremy actually prefers existing (or so we are assuming), existence may be better for him.

What, then, if Jeremy were a non-actual, but possible person? Even if we ascribe (actual) benefits and harm only to actual people, we are still entitled to say that Jeremy *would have* benefited from coming into existence. And this is sufficient to bring Jeremy within the scope of our moral concern. In fact, as I shall argue in Chapter 9 (Section 9.7), justice requires that we take into account the welfare of non-actual, possible individuals. Thus, an outcome may be worse for not including an individual that could have existed.

What, then, about the other modal distinction, that between necessary and contingent people? Does it appropriately distinguish those we can benefit and harm from those we cannot? Recall that a person is necessary vis-à-vis a particular comparison of outcomes if she exists in all of them; and that she is contingent if she exists in some but not all. The suggestion that contingent persons cannot be benefited or harmed, therefore, amounts to the claim that it cannot benefit or harm a person that an outcome in which she exists comes about rather than one in which she does not (and vice versa). Clearly this suggestion is incompatible with the Value of Existence View.

Heyd has argued that we can benefit and harm what he calls 'actual people', but not 'potential people'. His arguments, however, do not exploit this distinction, but trade instead on the difference between necessary and contingent people.[10] In fact, I have already dealt with his arguments in

---

[10] I shall return to Heyd's distinction between actual and potential people and its importance for population ethics in Chapter 9 (Section 9.6).

discussing the Metaphysical Argument. What ensures that existence cannot be better for a person than non-existence, according to Heyd, is the fact that in one of the outcomes considered she does not exist and so cannot have any properties, including, respectively, the relational property of being worse (or better) off and of having zero value. Similarly, the fact that, in one of the outcomes, she does not exist makes her a contingent person.

What I have argued, then, is that we can in fact benefit and harm not only necessary, but also contingent, people. We can do so by bringing them into existence.

5.7 Frustrationism

Let me consider a final objection to my argument for the Value of Existence View. When exploiting the Satisfaction Account of Preferences, I suggested that when we cause a person to exist, we benefit her to the extent her preferences are satisfied. However, this is not a case of simply satisfying her preferences; rather, it is a case of *creating* (satisfied) preferences. Does this somehow diminish the value of the satisfactions we bring about?

The view normally taken on the value of preference-satisfaction is 'satisfactionism'. According to this view, positive value attaches to satisfied preferences (it is more valuable that a preference is satisfied than that it never exists).[11] So if a person's preferences are (largely) satisfied, we can claim that she has benefited from coming into existence.

Frustrationists deny these claims. They believe that the only value involved in satisfying a preference is that it is *not frustrated*. So the satisfaction of a preference produces not positive value, but zero value; that is, the value of satisfying a preference equals that of not having it. The frustration of a preference, on the other hand, has negative value.[12]

According to frustrationists, then, satisfying one's existing preferences is valuable in the limited sense that one thereby avoids intrinsic harm, but there is no value involved in creating preferences that are then satisfied: the package *creating and satisfying* a preference creates no positive value. But it is exactly this package that we bring about, when we cause a person to exist. So we cannot benefit a person by causing him to exist; at best, we will not harm him.

---

[11] Of course, satisfactionism should not be confused with the Satisfaction Account of Preferences.

[12] For a defence of frustrationism, see Fehige (1998). Actually, Fehige calls this view 'antifrustrationism', but I shall opt for the shorter 'frustrationism'. For a somewhat sympathetic discussion (under the name of the 'moral ledger model'), see Singer (1993: 128–31).

Frustrationism is connected with a view about our moral reasons for bringing people into existence that many people find appealing. Everything else being equal, if a person will have a life that is worth not living, we have a moral reason not to bring her into existence, while there is no level of welfare that she could have that will give us a moral reason to bring her into existence.[13]

In what way are frustrationism and this apparently attractive view connected? According to frustrationists, we harm a person by bringing her into existence if she turns out to have frustrated preferences. Because the frustration of her preferences will have negative value for her, and because preference-satisfaction only has zero value, this negative value cannot be compensated for by positive value.

On the other hand, we cannot benefit a person by bringing her into existence, precisely because there is no positive value to be had in her life. Even if all her preferences were satisfied, this would have only zero value. So there is no level of welfare that a person can have that would give us a reason to bring her into existence.

The only problem with this promising theoretical development is that frustrationism is implausible—indeed, deeply counterintuitive. In practice, it entails that we always harm children by causing them to exist, no matter how happy they seem, since in the nature of things they will always have at least *some* frustrated preferences. Other things being equal, it therefore will be wrong to have a child whose life is much better than the life of anyone we know. Surely, this cannot be right. So in accounting for the value of preference-satisfaction we should reject frustrationism. And we may then claim that coming into existence *can* benefit (or harm) a person.[14]

---

[13] Jeff McMahan (1981: 100) has dubbed this asymmetrical view about causing happy and miserable people to exist the 'Asymmetry'. I critically discuss a very similar view in Chapter 9 (Section 9.2).

[14] The frustrationist might modify his theory and claim that frustrationism is true regarding some preferences, but not all. In that case he is a partial frustrationist. Here is a case in which frustrationism does seem plausible:

> I shall inject you with an addictive drug. From now on, you will wake every morning with an extremely strong desire to have another injection of this drug. Having this desire will be in itself neither pleasant nor painful, but if the desire is not fulfilled within an hour it will then become very painful. This is no cause for concern, since I shall give you ample supplies of this drug. Every morning, you will be able at once to fulfil this desire. The injection, and its after effects, would also be neither pleasant nor painful. You will spend the rest of your days as you do now. (Parfit 1984: 497).

Regarding your preference for another injection, the frustrationist seems to be right in claiming that the only value involved in satisfying it is that it is not frustrated. In other words, it would be just as good for you (or perhaps slightly better) if you did not have the preference.

Parfit, himself, uses this example to suggest that if one holds a preference theory of welfare, one should hold a global version of this theory. Even if you have a strong preference satisfied every day when you have another injection, you would (presumably) prefer never to have become addicted. That

Finally, it should be noted that frustrationism, if it were accepted, would not undermine the part of the case for the Value of Existence View that claims that it can harm a person to come into existence. In fact, the main problem with frustrationism is that it implies that people are harmed in this way all too often.

5.8 An Alternative Defence

To clarify my defence of the Value of Existence View, it may be helpful to compare it to an alternative defence, and point out why I am reluctant to use this alternative myself. As we have seen, Parfit holds that it cannot be better (or worse) for a person to come into existence than never to come into existence, because that would imply that it could be worse (or better) never to come into existence. However, Parfit does not take this to rule out the Value of Existence View. He argues that while the comparative claim that existence can be *better* (or worse) than never existing should be rejected, the non-comparative claim that coming into existence can be *good* (or bad) is indeed defensible (1984: 489–90).

It may be objected that Parfit does not succeed in defending the Value of Existence View on the basis of a non-comparative judgement. This is because claims about goodness (or badness) are themselves based on comparative judgements. Consider the following definition:

(3) x is good (bad), if and only if x is better (or worse) than non-x.[15]

Claim (3) implies that in order for a state of affairs to be good, it must be better that it obtains than that it does not. So in order for existence to be good, it must be better than non-existence, which is the comparative judgement that Parfit wants to avoid. Strictly speaking, what is needed is not (3) but:

(4) x is good (bad) for S, if and only if x is better (or worse) for S than non-x.

---

is, you have a global preference for not preferring and having a new injection every day. So according to a global preference theory of welfare, I will not make your life go better if I inject you with the drug and make you addicted. However, a partial frustrationist theory gives an explanation of why injecting the drug will not make your life go better that is just as plausible.

Partial frustrationism, though, would not undermine the claim that coming into existence can benefit a person. Even if frustrationism is plausible regarding some preferences, it is not plausible in a case where a child comes into existence and (globally) prefers existing, and has almost all of her preferences satisfied, and these preferences are (mostly) of the type of which satisfactionism is true.

[15] Similarly, Georg Henrik von Wright (1971: 34) defines good as follows: A state *p* is good, if it is unconditionally preferred to its contradictory non-*p*. And Broome (1993) argues that (moral) goodness is reducible to betterness. Actually, it seems possible that there can be a state *p*, such that *p* has zero value and non-*p* is bad. Therefore, (3) needs some revision, but this need not concern us here.

But the shift from (3) to (4) does not really help Parfit, since (4) implies that in order for existence to be good for S, it must be better for him than non-existence.

However, Parfit need not accept (4). He can define 'goodness' differently. More to the point, he can claim that a life that does not include any of what makes life worth living (and not living)—for example, pleasure or preference-satisfaction—is a life that has zero value. He can then define a 'good life' as a life that is better than a life that has zero value, and a 'bad life' as one that is worse.[16] And he can then claim that it is good (or bad) for a person to come into existence if and only if his life is a good (or bad) one. This claim is based on a comparison, but with a life that has zero value, not non-existence.

However, I do not believe that this can serve as an argument for the Value of Existence View. To defend the latter view, a comparison of existence and non-existence is needed. After all, the alternative to coming into existence is not a *life* with zero value; it is non-existence.

To illustrate this point, suppose I am considering whether I will benefit from going to sleep now. We might then define a good sleep as one in which I am better off than in, say, a state of unconsciousness (for example, I may be better off because I have pleasant dreams). Yet, suppose that the alternative to going to sleep now is not unconsciousness, but reading an excellent novel. Imagine also that reading it will give me more welfare than sleeping. While there is a sense in which it will benefit me to go to sleep (it is better than 'nothing'), this is not the sense we will usually be interested in, whether our concerns are prudential or moral. Rather, we want to identify the best option. And to identify the best option, we will need to compare sleeping with reading the novel.

Likewise, for our prudential and moral purposes here, the relevant alternative to existence is not a life with zero value, but non-existence. For instance, we want to be able to morally compare outcomes in which individuals come into existence and outcomes in which they do not. This does not mean that it is irrelevant to compare a particular life to a life that has no value when assessing the benefit of coming into existence. But the reason it is relevant to compare to a life in which there is no value, is that there is no value in never existing. In other words, a life in which there is no value is relevantly similar to never existing. But this claim, of course, involves a comparison of existence and non-existence. And so what we need, in order to defend the Value of Existence View, is a comparison of these two alternatives.

---

[16] Broome (1993: 78) suggests that this is what Parfit has in mind.

5.9 The Value of Existence View and Self-interests

It is now time to consider what the Value of Existence View implies for our self-interests. Since it may benefit a person to come into existence, it would be surprising if coming into existence could not be in our self-interest. After all, to say that something is in a person's self-interest is a way of saying that it would be good for her if it were to come about.

However, in the opening section of this chapter, I suggested that a person who does not (yet) exist cannot (yet) have a self-interest in existing.[17] But as I also suggested, once she exists, she will have interests, and so perhaps a self-interest in having come into existence. It may seem strange to say that we (now) have a self-interest in something that lies in the past, but, to the extent that it seems strange, I think that this is simply because it is not something we usually say. To say that something that lies in the past is in our present self-interest is just another way of saying that, from our present perspective, it was good for us that it came about, and surely this claim raises no problems.

Strictly speaking, the object of the self-interest in having come into existence does not just lie in the past; it lies also in the present and the future. This is because the value of coming into existence consists in the life one acquires or the benefits contained in it. So the self-interest has an entire life or the benefits contained in it as its object.

Consider now how we should assess a self-interest in having come into existence on the basis of my favoured view, the Prudential View. Since the value I gain from coming into existence is the benefits contained in my life, and since I am M-related to the people to whom these benefits befall (myself at different times), we should conclude that it is in my present self-interest to have come into existence (assuming, of course, that my life is worth living).

Note, though, that this self-interest may have different strengths at different times. Suppose that my life consists of forty good years, and then forty bad ones. Then, at the beginning of my life, my self-interest in having come into existence will be stronger than it will be towards the end of my life. This is because self-interests are M-relative. At the age of, say, twenty, I will be strongly M-related to myself at the times at which I will enjoy and have enjoyed various benefits, whereas I will be less related to myself later on, when

---

[17] Hare, with whom I agree on much regarding the issue of possible future people, denies this. He holds that such people have self-interests prior to their existence (1988: 217–18). But, as we shall see, nothing important hinges on this issue.

I am burdened by various harms. Therefore, the benefits will be weightier than the harms. But, at the age of seventy, for instance, it will be the other way around. I will be more strongly related to myself at the time of the harms, and so my self-interest in having come into existence will be weaker. If the last forty years are sufficiently bad, I shall cease to have a self-interest in having come into existence and, perhaps, even cease to be grateful for having done so.

There is a problem with the Prudential View that I have ignored until now, but it becomes particularly acute when applied to the benefit of having come into existence. Suppose that we assess this value on the basis of a single global preference, as I suggested we might do on the Object Account of Preferences. This will provide us with an assessment of the value of an entire life, but not with an assessment of the particular benefits it contains. How, then, do we discount these particular benefits to reach an assessment of our present self-interests, as required by the Prudential View? In fact, if the value of a life is to be determined on the basis of a global preference, it seems that we cannot assess the self-interest in having come into existence, since the global preference leaves no room for discounting. In order to discount, we need to be able to locate benefits at particular times, or at least in specific phases of a life, to be able to determine the extent to which the bearer of a self-interest is M-related to the beneficiary.

I do not know of any simple way of solving this problem. However, it seems to me that it should at least be possible to give a rough estimate of how the total value of a life should be distributed across particular phases. If this were not possible, we could not say that some parts of a life contribute more to its value than do others, and this strikes me as wrong. Looking back on my own life, it seems clear to me that some parts have made it more worth living than have others. Thus, it would appear that it must at least be possible to provide an estimate on how value is distributed. And so, it may be possible to discount benefits according to how strongly the M-relation obtains, even if any such measure will be rough.

Now, if we (or most of us) have a self-interest in having come into existence, what does this imply for our moral obligations to possible future people? Possible future people do not have present self-interests, but they have possible self-interests. And if we cause these people to exist, their self-interests will be actual, including the self-interest in having come into existence (or in not having come into existence). As I shall argue in Chapter 9, this provides a strong case for the view that we can increase the moral value of an outcome by causing more (happy) people to exist, even if the exact nature of a welfare function for 'different number' outcomes may elude us.

5.10 Summary and a Look Ahead

I have argued that the Value of Existence View can be defended on the basis of various theories of welfare. Furthermore, I have contended that the objections to this view that I have considered have failed or at least they are not conclusive. I have also suggested that, since we may benefit from coming into existence, we may have a self-interest in having done so, albeit a relative such interest.

In the next chapter, I begin to consider the importance of self-interests for morality and, in particular, justice. As I point out in Chapter 2, a moral theory that does not take self-interests into account would be crazy. This raises the question of how a moral theory should reflect the self-interests people or, more generally, sentient beings have. Morality, then, requires an account of what self-interests are. I believe the Prudential View provides such an account. However, there are many further questions to consider, including the question of how to distribute welfare or, more precisely, self-interest fulfilment among individuals.

II

Justice

6

Welfarism

6.1 Welfare, Morality, and Justice

Whatever else morality may include, it embraces a concern for self-interests. Imagine what morality would be like if it did not embody such a concern. The fact that torture causes suffering would not provide a reason to abstain from torturing people. Nor would the fact that certain experimental medical procedures may cause patients to become emotionally numb (and so incapable of experiencing pleasure) affect the rightness or wrongness of performing these procedures. Finally, the fact that in one outcome people are significantly worse off—for example, as a result of heavy pollution—than they would be in another outcome, would not provide a reason to prefer the latter outcome. All this is truly incredible. However, even though there is (almost) universal agreement that self-interests matter morally, there is widespread disagreement when it comes to the issue of *how* they matter and, more specifically, how they matter for the issue of just distributions.

In this second part of the book, then, I turn from the nature of self-interest to its importance for distributive justice. My concern is with how self-interest fulfilment should be distributed in cases of interpersonal (and, as we shall see, intrapersonal) conflict. Furthermore, my concern is with a particular aspect of distributive justice, namely with principles that rank outcomes in terms of their value. Such principles may therefore be called 'axiological', or 'theories of outcome value'.

Assuming that justice should regulate the distribution of self-interest fulfilment, our theory of justice will, of course, depend on the particular theory about self-interest we feed into it. According to the Prudential View, self-interests depend on two factors, namely benefits and Relation M. To avoid unnecessary complications, in the next four chapters, I shall focus only on benefits and how they should figure in a moral theory of the value of outcomes. Thus, in this chapter, I begin by developing an account of welfarism, which is the most ambitious account of the relation between benefits and outcome value.

Having developed an account of welfarism, I shall assess various welfarist theories of distributive justice, including egalitarianism and prioritarianism, in Chapters 7–9. In Chapter 10, I then assess the importance of Relation M for such theories. The account I develop there differs from welfarism proper in that it takes outcome value to be a function not just of welfare but also of Relation M. However, to avoid introducing too many complicating factors all at once, I shall postpone this discussion.

As I noted, welfarism is an ambitious doctrine—in fact, according to most moral philosophers, it is *too* ambitious. Yet, note that even if we reject welfarism, we will need an account of how benefits affect the value of outcomes. After all, even if we have other concerns besides welfare, we need to know how to assess outcomes in terms of *this* concern. And welfarism, properly developed, may be quite informative when developing such an account. For instance, it may inform us as to whether our concern for benefits should take an impersonal or a person-affecting form.

Since the distributive principles I consider are welfarist, they all take welfare to be the currency of distributive concern. That is, they all assess outcomes directly in terms of how *welfare* is distributed. But some political philosophers believe that our distributive principles should have a different currency. This is not because they deny that welfare is morally important, but simply because they believe that distributive principles that have other currencies are more plausible. Thus, resources (Dworkin 1981b), capabilities (Sen 1980), access to advantage (Cohen 1989), and opportunity for welfare (Arneson 1989; Vallentyne 2002), are some of the alternative currencies that have been suggested.

Nevertheless, I shall simply assume that welfare is the appropriate currency of distributive justice. Among other things, I do not want to introduce considerations of responsibility for distributive justice since it will unnecessarily complicate my discussion. Therefore, for example, I focus on equality and priority of welfare rather than equality and priority of opportunity for welfare. However, the issues I raise in relation to the two former principles are equally relevant for their opportunity-based versions.

My reason for focusing on welfare rather than resources (in some version or another) is by no means new or original and I shall mention it only very briefly. It is that unlike resources, welfare has intrinsic value. Thus, what matters to a person, ultimately speaking, is not that she has resources (capabilities etc.), but the welfare she derives from these resources. This, it seems to me, is a very good reason why welfare should be the currency of distributive justice.

To illustrate this point, suppose that we are egalitarians. And imagine that while two people have equal shares of resources, through no fault of her own, one of them has a significantly lower welfare than does the other. In fact, perhaps she is rather miserable. It seems clear to me that, insofar as we are egalitarians, this is exactly the sort of inequality we should be worried about. Now, as I said, I shall not develop this argument here, nor attempt to answer the criticisms that have been raised (see, for example, Dworkin 1981a). But it may be worth pointing out that, even if one happens to prefer a different currency, much of what I say about distributive justice will be relevant for the question of what sort of distribution of this preferred currency one should aim for. This is because versions of the principles I discuss can be constructed with other currencies.

6.2 Outcome Welfarism

Since my concern is with theories of outcomes, I shall call the kind of welfarism I am interested in 'outcome welfarism'. Furthermore, I shall take outcomes to consist of states of affairs. Thus, the state of affairs that I write this page is an outcome, and so is the state of affairs that you read it. So is the conjunction of the state of affairs that I write this page *and* the state of affairs that you read it. In addition, and perhaps more interestingly, the state of affairs that a woman has an abortion and the state of affairs that a country wages war on another are outcomes. Even the entire actual world (or the set of states of affairs that it includes) is an outcome. So, for that matter, is any possible world we can imagine.

I have elsewhere argued that it is surprisingly difficult to come up with a plausible definition of welfarism and that different versions have importantly different implications (Holtug 2003b). However, for present purposes, I shall adopt (one of) Sen's definition(s):

> *Outcome Welfarism.* The value of an outcome is an increasing function only of the individual benefits it contains.

The requirement that functions be increasing ensures that welfarist views satisfy:

> *The Pareto Principle.* Two outcomes, O_1 and O_2, are equally good if everyone has the same level of benefits in O_1 as in O_2, and O_1 is better than O_2 if, in O_1, everyone has at least as high a level of benefits as in O_2 and some have a higher level.[1]

This definition, I believe, has a couple of advantages compared to other doctrines of welfarism. Unlike the monistic welfarist doctrine that only welfare has intrinsic value (Moore and Crisp 1996: 598; Kagan 1998: 48; Sumner 1996: 186), it allows that distributive ideals such as equality and priority may directly affect outcome value, because it allows us to assign intrinsic value to, for example, *equality* in the distribution of welfare. Thus, it enables us to allocate intrinsic value to certain distribution-sensitive patterns that we may want the distribution of welfare to conform to.

Furthermore, unlike the welfarist doctrine that outcome value is a function only of welfare, where no restrictions are imposed on the nature of this function (Sen 1987: 39; Ng 1990: 171), Outcome Welfarism captures the intuition that welfarist views should, in some appropriate sense, be responsive to *increases* in benefits rather than to reductions. Consider the (repugnant) view that the lower the sum of welfare is in an outcome, the better this outcome is. If there are no restrictions on the welfare function, then this is a welfarist principle. But this seems wrong; welfarists consider benefits to be *good*-making properties of outcomes. And plausibly, Outcome Welfarism implies that this principle does not qualify as welfarist since it does not satisfy the Pareto Principle.[2]

6.3 Person-affecting Outcome Welfarism

So far, I have merely presented the welfarist doctrine. But what is its attraction? Wayne Sumner puts it well:

> The central thesis of welfarism is that *ethics has ultimately to do with ensuring that lives go well, or at least that they do not go badly.* Whenever we are told that we have a moral reason to do something we are therefore entitled to ask: 'Where is the good

---

[1] This version differs from standard versions of the Pareto Principle, since standard versions are formulated in terms of preferences rather than benefits: see, e.g., Broome (1991: 152). It corresponds to Broome's principle of personal good (1991: 165).

[2] However, for the suggestion that Outcome Welfarism may require *too* much responsiveness to increases in benefits, see Holtug (2003b: 164–9).

in it? Whose life will go better as a result? Who will be benefited (or saved from being harmed)?' And likewise, when we are told that we have a moral reason not to do something we may rightfully ask: 'Where is the harm in it? Who will be made worse off as a result?' Where there is no answer to this question, no linkage to benefits and harms, however remote or indirect, then the alleged reasons may be rejected as so many fictions. Now I find this an enormously attractive picture of the ultimate point of the whole ethical enterprise.   (Sumner 1996: 191–2)

In this attractive picture, outcomes are not *just* good or bad, they are good and bad in virtue of how they affect particular individuals for better or worse. Of course, Sumner is here addressing welfarism as a doctrine that covers the entire moral spectrum, and as such we may reject it even if we accept it as a doctrine only of outcomes. Note also that while Sumner takes welfarism to be a monistic doctrine, the defence he provides here applies equally to Outcome Welfarism.

Part of the attraction to which Sumner points, I believe, is that outcomes are claimed to be good and bad in virtue of being so *for individuals*. This is a *person-affecting* claim. To clarify, person-affecting approaches to ethics claim that what matters, morally, is what is good and bad (or better and worse) *for* people.[3] Thus, in a person-affecting approach, benefits are good *because* they are good for individuals. Such approaches should be contrasted with impersonal approaches, according to which benefits are good, period, and *therefore* it is good that (benefited) people exist. Thus, in impersonal approaches, the moral importance of individuals is that they are 'containers' of benefits.

Apart from Sumner, many others seem to assume a person-affecting approach to welfarism. For instance, Robert Goodin (1991a: 242) suggests that 'Where the utilitarian theory does draw the line is in insisting that to be good something must be good, somehow, *for* someone.' And Larry Temkin (1993b: 315) writes: 'It was an important step in moral philosophy when classical utilitarians emphasized the extent to which the value of things depended on their being good and bad *for* sentient beings.' Furthermore, Jonathan Glover (1992: 142) claims that when assessing harms, a 'comparative version of the person-affecting principle is perhaps a more palatable version of the impersonal approach'.

The critics of welfarism, on the other hand, sometimes find it most opportune to attack welfarism in its impersonal version. For instance, Tom Regan (1984: 205) complains that hedonistic utilitarians consider 'both moral agents and

---

[3] Parfit (1984: 393–4). Note that persons, according to a person-affecting approach, need not possess a great deal of psychological complexity. In fact, such an approach may involve the claim that all sentient beings are persons in the relevant sense.

patients . . . *mere* receptacles of what has positive value (pleasure) or negative value (pain). They have no value of their own; what has value is what they contain.' Later, he extends this complaint to preference utilitarianism as well (1984: 210). Nevertheless, although I think that Regan's most fundamental complaint about utilitarianism has to do with its aggregative nature, in the passage cited he clearly trades on intuitions about impersonal welfarism.

Note that the person-affecting claim differs from the subjectivist claim that in order for something to be good (or bad), it must be good (or bad) *according* to someone. To make this distinction clearer, suppose that you prefer that there be daffodils on other planets. Then, *according* to you, it would be good if the earth were not the sole planet to house daffodils. However, even if there are daffodils on other planets, presumably this is not *good* for you (you are not benefited). After all, your preference is not self-regarding, and (in all likelihood) you will never experience that it is satisfied.

The proposed person-affecting account of the attraction of welfarism adds something to Outcome Welfarism, as this doctrine seems neutral on the issue of impersonal versus person-affecting ethics. After all, the individual benefits Outcome Welfarism urges us to assess outcomes in terms of may be good, period, or good because they are good for their recipients. Therefore, in order for welfarism to present itself in its most attractive version, I shall develop the idea of a person-affecting welfarism further.

A person-affecting approach to ethics can take either a relational or a non-relational form. When ranking two outcomes, a non-relational approach will focus on whether they are *good* (or bad) for the individuals they contain. A relational approach, on the other hand, will compare them on the basis of their being *better* (or worse) than each other for their inhabitants. Which of these two person-affecting approaches we choose may make a difference if we believe that while it can be good for a person to come into existence, it cannot be better for her than never existing (Parfit 1984: 487–90). However, I have argued that the Value of Existence View needs to be supported by the relational claim that existence can be better (or worse) than non-existence. Therefore, it is a relational person-affecting approach I shall develop here.

In one version, this relational approach amounts to:

The Narrow Person-affecting Principle. An outcome, O_1, cannot be better (or worse) than another outcome, O_2, if there is no one for whom O_1 is better (or worse) than O_2.[4]

---

[4] The distinction between narrow and wide person-affecting principles derives from Parfit (1984: 393–401). I present a wide version below.

What the Narrow Person-affecting Principle does, of course, is to tie the betterness of outcomes to their value for the individuals for whom they are better. As Temkin has suggested, this principle has (at least initial) intuitive plausibility and can be invoked to (at least partly) explain a number of further moral intuitions. Consider, for example, the view that it cannot be better to respect people's rights in cases where doing so does not benefit anyone, including the people whose rights we respect. Likewise, this principle may be invoked to partially support the Pareto Principle, since it implies that a Pareto-inferior outcome cannot be better than a Pareto-superior outcome. Furthermore, it may be invoked to support the claim that if we add further happy individuals to an outcome then, everything else being equal, the new outcome that we bring about is at least as good as the former, less populated outcome.[5] Nevertheless, Temkin believes that ultimately it should be rejected. His best argument is based on the so-called Non-identity Problem, which is illustrated in Figure 6.1.[6]

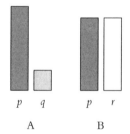

p q p r

A   B

Figure 6.1. The Non-identity Problem

In this figure, A and B are outcomes, column width represents the number of people in a particular group, whereas column height represents their level of welfare, and p, q, and r are distinct (and non-overlapping) groups of people. Suppose that p is a group of people who presently exist. They may adopt the 'live for today policy', which involves having their children immediately and

---

[5] The Narrow Person-affecting Principle is a version of what Temkin (1993a: 256–7) calls the 'Slogan'. Temkin's main interest is with a stronger version of the Slogan—a version he believes to underlie the so-called Levelling Down Objection to egalitarianism. I discuss this objection and the stronger version of the Slogan in Chapter 7 (Sections 7.4–7.6). For his account of the plausible moral judgements supported by the Narrow Person-affecting Principle, see Temkin (1993a: 249–55; 2003b: 71–8).

[6] This problem has been discussed extensively by moral philosophers since Parfit presented his pioneering work on the subject. See, for example, Parfit (1976; 1982; 1984: ch. 16); Heyd (1992: ch. 4); Hanser (1990); Holtug (2004; 2009); Kavka (1982); Roberts (1998: ch. 3); Roberts and Wasserman (2009); Temkin (1993a: 255–6); and Woodward (1986).

depleting natural resources for current uses. In that case, A would come about; they would enjoy a great many benefits, but their children would enjoy far less. Or they may adopt the 'take care of tomorrow policy', which involves waiting a few years before they have their children, and conserving the resources. The children they would then have are numerically different from those they would have in A. Furthermore, with the 'take care of tomorrow policy', these presently existing people would be slightly worse off, but their children would be much better off than their children would be in A. In other words, B would result (Temkin 1993a: 255–6).

Clearly, A is worse than B. B is more equal, better for the worse off and represents a higher total of welfare than does A. However, Temkin argues that according to the Narrow Person-affecting Principle, A cannot be worse.[7] According to this principle, in order for A to be worse, there must be someone for whom it is worse. So are there any such people? Clearly, A is not worse for p. Nor is it worse for q. This group has lives worth living and would not exist if B came about. Finally, Temkin (1993a: 255) argues that A is not worse for r, since if A obtains, r does not exist and so cannot be worse off.

However, what this shows is not that we should reject person-affecting approaches to welfarism, but merely that we should reject the Narrow Person-affecting Principle, thus interpreted. So consider instead:

> *The Wide Person-affecting Principle.* An outcome, O_1, cannot be better (or worse) than another outcome, O_2, if there is no one for whom, were O_1 to obtain, O_1 would be better (or worse) than O_2, and no one for whom, were O_2 to obtain, O_2 would be worse (or better) than O_1.

First, observe that this principle is clearly person-affecting, since it assesses outcomes merely in terms of whether, in these outcomes, individuals are better or worse off. Second, note that it is quite compatible with the intuitively plausible response to the Non-identity Problem, namely that A is worse than B. In order for A to be worse, either A must be worse for someone, were it to obtain, or B must be better for someone, were this outcome to obtain. And, as argued in Chapter 5, if the state of affairs that a person exists obtains, this state

---

[7] Strictly speaking, what Temkin says is that: 'Most believe that the "take care of tomorrow policy" should be adopted. But this is incompatible with [the Narrow Person-affecting Principle] . . . ' (1993a: 255). However, this principle is in fact quite compatible with the claim that the 'take care of tomorrow policy' should be adopted. After all, there may be more to morality than a theory of outcomes. Thus, perhaps the 'live for today policy' would be *wrong*, even if it would be *worse* for no one.

may be better (or worse) for her than the state of affairs that she does not exist. Now, since *r* have good lives in B, were B to obtain, this would be better for them. And since this would be better for *r*, the claim that A is worse than B is compatible with the Wide Person-affecting Principle.

The shift from the Narrow to the Wide Person-affecting Principle also enables us to deal with another problem facing the former principle, namely what we may call the Problem of Suffering (Holtug 1998: 170–1). This problem is illustrated in Figure 6.2.

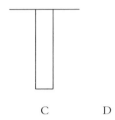

C   D

Figure 6.2. The Problem of Suffering

The line extending from the column represents the level where life ceases to be worth living, and so in C, people have terrible lives. In fact, their lives are so terrible that they are worth *not* living. In D, on the other hand, there are no people. Clearly, then, D is better than C. However, the Narrow Person-affecting Principle rules out this judgement, at least if it is interpreted along the lines suggested above. After all, there is no one for whom D would be better, were it to obtain. The Wide Person-affecting Principle, on the other hand, nicely accommodates the claim that D is better than C. It allows D to be better, since C would be worse for the people who would exist, were C to obtain. So the Wide Person-affecting Principle allows us to reach the right judgements regarding both the Non-identity Problem and the Problem of Suffering.

Furthermore, the Wide Person-affecting Principle is just as apt as the Narrow Person-affecting Principle when it comes to explaining the intuitions referred to above concerning rights, the Pareto Principle, and the value of adding further (happy) individuals to an outcome. For example, it implies that a Pareto-inferior outcome cannot be better than a Pareto-superior outcome and so at least partly justifies the Pareto Principle (although the Pareto Principle does of course imply the stronger claim that the Pareto-superior outcome is better). All in all, then, it seems that if we are to endorse a person-affecting welfarism, we should construe such a doctrine along the lines of the Wide Person-affecting Principle.[8]

Let us call a function of individual benefits that satisfies the Wide Person-affecting Principle a person-affecting function. We may then define:

> *Person-affecting Outcome Welfarism.* The value of an outcome is an increasing person-affecting function only of the individual benefits it contains.

Person-affecting Outcome Welfarism places two restrictions on functions of benefits, namely that they be increasing and that they be person-affecting. Note, however, that these two restrictions have a different scope. The former restriction introduces the Pareto Principle and this principle applies only to fixed populations; that is, comparisons of outcomes in which the very same individuals exist. The restriction that functions be person-affecting, on the other hand, introduces the Wide Person-affecting Principle and this principle applies to the comparison of fixed and variable populations alike.

6.4 On the Virtues of a Person-affecting Approach

The point of my developing Person-affecting Outcome Welfarism is that any distributive view that is welfarist in this sense can be justified in person-affecting terms; that is, in the kind of terms in which Sumner dipped his brush when painting his attractive picture of welfarism. Consider a particular distributive principle, such as:

> *Total Outcome Utilitarianism.* An outcome is intrinsically better, the larger the total sum of individual benefits it contains.

Clearly, this principle is compatible with Person-affecting Outcome Welfarism. After all, it renders outcome value a function only of welfare and it satisfies the Pareto Principle. Furthermore, Total Outcome Utilitarianism will never claim that an outcome is better (or worse) than another is unless it contains a greater (or lower) sum of individual benefits. And even if the greater (or lower) sum is due to contingent people, the Wide Person-affecting Principle will be satisfied. After all, the greater (or lower) sum can be due either to the presence of extra happy people in the better outcome, or to the presence of extra unhappy people in the worse outcome. If the former, the better outcome

---

[8] In fact, this conclusion is too hasty at this stage, since there are various person-affecting principles to consider, apart from the Narrow and the Wide Person-affecting Principles. I consider a number of these further principles in Chapter 9 and conclude that none is as plausible as the latter principle.

would be better for the extra people, were it to obtain, and if the latter, the worse outcome would be worse for the extra people, were that outcome to obtain. Either way, the Wide Person-affecting Principle is satisfied.

While Total Outcome Utilitarianism thus may be justified in person-affecting terms, it may also be justified in impersonal terms. In fact, the very same version of this principle can be justified in either approach. More precisely, the version of Total Outcome Utilitarianism we would reach in an impersonal approach is extensionally equivalent to the version we would reach in a (wide) person-affecting approach; they generate the same ranking of outcomes. This, however, does not imply that these two approaches are identical. After all, in a person-affecting approach, we will only be led to a version of Total Outcome Utilitarianism that is extensionally equivalent to the version reached in an impersonal approach if we believe that existence can be better (or worse) for an individual than non-existence. If we did not accept this claim, the Wide Person-affecting Principle would, for example, rule out the plausible judgement that in the Non-identity Problem (Figure 6.1), A is worse than B. The Wide Person-affecting Principle allows us to make this claim only on the assumption that B is better for r. With an impersonal approach, on the other hand, we need not worry about the claim that existence can be better or worse for an individual.

To explain why I consider the person-affecting approach intuitively more appealing, consider again the Problem of Suffering (Figure 6.2). According to Total Outcome Utilitarianism, D is better and C worse because C contains a lower (in fact, negative) sum of individual benefits. In an impersonal approach, it does not in itself matter that C would be worse for the people who would exist if it were to obtain. Rather, C is worse simply because it renders the world, or this particular corner of the world, worse. In a (wide) person-affecting approach, on the other hand, the lower sum in C is tied to the fact that if C comes about, people will suffer terribly and *thus* be much worse off than in D. In other words, it is the fact that C is worse *for them* that makes C worse and D better. And this person-affecting explanation seems intuitively more appealing, or so it seems to me. The 'worseness' of C is tied to the particular people for whom it is worse. This looks to be plausible because, after all, it is *for their sake* that we should want that D rather than C comes about.

6.5 Welfarism and Beyond

I have now argued that proponents of Outcome Welfarism should opt for Person-affecting Outcome Welfarism. However, I have by no means provided a full defence of this doctrine. This doctrine (indeed, any version of welfarism) rules out a great many moral ideals. Depending on which theory of welfare we assume, we may find it difficult to incorporate ideals such as autonomy, desert, integrity, and many others in our theory of outcomes (Temkin 1993a: 258–77). But note that some such values may be contained in our theory of welfare if, for example, we hold an objective list theory, where such items may figure on our list of objective values; or if we hold a preference theory, according to which various moral ideals are valuable insofar as they are (appropriately) preferred.

Nor shall I provide a full defence of Person-affecting Outcome Welfarism.[9] Nevertheless, as I have argued, the discussion of welfarism has clarified a concern that everyone should have, regardless of other ones, namely that for welfare and the distribution thereof. For instance, as I have suggested, this concern should take a person-affecting form. And we may, of course, expand our axiology with other moral values, if we so desire.

Furthermore, it is worth re-emphasizing that Person-affecting Outcome Welfarism is an axiological doctrine only, which means that it is compatible with the introduction of non-welfarist values elsewhere in our moral theory. To see this, consider first consequentialism, which is the theory that provides the closest 'fit' between our axiology and our full-blown morality. According to act-consequentialism, an act is right if and only if it brings about an outcome at least as good as that of any other available act, as judged from an impartial (agent-neutral) perspective.[10] Thus, there are two distinct features in consequentialism. According to the first, an agent should bring about the best possible outcome. And according to the second, this outcome is the one that is best, as judged from an impartial (agent-neutral) perspective. This means that the ranking of a particular outcome does not vary from person to person, depending on their particular circumstances (Scheffler 1982a: 1). In the following, I shall simply assume an agent-neutral ordering of outcomes (but I return to this impartiality-requirement in the next section).

While consequentialists require that we always bring about the best possible outcome, a moral theory need not have this particular structure. As pointed out in Chapter 2 (Section 2.1), some philosophers who consider consequentialism

---

[9] But for a critical discussion of one of Temkin's arguments, according to which welfarism implausibly rules out various moral ideals, see Holtug (2003a). Temkin responds to my criticism in Temkin (2003a). For other defences of welfarism, see Ng (1990) and Sumner (1996: ch. 7).

[10] There is, of course, no consensus on exactly what consequentialism is. Useful discussions—roughly along the lines suggested here—are available in Broome (1991: ch. 1); Carlson (1994: ch. 2); Kagan (1989: 1–4); Scheffler (1982a: 1–13); Sosa (1993); and Vallentyne (1987a). For brevity, I shall refer to act-consequentialism merely by the term 'consequentialism'.

too demanding suggest that agents have an (agent-relative) option not to bring about the best outcome, namely in cases where doing so would be unreasonably costly for the agent herself (Scheffler 1982a: ch. 3). For instance, an agent need not devote most of her time and money to help relieve famine in developing nations, because doing so would involve sacrificing more of her own welfare than we can reasonably expect from her. The upshot of this is that welfare will play a different role in a morality that includes options than in consequentialism. Since options reduce the moral requirements on agents generated by a concern for the welfare of others, there is a sense in which options may be said to increase agent autonomy or accommodate what Bernard Williams (1973c: 108–18) has called agent 'integrity'. And since options are compatible with the kind of (axiological) welfarism I have been discussing, my welfarist doctrine is compatible with these values of autonomy and integrity.[11]

Furthermore, just as morality may include options, it may contain (agent-relative) constraints. While consequentialists claim that we are always required to produce the best possible outcome, deontologists object that there are certain acts that are forbidden for an agent to perform, even if the outcomes they bring about are better than those of all alternative acts (Nozick 1974: 28–33; for a critique, see Holtug 2000). Thus, constraints may introduce concerns other than welfare and yet be compatible with a welfarist theory of outcomes. This is simply because constraints do not restrict theories of outcomes but rather the overall moral significance of such theories.

Finally, it is worth pointing out that even if we hold a welfarist-consequentialist moral theory as our criterion of rightness, it is plausible that an optimal decision-procedure will include values or concerns that do not figure in this criterion itself. Thus, liberty and autonomy, for example, may be part of a decision-procedure that maximally promotes the values our criterion of rightness requires us to promote. And so there are in fact various respects in which our moral theory may hold non-welfarist values, even if our axiology is purely welfarist. This is worth bearing in mind for readers who wish to combine the concern for welfare and distributions thereof with other moral concerns.

6.6 Impartiality

Apart from being welfarist in the sense specified above, the distributive principles I am concerned with all respect some important requirements of

---

[11] However, for an excellent criticism of options, see Kagan (1989).

impartiality. I now want to describe and to some extent motivate these requirements. The least controversial requirement is that, just like any other moral view, a distributive principle should be universalizable. That is, for any two cases to which a distributive principle ascribes different values, there must be a universal rule according to which these cases so differ (Hare 1963: 30).

The distributive principles I consider are also impartial in the stronger sense that they are agent-neutral. As I pointed out in the last section, this means that they generate rankings that do not vary from person to person. To see that agent-neutrality differs from universalizability, consider ethical egoism. As I construe the ethical egoist, he believes that the value of an outcome is a function only of a subset of the welfare it contains—namely, that consisting entirely of benefits to the individual assessing it. The egoist, then, holds a universal view. For any individual, x, the value of an outcome is a function only of x's welfare. However, ethical egoism is not an agent-neutral view. It lets the value of outcomes vary from person to person.

Agent-neutrality seems to me to be a plausible impartiality requirement in its own right. But note that, as I also pointed out in the last section, an agent-neutral welfarist theory of outcomes is compatible with both (agent-relative) options and (agent-relative) constraints. This should make my assumption of agent-neutrality more palatable to people who believe that morality has an agent-relative dimension.

By exposing welfarism to the requirements of universalizability and agent-neutrality, we can derive another requirement of impartiality; namely, anonymity. According to the requirement of anonymity, the value of an outcome is not affected by the permutation of benefits over individuals who exist in that outcome (Sen 1997: 10; Blackorby, Donaldson, and Weymark 1984: 332). Thus, if we have two outcomes, A and B, that include only two people, a and b, and a gets 2 units of welfare and b gets 1 unit in A, whereas a gets 1 unit and b gets 2 units in B, anonymity implies that A and B are equally good.

Anonymity is in some respects a stronger requirement of impartiality than both universalizability and agent-neutrality. As we have seen, ethical egoism can be construed as a universal view. But obviously, this view is not compatible with anonymity. Rather, according to ethical egoism, A and B are not equally good; A is better relative to a, and B is better relative to b. In this respect, then, anonymity is stronger than universalizability.

There is also a sense in which anonymity is stronger than agent-neutrality. Consider the view that the value of an outcome depends only on how many benefits accrue to people who are kings. This view is not only universal, it is also agent-neutral. It does not let the value of an outcome vary from person to person; it simply claims that, whoever you are, the value of an outcome depends only on the welfare of kings. However, clearly this view does not satisfy the requirement of anonymity. Suppose *a* is a king and *b* is not. This view then informs us that A is better than B. And this claim violates anonymity.

As mentioned, welfarism actually implies anonymity when combined with universalizability and agent-neutrality. Here is why. Consider again outcomes A and B. Assuming welfarism, the value of these outcomes is a function only of benefits. For example, A cannot be preferred on the basis of a claim about what *a* and *b* deserve (such a claim would introduce function variables other than benefits). Nor can A be preferred on the basis of the social roles of *a* and *b*; say, the fact that *a* is king and *b* is not. This too is ruled out by the claim that outcome value is a function only of individual benefits (and so not of social roles). Nor can A be preferred on the basis of the pattern of distribution, since that remains the same in both outcomes.

Rather, if it were to be claimed that A is better than B, the claim would have to depend simply on the fact that in A, it is *a* who gets 2 units and *b* who gets 1 unit rather than the other way around. But then the difference in value between A and B would depend simply on the numerical identities of the people to whom benefits accrue, and to allow values to depend simply on numerical identities is to violate the requirement of universalizability.

Note that this derivation of anonymity only works as long as we assume agent-neutrality. Consider again an agent-relative theory such as ethical egoism. This theory is universalizable. And it implies that, relative to *a*, A is better than B. Given this, we cannot use the requirement of universalizability to defend anonymity in the context of agent-relative theories.[12] But assuming agent-neutrality, anonymity follows.

6.7 Summary and a Look Ahead

In this chapter, I have developed an account of welfarism—Person-affecting Outcome Welfarism—according to which the value of an outcome is an

---

[12] Strictly speaking, ethical egoism is ruled out by welfarism alone, if we take welfarism to include the Pareto Principle, as I have done in my definition of Outcome Welfarism and Person-affecting Outcome Welfarism above. Yet, consider a principle according to which the best possible outcome is one that maximizes one's own welfare and cannot be Pareto-improved. This principle satisfies (Person-affecting) Outcome Welfarism, is universalizable, and yet violates anonymity. However, it is ruled out by the requirement of agent-neutrality.

increasing person-affecting function only of the individual benefits it contains. In various respects I have motivated this account of the welfarist doctrine, and in particular its reliance on a person-affecting approach to ethics. I have also pointed out that it is compatible with non-welfarist ideals in our overall morality. And finally, I have imposed some further requirements of impartiality that I believe our theory of outcomes should satisfy, namely universalizability, agent-neutrality, and (hence) anonymity. If we accept these requirements and Person-affecting Outcome Welfarism, what principle(s) of distributive justice should we hold? This is the topic of the rest of the book.

7

Egalitarianism

7.1 Welfare and Justice

While Person-affecting Outcome Welfarism and the requirements of impartiality I introduced in the last chapter impose a structure to which I believe our distributive principles should conform, they do not amount to a fully fledged (set of) such principle(s). In this chapter, I begin to consider various more specific welfarist principles of justice.

I should emphasize that the distributive principles I consider in this book are all distribution-sensitive in the sense that it matters how a particular sum of welfare is distributed on individuals. In this respect they differ from Total Outcome Utilitarianism. However, the assumption of distribution-sensitivity is not one I shall systematically defend. It relies on an intuition that distribution-*in*sensitive principles such as utilitarianism are unfair with respect to the plight of the worse off. While, because of the diminishing marginal utility of money (Hare 1981: 164–5), utilitarianism may tend to favour monetary equality, this tendency does not suffice to ensure a fair distribution of welfare.

It may be objected that on the assumption that individuals have identical utility functions (and so are equally good at converting money into welfare at each level of income), and that these functions imply the diminishing marginal utility of money (so that people gain more welfare from an additional monetary unit the poorer they are), utilitarianism favours both monetary and welfare equality.

However, as Amartya Sen (1997: 16–18) has argued, the tendency towards monetary equality does not always hold, because people do not in fact have identical utility functions. For example, some people may derive more welfare from a given level of income than others, because these others suffer from a serious disability that limits their options. In such cases, utilitarianism favours not only an unequal distribution of welfare, but also an unequal distribution of income.[1] Furthermore, even if an equal monetary distribution *did* obtain, these disabled people may, through no fault of their own, derive less welfare from their equal share, again because of their reduced set of options. Everything else being equal, this does not seem fair.

Therefore, my focus in this book is on distribution-sensitive principles, and I start with welfarist egalitarianism. First, I turn to the issue of how to define egalitarianism and of explaining how it differs from other distribution-sensitive principles, including prioritarianism. In part, this is motivated by recent discussions over just how egalitarianism and prioritarianism are to be distinguished, and if a principled distinction can even be made between them (Broome forthcoming; Fleurbaey forthcoming; Hausman forthcoming; Jensen 2003; Tungodden 2003). Then I argue that the so-called Levelling Down Objection is a serious challenge to egalitarianism. This objection has been countered in various ways by egalitarians and I shall consider it at some length, contending that they have not succeeded in rebutting it. More specifically, I submit that this objection cannot be rebutted on the basis of, for example, person-affecting egalitarianism or conditional egalitarianism. I also argue that, while some egalitarians have claimed the opposite, the Levelling Down Objection can in fact be supported by a plausible person-affecting principle. This principle is a stronger version of the Wide Person-affecting Principle I introduced in the last chapter. My main aim in this chapter, then, is to provide the theoretical basis for a rejection of egalitarianism. Having discussed this, I turn to prioritarianism in Chapter 8 and argue that this principle is superior to its egalitarian rival.

7.2 Egalitarianism

I have suggested that lack of distribution-sensitivity renders utilitarianism dubious. Nevertheless, we may differ on the issue of why this is so. Thus, egalitarians give one explanation, prioritarians another. In this section, I outline

---

[1] It can be shown that if one does not *know* anything about people's utility functions, everything else being equal, an equal distribution of a fixed sum of money maximizes the *expected* sum of welfare (Brandt 1979: 311–16). But first, this argument for monetary equality does not apply to cases in which we have reason to believe that people do not have identical utility functions, such as the one just described. And, second, while this is an argument for monetary equality, it is not an argument for equality of welfare.

what I take to be the welfare egalitarian doctrine in some detail. This will enable me to point out where it differs from prioritarianism and to identify the source of the Levelling Down Objection.

In its simplest form, what (axiological welfare) egalitarianism amounts to is this:

> *Overall Outcome Welfare Egalitarianism.* An outcome is intrinsically better, the more equal a distribution of individual benefits it contains.

This principle implies that what is problematic in Total Outcome Utilitarianism is that it does not pay any attention to the intrinsic value of equality. Yet, Overall Outcome Welfare Egalitarianism it not only simple, it is too simple. It is not sufficiently responsive to increases in welfare, and for this reason it does not satisfy Person-affecting Outcome Welfarism. For example, it does not differentiate between welfare-equality at different levels. It thus shows indifference where (if it is to be considered welfarist) it should show a preference. Since it is good that individuals are benefited, welfare-equality must be better the higher the level at which it obtains.

This is not to say, of course, that welfare-egalitarians cannot be welfarists. I have taken Overall Outcome Welfare Egalitarianism to be a complete distributive view in the sense that it generates an all-things-considered judgement on outcome value. But there is an alternative version of this view in which it merely orders outcomes *with respect to equality* and so may be combined with one or more further welfare axiological principles. Indeed, since presumably welfare-egalitarians take benefits to be the relevant distributive unit *because* benefits (unlike resources) have intrinsic value (Dworkin 1981a: 188–9; Broome 1991: 178), they are under considerable pressure to adopt a view that implies that, everything else being equal, it is better if there are more benefits. It hardly needs saying that one such view is (an appropriate *ceteris paribus* version of) Total Outcome Utilitarianism. And suitably combined, these two views imply that welfare-equality is better at higher levels.

Furthermore, if egalitarianism and (say) utilitarianism are *suitably* combined, the resulting view will satisfy the Pareto Principle and hence be welfarist. Let us call a view that combines a *ceteris paribus* version of Overall Outcome Welfare Egalitarianism and some other distributive principle(s) in such a way that the Pareto Principle is satisfied *Pareto Outcome Welfare Egalitarianism.* This, then, is the kind of egalitarian principle I shall be concerned with here.

In order to assess egalitarianism, we need to clarify this view in various respects. In particular, we need to explain in greater detail how it differs from prioritarianism. So, we need to ask what it is about egalitarian views that make them *distinctive*. Or, more precisely, what it is about egalitarian theories of outcomes that make them different from all other theories of outcomes.

It has been suggested that any measure of equality must satisfy the Pigou–Dalton principle of transfer, according to which, if the sum of benefits remains constant, equality is increased by a transfer of benefits from a better-off person to a worse-off person, as long as their relative positions are not reversed.[2] However, while perhaps this is a plausible restriction on measures of equality, it does not enable us to distinguish between egalitarianism and prioritarianism. To see this, consider:

> *Overall Outcome Welfare Prioritarianism.* An outcome is intrinsically better, the larger the sum of weighted individual benefits it contains, where benefits are weighted such that they gain a greater value, the worse off the individual is to whom they accrue.

I shall clarify and discuss this principle at some length in the next chapter but here, the point is merely that it satisfies the Pigou–Dalton principle. After all, a benefit of a fixed size will have greater (moral) value in the hands of a person who is worse off than in the hands of a person who is better off, everything else being equal.

Nor will it do simply to invoke the Pareto Principle to try to explain the difference between egalitarianism and prioritarianism. Admittedly, unlike Overall Outcome Welfare Prioritarianism, Overall Outcome Welfare Egalitarianism does not satisfy this principle. However, by definition, Pareto Outcome Welfare Egalitarianism does.

Nevertheless, it may be suggested that—contrary to what I have assumed so far—Pareto Outcome Welfare Egalitarianism is not a *substantially* egalitarian view. Therefore, the Pareto Principle may in fact serve to distinguish between prioritarianism and *substantial* egalitarian positions. Why might one think that Pareto Outcome Welfare Egalitarianism is not substantially egalitarian? Well, this principle weighs the value of equality against one or more other values. And the concern for equality will sometimes pull away from Pareto-improvements. Thus, what reason do we have to believe that a weighing of equality and other values will always satisfy the Pareto Principle? That is, unless

---

[2] This principle was originally formulated by Hugh Dalton, and it is generally assumed in measures of equality (see, e.g., Sen 1997: 145). The principle usually takes income as its currency, but for the purposes of our discussion here, the appropriate currency is welfare (for similar formulations, that take welfare to be the relevant currency, see Tungodden 2003: 19; and Vallentyne 2000a: 4).

we simply claim that the concern for equality only comes into play when our other concerns have been satisfied, in which case the concern for equality is reduced to a mere tie-breaker.

There are two types of egalitarian answers to the question of why we should expect a plausible egalitarianism to satisfy the Pareto Principle. According to the first, the Pareto Principle is held to be independently plausible and so a constraint on weightings of equality and other values (Broome 1991: 183–4). Therefore, Pareto Outcome Welfare Egalitarianism is the only plausible form of egalitarianism. This answer, however, does not really address the issue of whether such an egalitarianism is *substantially* egalitarian.

According to the second answer, the Pareto Principle is not taken as a constraint on how to weigh different values, but is satisfied as a result of the weighting itself. Thus, it may be pointed out that the Pareto Principle only forces us to hold an outcome O_1 better than another O_2 when O_1 is better for some and worse for none. So suppose that while an outcome A is Pareto-superior to another outcome, B, it is also less equal. For simplicity, let us assume that while there is perfect equality in B, some are better off but none are worse off in A than in B, as illustrated in Figure 7.1.

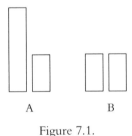

A   B

Figure 7.1.

Our *egalitarian* concern tells us to favour B. But in order for the inequality in A to be *great*, the extra benefits that accrue to some people must also be great. After all, it is these extra benefits that give rise to the inequality. Therefore, we may give substantial weight to equality and yet claim that in *these* cases, where the greater inequality in one outcome does not render anyone worse off than in the other outcome, increases in benefits outweigh decreases in equality (Parfit 1991: 30).

In other cases, where similar increases in inequality are not accompanied by large (or even any) increases in total welfare, the increase in inequality will be sufficient to render the outcome worse, even all things considered.

Examine Figure 7.2 (where the slashed line represents the average level of welfare in C).

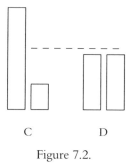

C   D

Figure 7.2.

In C, there is a *slightly* higher average and total of welfare than in D, but there is also *far* more inequality. Therefore, plausibly, the increase in benefits is outweighed by the increase in inequality. And so D is better than C. And since Pareto Outcome Welfare Egalitarianism is compatible with this pattern of responses to outcomes A–D, we are entitled to consider (appropriate versions of) Pareto Outcome Welfare Egalitarianism substantially egalitarian. And so, the Pareto Principle cannot even serve to distinguish prioritarianism from *substantial* egalitarianism.

I now want to suggest that egalitarianism is to be characterized in terms of what it is that egalitarians most fundamentally value. Egalitarians value equality, and equality is a *relation*.[3] But what does it mean that egalitarians *value* this relation? First, they value it *intrinsically*. That is, egalitarians value equality because they take it to be *good for its own sake* and not (merely) good because it tends to further some other goal; say, fraternity, political stability, or the general welfare. Thus, a utilitarian may have reasons to prefer some degree of equality, but surely that does not make her an egalitarian. To be an egalitarian, a person must value equality *for its own sake*.

Second, to qualify as an egalitarian, a person must value equality in the sense that she considers more equal outcomes *in one respect better* than less equal outcomes (Tungodden 2003: 6). However, as we have seen, she need not consider more equal outcomes better, all things considered. After all, clearly she may have other concerns.

---

[3] Thus, it is common to stress the *relational* nature of egalitarianism; see, e.g., Parfit (1991: 23); and Temkin (1993a: 200). Others, however, use 'egalitarianism' in a wider sense, where it includes at least one view that does not attach intrinsic value to relations between people, namely prioritarianism (see, e.g., McKerlie 1996: 277).

Combining these two claims, what we get is:

Outcome Welfare Egalitarianism. An outcome is in one respect intrinsically better, the more equal a distribution of individual benefits it contains.

Unlike Overall Outcome Welfare Egalitarianism, this principle does not generate an all-things-considered ordering of outcomes. Now, different measures of equality will rank outcomes differently and so there may be genuine disagreements about which outcomes are better than others with respect to this value. Nevertheless, I want to suggest that in order for a measure to be a measure of *equality,* it must imply:

The Perfect Equality Claim. An outcome in which everyone has the same share of benefits is more equal than an outcome in which individuals have different shares.[4]

Like the claim that, according to egalitarians, more equal outcomes are in one respect intrinsically better than less equal outcomes, the Perfect Equality Claim seems to me to be a part of our ordinary conception or folk theory of what (welfare) equality is.

While Outcome Welfare Egalitarianism and the Perfect Equality Claim each seem innocent enough, together they imply:

The Egalitarian Relational Claim. An outcome in which everyone has the same share of benefits is in one respect intrinsically better than an outcome in which individuals have different shares.

The Egalitarian Relational Claim seems to nicely capture an important relational aspect of egalitarianism. A principle that satisfies it will imply that an increase in an individual's welfare from n to $n+1$ intrinsically improves an outcome in one respect if everyone else is at $n+1$, but makes it intrinsically worse in one respect if everyone else is at n. Thus, the value of such an increase depends on the recipient's welfare level relative to that of others. However, as we shall see in Section 7.4, the Egalitarian Relational Claim is what renders egalitarianism vulnerable to the Levelling Down Objection.

In the following, then, I shall assume that egalitarians are committed to Outcome Welfare Egalitarianism, the Perfect Equality Claim, and (hence) the Egalitarian Relational Claim. Of course, these three principles amount only to a very limited characterization of egalitarianism. Thus, they only tell us how to rank equal outcomes against unequal ones, and only in one respect. Let me address these two limitations separately.

---

[4] See also Vallentyne (2000a: 4).

The proposed egalitarian principles do not tell us anything about how to rank various patterns of inequality. However, they are compatible with a number of further restrictions. For simplicity, let us momentarily assume that we hold an all-things-considered version of Outcome Welfare Egalitarianism; that is, Overall Outcome Welfare Egalitarianism. This version may satisfy, for example, the Pigou–Dalton principle. However, I do not intend to specify the egalitarian ordering of different patterns of inequality further here because the characterization I have already provided suffices to distinguish egalitarianism from other distributive views, including prioritarianism. According to prioritarians, the moral value of a further benefit to an individual depends on this individual's level of welfare, not on the welfare levels of others. Here, there is no commitment to the intrinsic value of equality or to the Egalitarian Relational Claim.[5] I shall develop this point in greater detail in Chapter 8 (Section 8.2).

My characterization of Outcome Welfare Egalitarianism is also limited in the sense that it does not tell us anything about how to order outcomes *all things considered*. As we have seen, egalitarians will not want to claim that equality is all that matters; they will want to combine the concern for equality with certain other distributive concerns.

This problem, of course, is remedied by Pareto Outcome Welfare Egalitarianism, which while it implies that some unequal outcomes are better than some equal outcomes, nevertheless satisfies the Egalitarian Relational Claim. This is because I have defined Pareto Outcome Welfare Egalitarianism as a principle that combines egalitarian and non-egalitarian concerns such as to satisfy the Pareto Principle, and I have characterized egalitarian concerns in terms of this relational claim. Thus, Pareto Outcome Welfare Egalitarianism implies that an outcome in which everyone has the same share of welfare is *in one respect* intrinsically better than an outcome in which individuals have different shares.

To put it differently, we might say that egalitarians are committed to a particular *reason* for holding the specific all-things-considered ordering that they hold. Of course, egalitarians do not share all their reasons (then they would hold the same all-things-considered orderings), but they have at least

---

[5] Broome suggests that while both prioritarianism and egalitarianism satisfy the Pigou–Dalton principle of transfer, the former view also generates a strongly separable ordering, whereas the latter view does not (Broome forthcoming: 2). The claim that egalitarianism does not satisfy strong separability reflects the fact that equality is a *relational* value. Yet, Broome does not capture the point that there is a particular *reason* why Outcome Welfare Egalitarianism and Overall Outcome Welfare Egalitarianism violate strong separability. I argue this point in Holtug (2005).

one reason in common. And this reason is itself an axiological ordering, albeit a partial ordering of outcomes in one respect only.[6]

However, why be concerned about egalitarianism in this sense? Marc Fleurbaey considers what he calls the minimal egalitarian statement that 'unequal distributions have something bad that equal distributions do not have' (Fleurbaey forthcoming: 3), but claims that this statement has almost no implications for the social ranking. Obviously, what Fleurbaey calls the minimal egalitarian statement is very similar to the Egalitarian Relational Claim. So what, exactly, is the supposed problem with this statement? Fleurbaey stresses that 'it is important to distinguish disagreements about the social ranking from disagreements about the *reasons* supporting the social ranking. Only the former have practical implications and are directly relevant for the policy-maker' (Fleurbaey forthcoming: 2). In other words, what is important for the policy-maker is the social ranking, and the minimal egalitarian statement says almost nothing about that.

Let me make two brief points here. First, the Egalitarian Relational Claim *is* defined in terms of a ranking of outcomes, although a partial ordering in one respect only. Nevertheless, presumably Fleurbaey will claim that what is important for the policy-maker is the all-things-considered ordering. This brings me to my second point. There is, of course, a sense in which it is true that what has practical implications for individuals is the all-things-considered ordering. What should be implemented is the all-things-considered ordering and in its implementation, the implications of each separate reason that supports this ordering are not felt by anyone. Nevertheless, the policy-maker, or anyone else for that matter, may want to know why she should implement a particular ordering, or whether an ordering that already is implemented is justified, and to answer these questions, she will need to invoke reasons. So distinctions in terms of reasons certainly have real importance.

Another implication of accounting for egalitarianism in terms of reasons is that we may find egalitarians and non-egalitarians endorsing identical all-things-considered orderings. In fact, as we shall see in Chapter 8 (Section 8.2), we may even find egalitarians and prioritarians in agreement here (Fleurbaey forthcoming: 9; Jensen 2003: 101–3; Tungodden 2003: 30–1). The difference, of course, will consist in their reasons for endorsing a particular ordering.

But note that this talk of different reasons for accepting a particular ordering, all things considered, is in no way mysterious. For example, several reasons

---

[6] This ordering is partial because the Egalitarian Relational Claim implies only that *equal* outcomes are in one respect intrinsically better than *unequal* outcomes. Thus, it does not tell us how to rank unequal outcomes against other unequal outcomes.

have been given for accepting Rawls's difference principle. One of these reasons appeals to Rawls's contract argument, whereas another appeals only to the 'intuitive' case for giving priority to the worst off in cases where they are not themselves responsible for so being (Barry 1989a: 213–14; Kymlicka 1990: 55). So, do two people who both hold the difference principle, but for each their reason, hold the same view? In a sense yes, and in another sense no. In order to bring out the full extent of their commitments, we shall have to refer to their reasons for holding the difference principle. Likewise, in order to describe the distinctions between egalitarians and other theorists, we shall have to refer to *their* reasons for ordering outcomes in the manner they do.

In this account of egalitarianism, then, it may not always be possible to determine whether an all-things-considered ordering that a particular person holds is egalitarian or not. Furthermore, turning from the person who holds this ordering to the ordering itself, there may be no determinate answer to the question of whether it is egalitarian or not. This may seem to be a rather impractical implication.

However, first, there is nothing that this characterization of egalitarianism prevents us from saying. Even if we cannot always determine whether a particular ordering is egalitarian, we can explain exactly why this is so and what the implications of this ordering are. We can, for instance, say that it is *compatible* with egalitarianism.

Second, as I have stressed, it seems to me that to be worthy of the predicate 'egalitarian', a principle must involve a commitment to Outcome Welfare Egalitarianism, the Perfect Equality Claim, and so the Egalitarian Relational Claim. Therefore, in order to be justified in calling a certain distributive view egalitarian, we must understand it as including a particular (egalitarian) reason for accepting it.

Finally, as already mentioned, the feature I have called the Egalitarian Relational Claim is what invites the Levelling Down Objection, and so drawing the distinction between egalitarianism and prioritarianism in terms of it ensures that this distinction has real theoretical interest.

Like other distribution-sensitive principles, egalitarianism needs a temporal focus. That is, egalitarians need to specify how much of different individuals' lives we should focus on when determining the degree of inequality between them. To illustrate this point, we may hold that what matters is that, at any particular point in time, individuals should be equally well off. Alternatively, we may hold that what matters is that there are equal amounts of welfare in their entire lives. According to this latter view, it does not detract from the value of an outcome if individuals are not equally well off at some time, as long as, at the end of their lives, equal amounts of welfare have accrued to them. For now, I shall assume this latter 'whole lives' view, but the points I shall make about egalitarianism in the following sections apply equally to other versions of egalitarianism. In Chapter 10, I return to the question of the temporal scope of distributive justice.

7.3 The Value of Equality

I have defined Outcome Welfare Egalitarianism as the view that an outcome is in one respect intrinsically better, the more equal a distribution of individual benefits it includes. This may seem to suggest that equality has (intrinsic) *positive* value. However, we cannot just assume that egalitarians hold such a view. Alternatively, they may claim that inequality has (intrinsic) *negative* value.

It may seem that there is no important difference between these two views on the (dis)value of (in)equality. Thus, Parfit claims that egalitarians believe that equality has value, and that 'it would be pedantic to claim instead that *in*equality has *dis*value' (1991: 5). Yet, this is not so. Consider an outcome in which everyone has a life that has zero value. If we hold that equality has positive value, we shall hold that this outcome contains such value (Persson 2001: 31). And so, presumably, if God or someone else could create it, everything else being equal, he would have a reason to do so. This seems wrong. Admittedly, it might be worse if, besides having a zero sum of individual welfare, this outcome also contained inequality. But this claim is also captured by the view that inequality has disvalue. And if we hold this latter view, we avoid the claim that the outcome in which everyone has a life that has zero value has intrinsic positive value. Rather, it has zero value. This egalitarian view of value, then, seems superior. However, my point here is merely that an egalitarian may hold either of these views and that Outcome Welfare Egalitarianism should be read as neutral between them.

Another issue is whether egalitarians should hold a person-affecting or an impersonal version of this view. Impersonal egalitarians locate the badness of inequality in non-individual entities such as relations between individuals, groups, or outcomes.[7] Person-affecting egalitarians, on the other hand, claim that the badness of inequality resides in the individuals for whom it is bad (Broome 1991: ch. 9). That is, it negatively affects an individual's welfare to

---

[7] For impersonal versions of egalitarianism, see Persson (2003); Scanlon (1988: 81); and Temkin (1993a: ch. 9). For a criticism of Temkin's argument for impersonalism, see Rabinowicz (2003).

be worse off than others are. And this effect on welfare is quite independent of the impact her being worse off than others has on her mental states, preference satisfaction, and the like. It simply flows from the fact that she is worse off than they are.

I believe that the value of equality is most plausibly accounted for in impersonal terms. To see this, consider two populations, inhabiting different continents, that have no contact with each other and are quite unaware of the other's existence (the continents might be Europe and America, for example, two thousand years ago). Suppose also that while one population was previously better off than the other was, the level of the better-off population has now been reduced (say, as a consequence of an earthquake) such that it equals the level of the worse-off population. This means that, in terms of equality, the world has improved (at least on the assumption that there are only these two populations).

Now, is it really plausible to claim that the increase in equality has improved the welfare of the worse off? They are, after all, quite unaware of what has happened. More generally, the reduction in the welfare of the better-off population has not caused a change in any intrinsic properties of the worse-off individuals. Therefore, it seems reasonable to claim that their welfare has not been affected (Parfit 1991: 29).[8] And since person-affecting egalitarianism implies that it has, we should reject such egalitarianism.

However, it may be objected that the case of the isolated populations does not really address the concerns of all person-affecting egalitarians. This is because such egalitarians may claim that relations of equality are valuable for individuals only when they obtain between members of a particular society, not when they hold between members of distinct societies. Thus, according to what we may call the 'Social Equality View', equality in an outcome only has intrinsic value in a context of social cooperation, where people are working to better their situation (Norman 1998: 50). The point is that person-affecting egalitarians may make use of the Social Equality View and so claim that in the case of the two isolated populations, members of the worse-off population do not experience an increase in their welfare because that would require a scheme of social cooperation with the better-off population.

---

[8] However, there are theories of welfare that may allow us to deny this claim. An objective list theory, for example, may include values of which it is true that we can have changes in their quantity irrespective of changes in the intrinsic properties of the individuals to whom they accrue. Furthermore, some preference theories claim simply that an individual benefits insofar as her preferences are satisfied. If, then, some of the worse-off individuals prefer that people in the world are equal, they are rendered better off by the reduction in the level of the better off.

Nevertheless, how plausible is the claim that inequality negatively affects the welfare of its victims, albeit only in a context of social cooperation? Let us consider a new case in which a decrease in welfare occurs in a *particular* society, whose members are working together to better their situation. Suppose that a person experiences a reduction in the quality of his mental states such that his level of welfare is reduced to the level of everyone else's.[9] Accept also that the reduction in the quality of this person's mental states has no behavioural manifestations. Then other people's intrinsic properties are not affected and it seems doubtful that they have benefited from the increase in equality. In fact, even if the change in this person's welfare *did* have behavioural manifestations and caused a change in other people's intrinsic properties, it seems to me that we can imagine cases in which it is doubtful that they have benefited, and especially benefited from the *increase in equality*.

So the claim that equality only has value in a context of social cooperation does not appear to help person-affecting egalitarians much. Therefore, in the following, I shall assume an impersonal version of egalitarianism, unless otherwise indicated.

7.4 The Levelling Down Objection

Outcome Welfare Egalitarianism and the Perfect Equality Claim imply that it is in one respect intrinsically better if inequality is eliminated, even if it does not involve making the worse off better off, but only involves making the better off worse off. After all, together, these two principles imply the Egalitarian Relational Claim, according to which an outcome in which everyone has the same share of welfare is in one respect intrinsically better than an outcome in which people have unequal shares.

Of course, egalitarians need not claim that it is better *all things considered* to increase equality by harming some and benefiting none. Obviously, Pareto Outcome Welfare Egalitarianism implies that this would in fact be a change for the worse. Nevertheless, since Pareto Outcome Welfare Egalitarianism incorporates the three egalitarian principles mentioned above, it implies that an elimination of inequality that harms some and benefits none is *in one respect* intrinsically better. It is intrinsically better regarding equality. But how *could*

---

[9] Even if we do not hold a mental state theory of welfare, surely a reduction in the quality of a person's mental states may cause a reduction in her welfare (say, because she has a preference for pleasurable mental states, or because pleasant mental states are items on an objective list).

this in any respect be better? It would benefit *no one*, not even the worse off. This constitutes the gist of the Levelling Down Objection (Parfit 1991: 17).

To illustrate the objection, consider the outcomes in Figure 7.3.

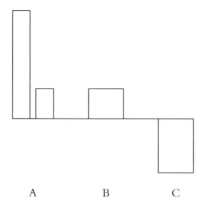

A   B   C

Figure 7.3. Levelling Down

For egalitarians, B must in one respect be intrinsically better than A, namely regarding equality, although it is better for no one. Furthermore, C must in one respect be intrinsically better than A, although everyone suffers terribly (has negative welfare) in C. These judgments illustrate the force of the Levelling Down Objection.[10]

I believe that there are two distinct concerns of ours from which the Levelling Down Objection derives its force. The first is a somewhat general moral concern. There is a strong tendency to think that the value of outcomes must be tied to value for individuals. Roughly, an outcome cannot be better (or worse) than another in any respect unless there is someone for whom it is better (or worse). A problem that levelling down poses for the egalitarian, then, is that it renders no one better off and yet it may involve an improvement in equality.

Therefore, part of the intuitive force of the Levelling Down Objection derives from the fact that the link between equality and improvements in welfare is purely contingent. Equality can come about in different ways and

---

[10] In his discussion of this objection, Parfit (1991: 18) claims that it is only what he calls telic egalitarianism that is vulnerable to it, not what he calls deontic egalitarianism. Telic egalitarianism is the view that it is in itself bad if some people are worse off than others are (which is similar to what I have called Outcome Welfare Egalitarianism). Deontic egalitarianism is the view that inequality is unjust, where injustice necessarily involves wrong-doing. However, there are versions of deontic egalitarianism that are vulnerable to a very similar objection; see Lippert-Rasmussen (2006).

some of these ways do not involve benefits to individuals. I shall discuss the basis of this intuition and the precise relation between morality and benefits it expresses in much greater detail in following sections. But for now, the rough description I have just provided will suffice.

The other concern from which the Levelling Down Objection derives its force is the following. Cases of levelling down suggest that the concerns that motivate us to be egalitarians may not really be captured by egalitarianism. Surely, part of what motivates our concern for equality is a concern for how those who are worse off—or worse off than others—*fare*. Our concern for equality, then, in one way or another reflects a concern for the worse off. But we may wonder whether egalitarianism adequately encapsulates this concern. Consider, for instance, a move from A to C. Equality is supposed to capture our care for the worse off but with respect to equality, C is better than A. The problem, of course, is that the move from A to C does not seem in any way to respond to our concern for the worse off. In fact, the worse off in A are much worse off in C.[11]

It may be thought that unlike impersonal egalitarians, person-affecting egalitarians are invulnerable to the Levelling Down Objection. Consider again A and B in Figure 7.3. Assuming that inequality is bad for the worse off, the move from A to B will in fact benefit these very people (and so Figure 7.3 inadequately represents such cases of 'levelling down', because it suggests that the welfare of these people is not affected). They are no longer worse off than others are and so their welfare is increased. Therefore, the Levelling Down Objection appears to lose its force. Levelling down *does* benefit some and so *can* be in one respect better.

However, person-affecting egalitarianism does not avoid the Levelling Down Objection. Consider D and E in Figure 7.4.

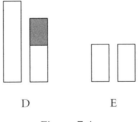

Figure 7.4.

<hr />

[11] Note that even Pareto Outcome Welfare Egalitarians cannot claim that their concern for *equality* is what motivates their concern for the worse off in the comparison of A and C; rather, their consideration for efficiency is what motivates this concern.

In D, the second group has a certain undiscounted level of welfare, which is the welfare they would have had, had they not been worse off than the first group. Their undiscounted welfare is represented by the second column (including both the white and the grey areas). But since the second group is worse off than the first group, their actual welfare is less than their undiscounted welfare. The difference between their undiscounted and their actual welfare is the grey area. In other words, the second group's actual welfare in D is simply the white area.

Suppose now that the undiscounted welfare of both groups is reduced, but the first group's welfare more so than the second group's. In fact, both groups now have a level of undiscounted welfare that equals the level of actual welfare the second group had in D. That is, E results. Since neither group in E is worse off than the other, neither group's welfare should be discounted. Thus, what we have is a case of levelling down. Unlike D, E is perfectly equal, but it is better for no one (see also Rabinowicz 2003: 84). Person-affecting egalitarianism, then, is not immune to the Levelling Down Objection.

Nor, for that matter, is the Social Equality View. Of course, the proponent of the Social Equality View may stress his point that equality is valuable only in situations where cooperation is to the mutual advantage of those who cooperate. This may seem to suggest that equality is valuable only when individuals *benefit*. However, the baseline for assessing such a condition of mutual advantage is the situation in which individuals do not cooperate. That is, cooperation is mutually advantageous if it leaves people better off than if they did not cooperate. And this is simply not relevant when assessing equality in other outcomes. We may have two outcomes such that (a) in both outcomes people are better off than if they did not cooperate, (b) in one outcome some are better and none worse off than in the other, and (c) in the other outcome there is greater equality. We will then have an outcome that involves mutually advantageous cooperation *and* levelling down.

According to the Social Equality View, the value of equality is conditional on social cooperation. As we have seen, this view does not avoid the Levelling Down Objection. However, there is a different conditional egalitarian view that does just that. I consider this view in section 7.7.

7.5 The Strong Wide Person-affecting Principle

I suggested that one of the reasons why the Levelling Down Objection seems so persuasive is that we have a strong tendency to think that the value of outcomes must be tied to value for individuals. Roughly, an outcome cannot be better (or worse) than another in any respect, unless there is someone for whom it is better (or worse). And since levelling down benefits no one, it cannot seem to make an outcome better in even one respect.

Outcome values, then, do not enter the scene out of nowhere; they crucially depend on how individuals are affected for better or worse. And the problem with egalitarianism is that the link between equality and benefits is purely contingent. But, in order for the idea that outcome values are tied to values for individuals to support the Levelling Down Objection, clearly this idea must be spelled out in greater detail. It is fine to say that outcome values depend *crucially* on values for individuals, but unless we are able to specify the nature of the relation with greater precision, we will not be able to tell just how supportive of the Levelling Down Objection this idea is. Plainly, this is a point the egalitarian may want to press. He may argue that the sort of relation between outcome values and benefits we must assume does not stand up to closer scrutiny.

In fact, this is exactly the strategy employed by Larry Temkin, who suggests that the Levelling Down Objection presupposes a principle he calls the 'Slogan'. He presents different versions of the Slogan, one of which coincides with what I have called the Narrow Person-affecting Principle. However, as Temkin realizes, the Narrow Person-affecting Principle cannot support the Levelling Down Objection. After all, this principle is compatible with the claim that levelling down can be *in one respect* better, even if it cannot be better all things considered.

To see this, compare again A and B in Figure 7.3. According to the Narrow Person-affecting Principle, B cannot be better than A. And this is quite compatible with Pareto Outcome Welfare Egalitarianism, which implies that while B is in one respect better, A is better all things considered.

Therefore, Temkin (1993a: 256) suggests that the Levelling Down Objection presupposes a stronger version of the Slogan, which is equivalent to:

The Strong Narrow Person-affecting Principle. An outcome, O_1, cannot be *in any respect* better (or worse) than another outcome, O_2, if there is no one for whom O_1 is *in any respect* better (or worse) than O_2.

Obviously, this principle implies that there is no value to be found in levelling down. Since B is better for no one in any respect, it cannot be in any respect better. And so, equality cannot be a value that renders an outcome in even one respect better than another.[12]

---

[12] Temkin suggests that the Narrow Person-affecting Principle derives much of its plausibility from the Strong Narrow Person-affecting Principle. Suppose we have a case in which an outcome is worse

However, Temkin believes that the Strong Narrow Person-affecting Principle is implausible. And we have already encountered one of his reasons for so believing. Just like the Narrow Person-affecting Principle, the Strong Narrow Person-affecting Principle gets us into trouble when applied to the Non-identity Problem. If we can bring about one of two (non-overlapping) groups of people, where the first group is significantly worse off than the second group (but the first group nevertheless has lives that are worth living), everything else being equal, the Strong Narrow Person-affecting Principle implies that it cannot be in any respect worse to bring about the first group. But since it seems fairly clear that it *is* worse to bring about the first group, we should reject the Strong Narrow Person-affecting Principle. And so this principle cannot support the Levelling Down Objection.

Thus far, I agree with Temkin. However, as I argued in Chapter 6 (Section 6.3), the proper response to the Non-identity Problem is not to abandon a person-affecting account of the value of outcomes, but to opt for the Wide Person-affecting Principle. This principle enables us to claim that it is worse to bring about the worse-off group because, if we were to bring about the better-off group, this would be better for *them*.

Like the Narrow Person-affecting Principle, and for the same reason, the Wide Person-affecting Principle cannot support the Levelling Down Objection. But as in the case of the former principle, a stronger version is available that can:

> *The Strong Wide Person-affecting Principle.* An outcome, O_1, cannot be *in any respect* better (or worse) than another outcome, O_2, if there is no one for whom, were O_1 to obtain, O_1 would be *in any respect* better (or worse) than O_2, and no one for whom, were O_2 to obtain, O_2 would be *in any respect* worse (or better) than O_1.[13]

than another is for no one in any respect. And suppose we claim that while such an outcome cannot be worse, all things considered, it *can* be worse in some respect (a claim that is compatible with the Narrow Person-affecting Principle but not with the Strong Narrow Person-affecting Principle). Temkin's (1993a: 257) point is that if this outcome can be in one respect worse, we are left wondering why it cannot be worse, all things considered. This must be due to the fortunate presence of some other factor, either in this or the alternative outcome, that outweighs (or cancels) the respect in which this outcome is worse. But how can we rely on there always being such a factor?

On further reflection, perhaps the presence of such a factor can be explained. Examine, for example, Pareto Outcome Welfare Egalitarianism once more. A proponent of this view will claim that, in Figure 7.3, A is in one respect worse than B, but that A is better, all things considered. More generally, she will claim that a Pareto-inferior outcome (such as B) is always worse, all things considered, even if it is more equal. Therefore, according to such egalitarians, if an outcome is worse for no one, it can be in one respect worse, but not worse all things considered. Furthermore, this is not due to the *fortunate* presence of some factor, but to the relative weights of equality and increases in benefits.

[13] See also Holtug (1998, 2003a; 2006a). As Glen Newey has pointed out, my formulation of a principle similar to this in Holtug (1998) was unfortunate.

Clearly, this principle does not get us into trouble when applied to the Non-identity Problem. It is compatible with the claim that it is worse to bring about the worse-off group, both in one respect and all things considered, because if we bring about the better-off group, this is better for them. Nor does this principle get us into trouble when applied to the Problem of Suffering. Finally, it *does* imply that it cannot be in any respect better to level down. Consider again Figure 7.3. B cannot be in any respect better than A since, were B to obtain, there would be no one for whom this outcome would be in any respect better than A, and were A to obtain, there would be no one for whom this outcome would be in any respect worse than B.

Since the Strong Wide Person-affecting Principle implies that there is no value to be found in levelling down, Temkin's claim that the Levelling Down Objection presupposes the Strong Narrow Person-affecting Principle cannot be correct. Furthermore, since the Strong Wide Person-affecting Principle avoids the problems so far encountered by the Strong Narrow Person-affecting Principle, it seems to be just the principle needed to meet Temkin's objection.

Having established the existence of a principle that appropriately explains the relation between outcome values and values for individuals required by the Levelling Down Objection, we may of course wonder what reasons we have to accept this principle. Let me briefly rehearse some of the reasons I have identified for accepting such a principle so far.

The Strong Wide Person-affecting Principle shares certain attractive features with the Wide Person-affecting Principle (for my discussion of these features with respect to the latter principle, see Chapter 6, Section 6.3). It allows us to deal with the Non-identity Problem and the Problem of Suffering in person-affecting terms. Furthermore, it explains at least part of the attraction of the Pareto Principle and the claim that if we add further happy individuals to an outcome then, everything else being equal, the new outcome that we bring about is at least as good as the former, less-populated outcome. Similarly, it accounts for the intuition that it is not better to respect a person's rights in a case in which this is better for no one, not even this person herself. And Temkin (1993a: 249–55) provides further examples of cases in which our intuitive responses seem to presuppose some kind of person-affecting principle, where the Strong Wide Person-affecting Principle explains these responses just as plausibly as the principles considered by him.

However, since the Strong Wide Person-affecting Principle shares the attractive features mentioned with the Wide Person-affecting Principle, we have as yet been offered no reason to accept one of these principles over the other. In order to find such reasons, we must look at cases in which they diverge. And, of course, levelling down is just such a case. Unlike the Wide

Person-affecting Principle, the Strong Wide Person-affecting Principle implies that levelling down cannot in any respect be a change for the better.

It may be objected that since the Strong Wide Person-affecting Principle is supposed to support the Levelling Down Objection, we cannot appeal to that objection when making the case for this principle. That would be viciously circular. But to raise such an objection would be to misunderstand my argument. I have considered Temkin's claim that once we attempt to specify the relation between outcome values and values for individuals that must be assumed by the proponent of the Levelling Down Objection, we realize that this cannot be done in a satisfactory manner. Against this, I have argued that while, indeed, the Strong Narrow Person-affecting Principle (or the Slogan) should be rejected, the Strong Wide Person-affecting Principle provides a plausible specification of the relevant relation.

Furthermore, I have argued that because of certain attractive features shared by the Wide Person-affecting Principle and the Strong Wide Person-affecting Principle, we have a reason to hold one of these two principles. And finally, I have contended that, *insofar as* we are impressed by the Levelling Down Objection, of these two principles we have most reason to hold the Strong Wide Person-affecting Principle. This principle *explains* our worries about levelling down.

7.6 Possible People and Moral Ideals

In response to my criticism, Temkin has argued that '*substantive interpretations of the [Strong Wide Person-affecting Principle] are neither obvious nor uncontroversial.* Thus, rhetorical appeals to the [Strong Wide Person-affecting Principle] are unwarranted in support of significant moral positions' (Temkin 2003a: 21–2). By a *substantive* interpretation of the Strong Wide Person-affecting Principle, Temkin means a version of this principle that specifies the theory of welfare we should read into it. Clearly, the implications of the Strong Wide Person-affecting Principle will depend on the theory of welfare assumed, and so, ultimately, it must be shown that there is a plausible theory of welfare that gives rise to a plausible version of this principle.

Let me make two general comments and then move on to some of Temkin's more particular worries. First, surely Temkin is setting his standards too high in the passage quoted above. There are substantive principles that are plausible and yet not *obvious* or *uncontroversial*. Certainly, to the extent they are plausible, we do have a reason (albeit a defeasible one) to accept them.

Second, while ultimately it must be shown that there is a cogent theory of welfare that gives rise to a plausible version of the Strong Wide Person-affecting Principle, I believe that at least part of the intuitive appeal of this principle is quite independent of any particular theory of welfare. The Strong Wide Person-affecting Principle is defined by its structure. It structures our judgements about outcomes by linking them to our judgements about welfare. The structure is the same, whichever theory of welfare we might decide to accept, and it is independently plausible.

By way of analogy, consider the Pareto Principle. Or examine the utilitarian doctrine, according to which the interests of each individual should have equal weight. Since these principles have independent plausibility; that is, have some credibility even before we know which theory of welfare to feed into them, we should not be surprised that the Strong Wide Person-affecting Principle is also independently plausible. Perhaps Temkin is willing to grant this, since he says that he finds the Levelling Down Objection and the Slogan, which he takes to be at the heart of this objection, '*extremely* plausible' (1993a: 248). In any case, since I do not want to assume any particular theory of welfare, I shall rely only on the intuitive force the Strong Wide Person-affecting Principle has in virtue of its structure.[14]

One of Temkin's more particular worries about my use of the Strong Wide Person-affecting Principle concerns the fact that I combine it with the Value of Existence View or, more precisely, with the claim that existence can be better (or worse) for an individual than never existing. As we have seen, this claim is necessary in order for the Strong Wide Person-affecting Principle to be compatible with the intuitively right answers to the Non-identity Problem and the Problem of Suffering. In fact, Temkin seems to have two distinct worries here. First, the Value of Existence View is itself highly controversial. And second, when combined with the Strong Wide Person-affecting Principle, it implies that:

> for *each* of the possible people who might exist, one should be concerned about *that person*, and have *some* reason to bring *that* person into existence and to promote *that person's* welfare, even if there are other possible people one could bring into existence instead who would be *much* better off in *all* respects.   (Temkin 2003a: 23)

While, indeed, the Value of Existence View is controversial, I argued at length in Chapter 5 that we should accept it. Therefore, I shall not elaborate further on this point here.

---

[14] But for an attempt to support the Strong Wide Person-affecting Principle on the basis of just such a theory of welfare, see Holtug (2003a).

Regarding Temkin's second worry, note that the Value of Existence View and the Strong Wide Person-affecting Principle in fact do not imply that we have reason to bring people into existence, let alone that we ought to have particular concerns in this respect. After all, the Value of Existence View involves prudential not moral value, and the Strong Wide Person-affecting Principle allows us to give moral value to the existence of extra people but does not imply that we *should* do so.

Nevertheless, perhaps Temkin's point is that in order for the Value of Existence View and the Strong Wide Person-affecting Principle to be compatible with the right answers regarding the Non-identity Problem (and the Problem of Suffering), we must assume that the existence of extra people can make an outcome better (or worse). This still does not imply that we have a reason to bring people into existence, but at least it draws us closer to that claim. It may be awkward to hold that while the existence of extra (happy) people makes an outcome better, this fact provides no reason at all to bring about the outcome.

As I shall argue in Chapter 9, the claim that the existence of extra people can make an outcome better or worse is in fact a plausible one. Therefore, this implication is one that we should in any case welcome. It enables us to give better answers to various problems in population ethics than we otherwise could. However, my defence of this claim will have to wait until Chapter 9.

Temkin also stresses that in my view, the pro tanto reason to bring about an individual does not go away even if there are other individuals we could bring about instead who would be much better off. In terms of betterness (rather than reasons), we can translate this into the claim that it is in one respect better to bring about the former individual (it is better for her), even if it is better, all things considered, to bring about the happier individuals. But this strikes me as quite unproblematic. If, as I shall argue, we can improve an outcome by bringing new individuals into existence, it is hardly surprising that different possible individuals may give rise to competing claims that we need to weigh against each other. Just as conflicts between existing individuals require us to weigh up their interests.

Those of Temkin's worries I have commented on so far should perturb even welfarists (or rather, they should do so had we not found a way of dealing with them). They challenge the welfarist on her own turf, so to speak. This is because they simply concern the issue of how benefits should be distributed and not the viability of non-welfarist ideals such as, for instance, desert and liberty. But as Temkin (1993a: 258–77) also points out, the Strong Wide Person-affecting Principle has other controversial implications, in that it rules out not only equality but also a great many other popular moral ideals. Exactly which ideals are ruled out will depend on the particular theory of welfare we hold. For example, assuming hedonism, the Strong Wide Person-affecting Principle rules out that an outcome can be better than another *merely* because it includes more autonomy whereas, assuming an objective list theory, it need not rule this out. This is because the latter theory of welfare may take autonomy to be an intrinsically valuable element in the good life.[15]

Although the Strong Wide Person-affecting Principle excludes various non-welfarist ideals, this need not really worry us here because our aim is to develop a *welfarist* theory of outcomes. Clearly, ideals such as desert and liberty are ones that hard-nosed welfarists will in any case want to do without.[16]

Nonetheless, I have suggested that my discussion would be relevant even for those who do not buy the whole welfarist package but nevertheless believe that there is a part of morality that behaves as this doctrine prescribes. And it may seem that this suggestion is now jeopardized, at least with respect to my discussion of the Levelling Down Objection. If our concern about levelling down is motivated by the Strong Wide Person-affecting Principle and this principle is welfarist in nature, then non-welfarists may clearly want to reconsider their worries about levelling down.

However, there are two reasons why my discussion of the Levelling Down Objection may have some appeal even for people who are attracted to (apparently) non-welfarist moral ideals. First, in line with my discussion of the compatibility of Person-affecting Outcome Welfarism and (seemingly) non-welfarist ideals in Chapter 6 (Section 6.5), there are various ways in which a proponent of the Strong Wide Person-affecting Principle can allow such ideals to play a role in morality. He may hold an objective list theory of welfare, where ideals such as, say, autonomy and liberty, are on the list of intrinsic values. Or he may hold a preference theory of welfare, according to which various moral ideals are valuable insofar as they are (appropriately) preferred.[17]

---

[15] For an alternative to Temkin's Slogan, one which rules out egalitarianism but does accommodate various non-welfarist ideals, see Doran (2001).

[16] For a critical discussion of Temkin's worries about the incompatibility of principles such as the Strong Wide Person-affecting Principle and various (apparently) non-welfarist ideals, see Holtug (2003a).

[17] Of course, the egalitarian may similarly argue that *her* (egalitarian) ideal is valuable insofar as it is (appropriately) preferred. We might then suspect that equality can never be reached without some people becoming better off in one respect, since their preference for equality is satisfied. If this were true, then the Strong Wide Person-affecting Principle would have no bite against egalitarianism. But first of all, it might have been the case that no one preferred equality. Then bringing it about would not automatically make anyone better off. So equality can be reached without anyone benefiting.

Second, it seems plausible that there are restrictions on the sort of preferences that can give rise to welfare. One such restriction may be that the preferrer *experiences* that her preference is satisfied.

Furthermore, he may hold that even if the Strong Wide Person-affecting Principle rules out that a particular moral ideal can contribute to the value of an outcome, this ideal may nevertheless be captured by moral options or constraints. Finally, even if a certain moral ideal does not figure on our list of outcome values, it may very well figure in a decision-procedure designed to promote just these values.

Second, as I pointed out above, the Strong Wide Person-affecting Principle is not the only concern that may motivate the Levelling Down Objection. I suggested that at least part of what motivates our regard for equality is a concern for how those who are worse off—or worse off than others—fare. As mentioned, we may wonder whether egalitarianism really captures this concern. After all, equality may be improved by levelling down. So suppose that inequality is eliminated, but at the cost of rendering everyone worse off. In fact, everyone now has a life that is clearly worth *not* living. How many of us can truly say that while the worse off are now much worse off than they were before, this *apparently* egalitarian concern of ours is accommodated by the change in welfare levels?

These points about how even those who are attracted to non-welfarist ideals may have confidence in the Levelling Down Objection will clearly not convince all egalitarians. For example, not all those initially attracted to egalitarianism will find that their trust in this view fades when they realize that it captures the concern for the worse off in a rather limited way (Temkin 1993a: 282). But I believe that many will begin to wonder whether this view really embraces their commitments. Especially if another view is presented that provides a better expression of the concern for the worse off. I consider such a principle in Chapter 8.

Assuming such a restriction, then if equality comes about and satisfies some people's preferences, this will not make them better off if they are not aware that their preferences are satisfied. So if, for instance, people on another continent are made worse off such that they reach our level of welfare, but we have no contact with these people, no one would become better off, even if their preference for equality was satisfied. So again, equality can be reached without anyone becoming better off in any respect.

Another possible restriction on preferences is that they be self-regarding. And people's preference for equality need not satisfy this requirement. So, assuming the self-regarding restriction, equality can be reached without anyone becoming better off in any respect, since the satisfaction of people's preferences for equality need not in any way benefit them.

Third, and most importantly, we can have cases of levelling down in which, although the preferences of some for equality are satisfied, other of their preferences are frustrated such that they do not benefit, all told. Therefore, equality can be reached without anyone becoming better off, even if we accept a preference theory of welfare. Such cases might be rare, but this should be of no comfort to the egalitarian. The fact that there can be such cases is what makes egalitarianism look dubious.

7.7 Conditional Egalitarianism

I have argued that the concerns that motivate the Levelling Down Objection are forceful ones. Let me therefore now consider a way in which the egalitarian may in fact render her position invulnerable to this objection. Thus, in a strategy sometimes used by egalitarians to avoid the Levelling Down Objection, it is claimed that while equality has intrinsic value, it has this value only conditionally. That is, equality is valuable for its own sake, but only if certain further conditions are satisfied. Thus, it has been suggested by Andrew Mason that equality has intrinsic value only if it benefits someone (Mason 2001: 248).[18] Let us call this view 'Conditional Egalitarianism'.

The claim that the equality contained in an outcome *benefits* someone makes sense only when we compare this outcome to at least one other outcome, relative to which this individual is better off. Mason (2001: 248) compares the relevant outcome to all other outcomes that are empirically possible, but this will not do for present purposes. This is because I want to be able to compare outcomes quite generally (that is, irrespective of whether they are empirically possible or not).[19] Rather, we should say that greater equality in one outcome than in another cannot render the former outcome intrinsically better in respect of equality unless its greater equality is better for at least one person. This view claims that while equality and improvements in benefits are only contingently related, the *value* of equality is necessarily related to such improvements. It therefore implies that levelling down cannot improve an outcome with respect to equality. More generally, it implies that a Pareto-inferior outcome cannot be better with respect to equality than a Pareto-superior outcome.[20]

Conditional Egalitarianism differs from the account of egalitarianism I developed in section 7.2, in that it does not satisfy Outcome Welfare Egalitarianism and the Egalitarian Relational Claim. This is why it is not vulnerable to the Levelling Down Objection.

Let me propose the following more formal characterization:

Conditional Egalitarianism. An outcome, O_1, is intrinsically better with respect to equality than another outcome, O_2, if and only if (a) O_1 is more equal than O_2,

---

[18] Mason distinguishes between two versions of this view, but the points I shall make apply to both versions, so I do not need to distinguish between them here.

[19] Nevertheless, the objections I shall raise are equally problematic for Mason's version of Conditional Egalitarianism.

[20] Prior to Mason, Temkin briefly discussed the possibility of Conditional Egalitarianism in Temkin (2000: 156–7).

(b) at least one individual has more benefits in O_1 than in O_2, and (c) the extra benefits that accrue to this individual in O_1 render O_1 more equal than it would have been, had these extra benefits not accrued to her in O_1.

Note that I do not simply claim that the more equal outcome must be better for someone, but further require that the extra benefits that accrue to her must in fact contribute to the increase in equality. To put it differently, she must in fact benefit from the increase *in equality*. To illustrate this point, compare the following two outcomes: (3, 1) and (2, 2), where the numbers refer to individual welfare levels. Here, the extra benefit that accrues to the second individual in the latter outcome is part of what creates the increase in equality. After all, (2, 2) is more equal than the outcome that results if we hold everything in the second outcome constant, except the extra benefit to the second individual, namely (2, 1). Therefore, (2, 2) is in fact intrinsically better with respect to equality than (3, 1), according to Conditional Egalitarianism.

Having thus explained the content of the (c)-clause, let me also motivate it. Consider the following two outcomes: (1, 1, 1, 1, 10, 10) and (1, 1, 1, 1, 1, 11). The difference between them is that in (1, 1, 1, 1, 1, 11), one individual (the second-to-last) has been reduced to the level of the worst off, whereas another individual (the last) has experienced a slight increase in her benefits. Now, many measures of equality imply that (1, 1, 1, 1, 1, 11) is more equal than (1, 1, 1, 1, 10, 10).[21] Furthermore, there is one individual who is better off in (1, 1, 1, 1, 1, 11). Therefore, if Conditional Egalitarianism did not include the (c)-clause, it would imply that (1, 1, 1, 1, 1, 11) is intrinsically better with respect to equality than (1, 1, 1, 1, 10, 10).

However, the fact that one individual is better off in (1, 1, 1, 1, 1, 11) than in (1, 1, 1, 1, 10, 10) actually pulls *away* from equality. In other words, (1, 1, 1, 1, 1, 11) would have been even more equal if this individual had not been better off than she is in (1, 1, 1, 1, 10, 10). Hence it is quite obscure how benefits to *her* can confer intrinsic value on the increase in equality in (1, 1, 1, 1, 1, 11).

---

[21] One reason is that those who are worse off in (1, 1, 1, 1, 10, 10) are worse off than more people than those who are worse off in (1, 1, 1, 1, 1, 11). Everything else being equal, they may therefore be said to have stronger equality-based complaints. Another reason is that the average level of welfare is lower in (1, 1, 1, 1, 1, 11) than in (1, 1, 1, 1, 10, 10). This means that the worst off in (1, 1, 1, 1, 1, 11) are closer to the level they would have if the welfare in (1, 1, 1, 1, 1, 11) were distributed equally, than the worst off in (1, 1, 1, 1, 10, 10) are to the level they would have if the welfare in (1, 1, 1, 1, 10, 10) were thus distributed. It can be argued, therefore, that the equality-based complaint is slighter in (1, 1, 1, 1, 1, 11). And even if (1, 1, 1, 1, 1, 11) includes an extra individual who is worse off, the fact that the average is lower in (1, 1, 1, 1, 1, 11), or the fact that there are fewer individuals the worse off are worse off than (or both these facts), may compensate for this. For these and other reasons, many measures of equality imply that (1, 1, 1, 1, 1, 11) is more equal than (1, 1, 1, 1, 10, 10).

This is why I have imposed the requirement that not only must the more equal distribution be better for at least one individual, it being better for her must be at least part of the explanation of why it is more equal. Since (1, 1, 1, 1, 1, 11) would have been even more equal if the last individual had not benefited—(1, 1, 1, 1, 1, 10) is more equal—(1, 1, 1, 1, 1, 11) is in fact not intrinsically better with respect to equality than is (1, 1, 1, 1, 10, 10), according to Conditional Egalitarianism. This, then, is what motives the (c)-clause.

I now want to present two objections to Conditional Egalitarianism—indeed, reasons why I think this view should be rejected. According to the first, Conditional Egalitarianism violates the transitivity of the betterness relation. More precisely, since we are now concerned only with the value of equality, it violates the transitivity of the 'x is better than y with respect to equality' relation. The ordering generated by this relation is the ordering that results on the assumption that only equality holds intrinsic value. Note that this relation orders outcomes with respect to the *value* they have in virtue of the degree of equality they exemplify, not simply in terms of how equal they are. To illustrate: while (1, 1) is more equal than (2, 1), it is not *better* with respect to equality, according to the conditional egalitarian. This, of course, is because no one benefits from the more equal former outcome.

Consider the following three outcomes:[22]

A: (5, 5, 5, 5)

B: (10, 10, 4, 6)

C: (30, 20, 10, 5)

First compare A and B. A is more equal and contains an individual who is better off than in B (the third individual). Furthermore, the fact that this individual has more benefits in A than in B contributes to the greater equality in A, since (5, 5, 5, 5) is more equal than (5, 5, 4, 5). Therefore, Conditional Egalitarianism implies that A is better with respect to equality than B.

Now compare B and C. The differences in benefits are both fewer and on average smaller in B. And the individual who is better off in B than in C—the fourth individual—is in fact below the average in B. For these reasons, it is plausible to claim that B is more equal than C. Let us assume that this is so. In addition, it is plausible to claim that the extra benefit to the fourth individual in B renders B more equal than it would have been, had this extra benefit not accrued to him here. That is, (10, 10, 4, 6) is more equal than (10, 10,

---

[22] Like me, Mason points out that the 'betterness with respect to equality' relation is intransitive. However, his example relies on his baseline for assessing improvements in benefits, namely empirically possible outcomes, so I cannot use it.

4, 5). This is because, while the extra benefit to the fourth individual in the former outcome increases the inequality between him and the third individual by one, it also *decreases* the inequality between him and *each* of the first and the second individuals by one. It is therefore plausible to claim that, according to Conditional Egalitarianism, B is better than C with respect to equality.

Assuming, then, that A is better than B and B is better than C with respect to equality, it follows that A is better than C in this regard. However, according to Conditional Egalitarianism, A *cannot* be better than C with respect to equality. After all, no one benefits from the higher degree of equality in A (in fact, C is Pareto-superior). Thus, Conditional Egalitarianism violates the transitivity of the 'x is better than y with respect to equality' relation.[23]

It may be objected that there is no reason to believe that 'betterness with respect to equality' is transitive. This objection may be, but need not be, combined with the (perhaps more controversial) claim that even 'betterness all things considered' is not transitive. However, as I pointed out in Chapter 1 (Section 1.5), I am simply assuming that 'x is better than y' and 'x is better than y with respect to z' are transitive relations. Like 'pollutes more than', 'is better than' is a comparative and I have suggested that comparatives are transitive. Furthermore, we can specify *respects* in which objects pollute more or are better than others are. For instance, an object may pollute more with respect to CO_2 than another, just as a distribution may be better with respect to equality than another is. And just as it is part of the meaning of 'pollutes more with respect to CO_2 than' that this relation has the property of being transitive, it is part of the meaning of 'is better with respect to equality than' that this relation has the same property.[24]

A second worry about Conditional Egalitarianism is that we seem to need some sort of explanation of *why* equality only has intrinsic value when it benefits at least one individual. Suppose someone were to suggest that equality has intrinsic value, but only on Tuesdays. Surely we would want to know why equality has such value on Tuesdays but not, say, Wednesdays. In other words, what is so special about *Tuesdays*?

In fact, there are two aspects of Conditional Egalitarianism that need to be explained. One is that an equality-increasing gain in benefits is a necessary condition for the intrinsic value of equality. The need to explain this condition is rendered more urgent by the fact that, just like the relation between Tuesdays

---

[23] For earlier discussions of how the combination of egalitarian and paretian principles can generate intransitivities in the betterness ordering, see, e.g., Mackie (1985); Tungodden and Vallentyne (2005); Wheale (1980); and Williams (1995: 277–9).

[24] For a an indirect defence of the transitivity of 'x is better than y with respect to z', see Holtug (2007a: 52–6), which includes a more elaborate discussion of Conditional Egalitarianism.

and the value of equality, the relation between benefits and the value of equality seems *surprising*. The second aspect that needs to be explained is why *at least one* individual must be benefited by equality. Why not require that, say, 10 per cent of the population must benefit? Unless such an explanation can be provided, there will be an air of arbitrariness to the claim that equality must benefit *at least one*.

The relation between equality and benefits required by Conditional Egalitarianism for intrinsic value is that any increase in equality must be at least partly due to an increase in at least one individual's benefits. But how does this increase in benefits manage to confer intrinsic value (that it would not otherwise have) on *equality*? Of course, an intrinsically valuable state of equality and the state that confers value on it, namely that benefits are increased, are not independent states. Rather, Conditional Egalitarianism requires that the former state at least partly consists in the latter state. But this does not *explain* why an equality-increasing gain in benefits is a requirement for the intrinsic value of equality.

How might the conditional egalitarian respond to the challenge of explaining his view? One suggestion is that he may simply appeal to a person–affecting principle, such as the Strong Narrow Person-affecting Principle. The Strong Wide Person-affecting Principle would do equally well, but since we are not now addressing the issue of possible people, we need only consider the simpler narrow version. The objections I shall raise against egalitarians who invoke a person-affecting principle will in any case apply to egalitarians who invoke either of these versions.

According to the Strong Narrow Person-affecting Principle, then, an outcome cannot be better (or worse) than another in any respect unless there is someone for whom the former outcome is better (or worse). The conditional egalitarian might invoke this as a requirement that must be satisfied by any plausible distributive principle, and then claim that this is why equality does not preserve its value when it does not increase anyone's benefits. Not only does this imply that additional benefits are a condition for the intrinsic value of equality, it also implies that such additional benefits must accrue to *at least one* individual. And so the conditional egalitarian can invoke the very principle that explains (at least part of) the force of the Levelling Down Objection in the first place.

However, Conditional Egalitarianism cannot be explained by invoking the Strong Narrow Person-affecting Principle. This is because Conditional Egalitarianism does not simply require that additional benefits must accrue to an individual in order for equality to be intrinsically valuable, but that *these extra benefits must themselves contribute to the increase in equality*. And the requirement that these benefits must be equality-increasing, of course, does not follow from the claim that at least one individual must benefit.

Furthermore, it is worth pointing out that by simply invoking the Strong Narrow Person-affecting Principle, one fails to explain why *equality* requires equality-increasing benefits in order to generate intrinsic value. More precisely, one does not explain how this requirement flows from a concern about equality. Rather, one simply revises this concern to meet what is considered an independently plausible requirement. Now, I am not suggesting that this manoeuvre is illegitimate as such. But it may also not explain much. By analogy, suppose we were to hold that the flourishing of the biotic community has intrinsic value, and then claim that this value must conform to the Strong Narrow Person-affecting Principle. Thus, it may be intrinsically good if some exotic plant species survives, but only if its survival is accompanied by a gain in benefits for at least one individual—a gain perhaps causally unrelated to the survival of the species. This would be a surprising connection between environmental values and benefits and the surprise is not explained away by simply imposing the Strong Narrow Person-affecting Principle as a condition for environmental (and other) value.

Also, it seems to me that a principle is better justified if it meets a requirement without *ad hoc* revision. The principle and requirement can then be said to be mutually supportive. To illustrate this point, consider prioritarianism. Roughly, since it values only individual benefits, albeit with priority to the worse off, there cannot be an increase in prioritarian value in the absence of an increase in benefits. Thus, prioritarianism does not need to be modified to conform to the Strong Wide Person-affecting Principle.[25] Rather, conformity to this principle flows from the concern with priority itself.

Therefore, I believe that Conditional Egalitarianism cannot be explained by invoking the person-affecting principles under consideration. While there are other ways in which one may try to explain Conditional Egalitarianism, I shall not go further into this here. I have elsewhere argued that none of these alternative explanations in fact provides a plausible account of the puzzling relation between benefits and the intrinsic value of equality (Holtug 2007a: 56–61).

So not only does Conditional Egalitarianism generate an intransitive ordering of 'better with respect to equality', it requires explanation but cannot really be explained either. In the following, then, I shall disregard Conditional Egalitarianism.

---

[25] Prioritarianism does not conform to the Strong *Narrow* Person-affecting Principle. Among other things, prioritarianism allows us to reach the right conclusion with respect to the Non-identity Problem. I return to these issues in Chapters 8 and 9.

7.8 Racial Segregation and Levelling Down

Instead of trying to revise egalitarianism such as to avoid the Levelling Down Objection, the egalitarian may simply accept the claim that, despite appearances to the contrary, there is some intrinsic value to be found in levelling down. He may argue that when described in abstract terms, levelling down may not seem to have anything to be said for it, but that there are more fully described cases in which levelling down indeed seems to have some value, or even to be appropriate. Jonathan Wolff has described just such a case:

> You are the mayor of a small town in the Southern states of the US. Your town has a swimming pool which is open to all. Against your opposition, your state Senate passes a new law: swimming pools must be racially segregated. If there is only one pool, then it must be made available to whites only. As mayor, you do not have funds to build another swimming pool, but in any case object to racial segregation. However, if you try to disobey the new law, you will be removed from office and replaced with a state official. But rather than allowing a whites-only swimming pool you decide to shut it down completely. Your opponents then accuse you of levelling down.   (Wolff 2001: 25)

In any real-life scenario, it is difficult to imagine that African-Americans are not in any way benefited by the closing of the swimming pool. After all, racial segregation is bound to cause African-Americans to feel that they are being treated unfairly and may very well affect their sense of self-worth. Furthermore, it may affect the attitudes of Caucasians, who may come to internalize the attitudes expressed in racial segregation, and thus further harm African-Americans.

However, in order for this to be a case of levelling down, we must simply assume that African-Americans are not in any way benefited if the swimming pool is closed, even in the long run. Now, Wolff's point is that even if we assume that you level down when you close the pool, it seems that you would be justified in so doing. In fact, the egalitarian need not claim that it is better to do so, all things considered, but merely that it is *in one respect* better.

It seems to me that there are three reasons why the existence of cases such as this does not refute the Levelling Down Objection. First, we may wonder whether there really *is* any value to be found in the levelling down it involves. Once we fully realize that closing the swimming pool will *in no way* benefit African-Americans, even in the long run, is it really so clear that closing it is in one respect better? At least in my own case, the intuition that there is something good about closing the pool begins to fade once I realize that this is what we must assume.

Second, even if we were to accept that in the swimming pool case there is something good about levelling down, we are still left with many other cases of levelling down that do not exhibit a similar pull on us. Wolff suggests that the swimming pool case is convincing because there are 'symbolic factors in play, which send messages of deep political inequality' (2001: 31). But clearly many cases of levelling down do not involve such factors. So we would need a different explanation of why levelling down is supposed to be of value in these cases.

Third, even if we were to accept that in the swimming pool case there is some reason to level down, this need not be because the outcome in which levelling down takes place is in any respect better than the outcome in which it does not. These reasons need not be based on the value of outcomes. In fact, racism seems to be just the sort of issue many ethicists and political theorists will want to deal with in terms of moral *constraints*. Along such lines, it may be claimed that racist acts and policies are wrong because they exhibit lack of respect for certain people where these people are in fact entitled to equal respect. And such claims need not be based on comparisons of outcome values. Therefore, the intuitive case for levelling down may not be relevant to our theory of outcomes. I conclude, therefore, that the egalitarian has not offered us a plausible answer to the Levelling Down Objection.

7.9 Summary and a Look Ahead

In this chapter, I examined (welfare) egalitarianism. First, I suggested that in order to qualify as an egalitarian, a person must assign *intrinsic* value to equality. I then argued that egalitarian views satisfy Outcome Welfare Egalitarianism, the Perfect Equality Claim, and (hence) the Egalitarian Relational Claim. In this respect, they differ, for instance, from prioritarianism.

I also pointed out that, because of their commitment to the Egalitarian Relational Claim, egalitarian principles invite the Levelling Down Objection. Egalitarians may try to avoid this objection by claiming that certain conditions have to be satisfied in order for equality to have intrinsic value, and that these conditions are not satisfied in cases of levelling down. I considered such different conditions and argued that none gives rise to a plausible egalitarian view.

Furthermore, I considered Temkin's claim that the Levelling Down Objection presupposes a dubious principle he calls the Slogan. Against this, I argued that the Strong Wide Person-affecting Principle is as supportive of the Levelling Down Objection as is the Slogan, and that it avoids the problems Temkin sets up for the latter principle. Or rather, it avoids those problems that will seem troubling even to welfarists. I also suggested that even if we are attracted to certain non-welfarist ideals, our concerns about these ideals need not be incompatible with the Strong Wide Person-affecting Principle. Finally, I submitted that our worries about levelling down may have different sources, and so that levelling down may trouble us even if we do not accept this principle.

The Levelling Down Objection is not a decisive objection to egalitarianism. But to many of us, it is rather powerful. And our worries about egalitarianism may be further fuelled if we can find an alternative view that better captures our concerns for the worse off. In Chapter 8, I shall examine prioritarianism, a principle that holds the promise of doing just that.

8

Prioritarianism

8.1 From Equality to Priority

In the last chapter, I pointed out that egalitarianism provides a possible diagnosis of what is troubling about the lack of distribution-sensitivity in utilitarianism. The latter view does not pay any attention to the intrinsic value of equality. However, I also mentioned that egalitarianism is vulnerable to the Levelling Down Objection. In light of this, I now turn to a third welfarist distributive principle—a principle that both provides a diagnosis of what is troubling about utilitarianism *and* avoids this objection. I argue that it is a principle we have good reasons to accept.

According to Overall Outcome Welfare Prioritarianism, an outcome is intrinsically better the larger the sum of weighted individual benefits it contains, where benefits are weighted such that they gain a greater value, the worse off the individual is to whom they accrue.[1] Like egalitarianism, this view provides a possible diagnosis of what is troubling about the lack of distribution-sensitivity in utilitarianism. Utilitarians are merely concerned with the sum of welfare and so do not exhibit a special concern for the worse off. A benefit of a fixed size matters the same no matter how well off the individual is to whom it accrues.

I have so far only provided a rough account of prioritarianism and I shall clarify this principle shortly. But first, I want to point to its intuitive

[1] The term 'prioritarianism' is derived from Parfit's so-called teleological (or telic) priority view, according to which 'benefiting people matters more the worse off these people are' (Parfit 1991: 19). Unlike the teleological priority view, Overall Outcome Welfare Prioritarianism allows for the possibility that benefits to individuals who are not persons may contribute to the value of an outcome (although this makes no difference in the present context where I have argued that only persons—sentient beings—are capable of benefiting). Furthermore, unlike the teleological priority view, Overall Outcome Welfare Prioritarianism rather straightforwardly lets natural distributions fall under the scope of the principle. For example, it implies that an outcome is better if, as a result of a natural lottery, a certain sum of benefits is distributed such that everyone has equal shares than if it is distributed such that some have greater shares than others.

appeal. Just as many egalitarians have been led to egalitarianism by pondering on the inadequacies of utilitarianism, many prioritarians have been led to prioritarianism by pondering on egalitarianism. Along such lines, Joseph Raz nicely captures the intuitive case for prioritarianism:[2]

> What makes us care about various inequalities is not the inequality but the concern identified by the underlying principle. It is the hunger of the hungry, the need of the needy, the suffering of the ill, and so on. The fact that they are worse off in the relevant respect than their neighbours is relevant. But it is relevant not as an independent evil of inequality. Its relevance is in showing that their hunger is greater, their need more pressing, their suffering more hurtful, and therefore our concern for the hungry, the needy, the suffering, and not our concern for equality, makes us give them priority.   (Raz 1986: 240)

The above passage suggests that our concern is for the fate of the worse off rather than for a somewhat abstract relation such as equality. When we encounter the hungry, the needy, the sufferers, we are worried about their being badly off. We want them to be better off. A concern for equality, on the other hand, does not in itself suggest that they should be better off, but rather that they should be as well off as everyone else.

This point can be further developed. In Chapter 7 (Section 7.4), I suggested that at least part of what motivates us to be egalitarians is a concern for the worse off. As I also pointed out, this concern is not really captured all that well by egalitarianism. After all, the Levelling Down Objection shows that there are cases in which increases in equality are not accompanied by benefits to anyone, including the worse off. In fact, there are cases in which increases in equality seriously harm these unfortunate people. Egalitarianism, then, is hardly based on a concern for the worse off.

In the present chapter, I first give a more precise characterization of prioritarianism. I then consider whether this view is vulnerable to the Levelling Down Objection. Usually, it is held that prioritarianism stays clear of the objection, but this has been contested recently. However, I shall argue that not only does prioritarianism stay clear of the Levelling Down Objection, it also nicely accommodates the concerns from which this objection derives its force.

In later sections, I then compare prioritarianism to certain other views to which it is intimately related, namely leximin and sufficientarianism. These views also incorporate the idea that we should give priority to the worse

---

[2] Apart from Raz, the list of theorists attracted to prioritarianism includes Arneson (2000); Hooker (2000: 55–65); McKerlie (2006); Nagel (1991: 63–74); Parfit (1991); Scanlon (1982: 123); Scheffler (1982a: 31); Temkin (1993a: 247–8); and Tungodden (2003: 23–32).

off. Thus, I raise the issue of how, exactly, the idea of priority should be cashed out. Rather unsurprisingly, I argue that these alternative views are inferior to prioritarianism. Finally, I consider a couple of objections, namely that this principle's commitment to aggregationism renders it dubious and that it is implausible when applied to conflicts between human and non-human animals.

8.2 Prioritarianism

I need to clarify prioritarianism in various respects. According to prioritarians, a benefit morally matters more the worse off the individual is to whom it accrues. How does this view differ from egalitarianism? Egalitarians value equality, and equality is a relation. Prioritarians, on the other hand, do not value a relation. Rather, what they are concerned with are *absolute* levels of individual welfare (Parfit 1991: 22–4). A benefit that falls at a particular level of welfare has the same moral value no matter at what levels other individuals are. And the lower this particular level is, the greater the value of the benefit is.

This description of the value commitments of the prioritarian needs to be made more precise. Like the egalitarian, we should characterize the prioritarian in terms of her commitments with respect to intrinsic value. We should require that she favours giving priority to the worse off, not (only) because doing so will tend to further some other goal of hers, say, fraternity or political stability, but (at least in part) because she holds that, everything else being equal, an outcome in which a benefit falls at a lower level is *intrinsically* better than an outcome in which an equal benefit falls at a higher level.

I want to suggest that the best account of these value commitments is that the prioritarian ascribes intrinsic value to compound states of affairs, each consisting of the state that a benefit of a certain size befalls an individual and the state that this individual is at a particular welfare level, where this value increases when the size of the benefit increases but decreases when the level of welfare increases. Thus, the (compound) state that a benefit befalls an individual at a lower level is intrinsically better than the (compound) state that an equal benefit befalls an individual at a higher level.

Furthermore, like the egalitarian, a prioritarian may be a pluralist. That is, she may have concerns other than priority. If so, she may not accept Overall Outcome Welfare Prioritarianism, since this view imposes a prioritarian all-things-considered ordering on outcomes. But, qua prioritarian, she will hold that an outcome in which a benefit falls at a lower level is *in one respect* intrinsically better than an outcome in which an equal benefit falls at a higher level. Combining these claims (and introducing an additive function for interpersonal aggregation) we get:

> *Outcome Welfare Prioritarianism.* An outcome is in one respect intrinsically better, the larger the sum of weighted individual benefits it contains, where benefits are weighted such that they gain a greater value, the worse off the individual is to whom they accrue.

Note that, whereas Outcome Welfare Egalitarianism cannot reasonably be claimed to exhaust our axiological concerns, Outcome Welfare Prioritarianism may be claimed to do just that. For instance, unlike Outcome Welfare Egalitarianism, it favours equality at higher levels over equality at lower levels. After all, additional benefits increase the value of an outcome whatever the level at which they fall. So from now on, and for simplicity, unless otherwise indicated, I shall simply assume that prioritarianism implies an all-things-considered ordering of outcomes equivalent to the ordering with respect to priority generated by Outcome Welfare Prioritarianism (although, strictly speaking, prioritarians are only committed to the latter principle *qua* prioritarians). That is, from here on in I simply assume Overall Outcome Welfare Prioritarianism.

With this assumption, we can expose in greater detail the structure of prioritarianism, as well as the structural difference between egalitarianism and prioritarianism, to which I referred above. As Broome (1991: 179; forthcoming: 2) has pointed out, prioritarianism can be formally represented by an additively separable function of the form

$$G = f(w_1) + f(w_2) + \ldots + f(w_n)$$

where f is an increasing and strictly concave function of individual welfare (w_i). Thus, as I pointed out above, the contribution each individual makes to the value of an outcome depends only on her own welfare, not on the welfare of others. Importantly, it is here assumed that individuals have identical weight functions, in the sense that the moral value of a further unit of welfare is the same for *all* individuals who are at identical welfare levels. This assumption follows from the requirement of anonymity. If individuals did not have identical weight functions, there would be possible permutations of benefits over individuals that would affect outcome values.

In a sense, the claim that individuals have identical weight functions can be said to express an ideal of the moral equality of individuals. A benefit to an individual at a given welfare level is exactly as important as a similar benefit to any other individual at the same level, everything else being equal. But, of course, the claim that individuals are moral equals does not commit the prioritarian to *egalitarianism*, which encompasses the view that it is in one respect intrinsically better if individuals have more equal shares of welfare.

As pointed out above, prioritarianism implies that moral outcome value is a strictly concave function of welfare.[3] Thus, benefits *gradually* decrease in moral value, the higher the level at which they fall, as illustrated in Figure 8.1.

Moral outcome value

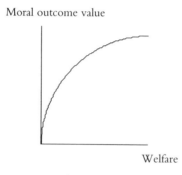

Welfare

Figure 8.1.

Also, prioritarianism is an *aggregative* principle, and I shall assume it implies that for any finite sum of benefits that fall at a lower level, it can be outweighed by a sufficiently large sum of benefits that fall at a (indeed any) higher level. In this respect, it differs from a principle that would give absolute priority to the very worst off.[4] I shall not defend this aggregative approach now, but will do so in Section 8.8.

More precisely, the sort of aggregative function applied to interpersonal (weighted) benefits is an additive function. Of course, other functions could be used, but for now I shall simply assume this particular one. However, in Chapter 9 (Section 9.4), I critically examine an averaging function.

---

[3] Note that while this function resembles the strictly concave function that represents the principle of diminishing marginal utility (according to which an extra monetary unit generates less welfare, the higher the level of income at which it falls), it differs in that it is not based on an empirical claim about the relation between income and welfare, but on a moral claim about the relation between welfare and outcome value.

[4] Thus, neither maximin nor leximin is a version of prioritarianism.

Another important issue concerns the *scope* of priority. I believe that priority has universal scope in the sense that it applies to welfare where and whenever it occurs. Although I shall not fully defend this claim in the present book, there are various *dimensions* for which I shall try to justify it. One such dimension concerns *levels* of welfare. Thus, I do not believe that there is a welfare threshold, over which priority sets out. I argue this in Section 8.7, in which I critically assess sufficientarianism, which is the view that there *is* such a threshold.

A further dimension in which I consider universal scope concerns the issue of what sort of *individuals* are entitled to priority. Thus, it may be suggested that some individuals, such as foetuses, non-human animals, and/or possible future individuals, fall outside the scope of prioritarianism. I briefly consider non-human animals in Section 8.9, where I argue that this is not the case. In Chapter 10 (Section 10.10), I argue that (conscious) foetuses are also included. And in Chapter 9, I discuss possible future individuals; but here, I do not reach a firm conclusion with respect to whether they fall within the scope of priority or not.

Just as I have assumed a 'whole lives' interpretation of egalitarianism, I shall assume a whole lives interpretation of prioritarianism. That is, I shall assume that an individual is worse off than another is—in the relevant sense—if and only if the former individual has less welfare in her life taken as a whole. So the fact that an individual is worse off than another at a particular point in time will not in itself imply that the former individual should have priority over the latter (at that time). I return to the issue of the temporal unit of distributive concern in Chapter 10, where I defend a more complex view.

Finally, as I pointed out in Chapter 7 (Section 7.2), prioritarianism satisfies both the Pareto Principle and the Pigou–Dalton principle of transfer.

Let us now return to the distinction between egalitarianism and prioritarianism. My characterization of the difference between these two principles is in terms of *reasons*.[5] Whatever particular all-things-considered ordering an egalitarian accepts, she will do so at least in part because she accepts the Egalitarian Relational Claim. Prioritarianism, on the other hand, does not involve a commitment to this claim. The moral value of a further unit of welfare to any individual depends only on the welfare level of that individual and the weight function. Of course, as I mentioned above, some may want to combine prioritarian and other concerns, and so the acceptance of Outcome Welfare Prioritarianism is *compatible* with a commitment to the Egalitarian Relational

---

[5] For the suggestion that the difference is to be explained in terms of reasons or justifications, see also Tungodden (2003: 24).

Claim. But it is not something to which one is committed in virtue of one's *prioritarian* concerns.

Note also that, as I indicated in Chapter 7 (Section 7.2), this way of construing the difference between egalitarianism and prioritarianism does not rule out that egalitarians may in fact endorse a prioritarian ordering of outcomes, all things considered. But since only egalitarians will endorse this particular ordering, in part because they endorse the Egalitarian Relational Claim, egalitarianism and prioritarianism are *distinct* views.

Nevertheless, Marc Fleurbaey denies that egalitarianism and prioritarianism are *fundamentally* different views. Thus, he argues that not only egalitarians, but also prioritarians, attach value to equality (forthcoming: 6–7). More precisely, assuming that the resulting ranking of outcomes is continuous, a prioritarian view can be represented by a function of the form

$$W = T \times (1 - IN)$$

where T is the total sum of welfare, and IN is an inequality index that satisfies the Pigou–Dalton principle. Fleurbaey provides the following proof. We choose W as a function that represents the prioritarian ordering of outcomes and implies that whenever an outcome holds an equal distribution of welfare, W equals T. According to Fleurbaey (forthcoming: 7), it can be shown that such a function exists. We then adopt the following inequality index:

$$IN = 1 - (W/T).$$

This is held to be a reasonable inequality index because, first, $IN = 0$ when the distribution is equal. And second, IN satisfies the Pigou–Dalton principle. After all, a prioritarian view satisfies this principle and so any Pigou–Dalton transfer increases W (while T is held constant) and so decreases IN. The point, of course, is that by reversing IN, we get $W = T \times (1-IN)$, which is what had to be proved.

In other words, just as Pareto Outcome Welfare Egalitarianism can be divided into parts, some of which are egalitarian and others are not, so can prioritarianism. However, the egalitarian value to which Fleurbaey thinks the prioritarian is committed is instrumental, not intrinsic (forthcoming: 6). More precisely, Fleurbaey thinks the prioritarian is committed to the instrumental value of equality in a logical sense of 'instrumental value'. Prioritarians hold equality to be instrumentally good in that an equal distribution of welfare is held to be intrinsically better than an unequal distribution of the same sum; prioritarianism logically implies that the best possible distribution of a given sum is an equal distribution. This logical sense of 'instrumental value' should be distinguished from its more ordinary causal sense, where an entity has instrumental value insofar as it causally produces some (intrinsic) value.

In fact, prioritarians hold that equality has instrumental value not only in the logical sense, but also in the causal sense. Equality has instrumental value in the causal sense because at least certain ways of increasing equality—giving to the worse off rather than the better off—will promote intrinsic prioritarian value.

But even if prioritarians are committed to the instrumental value of equality in both these senses, this does not make them *egalitarians*. Egalitarians hold that equality has *intrinsic* value and this implies (among other things) that egalitarians consider levelling down to be in one respect intrinsically good. Prioritarianism has no such implication.

Nevertheless, even if prioritarians are not *committed* to egalitarianism, some may well be egalitarians. I have already conceded this much in the case of *pluralist* prioritarians, who combine Outcome Welfare Prioritarianism and egalitarian concerns. But the point here is that even proponents of Overall Outcome Welfare Prioritarianism may in fact be egalitarians. This much seems to follow from the availability of Fleurbaey's inequality index, IN. According to IN, inequality reduces to zero when individuals have the same shares, in accordance with the Perfect Equality Claim. And so, if an overall outcome welfare prioritarian holds Outcome Welfare Egalitarianism with respect to IN, she will indeed be an egalitarian. But, of course, she *need not* hold Outcome Welfare Egalitarianism with respect to IN. So once again, we reach the verdict that prioritarians are not committed to egalitarianism *qua* prioritarians.

While some prioritarians may thus be egalitarians, unless otherwise indicated, I shall assume that prioritarians hold their prioritarian views simply because they take benefits to have greater intrinsic value at lower levels, not partly because they consider more equal outcomes in one respect intrinsically better than less equal outcomes.

8.3 Prioritarianism and the Levelling Down Objection

The claim that prioritarianism is not susceptible to the Levelling Down Objection has been contested and so I need to consider it in greater detail. Consider again levelling down (Figure 8.2).

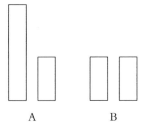

Figure 8.2. Levelling Down

In B, none are better off than in A, and so, according to the prioritarian, levelling down cannot improve an outcome, all things considered. Here, she is in agreement with Pareto outcome welfare egalitarians. But whereas these egalitarians accept the Egalitarian Relational Claim, and so hold levelling down to be in one respect intrinsically good, the prioritarian does not even do that. In levelling down, there is *nothing* of what prioritarians intrinsically value, namely compound states of affairs, each consisting of the state that a benefit of a certain size befalls an individual, and the state that this individual is at a particular welfare level. After all, in levelling down, the former state will not obtain, and so neither will the compound state.

However, as I said, the claim that there is no feature in prioritarianism that favours levelling down may be contested. Consider again the prioritarian function; W. Fleurbaey argues that when a distributional change implies that W is reduced in spite of a decrease in IN, the prioritarian must hold that the change worsens things *in spite* of the fact that something good happens on the IN side. Thus, Fleurbaey (forthcoming: 13) concludes that 'insofar as prioritarians give instrumental value to equality, as shown above, they should also be subject to *a similar kind of criticism* [the Levelling Down Objection]' (my emphasis).

Presumably, the sort of case Fleurbaey has in mind here is a case of levelling down. So let us assume that the welfare level of the better off is reduced to the level of the worst off, resulting in decreases in W, T, and IN. T is reduced because there is a decrease in the sum of welfare, and W is reduced because there is a decrease in the sum of *weighted* welfare. And since there is now perfect equality, IN reduces to zero. In other words, levelling down improves an outcome in one respect, namely regarding IN.

However, the *mere fact* that prioritarianism can be split into separate components such as to give rise to an extensionally equivalent ordering does not show that prioritarianism, or anyone who holds it, attaches any relevant kind of value to these separate components. And so, the fact that IN decreases in the case described above does not imply that prioritarians are committed to the claim that there is, in any interesting sense at least, something good about levelling down.

It may be helpful to consider the following analogy. Total Outcome Utilitarianism can be represented by

$$U = w_1 + w_2 + \ldots + w_n.$$

Furthermore, U is equivalent to the following function of average welfare:

$$V = n \times AVE,$$

where

$$AVE = (w_1 + w_2 + \ldots + w_n)/n.$$

Does this mean that total outcome utilitarians are committed to the claim that an outcome that has a higher average welfare than another is in one respect better? Obviously not. Consider Figure 8.3.

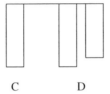

C   D

Figure 8.3. Hell Plus

All the people in these two outcomes have horrible lives, much worse than nothing. But the extra people in D have lives just slightly less horrible than the lives of the people who also exist in C (the first group).[6] Importantly, the move from C to D decreases V in spite of the fact that AVE increases (people are, on average, slightly better off in D). So, in Fleurbaey's line of reasoning, total outcome utilitarians must admit that while V decreases, something good is happening on the AVE side.

But, obviously, total outcome utilitarians do not consider D to be in any respect better than C is. More precisely, they will hold that D is not intrinsically better in any respect. Furthermore, in Hell Plus cases, AVE does not have instrumental value in the causal sense. While certain ways of increasing AVE will also increase the total of benefits, the move from C to D does not do that.

---

[6] The case of Hell Plus is inspired by a very similar case described by Parfit (1984: 393).

What about instrumental value in the logical sense, then? Admittedly, total outcome utilitarians will take AVE to have instrumental value in the sense that, holding n constant, an increase in AVE increases the value of V. But this just means that if we held the number of people in C constant, any increase in AVE would intrinsically improve the outcome. And surely, the mere fact that there are such *other* outcomes that are intrinsically better than C does not imply that, in any interesting sense at least, D is better than C.

Likewise, prioritarians do not consider B in any respect better than A. As we have seen, they will hold that B is not intrinsically better in any respect. Furthermore, in levelling down cases, decreases in IN do not even have instrumental value in the causal sense. While certain ways of decreasing IN will also increase prioritarian intrinsic value, the move from A to B does not do that. Of course, prioritarians will take decreases in IN to have instrumental value in the (logical) sense that, holding T constant, such a decrease increases the value of W. But this just means that if we held T constant, any decrease in IN would intrinsically improve the outcome. And again, the mere fact that there are such *other* outcomes that are intrinsically better than A does not imply that, in any interesting sense, B is better than A. A prioritarian will happily admit that there are such better outcomes, but surely this does not weaken her position. It is a far cry from claiming that B is in one respect intrinsically better than A, which is what the egalitarian claims. And so the 'similar criticism' Fleurbaey believes prioritarianism to be vulnerable to is really not similar at all.

Therefore, I regard that my claim that prioritarianism stays clear of the Levelling Down Objection has not been refuted. Just as Hell Plus cases are troublesome for average but not total utilitarians, levelling down cases are troublesome for egalitarians but not for prioritarians.

As I pointed out in Chapter 7 (Section 7.4), I consider that there are two separate concerns from which the Levelling Down Objection derives its force. Thus, I suggested that part of what motivates us to be egalitarians is a care for how those who are worse off—or worse off than others—fare. Obviously, prioritarianism nicely captures the concern for individuals who are badly off. It gives extra weight to benefits to these unfortunate individuals and so expresses the idea that it is especially important that *they* should fare better. And while it does not assess the value of a change to a worse-off person in terms of how her welfare level compares with the level of others, it will tend to favour benefits to those who are worse off than others are. If we can confer a benefit of a fixed size on one out of two individuals, and one is worse off than the other is, it implies that, everything else being equal, it is better to confer it on the former.

Furthermore, as we shall now see, prioritarianism also embraces the other concern from which the Levelling Down Objection derives its force.

8.4 Impersonal and Person-affecting Values

I have suggested that there is a strong tendency to think that the value of outcomes must be tied to value for individuals and that, in part, this is why the Levelling Down Objection seems so forceful. Furthermore, in Chapter 7 (Section 7.5) I fleshed out the required relation between outcome values and welfare values by introducing the Strong Wide Person-affecting Principle. Egalitarianism does not satisfy this principle, because it implies that an outcome can be in one respect better than another, even if the former outcome renders none better off and the latter none worse off. The problem with egalitarianism, then, is that the link between equality and improvements in welfare is purely contingent. Equality can come about in different ways and some of these ways involve benefits to individuals, whereas others do not.

Prioritarianism, on the other hand, does satisfy the Strong Wide Person-affecting Principle. In order for prioritarianism to imply that an outcome is intrinsically better (or worse) than another, in any respect or all things considered, it would have to be better (or worse) for someone were it to obtain, or the other outcome would have to be worse (or better) for someone were that outcome to obtain.

Nevertheless, while prioritarianism is thus compatible with the Strong Wide Person-affecting Principle, there is a sense in which it is not a person-affecting principle. It implies that a benefit of a fixed size has a higher moral value if it falls at a low level of welfare than if it falls at a high level. But this extra value that is realized at the low level is not a value *for anyone*. Thus, there is a sense in which prioritarians are committed to the existence of impersonal values (see also Persson 2001: 28–9; 2008: 301; Temkin 2000: 151–3).

What I have suggested is that prioritarians ascribe intrinsic value to compound states of affairs, each consisting in the state that a benefit of a certain size befalls an individual, as well as the state that she is at a particular welfare level. Obviously, both these constituent states concern individual welfare.[7] However, only one

---

[7] I do not mean to imply that prioritarians cannot ascribe intrinsic value to anything but the compound states of affairs under consideration. For instance, they may hold that besides such compound states, one of the constituents, namely the state that a benefit of a certain size befalls an individual, has intrinsic value. This would explain why they are concerned with the *welfare* of the worse off. My point here is merely that, *qua* prioritarians, they ascribe intrinsic value only to the compound state of affairs.

of them involves an *increase* in benefits. And it is the other state, the welfare level, which gives rise to the impersonal value described above. We might say that the moral value of a benefit reflects not just the size of the benefit but also the context in which it falls, where the context is the welfare level. The context determines the urgency of the benefit. This is why the intrinsic value of a compound state varies with the context; that is, with what we may call the impersonal element. But it is not as if the impersonal element is a separate intrinsic value that can somehow be isolated from the value of the compound state. Rather, the compound state simply has a specific intrinsic moral value that reflects both of its constituents, namely the benefit and its context.

It is the impersonal element, or the context, that ensures that a benefit of a fixed size will have different values in different circumstances, where this difference in value is not a difference for anyone. While prioritarians thus are committed to the existence of an impersonal element in intrinsic value, they are not committed to the existence of intrinsic values that contain *only* impersonal elements. In fact, they are committed to the claim that if an outcome is intrinsically better than another is, then, compared to this other outcome, the better outcome *necessarily* includes improvements in individual welfare. In this respect, prioritarians differ from egalitarians. Egalitarians are committed to the intrinsic value of states of affairs that are only contingently linked to welfare improvements, namely states of equality.

Nevertheless, does the impersonal element in prioritarianism somehow compromise this position? Ingmar Persson suggests that it undermines the prioritarian's reliance on the Levelling Down Objection to defeat egalitarianism. Thus, he argues that with respect to the impersonal value to which prioritarians are committed, there is a change when levelling down occurs (2008: 301). This change consists in the fact that when levelling down occurs, the average moral weight of benefits is raised. After all, since these benefits now on average fall at lower levels, their average moral weight has been raised. And, according to prioritarians, this is a good feature of the levelled down outcome.[8] However, if this is a good feature of the levelled down outcome, then this outcome is *in one respect* better, and so prioritarianism does not avoid the Levelling Down Objection after all. Furthermore, prioritarianism implies that it is always in one respect worse to benefit individuals, everything else being equal, because doing so will decrease the average moral weight of benefits. But this is absurd.

---

[8] Persson (2008: 301) also considers the possibility that the impersonal value of prioritarianism should be described as a bad feature that is reduced in a levelled down outcome, but this need not concern us here.

I believe that prioritarians should firmly deny these implications. More specifically, we need to keep two issues apart. One is the question of whether prioritarians are committed to the existence of impersonal values. I agree with Persson that they are (in the sense specified above). The other issue is what this value consists in. Here, Persson claims that it consists in the average moral weight of benefits and this I deny.

Compare the following two outcomes: (2, 1) and (1, 1). The first unit that accrues to each individual in these two outcomes corresponds to a compound state that consists of the welfare unit and its context. And each of these compound states has a certain positive intrinsic value. In fact, they all have the same value. Then there is also an additional unit of welfare that accrues to the first individual in the first outcome. This unit also corresponds to a compound state that has a positive value, although a smaller such value than the former compound states. While the states described here consist of both benefits and their contexts, there is no respect in which the second, levelled down outcome is better. The only difference with respect to intrinsic value is that the first outcome includes an additional compound state with positive value. So the Levelling Down Objection is countered.

Now consider Persson's more specific claim that the impersonal value to which prioritarians are committed is the value associated with the average moral weight of benefits. Since this value is higher in (1, 1) than in (2, 1), prioritarians must claim that (1, 1) is in one respect better. But why assume that the average moral weight of benefits is something to which prioritarians ascribe intrinsic value? We have just seen that prioritarians can model impersonal value in a way that does not assign any intrinsic value to levelling down, not even in one respect. Nevertheless, Persson may argue that, *necessarily*, prioritarians must value the average moral weight of benefits. This is because the prioritarian function can be construed as a function of such value. Thus, the prioritarian function,

$$G = f(w_1) + f(w_2) + \ldots + f(w_n),$$

is equivalent to

$$G^* = AVE\text{-}V(w_1 + w_2 + \ldots + w_n),$$

where AVE-V is the average moral value of welfare units. And since levelling down implies an increase in AVE-V, it is in one respect a change for the better. And so prioritarianism is vulnerable to the Levelling Down Objection.

However, since this objection to prioritarianism is similar to Fleurbaey's, I can make a similar reply. The fact that the prioritarian function can be split into different components does not show that prioritarians are committed to the independent value of each of these components. Just like total utilitarians are not committed to the claim that increases in average welfare are in one respect a change for the better, even though total utilitarianism can be represented as a function of average welfare. And while the prioritarian function would not work if it did not imply that benefits on average have less weight in the levelled down outcome, this does not imply that the average weight of benefits is something to which prioritarians must ascribe intrinsic value. As I have argued, they may construe their intrinsic value commitments differently.

Another observation Persson (2001: 28) makes, with respect to the impersonal aspect of prioritarianism, is that it is incompatible with the following:

> *The Person-affecting Improvement Principle.* If an outcome, O_1, is in some respect better (or worse) than another outcome, O_2, the betterness (or worseness) of O_1 for some (collective) is greater than the betterness (or worseness) of O_2 is for any (collective).

This principle provides a much stronger link between outcome values and individual welfare than does the Strong Wide Person-affecting Principle. It links the value of outcomes to the *size* of benefits. Consider the two outcomes in Figure 8.4 (where the slashed line represents the average level of welfare in A).

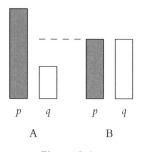

Figure 8.4.

Prioritarians and egalitarians hold that B is better than A, but this judgement is ruled out by the Person-affecting Improvement Principle. There is no individual or group of individuals for whom B is better to a greater extent than A is better for any individual or group. Thus, while B is better for q, A is to the same extent better for p. More precisely, the sum of benefits that accrues to q when we go from A to B equals the sum of benefits that accrues to p when we go from B to A.

In fact, the Person-affecting Improvement Principle implies that just as B cannot be better than A, A cannot be better than B. More generally, while it does not directly imply Total Outcome Utilitarianism, it is closely related to this principle.

Persson's point is that since prioritarianism is incompatible with the Person-affecting Improvement Principle, the prioritarian cannot invoke this principle in defence of the Strong Wide Person-affecting Principle. Thus, the prioritarian will have to reject what is a conclusive reason for accepting the latter principle (Persson 2001: 29).[9] And the Strong Wide Person-affecting Principle, of course, is what is supposed to explain at least part of the force of the Levelling Down Objection.

However, it seems to me that the Strong Wide Person-affecting Principle is quite capable of standing on its own when explicating the force of the Levelling Down Objection. I have suggested that this objection trades on the fact that in egalitarianism, the link between outcome value and improvements in welfare is entirely *contingent*. In other words, one problem with egalitarianism is that equality can be improved in the absence of increases in welfare. And this is exactly the feature that is ruled out by the Strong Wide Person-affecting Principle, which claims that an outcome cannot be improved in any respect in the absence of such increases in welfare.

Therefore, the Strong Wide Person-affecting Principle provides a plausible diagnosis of (part of) what is troubling about levelling down. And so prioritarians do not need to invoke the Person-affecting Improvement Principle to defend their commitment to the Strong Wide Person-affecting Principle.

Temkin (2000: 152) suggests that there is in fact a stronger relation to be found between the Strong Wide Person-affecting Principle and the Person-affecting Improvement Principle—a relation I have so far ignored. He claims that reflections on these two principles suggest that those who are attracted to the former should also be attracted to the latter, and that those who reject the latter should also reject the former. Therefore, since prioritarians reject the Person-affecting Improvement Principle, they should also reject the Strong Wide Person-affecting Principle.

However, I have argued that the relation between these two principles is not as strong as suggested by Temkin. A prioritarian may have reasons to hold the Strong Wide Person-affecting Principle that are quite independent of the Person-affecting Improvement Principle. For example, she may hold the former principle because it nicely explains her worries about levelling down, as well as about various other cases in which certain (alleged) values are increased

---

[9] Strictly speaking, Persson does not consider the Strong Wide Person-affecting Principle, but a principle similar to the Slogan. However, in the present context, this difference does not matter.

in the absence of benefits.[10] And these worries, as I have argued, need not hinge on the Person-affecting Improvement Principle. Furthermore, she may simply believe that the structure imposed on our axiology by the Strong Wide Person-affecting Principle has independent plausibility (just as some of us believe that the structure imposed by the Pareto Principle has independent plausibility).

In conclusion, prioritarianism not only avoids the Levelling Down Objection, it fully accommodates both of the concerns from which this objection derives its force. It captures our concern for the worse off and our person-affecting concerns.

8.5 Relational Justice

I have now argued that prioritarianism handles levelling down cases better than does egalitarianism. This, I believe, gives us a reason to prefer the former view to the latter, although this reason is not conclusive. Nevertheless, it may be suggested that there are also important aspects of our moral thinking that would be lost if we were to abandon egalitarianism in favour of prioritarianism. Thus, Temkin invites us to consider the following case of a 'typical' impoverished person in the United States:

> Ruth is not wretched, but she is a single parent of four, works at two jobs, drives an old car, wonders how she will meet the payments on her two bedroom apartment, and has no idea how her children will afford college on her $20,000 income. Many are deeply moved by the plight of people like Ruth in a land where *so* many others live in half million dollar homes, own fancy new cars, send their children to private schools, take expensive vacations, and have annual household incomes well over $100,000. Is it not clear that the extent to which many are moved by Ruth's situation is heavily influenced not merely by how she fares in *absolute* terms, but by how she fares *relative to the other members of her extraordinarily well-off society*?   (Temkin 2003b: 70)

If I understand him correctly, Temkin's point is that the motivational pull Ruth's situation exercises on us is so strong in part because she lives in a society where so many people are much better off than she is. Had her circumstances been the same, but everyone else been much worse off than she is, then we would not have been equally motivated to help her (Temkin 2003b: 70–1).

I am inclined to think that Temkin is right about this. But the question is whether it really shows that, in our moral thinking, we are committed to the

---

[10] In fact, Temkin himself gives examples of such cases in Temkin (1993a: 249–55; 2003b: 71–8).

value of equality. Let me point to two other features that may help explain our motivational patterns in this sort of case. First, since we are told that there are people (indeed, many of them) who are much better off than Ruth, we tend to focus on how grand it must be for them to be this well off. Being presented with the further details of such lives (half-million dollar homes, fancy new cars, etc.), we imagine this rather vividly! We then think of poor old Ruth, worried sick about how to make ends meet, and imagine how grand it would be if *she* were this well off.

If, on the other hand, we are presented with a case in which Ruth is better off than everyone else, we are not as inclined to focus on the sort of life the rich lead, and thus not as inclined to imagine what it would be like for Ruth to lead such a life. Nevertheless, if someone were to prompt us to vividly imagine how nice such a life would be for Ruth (not having to worry about house and car payments, education for her kids, etc.), arguably, the thought of helping Ruth would start to exercise a greater pull on us. The point, of course, is that this explanation of the difference in motivational pull in the two cases does not rely on the thought that *equality* matters.

Second, and more importantly, motivational pulls may have a tendency to weaken when they are confronted with stronger motivational pulls. By way of illustration, suppose that I feel like having a drink and happen to remember that there is an ice-cold beer in the fridge. Strongly motivated, I open the fridge. I then notice that sitting on the shelf just next to the beer is a delicious bottle of Chardonnay. Realizing that I would much rather have the wine, my motivation to have the beer instantly drops. However, it then hits me that the wine is for the guests I am having over later tonight. Slightly annoyed, I grab the beer. I know that I shall not enjoy *the beer* any less just because I cannot have the wine, but my motivation to have it has nevertheless dropped, as I cannot help thinking of the wine I could have had instead.

Now consider the situation of Ruth. Since Ruth is worse off than most others are she is, if not first in line, then at least in the front part of the queue with respect to whom we most want to help. As prioritarians, we have a stronger urge to help her than we have to help all those who are better off than she is. So, in terms of our motivation in this case, she does not face much superior competition. If, instead, we imagine that Ruth is better off than everyone else is, she is no longer in the front part of the queue. Rather, she is now at the very back. And so, in terms of our motivation to help, she does indeed face superior competition, and lots of it. Therefore, even if she is the only person we *can* help, we may be less motivated to do so. Not because we believe that it is morally less important to help her than it was in the former case, but because we cannot help thinking of how much *better* it would be if we could help some of those people who are much more unfortunate than she is. Importantly, this explanation of our motivational structure does not rely on the thought that *equality* matters, but merely on the thought that priority does.

I do not mean to suggest that the account of our motivational patterns I have just sketched is clearly right and that Temkin's is clearly wrong. In fact, it seems to me that it would be difficult to determine which explanation is the best. Nevertheless, I believe that I have provided a somewhat plausible alternative explanation. And the fact that such an explanation can be given weakens Temkin's case for claiming that in our moral thinking, we are committed to the value of equality.[11]

Consider also another case. Compare an outcome in which a child gets a small sweet and an outcome in which a child gets a small sweet and another child gets a large sweet. Suppose also that in the second outcome, there is no way of dividing the sweets more equally between the children. It may seem that there is an injustice present in the second outcome that is not present in the first outcome. And, indeed, it is not difficult to understand if the child who receives the smaller sweet will feel some resentment. The point is not that her sweet is too small (which may of course also be true), but that it is unfair that she should have such a small sweet when the other child receives a much larger sweet. It is a point about relational justice.[12]

I feel the force of the objection, but let me briefly suggest some responses prioritarians may make. First, insofar as the child who receives the lesser sweet *feels* bad, whether because she feels unjustly treated or for some other reason, this should be factored in. I suspect that, in many actual cases, we should probably refuse to distribute the non-divisible sweets unequally because the harm outweighs the benefits involved. Nevertheless, let us assume for the sake of argument that the child who receives the smaller sweet does not know that a larger sweet is received by another child and therefore does not suffer any harm. On this assumption, the objection does seem to me to lose some of its intuitive force.

Second, even prioritarians may concede that the unequal distribution of the sweets is regrettable, everything else being equal. Consider the fact that

[11] Yet perhaps Temkin is not appealing to our *motivations* but to our *reasons* to help Ruth. Perhaps he takes us to believe that there is a stronger reason to help Ruth if she is worse off than most others are than if she is better off than most others are. But it is not clear to me that this is what we (or most of us) believe. Alternatively, we may accept that whereas the reason to help Ruth does not change, this reason's relative position in our total pattern of reasons *does* change. That is, it may go from being one of our strongest moral reasons to being one of our weakest. Again, I do not want to claim that this account is superior to Temkin's, merely that it does not seem inferior.

[12] This objection was suggested to me by an anonymous reader for Oxford University Press.

in the natural lottery, some people are born with severe untreatable diseases, whereas others are born healthy. Even if there is nothing we can do about this, prioritarians will consider it regrettable. It would be better if the benefits and burdens were distributed more equally. Not because this would be more equal, but because the worse off would then be better off. Likewise, prioritarians will consider it regrettable that the sweets cannot be distributed more equally.

Third, prioritarians may emphasize that it is morally arbitrary that *this* child should receive the smaller sweet. There is, after all, no reason why the small sweet should go to her rather than to the other child. These two outcomes are equally good in prioritarian terms (or so we are assuming). She may therefore complain that if two outcomes are equally good morally but one is worse for her than the other, she should at least have a just chance of having the outcome that is better for her come about. In the particular case under consideration, this could involve flipping a coin.

Note that egalitarians may have to appeal to a similar procedure to fully do justice to our intuitions about the case. After all, it is not more equal that the larger sweet goes to one child than to the other. But if a fair procedure is required for bringing about justice in this case in which the two available outcomes are equally good, then why insist that there is a separate kind of injustice involved, namely one consisting in the fact that one child is *worse off than another*? The lack of a fair procedure may explain the injustice taking place. And this explanation, of course, does not differentiate between egalitarianism and prioritarianism. With respect to either principle, it requires that it is supplemented with a tie-breaker between equally good outcomes, either as a part of our theory of outcomes itself or as a constraint on arbitrary discrimination between individuals.

I am not here arguing that we should in fact supplement our principles of justice in this manner, merely that to the extent we find it *unjust* to give one child a small sweet and another child a large sweet, this may best be explained by such a supplement. A supplement that is in itself neutral between egalitarianism and prioritarianism.

8.6 Overall Outcome Welfare Leximin

So far, I have been concerned with the nature of prioritarianism (and its merits relative to those of egalitarianism). I now want to examine two principles that are intimately related to prioritarianism. They differ from prioritarianism only in that they rely on a different conception of priority. The first principle gives absolute priority to a worst-off individual, whereas the second principle holds that there exists an absolute welfare threshold, above which priority no longer applies. I shall argue that each of these principles faces various difficulties to which prioritarianism is immune. Thus, my discussion will serve to justify the particular interpretation of *priority* to which prioritarians ascribe.

Consider first:

> *Overall Outcome Welfare Leximin.* Of two outcomes, O_1 and O_2, both of which contain n individuals, O_1 is intrinsically better than O_2 if and only if (a) the worst-off individual in O_1 is better off than the worst off individual in O_2, or (b) in the case of equal welfare of the worst-off individuals in the two outcomes, the second worst-off individual in O_1 is better off than the second worst-off individual in O_2, or . . . (n) in the case of equal welfare of the worst-off individuals in the two outcomes, and of the second worst-off individuals in the two outcomes . . . and of the (n-1) worst-off individuals in the two outcomes, the best-off individual in O_1 is better off than the best-off individual in O_2.

The main idea is fairly clear. Suppose we want to improve a society as much as possible. Overall Outcome Welfare Leximin informs us that, among the different possible outcomes that we can bring about, we should choose the one in which the worst off are best off. If there are several outcomes in which the worst off are best off, we should choose the one in which the second worst off are best off (and so on). Thus, this principle gives *absolute priority* to the very worst off, but also gives some weight to the welfare of others.

It may be wondered whether Overall Outcome Welfare Leximin can be classified as a version of prioritarianism. It certainly captures the idea that we should give priority to the worse off. And it embraces the idea that intrinsic value should be ascribed to compound states of affairs, consisting of the state that a benefit of a certain size befalls an individual, and the state that this individual is at a particular welfare level, where this value increases when the size of the benefit increases but decreases when the level of welfare increases.

However, Overall Outcome Welfare Leximin does not have the aggregative feature I have claimed to be distinctive of prioritarianism. Unlike prioritarianism, it does not allow for trade-offs between benefits at different welfare levels when comparing the intrinsic value of outcomes. An outcome in which the worst off are better off than in another outcome is always better, quite independently of the welfare of anyone else. While intimately related to prioritarianism, then, Overall Outcome Welfare Leximin is not a version of this view. Yet, it is a mere terminological decision on my part to define prioritarianism such that it excludes Overall Outcome Welfare Leximin. Clearly, there is a sense in which these two views belong in the same 'family' of views.

Overall Outcome Welfare Leximin is, of course, reminiscent of Rawls's difference principle (1971: 302–3). However, there are also a number of disparities. First, whereas the difference principle takes social primary goods to be the relevant unit of distributive concern, Overall Outcome Welfare Leximin takes welfare to be the relevant unit. Second, whereas the difference principle applies only to the basic structure of society, Overall Outcome Welfare Leximin has a wider scope. Third, whereas Overall Outcome Welfare Leximin clearly has a leximin structure, it is not clear that the difference principle does.[13] Finally, whereas the difference principle applies to (representative members of) groups, Overall Outcome Welfare Leximin applies to individuals.

Let me briefly point out why I believe that a principle of distributive justice should apply to individuals rather than groups. There are different ways in which the welfare situation of a group can be measured, but for simplicity let us assume a measure of average welfare. Thus, the higher the average level of welfare, the better off the group is. Suppose we combine the distributive focus on the average welfare of groups with egalitarianism. And suppose that a society consists of only two groups. We will then claim that the greater the distance between the average welfare in these two groups, the greater the inequality. However, if we are worried about inequality *between* groups, why not worry about inequality *within* groups? A given level of average welfare in a group is compatible with both equality and inequality in that group. But as long as the average welfare is not affected, increases in inequality within a group will not matter. This seems arbitrary.[14]

Obviously, a similar point applies to prioritarianism and to leximin. If we give priority to worse-off groups rather than worse-off individuals, a reduction in the welfare of the worst-off members of a worse-off group may not matter, as long as the average welfare in the group is not affected. Again, this seems arbitrary. So we should give priority to individuals, not to groups.

Why would anyone hold Overall Outcome Welfare Leximin? I can think of several possible rationales but ultimately, I find them unpersuasive. The

---

[13] In one place, Rawls writes that 'the difference principle is a strongly egalitarian conception in the sense that unless there is a distribution that makes both persons better off . . . an equal distribution is to be preferred' (1971: 76). This statement is incompatible with leximin in that it rules out improvements to others than the worst off in cases, in which the worst off are not affected. Thus, it violates the Pareto Principle. But elsewhere, Rawls writes that 'the difference principle is compatible with the principle of efficiency' (Rawls 1971: 79).

[14] See also Temkin (1993a: 101–2). For a discussion of whether a version of the difference principle that deviates significantly from leximin is ultimately possible, see Tungodden and Vallentyne (2006).

first rationale appeals to Rawls's contract argument. It may be suggested that the parties in the original position would adopt not the difference principle, but the somewhat similar Overall Outcome Welfare Leximin. The second rationale is also based on a Rawlsian argument for the difference principle. It may be reasoned that the effects of the natural and social lotteries should be neutralized, so that, initially, an equal distribution is to be preferred. Yet, it would be irrational not to accept Pareto-improvements on an equal distribution. And we should then proceed to the particular Pareto-superior distribution in which the worst off are best off (and, in case there is no one such distribution, the one in which the second worst off are best off, and so on), because no one can have a reasonable complaint about this distribution.[15]

The third rationale is similar to the second and is based on work by Thomas Nagel. It relies on the ideal of unanimity, according to which an outcome should be acceptable to each and every individual involved (Nagel 1979b: 122–3). There may not be such an outcome, but then the best outcome is the one which is least unacceptable to the individual for whom it is most unacceptable. And this will be the outcome in which the worst-off individual is best off. As I said, I do not find any of these rationales for Overall Outcome Welfare Leximin persuasive, but I shall not elaborate on that point here.[16] Rather, I want to suggest that, in any case, this principle has implications that are quite unacceptable.

One such implication simply follows from the claim that the very worst-off individuals have absolute priority. Consider Figure 8.5.

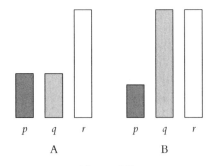

Figure 8.5.

[15] According to Brian Barry, this second argument is implicit in *A Theory of Justice*, see Barry (1989a: 213–4). See also Kymlicka (1990: 55).

[16] For a good criticism of the first argument, see Hare (1989). For a sound criticism of the second and third argument, see McKerlie (1994).

Suppose that p is a group of people who suffer from a painful disease and so are very badly off. Imagine also that the people in the q-group suffer from a disease that is almost but not quite as awful, whereas the people in the r-group are healthy. A treatment is available for both diseases. The treatment for the p-people will increase their welfare slightly, whereas the treatment for the q-people will completely cure them. Unfortunately, resources are limited and it is only possible to pay for one of these treatments. If the p-people are treated, A will result, whereas if the q-people are treated, B will result. To which group of individuals is it best to offer a treatment?

According to Overall Outcome Welfare Leximin, it is better to treat the p-people and so to bring about A. After all, the worst-off individuals are better off in A than in B. However, the q-people are only slightly better off in A (their worst outcome) than the p-people are in B (*their* worst outcome), and q-people are in fact very badly off in A. Furthermore, we can hugely increase the welfare of the q-people but only slightly increase the welfare of the p-people. So it seems better to treat the q-people. After all, if we are concerned about the welfare of the worst off, it seems that we should also be concerned about the welfare of individuals who are *almost* as badly off (to a limited degree, even the proponent of Overall Outcome Welfare Leximin will agree). And if we are also concerned about *them*, it intuitively seems that huge increases to these individuals can outweigh slight increases to the worst off.

Overall Outcome Welfare Leximin also has another troubling feature, namely that it is, in a certain sense, innumerate. Suppose we increase the number of people in q, while maintaining the assumption that we can either treat all the people in p or all the people in q, but cannot do both. No matter how many people we add to q, Overall Outcome Welfare Leximin will still imply that it is better to treat the p-people. This is what renders the worst off best off. In fact, since Overall Outcome Welfare Leximin applies to individuals rather than groups, we can simultaneously reduce p to a single person and we will still get the result that it is better to treat p. Surely, this cannot be right (McKerlie 1994).

Of course, we can move from Overall Outcome Welfare Leximin to a *ceteris paribus* version of this principle and then combine it with one or more others, such as to avoid these troubling implications. Thus, perhaps leximin captures one aspect of distributive justice (in our theory of outcomes) but not all aspects.[17] So perhaps a *ceteris paribus* version of leximin is *part* of a plausible theory of outcomes that is not innumerate and implies that, all things

---

[17] For instance, leximin could be said to capture Nagel's idea of unanimity, according to which an outcome should be acceptable to everyone, *including* the worst off.

considered, B is better than A. Thus, appropriately combined, a *ceteris paribus* version of leximin and a *ceteris paribus* version of utilitarianism will be such a theory.[18]

Now, it seems to me that the most plausible such combined theory will in fact be extensionally equivalent to prioritarianism. Its leximin component will give rise to some priority at all welfare levels (such that for any welfare level, a benefit at that level has greater moral value than an equal benefit at a higher level), but its utilitarian component will rule out giving absolute priority at any level. And so, unlike Overall Outcome Welfare Leximin itself, it will allow trade-offs between benefits at different welfare levels when comparing the intrinsic value of outcomes. Thus, as it turns out, (appropriately) combining *ceteris paribus* versions of leximin and utilitarianism is simply one way of arriving at prioritarianism.

To say that this is simply one way of arriving at prioritarianism is not to deny that the considered combination of views is a distinct position. Just as (any specific version of) Pareto Outcome Welfare Egalitarianism includes not just a particular ordering of outcomes but also an egalitarian reason for accepting it, the combined view under consideration can be distinguished from extensionally equivalent ones in terms of the reasons for accepting a prioritarian ordering. Nevertheless, it would appear that this particular way of arriving at the prioritarian ordering is not the most plausible one, and therefore I shall not attempt to develop it further here.

8.7 Outcome Welfare Sufficientarianism

The lesson learnt from the discussion of Overall Outcome Welfare Leximin is that we should not give absolute priority to the worst off. While such individuals should have priority over individuals at higher levels, benefits to the former can nevertheless be outweighed by (sufficient) benefits to others who are also badly off. Of course, prioritarianism accommodates this point, but so does the following principle:

> *Outcome Welfare Sufficientarianism.* An outcome is in one respect intrinsically better, the larger the sum of weighted individual benefits it contains, where benefits are weighted such that they (a) have zero-value when they fall at or above a

---

[18] Of course, we may instead substitute the *ceteris paribus* version of utilitarianism with a similar version of prioritarianism. But I find it difficult to see what the purpose of such a 'double counting' of priority would be.

specific threshold of individual welfare, *l*, and (b) have positive value when they fall below *l*, where this value decreases the closer to *l* they fall.

Outcome Welfare Sufficientarianism expresses the idea that benefits become increasingly less important, morally speaking, the better off an individual is, and that there is in fact some level of welfare where further benefits simply have no moral value at all. Of course, a benefit of a fixed size has the same value for the individual to whom it accrues no matter what level of welfare she is at, but its moral value decreases the better off she is. At some point, priority sets out and this is where the threshold is (Benbaji 2005; Crisp 2003; Frankfurt 1987; Rosenberg 1995; Tungodden 2003: 23–32).[19] Graphically, this can be represented as in Figure 8.6 (where the slashed line represents the welfare threshold).

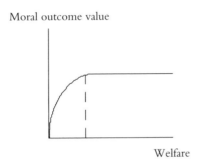

Moral outcome value

Welfare

Figure 8.6.

Note that this graph is similar to that of prioritarianism, up to the point where the threshold is reached (this first part of the curve is strictly concave). Thus, Outcome Welfare Sufficientarianism is in a sense Outcome Welfare Prioritarianism, but where priority has a narrower scope. So while intimately related to the latter principle, Outcome Welfare Sufficientarianism nevertheless is not a version of prioritarianism as I have defined it. I have claimed that in prioritarianism, priority has universal scope as regards welfare levels.

As mentioned, Outcome Welfare Sufficientarianism enables us to avoid the problems we encountered with Overall Outcome Welfare Leximin. Consider again Figure 8.5. Since we are assuming that both the *p*-people and the *q*-people are quite badly off, both groups of people are entitled to priority (that is, both groups are below the threshold, or so we may assume). And since

[19] Frankfurt, it should be noted, is concerned with monetary rather than welfare priority.

the p-people are only slightly worse off in B than the q-people are in A, and the q-people are much better off in B than the p-people are in A, it is better to benefit q. In other words, while the p-people have greater priority, this fact is outweighed by the fact that the q-people can be benefited much more. Additionally, Outcome Welfare Sufficientarianism is not innumerate.

Also, it may be suggested that Outcome Welfare Sufficientarianism captures our intuitions about other cases of conflict. Thus, Harry Frankfurt (1987: 32–3) suggests that whereas we are disturbed by inequalities between the poor and the rich, we are not disturbed by inequalities between the rich and the well-to-do. Here, Frankfurt considers income levels rather than welfare, but his point can be put in terms of either of these distributive units. Thus, regarding welfare levels, it may be proposed that we are not disturbed by inequalities above the threshold. Since the well off have enough welfare to live decent (or perhaps comfortable) lives, there is no reason to worry about them. Increases to them have zero value, morally speaking.

Obviously, the implications of Outcome Welfare Sufficientarianism will differ in important respects, depending upon where the threshold is set. Therefore, it is crucial that the proponent of this principle can provide some sort of reason for choosing the particular level she chooses. But what might such a reason look like?

Let me briefly consider three suggestions as to where the threshold should be set. Frankfurt (1987: 37) submits that the threshold is reached when an individual is (or reasonably ought to be) content with what he has. I believe that this suggestion has various drawbacks. First, since the threshold is set not with respect to welfare but with respect to contentment, the resulting principle is not a welfarist one. Obviously, this is not a problem for the principle *itself*, but in the present context of welfarist principles of distributive justice, it will not do.[20] Second, whatever plausibility this suggestion has when we assume, as Frankfurt does, that money is the relevant distributive unit, it loses when it is applied to welfare instead. While there may be some level of income at which no further amount of money would contribute anything much to our happiness, obviously this will not be so with respect to welfare. Prudentially, each unit matters just as much as the previous one.

Third, insofar as there were to exist a level at which people are content, presumably it would vary from person to person. This means that the threshold

---

[20] Alternatively, we might introduce a 'contentment theory of welfare', but then the threshold cannot be fixed at the level at which we are simply 'content'. In order to formulate Outcome Welfare Sufficientarianism, we need there to be welfare levels both over and under the threshold, as there will not be if, at the threshold, we reach maximum contentment.

is relativized to individuals. Therefore, a benefit may have moral value if it accrues to one individual, but not if it accrues to another, *even though they have identical levels of welfare*. So, in a way, individuals are penalized for their modesty (for a somewhat similar criticism of Frankfurt, see Goodin 1987: 49). Frankfurt may of course reply that *reasonable* contentment is not relative to individuals, but then we would need an account of 'reasonable contentment'. And Frankfurt does not provide such an account himself, nor is it clear what one would look like.

Finally, it seems awkward to rely on two different distributive units; one that settles welfare weights (contentment) and another that gives value to outcomes (welfare). If further benefits do not matter (morally) once an individual is content, then it would seem that this is because contentment is what really matters. But if this is so, then why hold welfare to be the unit that gives value to outcomes?

Perhaps a better suggestion is to fix the threshold relative to *needs*. Where contentment relies on preferences and varies from person to person, needs are similar for everyone, or so it may be argued. Thus, everyone needs water, food, shelter, and health. Indeed, it may be argued that needs are a more appropriate distributive unit than satisfaction of preferences. Along these lines, Scanlon suggests that even if a person would be willing to forego a decent diet in order to build a monument to his god, it is morally more important to provide him with food than to help him satisfy his religious desires (1975: 659–60; see also Nagel 1986: 166–75). Needs are morally more urgent than (mere) preferences.

The idea that the threshold should be fixed in terms of needs may seem to have some intuitive plausibility. Thus, it may be argued that priority should be given to those who do not have their basic needs satisfied, but that once an individual has reached this level, priority sets out. We should be concerned about people having a decent minimum of basic necessities, but not be worried about the distributive shares of individuals who are above that level.

However, this suggestion suffers from drawbacks similar to those of the previous one. First, since the threshold is set with respect to needs rather than welfare, the resulting principle is not a welfarist one.[21] Second, this principle implies that we will have cases in which a benefit has moral value if it accrues to one individual, but not if it accrues to another, *even though they have identical levels of welfare*. Finally, we will be relying on two different distributive units;

---

[21] Again, of course, this problem would be fixed if we were to adopt an appropriate theory of welfare, in this case a 'need-based theory'. (For the suggestion that needs should play an important role in our account of welfare and of practical rationality, see Copp 1993.)

one that settles weights (needs) and another that gives value to outcomes (welfare). This last point is particularly disturbing. If we set the threshold in terms of needs, presumably this is because we believe that it is especially important to take care of the needs of the worse off. But then why give weight to welfare rather than needs?

Unlike the previous two, the third suggestion does not answer the question of whether an individual has reached the threshold on the basis of facts (only) about this individual. Thus, Roger Crisp proposes that Outcome Welfare Sufficientarianism is based on the virtue of *compassion*. Furthermore, he submits that our compassion is limited to the worse off. Once an individual reaches a certain level of welfare, compassion sets out (Crisp 2003: 758). And thus this is where the threshold is.

However, it seems to me dubious that compassion sets out above a certain level of welfare.[22] Suppose that a given individual—Amy—is at the threshold level. For the sake of argument, let us assume that this level is fairly high. So Amy is quite well off. Imagine also that, due to some (very fortunate) changes in the world economy, everyone else becomes much better off than Amy. So everyone but her now has a life of extreme luxury and happiness. It would appear that, in such a case, we would not only regret the fact that Amy was 'left behind', and so value further benefits to her. We would also attach greater value to benefits to her than to (further) benefits to others. So if we were in a position to redistribute, we would want to favour Amy, everything else being equal.

Even, then, if we were to grant Crisp that compassion is at the heart of priority, we need not agree that there is a level at which compassion sets out. It seems to me more plausible to claim that our compassion is simply greater, the worse off an individual is. Given this, the virtue of compassion is better captured by prioritarianism.

Admittedly, when individuals are very well off, we may *feel* no compassion for them at all, but I suggest that this is because two potentially misleading features affect our emotions. One is that when some people are much worse off than others are, we are inclined to focus only on *their* misfortune. However, when there are no such others to 'steal' our attention, we realize that our compassion reaches out even to those who are very well off. The other relevant

---

[22] Perhaps I should qualify this claim. In the dictionary sense, 'compassion' is a feeling directed at the *suffering* of others (see, e.g., *The Advanced Learner's Dictionary of Current English*). And if this is what we mean by 'compassion', clearly there are increases in welfare that cannot be objects of this virtue. However, this conception of compassion cannot be what Crisp has in mind. After all, an individual need not actually *suffer* in order to have a low welfare level. Perhaps her life just consists in a few simple joys and nothing else.

feature is that compassion is relative to welfare levels; we should thus not expect to feel a *great deal* of compassion for individuals who are doing very well with respect to welfare. In fact, when individuals are very well off, our compassion may be so reduced that it almost *seems* as if we have none. And when both of these two features are at work at once, we may *feel* no compassion at all.

There is one final issue that I want to consider in this section. Outcome Welfare Sufficientarianism does not assign any weight to benefits above the threshold. Therefore, it does not satisfy the Pareto Principle and so it is not a version of Person-affecting Outcome Welfarism. In fact, it does not even satisfy the *Weak* Pareto Principle, according to which an outcome is better than is another if it is better for everyone. After all, if everyone is at or above the threshold, Outcome Welfare Sufficientarianism does not assign any value to increases to anyone. So even if we could hugely increase everyone's welfare level, it would not make for a better outcome. Surely, this cannot be right.

However, Outcome Welfare Sufficientarianism orders outcomes in one respect only and so may be combined with one or more other principles that *do* assign value to increases in welfare above the threshold. Along such lines, Crisp (2003: 758) suggests that it should be combined with a version of axiological utilitarianism. In the resulting view, priority is given to increases in welfare below the threshold, whereas equal increases have equal value from the threshold up. This view satisfies the (Strong *and* Weak) Pareto Principle(s).

Nevertheless, there are different ways in which the two principles can be combined. Crisp's suggestion is that non-trivial benefits below the threshold have absolute priority over benefits above the threshold (2003: 758–9). Presumably, the purpose of the requirement that benefits below the threshold should be *non-trivial* to have absolute priority, is to rule out that even the *tiniest* benefits below outweigh even the *greatest* benefits above. And, indeed, such an implication would be implausible. Yet, if one is troubled by the claim that trivial benefits below have absolute priority over huge benefits above, then why think that it completely changes the picture if we substitute 'non-trivial' for 'trivial' benefits in this claim? The difference between a trivial and a non-trivial benefit may be very slight indeed.

In reply to this objection, perhaps it may be suggested that the notions of 'trivial' and 'non-trivial' benefits appealed to here are vague. Thus, if we have a spectrum that covers all the possible sizes a benefit may have, there is a range in which it is neither determinately true that the benefits are trivial, nor determinately true that they are non-trivial. And so, between the largest (determinately) trivial benefit and the smallest (determinately) non-trivial benefit there is a range of indeterminacy. Due to this range of indeterminacy, the difference between the two benefits in question cannot be *too* slight.

Accordingly, it may seem less awkward that although a trivial benefit below the threshold does not have absolute priority over even the greatest benefit above, a non-trivial benefit below still has just that.

However, this reply introduces a new problem, namely what to say about trade-offs between benefits in the indeterminacy range that fall below the threshold, and benefits above the threshold. Do indeterminate benefits below have absolute priority over benefits above? If we answer, yes, then our original problem reappears at another level: while the largest possible trivial benefit below the threshold does not have absolute priority over benefits above, a *slightly* bigger benefit in the indeterminacy range does. If, on the other hand, we answer, no, then the original problem again reappears. The largest possible benefit in the indeterminacy range that falls below the threshold does not have absolute priority over benefits above, even though a *slightly* greater non-trivial benefit below the threshold does have such priority.

Perhaps, then, it is better to say that it is neither determinately true nor determinately false that benefits in the indeterminacy range that fall below the threshold have absolute priority over benefits above. Yet this leaves us with a problem: Crisp's combined principle does not always provide us with determinate answers, not because the empirical reality to which it is applied is complex, but for purely theoretical reasons. Of course, if the indeterminacy range is rather narrow, so is the range of cases in which the principle does not yield determinate answers. But if the indeterminacy range is narrow, then the difference between (determinately) trivial and (determinately) non-trivial benefits is correspondingly slight. Thus, again, it may seem strange that while a non-trivial benefit below the threshold has absolute priority over benefits above, a trivial benefit below does not.

I also have another worry about Crisp's combined proposal. Consider the following outcomes:

A: (8, 100)   C: (8, 8, 8, 8, 8, 100)

B: (10, 10)   D: (9.9, 9.9, 9.9, 9.9, 9.9, 10)

Assume that the threshold level is 10 and that an increase in welfare has to contain at least two units to amount to a non-trivial benefit. Clearly, then, Crisp's principle implies that B is better than A. After all, in the move from A to B, there is a (non-trivial) gain of two welfare units for the first individual and it falls below the threshold. Therefore, it has absolute priority over the loss of 90 units by the second individual above the threshold. Now consider C and D. Intuitively, it would seem that if B is better than A, then D is better than C. After all, in the move from C to D *five* people gain *almost* as much as *one* person does in the move from A to B, whereas one person loses 90 units in both moves. However, Crisp's principle does not imply that D is better than C. In fact, it says nothing about how to compare them. Crisp may of course invoke the utilitarian element in his principle to deal with trivial benefits below the threshold, but note that C has a higher total of welfare than does D, and so this element cannot explain why D is better.

Finally, since it implies that benefits above the threshold have equal value, Crisp's principle remains at variance with at least my intuitions about conflicts above the threshold. Consider Figure 8.7 (where the slashed line represents the average level of welfare in E, and the continuous line represents the welfare threshold):

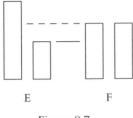

E   F

Figure 8.7.

Suppose that, as usual, the differences between the two groups do not in any way correspond to differences in desert or responsibility. In E, the first group just happens to be much luckier than the second group, although the second group is itself quite well off. In their forests, the first group has discovered some very special fruit trees. The fruits contain vitamins that not only vastly increase people's health, but also allow them to live much longer; say, two hundred years. Having heard the good news, the second group has searched their forests but only to find that they have not been blessed with any of those marvellous trees.

Nevertheless, the first group could decide to share their fruits with the second group. Unfortunately, there are not enough fruits such that both groups can obtain the maximal effect of the vitamins. But even so, if the fruits were shared equally, both groups would experience a significant increase in welfare (perhaps the individuals in both groups would undergo some improvements in their health and live 120 years). In fact, the increase that would be felt by the second group would exactly equal the loss that would be experienced by the first group. In other words, if the fruits were equally shared, F would result.

According to Crisp's pluralist account, E and F are equally good. This is because, above the threshold, an extra unit of welfare always counts the same. However, intuitively, F seems to be better than E. Indeed, I suggest that F is better for the same reason as an equal distribution of a particular sum is better below the threshold. Benefits matter more at lower levels. All in all, then, it seems to me that prioritarianism will handle cases of conflict both across and above the threshold better than Crisp's account.

Crisp has responded to my case of the fruit trees, suggesting that if we are inclined to consider F better than E, this just shows that the threshold has been set too low (personal communication). Thus, had the more unfortunate group in E nevertheless been at a suitably high level of welfare, we would no longer be inclined to believe that it would be better to distribute the fruits equally. In fact, no matter where we place the threshold, Crisp may reply that if we take an equal distribution above the threshold to be better, this is because the threshold is still too low.

I have some worries about this line of argument. First, sufficientarians cannot just dismiss cases in which this view seems to have implausible implications by saying that the threshold has been set too low. Surely it is up to them to point to a threshold and tell us why it is plausible.

Second, it would appear that the fruit tree scenario contradicts Crisp's suggestion even at very high levels. Suppose that everyone in E lives for at least ten thousand years but that the lucky first group gets an additional ten thousand years. In F, on the other hand, the welfare is more evenly spread since each group gets an equal share of the fruits. Suppose also that E is the actual outcome. It seems to me that standing at the end of their lives and yearning for more excellent years to live, the second group may reasonably complain that it would be fairer and, indeed, better if the first group shared their fruits with them. Why should *they* (the second group) have to die now when there is an alternative outcome in which *everyone* has, say, three thousand happy years ahead of them (with no loss in total welfare)?

Finally, it is worth pointing out that if the threshold is set at a sufficiently high level, Outcome Welfare Sufficientarianism will have no distinctive practical significance whatsoever. If, for example, the threshold is reached only after two hundred years of pure ecstasy, no one will ever be above the threshold and so, for all practical purposes, Outcome Welfare Sufficientarianism will coincide with prioritarianism. It may be replied that, for practical purposes, prioritarianism does not differ much from utilitarianism either and so that a prioritarian would be ill-advised to push this point too far. However, it is hardly obvious that prioritarianism and utilitarianism do not differ much on a practical level. Furthermore, if they do not, this is primarily because it is very difficult to assess welfare precisely and so to know where utilitarianism and prioritarianism diverge in their practical recommendations. The practical implications of Outcome Welfare Sufficientarianism, on the other hand, would coincide with the practical implications of prioritarianism even if we had full knowledge of the possible welfare distributions.

8.8 Aggregation

I have argued that prioritarianism is superior in various respects to both Overall Outcome Welfare Leximin and Outcome Welfare Sufficientarianism. Yet, it may be suggested that the latter principles have an advantage in that they include certain non-aggregative features. Crisp (2003: 754) criticizes prioritarianism for 'aggregating all the way up', and Overall Outcome Welfare Leximin altogether resists trade-offs between different welfare levels. In light of this, consider the World Cup Case, which is from Scanlon:

> Suppose that Jones has suffered an accident in the transmitter room of a television station. Electrical equipment has fallen on his arm, and we cannot rescue him without turning off the transmitter for fifteen minutes. A World Cup match is in progress, watched by many people, and it will not be over for an hour. Jones's injury will not get any worse if we wait, but his hand has been mashed and he is receiving extremely painful electrical shocks. Should we rescue him now or wait until the match is over? Does the right thing to do depend on how many people are watching—whether it is one million or five million or a hundred million? (Scanlon 1998: 235)

The point, of course, is that principles such as prioritarianism that permit trade-offs between the relevant welfare levels will imply that there must be *some* possible number of viewers such that their aggregated benefits outweigh Jones's pain. And, it may be argued, this just shows that prioritarianism cannot be correct.[23]

There are a couple of assumptions we should make in order to 'purify' the World Cup Case. We should assume that none of the millions of people watching the game are as badly off as Jones, or at least that if they are as badly off, watching the entire match (without delay) will not make them any better off. We should also assume that if the transmission is interrupted, it will not cause the viewers too much distress. (Being quite a football fan myself, I am inclined to think that this assumption is rather unrealistic. After all, we are not talking about some trivial *third division* game.) What we need is a case in which, if the transmission is not interrupted, Jones will be very badly off and the viewers will be quite well off, whereas if the transmission is interrupted, Jones will be *much* better off and the viewers will only be *slightly* worse off.

[23] For a critical discussion of Scanlon's explanation of what is troubling about aggregation, see Parfit (2004a). Scanlon responds in Scanlon (2004: 130–4).

There are various things that can be said in defence of prioritarianism here. First, this principle *does* give priority to the worse off. To bring out this point more clearly, consider Total Outcome Utilitarianism. Total Outcome Utilitarianism implies that it would be better to continue the transmission if only the sum of welfare thus gained by the viewers is greater than Jones's loss. According to prioritarianism, on the other hand, it is not sufficient that the sum of welfare gained by the viewers is greater than Jones's loss. Since Jones is worse off, benefits to him have priority. How much the sum of welfare gained by the viewers must exceed Jones's loss will of course depend on the particular prioritarian weight function assumed.

Furthermore, we should note that there are severe problems in non-aggregationism. This much was revealed when we considered Overall Outcome Welfare Leximin and Outcome Welfare Sufficientarianism. By giving absolute priority to the worst off, or to individuals below a given threshold, we render small increases to them more important than huge increases to individuals who may be almost as badly off.

A further problem for non-aggregationism is that we seem quite happy to aggregate in many everyday cases. For instance, major public projects such as the building of a large bridge are generally accepted, although it is well known that there is a *very high risk* that it will result in severe injuries and even death. These risks are accepted because of the expected benefits, namely the convenience for many people of being able to get to their destination faster.

Nevertheless, it may be argued that there is a relevant difference between major building projects and the World Cup Case. While in major building projects, there is a high risk of injuries and death, this risk is distributed on a large number of individuals who voluntarily accept it. In the World Cup Case, the risks may *initially* also have been distributed on a large number of people (and voluntarily accepted), but it is *now* clear that it is Jones who will be harmed if the transmission is continued. Therefore, it may be argued, the sort of aggregation that is appropriate in the building project is not appropriate in the World Cup Case.

However, consider what we may call the 'Distributed World Cup Case'. Suppose that a large number of people are working on the transmission at the television station. And imagine that we know that there is a *very high risk* that *someone* will be pinned down under the electrical equipment and receive extremely painful electrical shocks, but we do not know who. Furthermore, for some reason, if Jones or someone else is trapped under the equipment, it will take an hour to get him out of there. However, if we now interrupt the transmission, the equipment can be secured such that no one will be hurt.

Intuitively, there does not seem to be much difference between the World Cup Case and the Distributed World Cup Case. Intuitively, just as it is better to interrupt the transmission and save Jones in the World Cup Case, it is better to interrupt the transmission and ensure that no one is hurt in the Distributed World Cup Case.

But the Distributed World Cup Case, of course, has the feature that is supposed to explain the difference between the World Cup Case and the building of a large bridge. The risk is (voluntarily) distributed on a large number of people. On further reflection, then, it is not clear that this feature plays the role it must play if it is to explain the difference between the World Cup Case and major building projects. Of course, there might be something about building projects that gives this feature a special significance it does not generally have, but I cannot think of what it would be. So it seems to me that we should not rely too heavily on our non-aggregationist intuitions about cases such as the World Cup Case. Our total pattern of intuitions is much more complex and may well favour aggregationism overall.[24]

In addition, consider again what I called the 'Inadequate Comprehension Factor' in Chapter 4 (Section 4.12). When very large numbers are at stake, it is difficult to get an intuitive feel of them. Therefore, we may tend to underestimate the amount of harm or frustration that would be realized if the transmission is interrupted and so its moral importance.

Finally, to those who remain unpersuaded, it is worth pointing out that the prioritarian can accommodate the claim that Jones should be helped immediately in the World Cup Case. A constraint may be introduced that implies that it would be wrong not to help Jones straightaway. As I have already indicated several times, constraints do not constrain our theory of outcomes, and so such a constraint is quite compatible with a prioritarian welfarist theory of outcomes. And, of course, if we were to abandon the welfarist requirement, Outcome Welfare Prioritarianism could be combined with one or more other principle(s) of outcome value such as to give rise to a theory that implied that it would be better to help Jones immediately.

Also, it could be argued that even if it were *better* to continue the transmission (as implied by prioritarianism) and *wrong* not to do so, a plausible decision-procedure would rule out this option. That is, the best possible set of rules and dispositions we could inculcate in ourselves and each other would rule out our ignoring the suffering of Jones.

---

[24] For a more general defence of aggregationism, see Norcross (1997).

8.9 Moral Standing

There is also another scope-related feature of prioritarianism that many people may find disturbing. If foetuses and non-human animals fall within the scope of this principle, it may seem as if they have priority over the rest of us. After all, it may seem plausible that both foetuses and many non-human animals are worse off than we (or most of us) are (Holtug 2007b: 11–12). This may be true even of humans who are in fact quite badly off (relative to most other members of our species). Therefore, it would seem that prioritarianism implies what Peter Vallentyne (2006: 212) has dubbed the 'Problematic Conclusion', according to which 'morality requires a massive shift of resources away from most humans—even most of those with significantly diminished human lives—to most mice' (and other sentient non-human animals). Or rather, since my account of prioritarianism is concerned only with axiology, it implies that such a redistribution would be a change for the *better*.

Now, there are two reasons why the issue of foetuses is a bit tricky. First, since some foetuses are not (yet) conscious, the question of their moral standing raises the issue of the moral standing of possible persons. I shall return to this in Chapter 9. Second, I have not yet addressed the issue of what the appropriate temporal unit of prioritarian concern is (but shall do so in Chapter 10). We should give priority to the worse off, but are the worse off those who are worse off at particular points in time, or those who are worse off over their whole lives? If, as I have so far assumed, they are those who are worse off over their whole lives, then there is no reason to think that, in general, (conscious) foetuses are worse off than the rest of us. While they may be worse off now, they have a whole life of benefits ahead of them. Therefore, for now, I shall concentrate on non-human animals.

However, the issue of non-human animals cannot be considered in isolation from the issue of humans with similar cognitive capacities; that is, humans with severe cognitive disabilities. Nevertheless, I take it that most prioritarians will not be troubled by the thought that humans with severe cognitive disabilities have priority over humans who do not have such disabilities and (for that reason) enjoy higher levels of welfare. In fact, my guess is that most prioritarians hold that people with cognitive disabilities *should* have priority over more fortunate members of our species. In any case, this is what *I* believe. This also explains my focus on the intuitively more troubling issue of giving priority to non-human animals.

Let me initially point out that egalitarianism, leximin, and sufficientarianism are not better equipped to address the issue of non-human animals than prioritarianism is. Consider first egalitarianism. In order to equalize the welfare of better-off humans and worse-off non-human animals, we must prefer slight increases to the latter even at the expense of huge increases to the former. Of course, egalitarians may have stronger conceptions of efficiency than the Pareto Principle, and so may hold that huge increases to better-off humans outweigh small increases to worse-off non-human animals all told, but this does not give them an advantage compared to prioritarians. Furthermore, both leximin and sufficientarianism seem far less plausible here. Leximin implies that even the slightest increase to worse-off animals has priority over even the largest increase to better-off humans. And sufficientarianism implies that small (but non-trivial) benefits to non-human animals below the threshold have priority over even the largest benefits to humans above the threshold (incidentally, a conclusion that Crisp seems prepared to accept; 2003: 761).

How might a prioritarian attempt to lessen the commitment to the welfare of non-human animals? That is, how might she resist the conclusion that it would be better to implement a massive shift of resources from (most) humans to (most) non-human animals? Here, I can be relatively brief, as I have considered this question at length elsewhere (Holtug 2007b).

There are a number of suggestions that I believe we should exclude in advance because they are either speciesist or imply that prioritarianism does not apply to severely cognitively disabled humans (Holtug 2007b: 12–14). Instead, it may be suggested that an individual's priority level should be fixed relative to what is (in some appropriate sense) normal for individuals with comparable psychological potentials.[25] This implies that a human (with normal psychological potentials) that is worse off than (similar) humans normally are, has priority over a dog (with normal dog psychological potentials) that is better off than (similar) dogs normally are, *even if the human is better off than the dog*.

One problem with this account is that it seems difficult to come up with a plausible account of potentials (Holtug 2007b: 14; McMahan 2002: 152). But apart from that, a further problem is that an individual's priority is rendered relative to what happens to be *normal* for individuals with similar psychological potentials. Suppose that, for some reason, there is a dramatic decline in the average level of welfare enjoyed by human beings. Perhaps some new horrible disease occurs. Imagine also that a small group of people is in fact immune to this disease. Nevertheless, since there is a dramatic drop in average welfare

---

[25] This suggestion is heavily influenced by McMahan's account of fortune. McMahan claims that an individual's fortune depends on whether his gains from life are below or beyond the norm for individuals with psychological potentials similar to his own (McMahan 2002: 145–65). However, McMahan's concern is not distributive justice but an assessment of the badness of death.

among individuals with comparable psychological potentials, each of these immune individuals will now experience a dramatic decline in priority. Since they are now much better off than comparable individuals normally are, they will have less priority than most non-human animals, namely all those non-human animals that are not equally well off relative to what is normal for individuals that have psychological potentials similar to *theirs*. But since no changes have occurred to either immune humans or non-human animals, such a change in priority between them seems absurd.

Consider instead a more sophisticated solution to the Problematic Conclusion, which is due to Peter Vallentyne. Vallentyne is concerned with the implications of egalitarianism rather than of prioritarianism, but his solution may easily be adopted by prioritarians as well. Very roughly, the core idea is that fortune—that which is to be equalized—is welfare relativized to degree of moral standing, where an individual's moral standing is grounded in her capacity for welfare (Vallentyne 2006: 228–35). Here, an individual's capacity for welfare is something that she can realize *now*. Therefore, even if a non-human animal has the potential for as much welfare as a human, namely if the animal is genetically enhanced, it does not now have the *capacity* to realize such a high welfare. Vallentyne fleshes out the core idea by suggesting that, for non-negative levels of welfare, fortune is welfare divided by degree of moral standing. Thus, assuming that most non-human animals will have a much lower moral standing than most humans will, they may well have equal fortunes, even if humans have a much higher welfare. For example, a non-human animal that has a moral standing of 0.01 and a welfare of 1 will have a fortune equal to that of a human who has a moral standing of 1 and a welfare of 100 (both have a fortune of 100). Therefore, according to Vallentyne, they are in the relevant sense equal. And, as a prioritarian may argue, they are entitled to equal levels of priority. Thus, no massive shift of resources from most humans to most non-human animals is warranted.

In fact, Vallentyne's suggestion is much more sophisticated than this, but for present purposes, no greater degree of sophistication is needed. This is because the objections I shall raise apply equally to Vallentyne's more sophisticated version. Also, what I shall consider is the prioritarian version of Vallentyne's idea, rather than the egalitarian version he himself considers. However, the objections I shall raise apply to both versions.

My first objection is that it is simply not plausible for a prioritarian (or for an egalitarian, for that matter) to sacrifice the welfare of individuals with a low moral standing to the extent suggested by Vallentyne's approach. It means that a *small* increase to a human who *is much better off* (in terms of welfare) may outweigh a *large* increase to a non-human animal that is *much worse off*.

Furthermore, a *small* increase to a *much better-off* human with normal cognitive capacities may outweigh a *large* increase to a *much worse-off* human with a severe congenital cognitive disability (and so a lower capacity for welfare and hence lower moral standing). And finally, a *small* increase to a *much better-off* healthy human may outweigh a *large* increase to a *much worse-off* human with an untreatable disease that continuously causes her to experience pain (where her capacity for welfare is therefore low). This strikes me as rather disturbing and in any case something a prioritarian will want to reject.

To emphasize further the point that individuals with a low(er) moral standing are being unreasonably sacrificed, it may be helpful to consider a case in which we, you and I, are at the less attractive end of the spectrum of welfare capacities. Suppose aliens arrive who have enormous capacities for welfare (they are—in *that* sense—utility monsters, to use Nozick's catchy phrase). It seems as if, according to the view under consideration, a massive shift in resources from us to them in appropriate circumstances would be an improvement, even if we are *much worse off* than they are, and in fact gain *greater* welfare from our resources than they would.

A second objection is that not only does Vallentyne's approach sacrifice the welfare of beings with low moral standing, it also implies that we can downplay the importance of welfare to certain individuals by ensuring that they *remain* at such a low moral standing. Suppose, for example, that by not adequately feeding a baby, we can ensure that she will develop a cognitive disability and in fact only reach a moral standing of 0.01. Had we adequately fed her, on the other hand, she would have reached a (normal) level of 1. This means that since we have not adequately fed her, we need only confer one unit of welfare on her in order for her to acquire a fortune equivalent to what normal humans need 100 units to acquire. And so by depriving her of what would have been a much better future for her, we enable ourselves to downplay the importance of benefits accruing to her and so, relatively speaking, to increase the importance of benefits to ourselves. Again, this does not seem right.[26]

I end my discussion of what prioritarianism implies for non-human animals here. I am prepared simply to apply this principle to the welfare of human and non-human animals alike; especially when keeping in mind that, because

---

[26] In his more sophisticated account, Vallentyne stresses that just like her present capacities, an individual's actual future capacities may influence her level of fortune (Vallentyne 2006: 232). However, since the baby is *in fact* not fed, her future capacities will always be limited. In other words, the fact that she *could* have had higher capacities does not boost her moral standing. Also, Vallentyne suggests that an individual may have a claim to having her capacities enhanced if they have been wrongfully thwarted (Vallentyne 2006: 231). But, the baby does not yet have these capacities and so it is not clear that they are thwarted. In any case, if we claim that they are thwarted, what reason can we give for why a non-human animal does not have *its* capacities thwarted when we refuse to enhance it?

of the generally superior psychologies of humans, it seems plausible that we will often be in a position to provide larger benefits to them, where such benefits may therefore outweigh slighter benefits to non-human animals. This is most obvious with respect to objective list theories that emphasize the value of autonomy, knowledge, and other items that require a high degree of psychological sophistication in order to be instantiated. But this is also likely to be the case according to preference theories that focus on the number, intensity, and sophistication of preferences, and also according to sophisticated versions of hedonism.

While the implications of prioritarianism with respect to non-human animals nevertheless may seem counterintuitive, the 'counterintuitiveness' may very well be due to speciesist—and so unreliable—intuitions about fairness. Thus, I do not find it counterintuitive that justice requires us to give priority to people who have severe cognitive disabilities and short lives, and are for this reason much worse off than others are.

A further issue, which I have mentioned but not discussed in this chapter, is what we should take to be the temporal unit of justice. I have merely assumed a 'whole lives' version of prioritarianism, and such a version tends to increase the extent to which humans are better off than non-human animals, since humans typically have longer lives. Thus, it is clear that, for instance, a 'time-slice' version of prioritarianism will imply a reduction in the extent to which non-human animals (on average) have priority over humans (Holtug 2007b: 19–21). However, I shall not consider this issue of the temporal unit of justice until Chapter 10, where I briefly reconsider the implications of prioritarianism with respect to non-human animals (Section 10.8).

Note also that since prioritarianism restricts only our axiological claims, some may wish to combine this principle with others that render our morality less demanding with respect to non-human animals than it otherwise would have been. For example, some may want to claim that morality includes (agent-relative) options, so that each of us may permissibly give some priority to our own interests over those of non-human animals. Yet, note also that this means that we will equally down-play the interests of other humans, and this of course is something that many prioritarians will be much less inclined to accept.

8.10 Summary and a Look Ahead

I have suggested that, just like egalitarianism, prioritarianism should be characterized in terms of the values it takes to be intrinsic. And I have submitted that prioritarians ascribe intrinsic value to compound states of affairs, each consisting in the state that a benefit of a certain size befalls an individual, and the state that the individual is at a particular welfare level, where this value increases when the size of the benefit increases, but decreases when the level of welfare increases.

The differences between egalitarianism and prioritarianism in terms of intrinsic value commitments further suggest variations in the orderings they generate. In Chapter 7, I argued that Outcome Welfare Egalitarianism satisfies the Egalitarian Relational Claim. Prioritarianism, on the other hand, does not satisfy this claim.

Both prioritarianism and egalitarianism provide a possible diagnosis of what is wrong with the missing distribution-sensitivity in utilitarianism. However, unlike egalitarianism, prioritarianism is not vulnerable to the Levelling Down Objection, or so I have argued. In fact, prioritarianism fully accommodates both of the concerns from which this objection derives its force. Therefore, in this respect at least, prioritarianism is preferable.

It may be objected that there are other respects in which prioritarianism does not do justice to our moral thinking. Thus, Temkin argues that our motivational patterns exhibit a concern for equality. However, I have suggested that these patterns may in fact be explained with reference to certain other features, namely some potentially misleading psychological tendencies that we have.

I have further argued that prioritarianism is more plausible than the conceptions of priority invoked by Overall Outcome Welfare Leximin and Outcome Welfare Sufficientarianism. I have also suggested more generally that, despite appearances to the contrary, the sort of aggregationism to which the prioritarian is committed is not implausible. Finally, I have proposed that the implications of prioritarianism for the relative weight of human welfare and non-human animal welfare are credible enough to be accepted.

Prioritarianism still needs to be further developed. I have not yet considered the issue of what the appropriate temporal unit of prioritarian concern is. This is one of the topics of Chapter 10. Furthermore, I have not yet considered what the implications of prioritarianism are for the issue of possible future people. It is to this issue that I turn now.

9

Population Ethics

9.1 Future Generations

It is often claimed that the world is (or is becoming) overpopulated. Thus, there are simply not enough resources—or our level of pollution is too high—to sustain the present rate of population growth (at least in the long run). However, in order to know whether the world is (or is becoming) overpopulated, we need to know what an appropriate population size would be (perhaps for a given pattern of distribution and a given level of technological development). And in order to know that, we need to ascertain how to assess the value of populations. That is, we need a theory of population ethics.

Population ethics is probably one of the most perplexing issues dealt with by contemporary moral philosophers. Multitudes of distributive principles have been devised to address this issue, but they all seem troubling in one or (typically) more respects. As we shall see, prioritarianism is no exception in this regard.

While it is sometimes assumed that population ethics is an intriguing but, for practical purposes, less important part of morality, this is by no means the case. Many of the choices we make, individually as well as collectively, affect both the identity and the number of people who come into existence. Obviously, these choices include our individual decisions about whether and when to reproduce. But they also include our collective (or political) decisions about whether to allow or even advance the use of contraceptives and abortion, whether families with children should have special benefits in society, and what should be done (if anything) to try to control population growth in developing nations.

Furthermore, many decisions that at first seem entirely irrelevant to population ethics turn out not to be; for example, decisions about how to develop infrastructure and transportation. Clearly, such decisions may affect the level of welfare enjoyed by future generations. Thus, had railroads never been built, chances are that people nowadays would have a lower level of welfare than the one we presently enjoy. And such decisions not only affect the welfare of future generations, they also affect their identities and size. Thus, railroads affect where people go and so whom they meet. Consequently, railroads also affect with whom they have children, and so the numerical identities of the children they have are impacted.[1]

It is also worth noting that our policies with respect to perhaps the two most important moral challenges facing us today, global poverty and global warming, will clearly have implications for who and how many will exist. In light of this, it seems clear that we need to address future generations in our principles of justice.

In previous chapters, I have suggested that we can increase (or decrease) the moral value of an outcome by causing extra happy (or unhappy) individuals to exist. For example, this claim was at the heart of my solution to the Non-identity Problem. However, the claim that the welfare of additional individuals contributes to the value of an outcome can be cashed out in a number of different ways, and in this chapter I consider some of them.

In particular, I examine the implications of prioritarianism when applied to population ethics. Usually, this principle is applied to fixed populations only, but in light of the urgency of problems such as global poverty and global warming, this extension in scope seems well worth pursuing. I focus especially on the problems to which prioritarianism gives rise in population ethics and what, if anything, can be done to solve them.

In previous chapters, I have argued that it can benefit (or harm) an individual to come into existence. Furthermore, I have assumed a welfarist framework for my theory of outcome value, and submitted that welfarism is most plausible when fleshed out in person-affecting terms. In the present chapter, I provide a person-affecting prioritarian account of the (moral) value of bringing new individuals into existence. First, I distinguish between various person-affecting doctrines that may be relevant when developing a prioritarian account of population ethics. Then I consider a problem that threatens the particular person-affecting prioritarian account I develop—indeed, a problem that bedevils several theories of population ethics—namely:

> *The Repugnant Conclusion.* A world populated by individuals, every one of whom has a life barely worth living, would be better than a world populated by, for example, ten billion individuals all of whom have very worthwhile lives—as long as the former population is sufficiently large.

---

[1] This follows from a plausible claim made by Kripke, namely that an individual would not have existed, had she not originated from the sperm and egg from which she in fact originates, see Kripke (1980: 113).

To illustrate, the Repugnant Conclusion (Parfit 1984: 388), portrayed in Figure 9.1, implies that B is better than A.

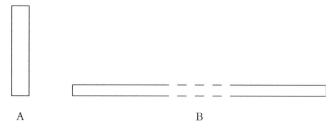

Figure 9.1. The Repugnant Conclusion

By assigning a sufficiently high value to the existence of extra individuals who have lives worth living, the person-affecting version of prioritarianism I develop implies that the higher quantity in B outweighs the higher quality in A. In fact, as we shall see, it also implies what I call the 'Super-repugnant Conclusion', according to which B can be better than A, even if A holds a higher total of welfare.

Note, incidentally, that in my description of the Repugnant Conclusion, I have made no claims about whether the two populations compared overlap (in the sense that there are particular individuals who exist in both). Figure 9.1 should be seen as compatible with comparisons in which they overlap and comparisons in which they do not. This is because I need to consider both kinds of comparison in what follows.

In the rest of the chapter, I consider various ways of dealing with the Repugnant Conclusion. And if this conclusion can be avoided, so can the Super-repugnant Conclusion. First, I consider the possibility of replacing the additive function in prioritarianism—according to which outcome value is an additive function of individual (weighted) welfare—with a non-additive function. I then consider various ways in which my favoured account of person-affectingness may be modified such as to avoid the Repugnant Conclusion. Furthermore, I consider the possibility of combining prioritarianism and a non-prioritarian distributive principle in order to render my account of population ethics more plausible. I argue that none of these strategies works.

Finally, I turn to the question of just how counterintuitive the Repugnant and the Super-repugnant Conclusions are. I argue that while their counterintuitiveness cannot easily be explained away, there are nevertheless theoretical reasons that speak in their favour. However, since I continue to find them rather counterintuitive, I do not end this chapter with a firm commitment to any particular fully-fledged distributive view in population ethics. The problem is that while prioritarianism has counterintuitive implications if it is applied to possible individuals (or more specifically 'different number' comparisons), it is not clear that any of the alternative views fares any better. We may of course then settle for an account of justice for 'same number' comparisons only. But in light of the urgency of some of the questions we need to address in population ethics, it is unfortunate if we cannot provide an account of justice in this sphere, prioritarian or otherwise.

9.2 Person-affecting Moralities

What is commonly referred to as 'person-affecting morality' is in fact a series of quite distinct but often conflated doctrines. These doctrines can be divided into two main types. According to the first—those incorporating a Person-affecting Restriction—the part of morality that concerns individual welfare should be cashed out in terms of what is good and what is bad (or what is better and what is worse) for individuals.[2] According to the second—following Narveson's Slogan—our duty is to make individuals happy, not to make happy individuals (Narveson 1967; 1976; 1978).

I have already considered some of the attractions of the Person-affecting Restriction. When discussing person-affecting and impersonal versions of welfarism in Chapter 6 (Section 6.3), I appealed to the view that outcomes are to be considered good and bad (only) in virtue of being so *for individuals*. And this view, of course, is simply a version of the Person-affecting Restriction that applies only to outcomes and restricts not just our claims about the outcome value of welfare but about outcome value quite generally.

However, there are a number of different person-affecting approaches that are compatible with the Person-affecting Restriction, and in Chapter 6 (Section 6.3), I argued for the Wide Person-affecting Principle. Unlike the Narrow Person-affecting Principle, this principle allows us to reach the right judgements with respect to the Non-identity Problem and the Problem of Suffering. Since I need to refer to these two problems a number of times in this chapter, it will be useful to introduce them (or more precisely their graphical representations in Figures 9.2 and 9.3) again.

---

[2] The term 'Person-affecting Restriction' is introduced in Glover (1977: 66) and employed in Parfit (1984: 394).

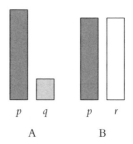

Figure 9.2. The Non-identity Problem

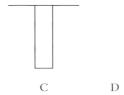

C   D

Figure 9.3. The Problem of Suffering

In Chapter 6, I also pointed out that a person-affecting account, along the lines of the Wide Person-affecting Principle, lets us give less abstract and intuitively more plausible accounts of the Non-identity Problem and the Problem of Suffering than an impersonal account does. More generally, it allows us to claim that outcomes are better or worse in virtue of being so *for* particular individuals rather than merely, say, for the world.

In addition to the Wide Person-affecting Principle, I have also embraced the Strong Wide Person-affecting Principle. Nevertheless, I shall consider only the former principle in the present chapter. This is because the stronger principle is unnecessarily specific for my purposes here.

In order to apply the Person-affecting Restriction to issues in population ethics, we need to know whether it can be good or bad (or better or worse) for individuals to come into existence. After all, it is only if this can be good or bad (or better or worse) for them that a person-affecting account allows us to claim that their coming into existence contributes to the value of an outcome. And, indeed, as I have argued in Chapter 5, it can be better (or worse) for an individual to come into existence than never to exist. Therefore, the Person-affecting Restriction is quite compatible with the claim that it may add to the value of an outcome to include extra (happy) individuals.

Although a person-affecting approach, involving the Wide Person-affecting Principle and the claim that existence can be better (or worse) than non-existence, is distinct from an impersonal approach, it nevertheless inherits many of the features of the latter that observers have generally found highly problematic. Indeed, it inherits some of the very difficulties that advocates of a person-affecting morality have usually hoped to *avoid*, and in particular the implication that it is good to bring into existence new, happy individuals, possibly even at our own expense, and that we may sometimes be obliged to do so (Heyd 1992; Narveson 1967; Roberts 1998; Wolf 1997).

The proponent of a person-affecting approach can of course try to avoid these implications in various ways. For example, it may be proposed that while existence can indeed be better (or worse) for an individual than can non-existence, these claims about individual *welfare* do not affect the value of *outcomes*. However, the price would be unacceptably high, not least because we would then have no way of solving the Non-identity Problem and the Problem of Suffering, or at least none within the context of person-affecting morality. After all, in the Non-identity Problem, for instance, B is better than A in virtue of being so for *r*.

Another suggestion, which at least enables us to solve the Problem of Suffering, would be to hold:

> *The Asymmetry.* While it detracts from the value of an outcome to add individuals whose lives are of overall negative value, it does not increase the value of an outcome to add individuals whose lives are of overall positive value.

This 'Asymmetry'[3] has famously been defended by Narveson (1967: 69–71). His defence consists in pointing out that if we cause a miserable child to come into existence, there will exist a child who will have a justified complaint, while if we refrain from causing a happy child to come into existence, this child will not exist and so can have no complaint. But as Timothy Sprigge (1968: 338) has pointed out, if it is claimed that causing the miserable child to come into existence gives this child a genuine reason to complain, then it would seem that by causing the happy child to come into existence, we give *this* child a genuine reason to be grateful. And there is no obvious reason we should be concerned with complaints (or harm) and not with gratitude (or benefit).

Of course, the proponent of the Asymmetry may simply claim that this doctrine is intuitively plausible. However, I have two reservations about this claim. First, I also have a second-order intuition according to which we should either attach value to the welfare of both miserable and happy possible future individuals, or to neither. At any rate, since in other areas of morality we do

---

[3] The label is McMahan's (1981: 100). Strictly speaking, McMahan formulates the Asymmetry in terms of reasons rather than the value of outcomes, but for the present axiological purposes, my formulation is more appropriate.

attach value to happiness, we seem to need an explanation of why we should not do so in the case of possible future individuals.

Second, the Asymmetry has some rather counterintuitive implications and therefore cannot be described, simply, as enjoying intuitive support. While it plausibly implies that an outcome is rendered worse by the existence of additional miserable individuals, it is incompatible with a person-affecting solution to the Non-identity Problem. It implies that, in Figure 9.2, the welfare of the r-individuals in B counts for nothing. Given the Asymmetry, then, there is no person-affecting basis for holding B to be better than A.

Another counterintuitive implication is the following. Suppose that, some time in the future, the last few inhabitants of earth can either cause the world to be fully populated again, or bring the existence of the human race to an end by refraining from having children. Let us assume that they will be equally happy themselves, whichever choice they make. It would then be better if they were to refrain from having children because, among the billions of people they could cause to exist, there would surely be a few (say one in every 100,000) who would be miserable; and while their misery would count against their being created, the happiness of the rest would count for nothing (Sikora 1978: 136–40).

It may be objected that surely the last few inhabitants will have an interest in having children, so the assumption that their welfare is not affected is implausible (Wolf 1997: 117). However, first, we can simply stipulate that their welfare would not be affected by childlessness. Second, even if these last few individuals did have an interest in having children, presumably the suffering of the far greater number of miserable individuals who would come into existence, if they decided to repopulate the world, would outweigh this interest. Consider Figure 9.4.

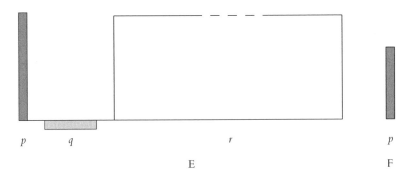

Figure 9.4. The Problem of Extinction

If the last inhabitants on earth—the p-individuals—repopulate the world, E will result. If they do not, F will. In E, while the p-individuals are better off, the q-individuals are clearly worse off. And in any plausible welfare function, the misery of the q-individuals outweighs the gain of the p-individuals (including total welfare, average welfare, and the assignment of priority to the worse off). Furthermore, assuming the Asymmetry, the welfare of the r-individuals counts for nothing. Therefore, F is better than E. But this is pretty counterintuitive, to say the least. Let us call this problem the 'Problem of Extinction'. It is another reason why the Asymmetry does not seem to be the solution for the proponent of a person-affecting approach.

There is a further (but related) difficulty usually associated with impersonal principles and inherited by a wide person-affecting approach. This is the Repugnant Conclusion referred to earlier. It is not that the Wide Person-affecting Principle *implies* the Repugnant Conclusion. Clearly it does not. However, the point of this principle is to allow us to take into account the welfare of all possible future individuals when assessing the value of outcomes, and if we do so, we shall have to confront the question of whether a sufficient number of individuals at a low level of welfare can outweigh a smaller number of individuals at a much higher level. The problem is not just to avoid the Repugnant Conclusion, but to avoid it while steering clear of various other unwelcome conclusions (Parfit 1984: part 4). And, as we shall see in the next section, assuming this kind of person-affecting approach, prioritarianism does indeed imply the Repugnant Conclusion.

The other main type of person-affecting doctrine to which I referred above—Narveson's Slogan—has been devised precisely to avoid the Repugnant Conclusion and other similar problems in population ethics. This Slogan has attracted the interest of many population ethicists and various suggestions have been made as to how to argue for it. The most common strategy is to restrict the scope of distributive principles so that they do not apply to all possible future individuals, but only to a particular sub-group thereof. For example, it may be proposed that only the welfare of individuals who now exist (and perhaps individuals who have existed in the past) matters. In fact, Narveson sometimes writes as if this is his view.[4]

However, this particular restriction is rather implausible in that it implies it is of no intrinsic significance whether future people are very happy or suffer terribly. And so we should dismiss any distributive principle that incorporates this restriction. In order to be even minimally plausible, a distributive principle

---

[4] For instance, he writes: 'moral questions *presuppose* the existence of people' (1976: 68).

that applies to population ethics must attach at least some (intrinsic) significance to the welfare of future generations.

Nevertheless, there are other, more sophisticated ways of restricting the scope of our principles. In fact, for each of the temporal and modal distinctions drawn between preferences in Chapter 2, there is a similar distinction to be drawn between individuals. And these distinctions may be claimed to be relevant for population ethics. Thus, just as one may claim that only present, necessary, or actual preferences matter for self-interest, one may profess that only present, necessary, or actual individuals matter morally.

In this chapter, then, I examine two suggestions involving modal distinctions. According to the first, we should attach value only to the welfare of actual individuals, not to the welfare of individuals that are merely possible. As you may remember, an individual is actual if and only if she exists in the actual world, whether she be past, present, or future (otherwise she is merely possible). According to the second, we should attach value only to the welfare of necessary individuals, not to the welfare of individuals who are merely contingent. To recapitulate, individuals are necessary in relation to specific comparisons of outcomes. Thus, an individual is necessary with respect to a particular comparison of outcomes if and only if she exists in all the outcomes compared (and she is contingent if she exists in some but not others).

Also, in my discussion of Narveson's Slogan, I give special attention to two recent, book-length attempts to defend it, authored by David Heyd and Melinda Roberts.

Note that while they are distinct person-affecting doctrines, Narveson's Slogan and the Person-affecting Restriction are compatible with each other. In fact, most of the attempts to capture Narveson's Slogan that I consider below, also satisfy the Person-affecting Restriction. In restricting the range of individuals to whom we owe concern, most of them evaluate outcomes only in terms of their being better or worse for (the restricted class of) individuals.

9.3 Prioritarianism and the Repugnant Conclusion

What does my favoured distributive principle—prioritarianism—imply if it is applied to the issue of possible future individuals? Assuming the person-affecting approach for which I have argued, our distributive principle(s) should accommodate the welfare we can bestow on such individuals by bringing them into existence. Existence can be better (or worse) for an individual than non-existence, and we should evaluate outcomes in terms of their being better (or worse) for the individuals they contain.

With a superficial reading of prioritarianism, it may seem as if this principle cannot morally accommodate the value of coming into existence. According to prioritarianism, the moral value of a further benefit in an individual's life depends on this individual's welfare level. But how, then, do we apply prioritarianism to possible future individuals? It may be argued that such individuals do not have a welfare level independently of the welfare we may bestow on them by causing them to exist. To bring out this point more clearly, consider again the 'whole lives' version of prioritarianism I have been assuming so far. According to this version, the lower the sum of welfare in a life, the greater the value of a further benefit. The point is that there is no lifetime level of welfare at which the benefit of coming into existence falls. Rather, the lifetime level *just is* the benefit that accrues to an individual from coming into existence, and so there is no welfare level, independent of this benefit, that can serve as a standard for how to weight the benefit.

Another way of expressing the point is this. According to prioritarianism, we should give priority to the worse off, but possible future individuals are not worse off. That would presuppose an independent welfare level and they have none.

However, I believe that we can in fact ascribe welfare levels to possible future individuals on the basis of which we can assign priority levels to them. Consider a possible future outcome in which an individual comes into existence. In this outcome, the individual will enjoy a certain sum of welfare. In keeping with a whole-lives version of prioritarianism, this welfare should be weighed according to how much welfare she would have had in her life, had this welfare not accrued to her. And had this welfare not accrued to her, because she had not been caused to exist, no welfare would have accrued to her. Furthermore, for her, the state in which no welfare accrues to her because she does not come into existence has zero value. More precisely, in the possible future outcome in which she comes into existence, the state of affairs that she does not come into existence has zero value for her. This is what I argued in Chapter 5 (Section 5.5). Therefore, the benefit of coming into existence falls at a level of zero value.

Nevertheless, while we thus can have a person-affecting prioritarian principle that accommodates the value of coming into existence, such a principle has a number of highly controversial implications. It implies that, everything else being equal, it is better to cause new individuals to come into existence than to bring about an equal benefit to individuals already in existence, assuming that these individuals already in existence have lives worth living. After all, since these individuals who already exist have lives worth living, the benefit we can bestow on them will fall at a level higher than zero and so will have less weight.

Furthermore, prioritarianism implies the Repugnant Conclusion. Why is this? Consider first how Total Outcome Utilitarianism suggests this conclusion. According to Total Outcome Utilitarianism, just as it does not matter how a particular sum of welfare is distributed on different individuals, it does not matter on how many individuals it is distributed. Therefore, a reduction in the quality of lives can be counterbalanced by a sufficiently large increase in the quantity of individuals. This is why it would be better if a sufficiently large population lived lives barely worth living than if a smaller population lived very worthwhile lives.

Like total utilitarianism, prioritarianism implies that quality can be counterbalanced by quantity. The extra benefits that are created by causing more individuals to exist can outweigh a reduction in the average level of welfare. Therefore, like utilitarianism, prioritarianism implies the Repugnant Conclusion. Furthermore, it would not take as many individuals living lives barely worth living, according to prioritarianism, as it would according to total utilitarianism, to counterbalance the value of the outcome in which ten billion people live very worthwhile lives. This is because, in prioritarianism, benefits are weighted such that they count more at lower levels. So the last unit of welfare that befalls an individual due to her coming into existence will not count as much as does the first unit. Hence, it can be better if many individuals exist and live lives barely worth living than if fewer individuals exist and live very worthwhile lives, *even if the total sum of welfare produced in the former outcome is somewhat smaller than in the latter outcome*. After all, the welfare units on average fall at lower levels in the former outcome than in the latter.[5] In other words, prioritarianism implies:

> *The Super-repugnant Conclusion.* A world populated by individuals, every one of whom has a life barely worth living, would be better than a world populated by (for example) ten billion individuals, all of whom have very worthwhile lives, even if the former population has a lower total sum of welfare—if only the former population has an appropriate size.[6]

What this suggests is that if the implications of total utilitarianism regarding possible future individuals are repugnant, the implications of prioritarianism

---

[5] Which is not to say that, according to prioritarianism, the average moral weight of benefits has intrinsic moral value; see Chapter 8 (Section 8.4).

[6] In order to have an appropriate size, the former population would have to be large enough to have a higher prioritarian value than the latter outcome would, but small enough to have a lower total sum of welfare.

are even more repugnant. Prioritarianism implies the *Super*-repugnant Conclusion.

Furthermore, prioritarianism does not only have implications regarding hypothetical cases, such as those envisaged in the Repugnant and the Super-repugnant Conclusions. Indeed, some may want to argue that, according to prioritarianism, it would be better to hugely increase population size than not to, even in the actual world. And this is so, even if it means a significant reduction in the standard of living enjoyed by the present and future generations. After all, increases in population size may be warranted even if they are accompanied by decreases in average and (even) total welfare. Thus, it may be suggested that prioritarianism (together with various facts about the world) implies:

> *The Disturbing Conclusion.* In the actual world, it would be better if the present generation were to increase vastly population growth than if it were not to do so, even to the level where this leads to a significant reduction in the average standard of living enjoyed by present and future generations.

Of course, we can certainly imagine circumstances in which prioritarianism has such an implication. However, it can be argued that these circumstances are not very likely to (actually) obtain. There are several reasons for this. The first is the theoretical point that although prioritarians cannot plausibly modify their view to accommodate the Asymmetry, prioritarianism implies what we may call:

> *The Weak Asymmetry.* Everything else being equal, it is better to avoid that a person comes into existence and has a life worth not living (at level $-n$), than to ensure that a person comes into existence and has a life worth living (at level n).

The Weak Asymmetry follows from prioritarianism, because, according to this principle, benefits (and the avoidance of harms) matter more at lower levels. So each negative unit of welfare counts more than each positive unit. Furthermore, if we bring a happy individual into existence, the units of positive welfare that are thereby created gradually count less as they are piled on top of each other, whereas if we bring a miserable individual into existence, the units of negative welfare that are thereby created gradually count more.

This weak asymmetry will tend to somewhat weaken what seems to be a formidable prioritarian case for population growth. After all, presumably, among the people we may create, some will have lives worth not living and, everything else being equal, the miserableness of such a life weighs more heavily than does the happiness of a happy person we can cause to exist.[7] In

---

[7] Note that unlike the Asymmetry, the Weak Asymmetry does not get us into trouble when applied to the Problem of Extinction. While, in Figure 9.4, the Weak Asymmetry implies that each of the units

fact, since the sort of population growth we are considering would lead to a significantly lower standard of living than that with which we are familiar today, presumably *many* of the lives we would create would be below the level where life ceases to be worth living.

Furthermore, since the standard of living of the present generation is rather unevenly spread (to say the least), many presently existing individuals are likely to fall below the level where life ceases to be worth living. And in prioritarianism, of course, such lives below zero are especially bad, since we should give priority to the worse off.

Finally, a significant decrease in the average standard of living is likely to lead to various kinds of conflict, including rebellion, theft, violence, and war. Especially since, as I have just pointed out, resources are very unevenly spread and so a significant reduction in the average standard of living will reduce some (many) individuals to a very low level indeed (Hare 1993: 79). Presumably, this would be so even if, when reducing the average standard of living, we *aimed* for an equal distribution. Many individuals would come to live at a level comparable to that of a poor, malnourished Ethiopian. So, in light of the further disastrous consequences of rebellion, violence, war, etc. for welfare, the sort of population growth now under consideration may not be a very good idea, even in prioritarian terms.

Therefore, it seems to me that the most troubling implications of prioritarianism in population ethics pertain to empirically unrealistic scenarios such as those envisaged in the Repugnant and the Super-repugnant Conclusion. Thus, it is primarily these conclusions I shall be concerned with in the remaining part of this chapter. However, since the Super-repugnant Conclusion is simply a version of the Repugnant Conclusion, I shall mostly be concerned with the latter. As I pointed out above, if prioritarianism can be revised such as to avoid the latter conclusion, the revised version will also avoid the former. Nonetheless, towards the end of the chapter, I shall reconsider the counterintuitiveness of both.

Before I move on, I need to consider a related problematic conclusion that is implied by both total utilitarianism and prioritarianism, namely what Broome (2004: 213; see also Carlson 1998) has dubbed:

> *The Negative Repugnant Conclusion.* A world populated by individuals, every one of whom has a life barely worth *not* living, would be worse than a world populated by (for example) ten billion individuals, all of whom have *extremely miserable* lives (lives very much worth *not* living)—as long as the former population is sufficiently large.

---

of negative welfare of q is weightier than each of the positive welfare units of r, it does not suggest that the suffering of q outweighs the happiness of r. It is quite compatible with E being better than F.

To illustrate, consider Figure 9.5.

Figure 9.5. The Negative Repugnant Conclusion

According to both total utilitarianism and prioritarianism, B is worse than A, even if people suffer much more in A. This is because, if sufficiently populated, B includes both a higher sum of negative welfare and a higher sum of weighted negative welfare than does A. And just like the Repugnant Conclusion, the Negative Repugnant Conclusion seems rather counterintuitive.

I once claimed that because only prioritarianism implies the Super-repugnant Conclusion, this principle is less plausible than total utilitarianism in the area of population ethics (Holtug 1999: 36). I now think this was a mistake. One reason is that while total utilitarianism seems superior to prioritarianism with respect to the Repugnant Conclusion, prioritarianism seems superior to total utilitarianism with respect to the Negative Repugnant Conclusion. After all, it will take more individuals in B to render this outcome worse than A according to prioritarianism, than according to total utilitarianism. As stated by total utilitarianism, the sum of negative welfare in B need only exceed the sum of negative welfare in A to render B worse. However, as maintained by prioritarianism, the units of negative welfare that accrue to individuals in A on average count more than do the units of negative welfare that accrue to individuals in B. This is because, on average, these units fall at lower levels in A. Therefore, in order for B to be worse, it is not sufficient that this outcome includes a higher negative sum of welfare. The negative sum in B must exceed the negative sum in A by a certain *amount*. Thus, prioritarianism does better than total utilitarianism does with respect to the Negative Repugnant Conclusion.

Note that insofar as we are prioritarians, we are likely to find the Negative Repugnant Conclusion more counterintuitive than the Repugnant Conclusion itself, where this may incline us to think that prioritarianism in fact does *better* than total utilitarianism does with respect to repugnant conclusions. However, the *reason* for finding the negative version more repugnant is that we may believe that welfare matters more at lower levels. After all, as prioritarians, we find it more important to raise an individual from, for example, -10 to -1 than to raise an individual from 1 to 10 (although, in each case, an individual is raised by nine units). And so there is a sense in which we will be more concerned about the difference between the worse off and the better off in the Negative Repugnant Conclusion than about the difference between the worse off and the better off in the (positive) Repugnant Conclusion. But of course, this reason will not appeal to hard-nosed utilitarians.

More generally, prioritarianism implies that the best possible distribution of a fixed sum of welfare is as flat a distribution as possible both concerning positive and negative welfare levels. So just as $(1, 1, 1, 1)$ is better than $(4, \star, \star, \star)$, $(-1, -1, -1, -1)$ is better than $(-4, \star, \star, \star)$, where '$\star$' refers to the non-existence of an individual in an outcome. We might say that prioritarianism favours a 'flattening out' of welfare. And while such flattening out seems troubling when it comes to positive welfare, it seems a welcome implication when it comes to negative welfare. Again, prioritarians may find the deviation from utilitarianism with respect to negative welfare more important than the deviation with respect to positive welfare, and so that prioritarianism compares favourably with the former principle in this regard.

Note, however, that there are also cases in which total utilitarianism implies that it would be good to eradicate negative welfare at high levels where prioritarianism has no similar implication. Consider the following two outcomes: $(-10, \star, \star, \star \dots \star, \star)$ and $(1, -1, 1, -1 \dots 1, -1)$. No matter how long the sequence in the latter outcome is, total utilitarianism implies that the former outcome is worse. After all, the sum in the latter outcome is zero, regardless of the length of the sequence. However, according to prioritarianism, the negative units in the latter sequence are weightier than the positive units and so this outcome has negative value. And if the sequence is long enough, the negative value of the latter outcome will exceed the negative value of the former.

This is not because prioritarians are less concerned about the negative welfare of the one individual in the former outcome (in fact they are more worried about it), but because they are (also) more troubled about the negative welfare of half of the individuals in the latter outcome. It is their greater concern for them than for the individuals who, after all, have positive welfare in this outcome that may incline prioritarians to the view that the latter outcome has negative value.

A further relative advantage of prioritarianism in the area of population ethics is that the Repugnant Conclusion may seem less disturbing when it is transformed to higher levels, where prioritarianism provides a plausible explanation of why this should be so. Consider again Figure 9.1. Now suppose we increase the welfare-level in A and B while keeping the difference in average welfare constant. Imagine, for instance, that while everyone in B has a *good* life, everyone in A has an *ecstatic* life. Here, the conclusion that there must be some number of individuals such that, if they populated B, B would be better than A, does not seem very disturbing (and in any case less disturbing than the 'original' Repugnant Conclusion). In a sense, Total Outcome Utilitarianism accommodates this claim. It would take fewer individuals in B at this higher level to counterbalance the value of A than it would at a lower level (because, when we raise the average by an equal amount in A and B, we raise this level for more individuals in B). However, this may not be the whole explanation of why 'repugnant' conclusions are less repugnant at higher levels. It seems to me that another reason is that the worse off are better off in higher than in lower level repugnant conclusions. Prioritarianism captures this reason by giving priority to the worse off. When we raise the average in both A and B, the increase in welfare that accrues to every individual in B falls at a lower level than the increase that accrues to every individual in A and so has greater moral value.

Finally, as I have already pointed out, a further attractive feature of prioritarianism, not shared by Total Outcome Utilitarianism, is that it implies the Weak Asymmetry. Nevertheless, the Repugnant and the Super-repugnant Conclusions are not welcome conclusions, and so it is worth asking if there are ways in which prioritarians who wish to provide an account of populations ethics may avoid them.

9.4 Additive and Non-additive Functions

One way in which a prioritarian may seek to avoid the Repugnant Conclusion is by revising her view, such that she no longer claims that outcome value is an *additive* function of weighted welfare.[8] For example, just like utilitarians, prioritarians may opt for an averaging function. According to what we may call Average Outcome Utilitarianism, an outcome is better the higher the average level of individual benefits it contains. Likewise, according to what we may term Average Outcome Welfare Prioritarianism, an outcome is better the larger the average of weighted individual benefits it contains, where benefits are weighted such that they gain a greater value, the worse off the individual is to whom they accrue.

---

[8] This move is similar to another move I considered in Chapter 4 (Section 4.11), according to which a proponent of the Additive Prudential View may contemplate giving up additivity to avoid the Repugnant Conclusion about Self-interest.

Obviously, both Average Outcome Utilitarianism and Average Outcome Welfare Prioritarianism avoid the Repugnant Conclusion. In Figure 9.1, A includes both a higher average of welfare and a higher average of weighted welfare than does B. However, both these principles are rather implausible. As I pointed out in Chapter 8 (Section 8.3), we cannot reasonably claim that it is always good to increase average welfare. That would imply that if everyone has a life much worse than nothing, we can improve the world by adding individuals who have slightly better lives, but are nevertheless below the level where life ceases to be worth living. We have thus raised the average (Parfit 1984: 422). And we have also raised the weighted average.

Furthermore, as this case also illustrates, both Average Outcome Utilitarianism and Average Outcome Welfare Prioritarianism violate the Wide Person-affecting Principle. While we increase the average welfare and the average weighted welfare by adding further miserable individuals, obviously there is no one for whom this is better. Thus, the claim that the more populated outcome is better violates the Wide Person-affecting Principle. In fact, this may be part of the explanation for why we find the claim implausible.

Finally, these two average principles imply what Gustav Arrhenius (2000: 66) refers to as:

> *The Sadistic Conclusion*. It can be better to add individuals who have lives worth not living to an outcome than to add individuals who have lives worth living.

Suppose a generation (*p*) is contemplating two population policies. Either they have a number of children who will, unfortunately, have lives worth not living, and in that case A will result. Or they have a much larger number of children who are worse off than they are but, nevertheless, have lives above the zero level. In that case B will result. Note that, by assumption, *p*'s welfare will not be affected by their choice. This case is illustrated in Figure 9.6.

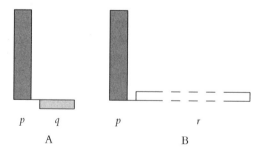

Figure 9.6. The Sadistic Conclusion

Here, both Average Outcome Utilitarianism and Average Outcome Welfare Prioritarianism imply that A is better than B, even though r will have lives worth living and q will have lives worth not living. This is because, assuming that r contains a sufficient number of individuals, r detracts more from the average welfare and average weighted welfare than does q.[9] For these reasons, and others, such average principles seem to me quite implausible.

Nevertheless, there are other non-additive functions one may employ. Consider, for example, what Thomas Hurka (1983: 497) calls a 'Variable Value View'. According to this view, the value of an additional individual at a given level of welfare varies with the number of individuals in the world. The more individuals, the less value this additional individual contributes. More precisely, outcome value is a strictly concave function of population size, as illustrated by the last of the graphs in Figure 9.7 (Hurka 1983: 500–2).

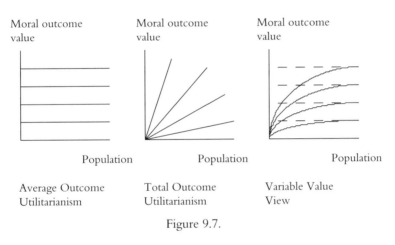

Figure 9.7.

Each of the strictly concave curves represents a given average level of welfare, such that a higher curve represents a higher average level of welfare than the curve(s) below. Furthermore, each curve asymptotically approaches a certain limit. Therefore, for a given average level of welfare, there is a certain level

---

[9] In Average Outcome Welfare Prioritarianism, it will take a larger number of individuals in r to render A better than B, than it will in Average Outcome Utilitarianism. Suppose that p consists of one individual at +7, q of one individual at −1, and r of two individuals at +1. According to Average Outcome Utilitarianism, A and B will then have equal value ([7+(-1)]/2 = 3 and [7+1+1]/3 = 3). However, according to Average Outcome Welfare Prioritarianism, B will be better than A. This is because a welfare level of −1 has a higher prioritarian *negative* value than a welfare level of +1 has prioritarian *positive* value. Therefore, relative to each individual in r, the individual in q detracts more from average *weighted* welfare than from average welfare. Two individuals at +1 will not detract as much from average weighted welfare as one individual at −1 does.

of moral outcome value this curve will approach but never reach. This is an important feature, because it enables Variable Value Views to avoid the Repugnant Conclusion. Suppose that the lowest curve represents the average welfare level of individuals living lives barely worth living. Then, if the value of the outcome in which ten billion individuals live very worthwhile lives is above the limit asymptotically approached by this curve, an outcome in which individuals live lives barely worth living cannot be better than the outcome in which everyone lives much better lives, no matter how many individuals the former outcome contains.

Variable Value Views are sort of a compromise between Average Outcome Utilitarianism and Total Outcome Utilitarianism in that, at low population levels, they mostly resemble Total Outcome Utilitarianism, and at high population levels, they mostly resemble Average Outcome Utilitarianism. Consider first Average Outcome Utilitarianism. The graph for this principle consists of a series of horizontal straight lines, where each line represents a given average welfare level. At any given such welfare level, we cannot increase outcome value by enlarging population size, which is why these lines are horizontal. As we can see, Variable Value Views resemble Average Outcome Utilitarianism at high population levels, where the curves representing the former views flatten out.

Total Outcome Utilitarianism, on the other hand, is represented by a series of straight lines that rise to the right. This is because, for each average welfare level, every additional individual contributes positively and equally to outcome value (we are assuming that each individual is at the average). As we can see, Variable Value Views resemble Total Outcome Utilitarianism at low population levels, where the curves representing the former views rise sharply to the right.

According to Hurka, Variable Value Views have various nice properties. Because they resemble Total Outcome Utilitarianism at low population levels, they will assign a high value to additional individuals if the existence of the human race is threatened; say, as a consequence of a nuclear holocaust (1983: 502). And because they resemble Average Outcome Utilitarianism at high population levels, at such levels, they will tend to condemn population increases that are at the expense of average welfare.

In order to gain similar advantages, a prioritarian may adopt a version of such a Variable Value View. She may interpret the curves in the last graph in Figure 9.7 as representing not average welfare but average *weighted* welfare. Thus, she may claim that outcome value is a strictly concave function of population size.

And so she reaps the benefits of the Variable Value View to which Hurka refers.

What should we think of such Variable Value Views? The exact implications will depend on the particular concave function assumed, but perhaps we can make the following general conjecture. Since Variable Value Views resemble Average Outcome Utilitarianism at high population levels, at such levels they are likely to inherit at least some of its problems (or similar ones). At least, I know of no Variable Value View that entirely avoids these and similarly grave difficulties.[10] And while, obviously, these points do not prove that a plausible such principle cannot be devised, it suggests to me that we should be sceptical of this possibility.

There are, of course, other possible functions that may be invoked—and various other attempts may be made—to avoid the Repugnant Conclusion.[11] Ultimately, I believe that each of these faces severe difficulties. But in light of my person-affecting approach to outcome value, one group of such attempts deserves further discussion here, namely those that invoke restrictions on the class of individuals whose welfare counts. All these alternative person-affecting approaches are available to a prioritarian, who will then simply apply her prioritarian principle to a smaller class of individuals than in the (wide) person-affecting approach I have considered so far. Nevertheless, since these approaches are also available to many other types of theorists, I shall not assume prioritarianism in the following sections, in which I discuss these various alternative person-affecting approaches. The objections I shall raise are quite general and so will apply whatever more particular theory of outcomes we may want to combine them with.

9.5 The Necessary-person-affecting Principle

According to Narveson's Slogan, our duty is to make individuals happy, not to make happy individuals. One way of defending the idea this slogan

---

[10] For an excellent critical discussion of two more particular Variable Value Views, see Arrhenius (2000: ch. 4).

[11] The list of such functions and attempts includes critical level theories (Blackorby, Bossert, and Donaldson 1997; Broome 2004), discontinuity theories (Crisp 1992: 149–52; Glover 1977: 69–71; Griffin 1986: 338–40), frustrationist theories (Fehige 1998), perfectionist theories (Parfit 1986b), and theories that deny the transitivity of the betterness relation (Persson 2004; Rachels 2001; 2004). Many of them are aptly criticized in Arrhenius (2000).

encapsulates is to appeal to the distinction between necessary and contingent individuals. Thus, it may be claimed that only the welfare of necessary individuals should be taken into account.[12] This is another idea often associated with person-affecting morality. For example, in one place, John Broome (1992: 124) calls a similar claim the 'person-affecting condition'. The point is that, relative to a comparison of an outcome in which a happy individual comes into existence and an outcome in which he does not, this individual is contingent; and so, everything else being equal, the outcome in which he comes into existence is not better than the outcome in which he does not.

More generally, we may appeal to:

> The Necessary-person-affecting Principle. An outcome, O_1, cannot be better (or worse) than another outcome, O_2, if there is no one who exists in both O_1 and O_2 for whom O_1 is better (or worse) than O_2.

Strictly speaking, this principle does not say that we should assign value to the welfare of necessary individuals, but clearly this is part of its motivation. Obviously, there are many ways in which this can be done but, assuming welfarism, the following claim should be relatively uncontroversial with proponents of the Necessary-person-affecting Principle:

> The Necessary-person Betterness Claim. An outcome, O_1, is better than another outcome, O_2, if, within the class of individuals who exist in both outcomes, (a) everyone in O_1 is equally well off, and (b) everyone is better off in O_1 than in O_2.

Note, first, that this claim does not have any implications for situations in which different necessary individuals have conflicting interests. And, second, that it only implies that an outcome is better than another when the Weak Pareto Principle—according to which an outcome is better than another if it is better for everyone—is satisfied with respect to necessary individuals. Nevertheless, some might claim that an outcome that is better for everyone need not be better itself, because it may increase inequality. But note, third, that the Necessary-person Betterness Claim only requires a weakly Pareto-superior outcome to be better, if all the necessary individuals who exist in this outcome are equally well off.

Now, how might we attempt to justify the Necessary-person-affecting Principle? As I pointed out in Chapter 5 (Section 5.6), David Heyd (1992: 97–103) has argued that we can benefit what he calls 'actual people', but not 'potential people'. I shall address this distinction of Heyd's in the next section,

---

[12] For good discussions of the moral relevance of the distinction between necessary and contingent individuals, and of the distinction, to be discussed in Section 9.7, between actual and merely possible individuals, see Arrhenius (2000: 139–45); and Bykvist (1998: 98–104).

but I shall consider his argument in this section because it does not really trade on an actual–potential distinction but rather on the distinction between necessary and contingent individuals.

In fact, we have already encountered Heyd's argument in my discussion of the value of coming into existence. According to this argument, an outcome in which an individual exists cannot be better (or worse) for her than an outcome in which she never exists, because in the latter outcome she has no properties. If one outcome is to be better (or worse) for her than another, she must exist in both; that is to say, relative to the comparison, she must be a necessary rather than contingent individual. But if we are to assess outcomes as better and worse on the basis of their being so for individuals, an outcome cannot be better (or worse) than another unless it is so for at least one individual who exists in both. Thus, we arrive at the Necessary-person-affecting Principle. However, as I argued in Chapter 5 (Section 5.5), Heyd's argument for the view that existence cannot be better (or worse) for an individual than non-existence does not succeed.

Nevertheless, even if it may be difficult to provide a rationale for it, perhaps we should simply accept the Necessary-person-affecting Principle because of its intuitive plausibility. Consider the Repugnant Conclusion. Assume that in Figure 9.1, A and B consist of non-overlapping groups of individuals. All of the individuals involved in the comparison of A and B will then be contingent, and so the Necessary-person-affecting Principle will rule out any suggestion that B is better than A. Equally, if we assume that there is an overlap between the populations of A and B, the principle will imply that B is not better than A, because B is not *better* for any of the individuals who exist in both.

Regrettably, however, the Necessary-person-affecting Principle is in fact highly counterintuitive. In the non-overlapping case, the Necessary-person-affecting Principle implies not only that B is no better than A, but also that A is no better than B—that is, that neither outcome is better. This is hardly a great improvement. It may be said that unlike certain other person-affecting views on outcome value, at least the Necessary-person-affecting Principle does not require us to bring about B rather than A if we are in a position to do so. But this point assumes that moral requirements are wholly determined by welfarist orderings of outcomes, and on this assumption the Necessary-person-affecting Principle would imply that we have no moral reason not to bring about B. Since neither A nor B is better, perhaps we should flip a coin. Again, while this may be an improvement, it is hardly a *great* improvement.

The Necessary-person-affecting Principle also gives us the wrong answers to the Non-identity Problem and the Problem of Suffering. Consider Figure 9.2.

Since only the *p*-individuals are necessary and they are better off in A than in B, this principle ensures that B is no better than A. Furthermore, since the *p*-individuals are in fact better off in A, and are equally well off there, the Necessary-person Betterness Claim implies that A is better than B. This should surely be denied.

Furthermore, reconsider Figure 9.3. Since the individuals who exist in C are contingent, C cannot be worse than D, even if everyone in C suffers terribly. This implication is itself unacceptable, but it gets worse. Consider the problem illustrated in Figure 9.8.

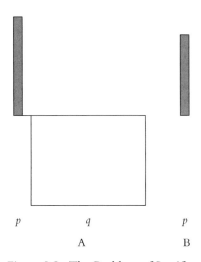

p   *q*   *p*

A   B

Figure 9.8. The Problem of Sacrifice

Since only the *p*-individuals are necessary, and since they are slightly better off in A than in B, the Necessary-person-affecting Principle implies that B cannot be the better outcome. Moreover, since the *p*-individuals are equally well off in A, the Necessary-person Betterness Claim implies that *A is better*. The fact that a huge group of individuals suffer horribly in A in no way affects this judgement.

Let me point to a final problem for the Necessary-person Betterness Claim, one reaching beyond its intuitive repugnance. Just as we saw that the Necessary Preference View violates the 'S has a stronger self-interest in x than y' relation (in Chapter 2, Section 2.6), the Necessary-person Betterness Claim violates the transitivity of the betterness relation (for a similar point, see Broome 1992: 125). Consider Figure 9.9.

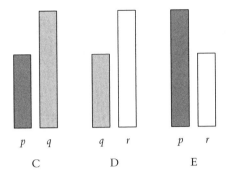

Figure 9.9. The Problem of Transitivity

When comparing C and D, only the *q*-individuals are necessary, and since they are better (and equally well) off in C, C is better than D. When comparing D and E, only the *r*-individuals are necessary, and since they are better (and equally well) off in D, D is better than E. The transitivity of the betterness relation then implies that C is better than E. However, since when comparing C and E only the *p*-individuals are necessary, and since they are better (and equally well) off in E, E is better than C. Thus, we have a contradiction.[13] All in all, then, it seems that we have ample reason to reject the Necessary-person-affecting Principle and its associate, the Necessary-person Betterness Claim.

9.6 Generocentrism

In his book, *Genethics*, the distinction Heyd takes to be morally relevant is not that between necessary and contingent individuals, but that between what he calls 'actual people' and 'potential people'. Since Heyd's use of the term 'actual

---

[13] Let me briefly mention two ways in which the proponent of the Necessary-person Betterness Claim may attempt to avoid this contradiction. First, as I have pointed out at various times, some theorists have denied the transitivity of the betterness relation which, of course, removes the inconsistency. But I have also suggested that we have reasons not to make this move. Second, one may relativize betterness to comparisons of sets of outcomes. Thus, relative to the set consisting of C and D, C is better than D; relative to the set consisting of D and E, D is better than E; and relative to the set consisting of C and E, E is better than C. Furthermore, there are no necessary individuals relative to the set consisting of C, D, and E, and so the Necessary-person Betterness Claim does not rank this set. Hence, there is no inconsistency. However, this move generates the same sort of problems we encountered for a similar relativization of the Necessary Preference View in Chapter 2 (Section 2.6).

people' differs from mine, I shall call what Heyd refers to as 'actual people' *agent-independent individuals*. I shall also call what he refers to as 'potential people' *agent-dependent individuals*. According to Heyd, then, while we can benefit or harm an agent-independent individual, we cannot benefit or harm an agent-dependent individual, and so we can owe moral concern only to the former. This view he refers to as 'generocentrism'.

An individual, S, is agent-dependent for a particular agent, A, if and only if the existence of S depends on the choices of A (Heyd 1992: 97–103). And S is agent-independent for A, if and only if S is not agent-dependent for A. So if, for example, you are trying to decide whether or not to have a child, this child is agent-dependent for you but agent-independent for, say, me. Therefore, according to Heyd (1992: 101, 105), you cannot benefit or harm it, for instance, by causing it to exist, whereas I can benefit or harm it—assuming that it becomes actual.

To appreciate the difference between the various modal distinctions, consider the following two possible worlds, World 1 and World 2, each of which contains three individuals:

World 1	World 2
s_1	s_1
s_2	s_2
s_3	s_4

Suppose, furthermore, that it is s_1 who decides whether s_3 or s_4 comes into existence, and that she will in fact decide that s_3 comes about (so that World 1 is the actual world). Then the following properties can be assigned to s_1–s_4:

s_1: actual, necessary, s_2–s_3–s_4–independent,
s_2: actual, necessary, s_1–s_3–s_4–independent,
s_3: actual, contingent, s_1–dependent, s_2–s_4–independent,
s_4: merely possible, contingent, s_1–dependent, s_2–s_3—independent.

As is obvious from this list of properties, generocentrism generates an agent-relative ordering of outcomes. Thus, since both s_3 and s_4 are s_1-dependent, their welfare should not affect s_1's ordering of World 1 and World 2. Since, on the other hand, s_3 and s_4 are both s_2-independent, presumably their welfare *should* affect s_2's ordering. Now, Heyd may be more concerned with the moral status of acts (or choices) than axiology, but since the axiological points I shall make about generocentrism can easily be transferred to the morality of acts, I can continue to stick with axiology.

The agent-relativity of generocentrism generates some puzzling conclusions. Suppose you are in the process of deciding whether or not to have a child.

You and I both donate a certain amount of money to this child, in such a way that the money will automatically be his if he comes into existence. Imagine also that he does in fact come into existence. The child is then you–dependent and me–independent. This means that relative to you, the welfare that accrues to him through your donation does not contribute to the value of the resulting outcome, whereas the welfare that accrues to him through my donation does. This strikes me as rather puzzling.[14]

Generocentrism is also troubled by many of the problems we have already encountered in examining other views. Thus where the Repugnant Conclusion is concerned, it provides no basis for ranking A and B in Figure 9.1, unless we are in a position to determine whether their inhabitants are agent-dependent or agent-independent. Suppose that, after the next ice age, only one person has survived and by the use of advanced *in vitro fertilization,* artificial wombs, and robot-parent technology, she can use harvested eggs and sperm to create either an A or a B future. Assume also that her own welfare will not be affected by her choice (perhaps making this choice will be the last thing she does). Here, since her own welfare will not be affected, and since the inhabitants of A and B are all her-dependent, generocentrism implies that, relative to her, neither of the outcomes in which she realizes A or B is the better outcome.

Better still, suppose that this person is a total utilitarian and, in the light of her beliefs, will feel better about bringing into existence the more populous B outcome. In this case, generocentrism implies that the outcome in which she realizes B is the better one.

Turning to the Non–identity Problem, imagine that in Figure 9.2, *p* represents a mother who intends either to have a child now or to wait a couple of months. If she has a child now (*q*), then due to the presence of certain chemicals in her body, this child will have a genetic disease that will cause him to have a life barely worth living. Since his disease is a serious genetic disorder, no one can improve his welfare above this level. If, on the other hand, she waits, she will have a different child (*r*), and since the chemicals will have left her body, she will have a child with much higher welfare. Furthermore, suppose that if she does not wait, because of his disease she will have to take care of her child for the rest of her life, and that this will in fact be so rewarding for her that, despite the pain of worrying about him, she will have a slightly better life than she would have if she were to wait and have another child. Here, since

---

[14] The problem can be avoided if, instead of relativizing value to agents, we relativize it to choices. Then, since your choice of having the child and your choice of donating the money are different options, the latter may contribute value to the relevant outcome. In one place, Peter Singer considers such a view; he suggests that we might 'count only beings who already exist, prior to the decision we are taking, or at least will exist independently of that decision' (Singer 1993: 103).

both q and r are p-dependent and p is better off in A, generocentrism implies that, relative to p, A is better than B (see also Petersen 2001: 413–14).

Now consider the Problem of Suffering. Suppose that, in Figure 9.3, a child who has a genetic disease rendering his life so terrible that it is much worse than no life at all populates C. A woman may decide either to have this child or to abstain from doing so. Since this child is her-dependent, generocentrism prevents her from saying that the outcome in which she has the child is worse. It may be objected that surely her own welfare will be negatively affected by having the child, but again we can imagine that taking care of the child will be very rewarding for her.

Finally, a version of the Problem of Sacrifice in which generocentrism generates the wrong result can easily be constructed. Thus, it seems quite appropriate when Heyd (1992: 142) himself points out that generocentrism allows us to adopt a policy of *après moi, le déluge*.

9.7 The Actual-person-affecting Principle

Apart from the distinctions already considered, another modal distinction can be invoked to support Narveson's Slogan. This is the distinction between actual and merely possible individuals, the claim being that only the welfare of the former matters (Bigelow and Pargetter 1988: 174; Feinberg 1980: 180; Steinbock 1992: 72; Warren 1978: 24).[15] If this last claim is correct, we need pay no attention to the welfare of individuals we choose not to bring into existence. So if we choose not to bring into existence additional happy individuals, the welfare we have failed to bring about does not matter, even when we compare this outcome with another outcome in which we do cause them to exist. On the other hand, if additional individuals are created, their welfare matters.

An implication of this approach, in the Problem of Suffering (Figure 9.3), is that if we bring about C, we have created the worse outcome. Thus, the distinction between actual and merely possible individuals may seem better placed to solve our problems than that between necessary and contingent ones.

More generally, we can appeal to:

The Actual-person-affecting Principle. An outcome, O_1, cannot be better (or worse) than another outcome, O_2, if there is no actual individual for whom O_1 is better (or worse) than O_2.

---

[15] In some of this work, however, it is not entirely clear whether the focus is on actual individuals *or* on actual preferences (Feinberg seems especially ambiguous in this regard).

Just like the Necessary-person-affecting Principle, this principle does not say that we should attach value to the welfare of the favoured class of individuals, but clearly this is part of the idea that motivates it. So let us add:

> *The Actual-person Betterness Claim.* An outcome, O_1, is better than another outcome, O_2, if, within the class of actual individuals, (a) everyone in O_1 is equally well off, and (b) everyone is better off in O_1 than in O_2.

Why claim that it is only the welfare of actual individuals that matters? The answer may seem obvious. Why on earth should we care about the welfare of individuals who will in fact never exist? However, the idea that merely possible individuals do not matter is not as attractive, let alone obvious, as it initially sounds. Consider Figure 9.10.

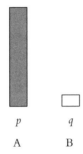

Figure 9.10. The Problem of Low Welfare

Suppose that B is the actual outcome, so that whereas q is actual, p is merely possible. The Actual-person-affecting Principle then implies that A cannot be better than B. After all, there is no actual individual for whom A is better than B. Furthermore, the Actual-person Betterness Claim implies that B is *better* than A. Importantly, these disturbing conclusions follow precisely because the welfare of merely possible individuals is not taken into account.

The actual-person-affecting approach also has a rather peculiar implication. Assume act-consequentialism. And imagine that A and B are the only outcomes we can bring about. In this case, since B is better it will be right to bring it about (and wrong to bring about A). But now suppose A is the actual outcome. Here p will be actual whereas q will be merely possible, and the Actual-person Betterness Claim will imply that A is better than B. Thus it will be right to bring about A (and wrong to bring about B). It would appear, then, that *simply by bringing about B* (and so making B actual), we can ensure that this act, which would otherwise have been wrong, is right.[16] But how could one make an act right merely by performing it?

The actual-person-affecting approach runs into further problems. We have already seen that on the assumption that B is actual, it gives the wrong answer to the Problem of Low Welfare. And if, in Figure 9.1, there is no overlap in the populations of A and B, and B is the actual outcome, it generates the Repugnant Conclusion. The Actual-person-affecting Principle implies that A is no better than B, and the Actual-person Betterness Claim that, in fact, B is better.

Nor does the actual-person-affecting approach allow us to solve the Non-identity Problem or even the Problem of Suffering. Suppose that, in Figure 9.2, A is the actual outcome. The Actual-person-affecting Principle will then indicate that B is no better than A.

As I pointed out above, the actual-person-affecting approach implies that, in the Problem of Suffering (Figure 9.3), it would be worse if we were to bring about C. And this, of course, is what we want to claim. However, assume that D is actual. The Actual-person-affecting Principle then suggests that D is no better than C. Thus, if we were to bring about D, we would not have brought about the better outcome. Finally, consider the Problem of Sacrifice (Figure 9.8). Assuming that B is actual, the Actual-person Betterness Claim implies that A is better than B, although *p* is only slightly better off in A, and A contains a huge group of individuals living miserable lives.

In the light of these difficulties, it seems to me that we should abandon the actual-person-affecting approach. The modal distinctions between actual and merely possible individuals, and necessary and contingent individuals, both generate implausible theories of outcomes if we base our axiology on them. Our judgements will then be modally *partial* in a manner that seems clearly *unfair*. Just like racism, sexism, and speciesism, modal partiality thus turns out to be a variety of arbitrary discrimination. Better, then, to embrace modal *impartiality* of the sort inherent in, for example, the wide person-affecting approach.

9.8 Personalism

In her recent book, *Child versus Childmaker*, Melinda Roberts first provides a preliminary sketch of what she considers a plausible 'person-affecting intuition',

---

[16] As I pointed out in Chapter 2, a similar criticism can be raised against the Actual Preference View (Section 2.5). See also Arrhenius (2000: 140–1); and Bykvist (1998: 103–4).

according to which 'the morally significant aspect of how we conduct ourselves as agents lies in the consequences our conduct has for each and every person who ever lives' (1998: 1, see also 2, 11). While this is clearly along the lines of the actual-person-affecting approach presented above, the theory she develops later in the book is not an actualist one and it is worth taking a closer look at it. Roberts calls her theory 'personalism'. The general idea is that we should assess outcomes by asking whether individuals are wronged in them.[17]

More precisely, personalism consists of the following four principles (Roberts 1998: 62–4):

N⋆: s is not wronged by agents in X *if* s never exists in X.

M⋆: s is not wronged by agents in X *if*, for each world Y accessible to such agents, s has at least as much well-being in X as s has in Y.

D⋆: s is wronged by agents in X *if* s exists in X and there is some world Y accessible to such agents such that:

   (i) s has more well-being in Y than s has in X;
   (ii) for each person s' who ever exists in X, *either s'* has at least as much well-being in Y as s' has in X *or s'* never exists in Y; *and*
   (iii) for each s' who ever exists in Y, s' exists at some time in X.

P⋆: X is permissible for agents at t *if and only if* no person who exists at or after t is wronged in X at or after t.

These principles deal with the moral status (permissibility) of acts bringing about outcomes rather than with axiology, but as Roberts (1998: 75–6) herself points out, we can use them to generate an axiology if we add a principle such as:

R⋆: X is worse than Y if someone is wronged in X and no one is wronged in Y.

Since the problems I shall discuss for the resulting ordering of outcomes are equally problems for personalism as a theory of the moral status of acts bringing about outcomes, this addition seems innocent enough.

Let us have a closer look at personalism. N⋆, in conjunction with P⋆ and/or R⋆, seems to nicely capture Narveson's Slogan. M⋆ captures the claim that an individual cannot be wronged if her welfare is maximized. D⋆ embraces the idea that an individual is wronged if she is 'gratuitously' rendered worse off than she could have been ('gratuitously', because no one benefits from her

---

[17] In fact, Roberts is not the only able defender of personalism. Thus, Peter Vallentyne writes, 'by and large, Roberts's Personalism seems exactly right' (Vallentyne 2000b: 646). And Broome suggests that, with respect to the intuition that it is (often) ethically neutral to add an individual to an outcome, 'Melinda Roberts gives a persuasive non-axiological account' (2004: 150).

being worse off). If, on the other hand, she is rendered worse off, but not gratuitously so, Roberts points out that we need a theory of fairness to settle the competing interests. Finally, P★ and R★ inform us that the moral and axiological status of outcomes is to be explained in terms of wrongings.

To understand these principles better, consider the outcomes represented in Figure 9.11 (the reason I call this the Extended Non-identity Problem will become apparent later).

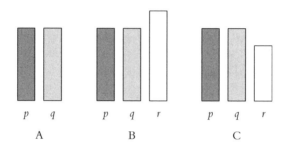

Figure 9.11. The Extended Non-identity Problem

M★ implies that neither p nor q are wronged in A; and N★ implies that r is not wronged there. So no one is wronged in A. Moreover, M★ implies that p, q, and r are not wronged in B; and D★ implies that r *is* wronged in C. The r-individuals are gratuitously rendered worse off than they could have been. So R★ implies that C is worse than both A and B.

As I said, personalism differs from an actual-person-affecting approach. Suppose C is the actual outcome. The Actual-person-affecting Principle then implies that C cannot be worse than A. Personalism, on the other hand, implies that C is worse. In fact, actual individuals have no special status in personalism. Rather, an outcome is assessed in terms of whether anyone who exists *in that outcome* is wronged. In itself, it is insignificant whether the outcome and its inhabitants are actual.

Still assuming the axiology provided by R★, an interesting feature of personalism is that, unlike the other principles considered so far, it violates the Person-affecting Restriction. It implies that C is worse than A even if there is no one for whom C is worse (and no one for whom A is better). Thus, the intuitive merit of the Person-affecting Restriction speaks against personalism. Roberts might say that while C is not *worse* for anyone, someone is *wronged* there, but even this strikes me as rather implausible. Suppose that, having realized that personalism renders both A and B permissible, we flip a coin and end up realizing A. We then congratulate ourselves for respecting r by not realizing C. C would, after all, wrong r. However, the sort of respect for r we have thus exhibited is clearly one which, putting myself in r's shoes, I would much rather do without: C is much *better* for r than A is. Thus, the claim that by bringing about A rather than C we respect r seems to me dubious, especially within the sort of welfarist framework I have assumed *and* to which Roberts is committed.

Furthermore, personalism does not do all that well when applied to the series of problems we have considered for other views. Examine the Repugnant Conclusion (Figure 9.1). Suppose that A and B consist of non-overlapping groups of individuals. Then M★ implies that no one is wronged in either A or B, and so we have no basis for saying that one is worse than the other is. In fact, even if we reduce the number of individuals in B so that it equals the number of individuals in A—even, indeed, if we reduce the number below this level—there will still be no basis for saying that the resulting outcome is worse. Thus, in the Problem of Low Welfare (Figure 9.10), there is no basis for saying that B is worse than A.

Now consider the Non–identity Problem (Figure 9.2). M★ implies that neither p nor q is wronged in A, and N★ indicates that nor is r. In B, neither q nor r is wronged. And while the p-individuals are worse off than they are in A, they are not wronged either. For D★ to suggest that p is wronged in B, all the individuals who exist in A must also exist in B, but the q-individuals do not satisfy this condition. It follows that no one is wronged in either A or B, and hence that there is no basis for saying that one outcome is worse than the other is.

Roberts basically bites the bullet with respect to the Non–identity Problem, but argues that most of the cases usually considered under this heading are in fact not like the problem represented in Figure 9.2. For example, she points out that the 'live for today policy' and the 'take care of tomorrow policy'—to which I referred when setting up the Non–identity Problem in Chapter 6 (Section 6.3)—are likely not to be the only options. Surely, she observes, there will be possible outcomes in which *some* of the q-individuals are better off than they are in A, and if there are, M★ will no longer imply that A wrongs no one (Roberts 1998: 96). More generally, Roberts (1998: ch. 3) suggests that such cases should be treated as she treats the Extended Non–identity Problem (Figure 9.11). If only A and C are accessible, there is no basis for calling C worse. If B is also accessible, D★ will imply that C is worse.

However, first, I have already expressed misgivings about the implications of personalism for the Extended Non–identity Problem. Second, as Roberts is prepared to admit, there are cases in which we cannot invoke further outcomes to save the day for personalism. Thus, I considered a case in which a woman can either have a child now who will have a serious genetic disorder, or have a child later who will not. Assuming that there is only so much that can be done for the former child, this child is bound to have significantly lower welfare, and yet personalism does not render this optimal outcome for him worse.[18]

Finally, consider the Problem of Extinction (Figure 9.4). Examine first the version in which the last few inhabitants will be equally happy, whether they repopulate the world or bring human existence to an end (so in terms of Figure 9.4, the p-individuals have equal welfare in E and F). On this assumption, D$\star$ implies that q is wronged in E. This is because, according to Roberts, we should assign zero welfare to individuals in outcomes in which they do not exist, and so the q-individuals have more welfare in F than in E. Therefore, (i) is satisfied in D$\star$, as are (ii)−(iii). In F, on the other hand, no one is wronged. N$\star$ implies that q and r are not wronged, and M$\star$ indicates that p is not. So R$\star$ implies that E is worse than F, and P$\star$ suggests that E is impermissible.

But even if we assume that the p-individuals are better off in E than in F, as represented in Figure 9.4, personalism may be in trouble. D$\star$ will then no longer imply that anyone is wronged in either of the two outcomes, because there is no one who is gratuitously worse off in either, and presumably Roberts would ideally wish to settle the conflict between p and q on the basis of a principle of fairness. Furthermore, as I pointed out in Section 9.2, for any plausible welfare function, the misery of the q-individuals in E outweighs the gain for the p-individuals. So E is worse, and indeed impermissible.[19] In other words, on the assumptions made, it is not only worse but also impermissible for us to bring about the continued existence of the human race. This strikes me as a rather extreme view.

Nevertheless, in response to my argument, Roberts has recently stated that she does not find it clearly incorrect to forbid the creation of miserable

---

[18] With respect to cases such as this, Roberts (1998: 98) responds that she finds them 'in all significant respects' analogous to a case in which a doctor performs heart surgery on a patient, thus causing him pain but saving his life. I find this rather surprising. After all, by performing the operation, the doctor presumably *increases* both total and average welfare, and possibly equality. On the other hand, by having the child with less welfare rather than the child with more, presumably the woman *decreases* both total and average welfare, and possibly equality.

[19] A further reason to suppose that Roberts is committed to the claim that E is worse is that she wants to include the value of equality in her theory of fairness. Arguably, F is more equal than E (depending on how we take this value to apply to variable populations; see Temkin 1993a: ch. 7). However, elsewhere Roberts proposes that personalism should be combined not with egalitarianism proper, but with a principle similar to leximin (Roberts 2002: 344−9). And it may be suggested that in terms of leximin, F is better than E because the worst off are better off in F. But this would be too swift. The reason why the worst off are better off in F is that those who are worst off in E do not exist in F. And it seems implausible to claim, as a general rule at least, that an outcome is better than another if it leaves out those who are worst off in the latter outcome.

individuals, even at the expense of many, many more happy ones. She questions 'the idea that we may permissibly make some individuals suffer rather dreadfully simply so that people to whom we owe nothing may eventually exist' (2004: 126).[20] However, there are three reasons why these comments fail to persuade me. First, Roberts's remarks seem to rely on some version of the Asymmetry, and I have already voiced my reservations about this doctrine. In particular, if we owe one group of possible future individuals 'nothing', why is it that we owe another group of possible future individuals—those who would be miserable—a great deal? Second, a version of the Problem of Extinction can easily be constructed in which the worst off do not suffer 'dreadfully', but only very moderately. And, finally, I simply continue to find the claim that it is worse to continue the existence of human kind very counterintuitive.

Let me briefly sum up my discussion of different person-affecting approaches to population ethics in the last few sections. Because a wide person-affecting prioritarian approach threatens to lead us to the Repugnant Conclusion, I have considered a number of alternative person-affecting principles that restrict the range of individuals to whom we owe concern. In effect these principles attempt to capture Narveson's Slogan. I have argued that none of the principles is plausible. All of them imply *versions* of the Repugnant Conclusion. All of them create several other problems. So none of these alternative person-affecting approaches seems to offer a viable option for the prioritarian seeking to avoid the Repugnant Conclusion.

9.9 Pluralist Prioritarianism and Transitivity

In this section, I want to examine the suggestion that prioritarianism should be combined with some further distributive principle in order to achieve a more suitable approach to population ethics. More precisely, the idea is that prioritarianism should be applied only to necessary individuals and this complementary principle only to contingent ones. If, then, this complementary principle does not generate various of the counterintuitive conclusions prioritarianism generates when applied to possible future individuals, then neither will the combined principle. At the same time, the advantages of prioritarianism will be preserved for necessary individuals.

For simplicity, I shall consider the suggestion that Outcome Welfare Prioritarianism should be joined with (an appropriate *ceteris paribus* version of) Total

---

[20] In this article, Roberts also considers versions of the Problem of Extinction that do not rely on the idea that miserable individuals can be traded off for happy ones.

Outcome Utilitarianism. Let us call the resulting view 'Pluralist Outcome Welfare Prioritarianism'. For reasons that have already surfaced in my discussion,
total utilitarianism may not be a better theory to apply to population ethics
than prioritarianism is. While the former does not imply the Super-repugnant
Conclusion, it is more vulnerable with respect to the Negative Repugnant
Conclusion. Nevertheless, the lesson to be learnt from studying Pluralist Outcome Welfare Prioritarianism can be generalized to cover other combinations
of views as well.

A problem with Pluralist Outcome Welfare Prioritarianism is that it violates
the transitivity of the betterness relation. To see this, compare the outcomes
represented in Figure 9.12.

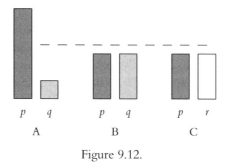

Figure 9.12.

The slashed line represents the average welfare in A. Since there are equal
numbers of individuals in these three outcomes, A holds a higher total than do
both B and C.

Now compare A and B. Since the same individuals exist in these two
outcomes, no one's existence is at stake. In other words, in this comparison, all
the people involved are necessary. So the benefits to p and q should be assessed
in accordance with prioritarianism. Although p loses slightly more in B than q
gains, q is worse off and so should be given priority. Therefore, B is at least as
good as A (in fact it is better).

When comparing B and C, we see that q exists in B, whereas r exists in
C. So their existences are at stake in this comparison. Therefore, the benefits
to them should be assessed in accordance with total utilitarianism. Since p is
equally well off in B and C, and the benefits to q in B count the same as the
benefits to r in C, C is at least as good as B (in fact they are equally good).

Since C is at least as good as B, and B is at least as good as A, transitivity
implies that C must be at least as good as A. But according to Pluralist Outcome
Welfare Prioritarianism, A might very well be better than C. Since q exists only

in A and *r* only in C, the benefits to these groups should count in agreement with utilitarianism. Although the benefit to *r* if C is brought about is greater than the benefit to *q* if A is brought about, *p* loses more in C than the difference between *r* and *q*. Furthermore, *p*'s gain from C to A counts with priority. We may imagine that *p* is still not very well off in C, such that all of this group's gain from C to A counts more than it would according to utilitarianism. (In terms of the graphics of Figure 9.13, this means that in A, *p* is at a level of welfare where the graph of the strictly concave (prioritarian) function is at least as steep as the graph of the linear (utilitarian) function.)

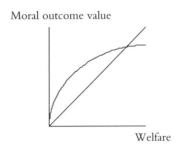

Figure 9.13.

Thus, not only is the gain in welfare larger if we go from C to A than if we go from A to C, it may even count for more than its actual size would suggest (of course, it may also count for *less*). Hence, the transitivity of the betterness relation is violated.

The reason why Pluralistic Outcome Welfare Prioritarianism generates intransitivity is that the weight it assigns to the welfare contained in an outcome depends upon the alternative outcome with which it is compared. The benefit that accrues to *q* in B may matter more when B is compared to A than when it is compared to C. This is because, when B is compared to A, *q* is taken to consist of necessary individuals that are entitled to priority, whereas when it is compared to C, it is taken to consist of contingent individuals, who are not thus entitled.

It may be objected that it is just the particular combination of prioritarianism and total utilitarianism that I have focused on that generates intransitivity. However, this is not so. As we have just seen, what generates the intransitivity is the fact that, in a particular outcome, the moral value of a benefit of a fixed size will depend upon which other outcome this outcome is compared to. More precisely, it will depend upon whether the benefit accrues to an individual who is necessary or contingent in the comparison. Since a pluralistic prioritarian approach consists in assessing benefits to necessary and contingent individuals differently (only the former can be assessed in terms of prioritarianism), any version of this approach will imply that the moral value of a particular benefit to an individual will depend on whether this individual, in the outcomes compared, is necessary or contingent. And so the feature that causes intransitivity will be present in all combinations of prioritarianism and utilitarianism.

Instead, it may be objected that if prioritarianism is combined, not with utilitarianism but with another principle, perhaps intransitivity can be avoided. However, this combination must also involve assessing benefits to necessary and contingent individuals differently. So, again, the feature that causes intransitivity is present. It seems, then, that intransitivities cannot be avoided.[21] More generally, intransitivities are likely to arise in many combined views that are applied to the issue of possible people, whether or not they include prioritarianism.

9.10 Reconsidering Our Intuitions

The wide person-affecting version of prioritarianism I have suggested implies the Repugnant and even the Super-repugnant Conclusions. I have considered various ways in which a prioritarian may attempt to avoid these conclusions. She may opt for a non-additive function, adopt an alternative person-affecting approach, or go for a pluralistic account. However, as I have argued, none of these options provides a viable alternative. Nor, of course, will it help the prioritarian to go for an impersonal account instead.

It seems, then, that we must address the Repugnant and the Super-repugnant Conclusions head on. In this section I consider only the former conclusion and then return to the latter conclusion in the next section. Not all theorists have found the Repugnant Conclusion repugnant (Attfield 1995: 162–9; Hare 1993: 68; Ryberg 1996: 172–4; 2004; Sikora 1978: 116–17; Tännsjö 1998: 160–3;

---

[21] It may be worth considering a view that is similar to, but nevertheless different from, Pluralistic Outcome Welfare Prioritarianism. Consider a restriction of the scope of prioritarianism such that this principle applies only to same-individual comparisons. Thus, prioritarianism should not be invoked at all in different-individual comparisons (this restriction differs from Pluralistic Outcome Welfare Prioritarianism, since the latter principle did apply prioritarianism (to necessary individuals) in different-individual comparisons). However, such a restriction of the scope of prioritarianism may easily lead to new intransitivities. After all, if prioritarianism is relevant only in comparisons that consist entirely of necessary individuals, and other principles are relevant when comparing outcomes that also consist of contingent individuals, the same outcome will vary in value when compared to various different outcomes. For a similar point, regarding other principles, see Temkin (1987: 170).

2002); and obviously if, on further reflection, the Repugnant Conclusion is acceptable, the fact that a wide person-affecting prioritarian approach invites this conclusion need not worry us after all.

We can, I think, distinguish between two versions of the view that the Repugnant Conclusion is not really repugnant. According to the first, once we fully understand what this conclusion amounts to, we cease to find it counterintuitive—or, at least, cease to find it *very* counterintuitive. According to the second version, while perhaps we continue to find it counterintuitive, certain theoretical considerations outweigh this intuition to such an extent that we should accept the conclusion.

The second of these options seems to me the most promising. To me the Repugnant Conclusion is stubbornly counterintuitive, especially in the version in which the lives in the more populous outcome are barely worth living because they last only, say, one minute, and consist in nothing but a slight pleasure; and, for that matter, in the version in which the more populous outcome holds a much lower average welfare because it is populated only by, for example, rabbits.

Let me, then, address the issue of counterintuitiveness first. If I understand him correctly, Torbjörn Tännsjö holds that the Repugnant Conclusion is not (very) counterintuitive. He writes:

> The view I am prepared to defend is somewhat pessimistic but still, I am afraid, realistic. My impression is that if only our basic needs are satisfied, then most of us are capable of living lives that, on balance, are worth experiencing. However, no matter how 'lucky' we are, how many 'gadgets' we happen to possess, we rarely reach beyond this level. If sometimes we do, this has very little to do with material affluence; rather, bliss, when it does occur, seems to be the ephemeral result of such things as requited infatuation, successful creative attempts and, of course, the proper administration of drugs. . . . Note also that many of the good things in life come with a price tag to be paid in terms of suffering. In many situations, we find ourselves momentarily below the line where our lives are worth living. Moreover, many people probably live lives that, on the whole, are worth not living. When this is acknowledged, the repugnant conclusion does not seem repugnant any more.   (Tännsjö 2002: 345)

Here, Tännsjö suggests that *our* lives are much like the lives of the individuals who inhabit B in Figure 9.1. He suggests that once we realize this, the Repugnant Conclusion ceases to seem repugnant. Since Tännsjö does not here refer to any theoretical reasons for accepting this conclusion, I shall assume that what he means is that the Repugnant Conclusion ceases to strike him as (very) counterintuitive.

What should we make of this argument?[22] I have elsewhere raised two objections (2002). First, Tännsjö's claims about our level of welfare seem to me to be not only somewhat, but *too* pessimistic. Thus it seems to me that my own life could be significantly worse than it actually is and yet worth living. However, Tännsjö has responded to this objection. He considers a case in which a person loses a limb and conjectures that in such a case, what will happen is that, after a while with low (in fact sub-zero) welfare, this person's welfare will again increase until it reaches its original level. To support this claim, he refers to conversations with people who have acquired (non-congenital) disabilities. He informs us that they have always reported that after a period with lower welfare, they have become as well off as they used to be (Tännsjö 2002: 347–9).

However, first, I am not sure that the available statistical evidence supports Tännsjö's claims about people with acquired disabilities (Brickman, Coates, and Janoff-Bulman 1978: 921). Second, it strikes me that the relevant question to pose is not whether these people have regained their original welfare level. Rather, it is whether, at some point after they acquired their disability, they have experienced a lower welfare level *and yet* found their life worth living. Finally, it seems to me that there is no particular reason to look to people with acquired disabilities to obtain the relevant evidence. In my own case, I can clearly recognize different periods in my life, some of which included higher welfare levels than others. I can also discern some periods in which my welfare has been lower than it has been on average over my life so far. And for what it is worth, it seems to me that at least some of these periods with below-average welfare have been intrinsically worth living.

My other objection to Tännsjö's argument for the intuitive acceptability of the Repugnant Conclusion is that he does not fully address what is repugnant about the Repugnant Conclusion. The repugnance lies in the combination of two features: the lives in B are barely worth living, *and* the lives in A are much better. Tännsjö only addresses the former, and this feature, taken by itself, is not repugnant (since whatever 'barely worth living' may turn out to involve, the lives in B *are* worth living). So it seems that Tännsjö does not explain away the repugnance.

Let me emphasize that I am not suggesting that it is *only* the difference in average welfare between A and B that renders the Repugnant Conclusion

---

[22] Incidentally, similar arguments appear in Attfield (1995: 162–9); Ryberg (1996: 164–74); and Sikora (1978: 116–17).

intuitively repugnant. To me, it makes an intuitive difference that the inhabitants of B have lives *barely worth living*. Had they had really great lives, and had the difference in average welfare between B and A been maintained, I would find the claim that B is better much less troubling. In fact, I would not find it troubling at all. (Incidentally, as we have seen, prioritarianism provides a nice partial explanation of why a 'repugnant' verdict at a higher level is more attractive.)

In response to my second objection, Tännsjö (2002: 350) has pointed out that he is quite prepared to focus on the comparison of A and B. He then points out that when he considers that (a) B might be pretty much like our world, (b) the Repugnant Conclusion is not considered repugnant at higher levels, and (c), according to Parfit, it takes ten billion individuals (rather than a lower number) in A to establish the Repugnant Conclusion, he does not find this conclusion repugnant. However, for those of us who consider the Repugnant Conclusion counterintuitive, these considerations may not help much. So I suggest that we examine the other sense in which the Repugnant Conclusion may be claimed not to be repugnant.

9.11 Should We Accept the Repugnant Conclusion?

Are there, then, other considerations that ease the acceptance of the Repugnant Conclusion, even if it is counterintuitive? I have argued that the person-affecting alternatives to the wide person-affecting approach are not very plausible. In fact, they strike me as less plausible than is the wide person-affecting approach, even if this approach is cashed out in terms of a principle (such as wide person-affecting prioritarianism) that leads us to the Repugnant Conclusion. Furthermore, it is not clear that there is a credible wide person-affecting distributive principle that avoids the repugnant verdict, and so perhaps we have overall reason to accept it?

A further theoretical reason for embracing the Repugnant Conclusion may be added. As Parfit and others have pointed out, if we deny this conclusion, we shall have to deny some very plausible judgements as well.[23] Consider Parfit's so-called Second Paradox, represented in Figure 9.14.

---

[23] See Arrhenius (2000), especially his second impossibility theorem (169–71); Kitcher (2000: 568–9); and Parfit (1986b: 156–60). Arrhenius, Kitcher, and Parfit, however, do not take their arguments to establish the acceptability of the Repugnant Conclusion. Tännsjö, on the other hand, does take such arguments to establish its acceptability.

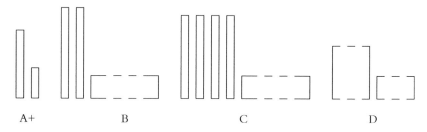

A+   B   C   D

Figure 9.14. Parfit's Second Paradox

In A+, there are two groups of individuals, both of which are very well off. Let us suppose that the least well-off group consists of the ten billion very happy individuals referred to in the Repugnant Conclusion (A in Figure 9.1). Furthermore, in A+, these individuals have an even higher level of welfare. Since A+ consists of this group at a higher level of welfare and a group that is even better off, we should claim that A+ is at least as good as A. Of course, it may be pointed out that A+ contains an inequality. However, even if we were to hold that equality has intrinsic value as, of course, I have argued that we should not, it is difficult to believe that the inequality contained in A+ would make this outcome worse than A. After all, everyone in A benefits and another group that is even better off comes into existence.

In B, everyone who exists in A+ is even better off than in A+, and they are now equally well off. Furthermore, a much greater number of individuals who are only slightly worse off than the worst off in A+, and so are in fact very well off, have been added. Here, we should claim that B is better than A+. Again, of course, the issue of equality may be invoked. It may be objected that the inequality in B is worse than the inequality in A+. But first, it is not clear that this is so.[24] And second, even if it were so, surely the disvalue of the additional inequality in B is outweighed by the fact that everyone in A+ is better (and equally well) off in B, and that the extra individuals in B have very worthwhile lives.

Now compare B and C. In a change from B to C, the best off would lose a little, but an equally large group of the worst off would gain a great deal. Clearly, then, C is better than B.

The rest of the argument involves mere repetition. By repeating the sorts of steps involved in the comparison of B and C a number of times, we reach

[24] As Parfit points out: while the gap between the best- and the worst-off individuals is slightly greater in B than in A+, only a small percentage of the individuals in B are better off than the rest are. Relative to the population size, nearly everyone is equally well off. In A+, though, half the population is better off than the other half is (1986b: 156).

the judgement that D is better than C. Then we reiterate the whole process, starting from D. Like A+, D consists of two groups, one of which is better off than the other. Only in D, the best-off group is worse off than the best-off group in A+, and the worst-off group is worse off than the worst-off group, also in A+. Therefore, by reiterating the process we end up with two groups, where the best-off group is worse off than the best-off group in D, and the worst-off group is worse off than the worst-off group in D. For the same reason as D is better than A+, this new outcome is better than D. And by further employing this process a number of times, we end up with everyone at the level where life is barely worth living. And since each move in the process has resulted in a better outcome, we end up with the claim that this last outcome is better than A+, which in turn is at least as good as A. Thus, we end up with the Repugnant Conclusion (Parfit 1986b: 156–60).

To reject this argument, we shall either have to deny that one improves an outcome by increasing the welfare of everyone and adding new happy individuals (as in the move from A+ to B), or deny that one improves an outcome by slightly decreasing the welfare of the best off while simultaneously greatly increasing the welfare of an equal number of worst off (as in the move from B to C). This is the crux of Parfit's Second Paradox, which suggests a further reason to accept the Repugnant Conclusion.

We should also consider the impact of what I called the Inadequate Comprehension Factor in Chapter 4 (Section 4.12). In that chapter, I argued that perhaps we are unable to fully fathom (except maybe abstractly) how much value would be realized by a large number of continuers. This may be part of the reason we find the Repugnant Conclusion about Self-interest counterintuitive. Likewise, we may be unable to fathom fully how much value would be obtained in an outcome in which a huge number of individuals have lives barely worth living. To the extent that we cannot fathom this, our intuitions about the Repugnant Conclusion are unreliable. Perhaps, then, we overestimate the repugnance of the Repugnant Conclusion.

Even if we were to accept the Repugnant Conclusion, what about the Super-repugnant Conclusion, which is also implied by the wide person-affecting version of prioritarianism? Here, total utilitarians may be eager to point out that at least their view does not entail *such* a counterintuitive conclusion. Total utilitarians will, of course, not prefer an outcome that not only contains a lower average of welfare, but also a lower total. Indeed, what intuitively appealing reason could there be to prefer an outcome in which everyone has a life barely worth living, to an outcome in which everyone is very well off if the former outcome holds a *lower* total of welfare?

It seems to me that there actually is such a reason that has some intuitive merit. Consider again Figure 9.1. While in A, everyone has a very worthwhile life, there are many individuals who never get anything; for instance, all the additional individuals in B. They are deprived of something they would otherwise have had. Just as an individual who dies prematurely is deprived of something he would otherwise have had. Therefore, there is a sense in which B may be claimed to be more *just* than A. More individuals get a share of the goods (the goods being, of course, welfare). And this will be so even if B were to hold a somewhat lower total of welfare than A.[25]

A further consideration is that the number of individuals required in B to counterbalance the value of A will depend on the particular prioritarian function assumed. The more priority we give to the worse off, the fewer individuals are required in B to render this outcome better than A.[26] So one way of softening the implications of prioritarianism with respect to the Super-repugnant Conclusion is to assign less priority to the worse off. But this suggestion may of course be less plausible in other moral spheres than it is in population ethics. We will then be assigning less priority to the worse off among existing individuals.

While there may be theoretical reasons for accepting the Repugnant and even the Super-repugnant Conclusions, I still find these conclusions rather counterintuitive. In fact, I find them counterintuitive to an extent such that it is difficult to simply condone a principle that implies their acceptance. Of course, the latter, more counterintuitive conclusion can be avoided if, for example, we adopt total utilitarianism rather than prioritarianism, but then again prioritarianism compares favourably with total utilitarianism with respect to the Negative Repugnant Conclusion, the Weak Asymmetry, and the explanation of why repugnant conclusions are less repugnant at higher levels. So it is not clear that this is a trade worth making, even if we confine ourselves to population ethics.

More generally, the problem is that there does not seem to be any principle that deals entirely convincingly with the issue of possible individuals. This leaves us with three options. First, we may argue that a particular principle

---

[25] It may be objected that the more people we cause to exist, the greater the number of possible individuals there will be. And since we increase the pool of possible individuals, we also add to the number of possible individuals who will *not* exist. However, we may instead assume a non-dynamic notion of 'possible individuals', such as all the individuals who could have come into existence since, say, the Big Bang. On this conception of possible individuals, we do not increase the class of merely possible individuals by having more children; quite to the contrary in fact.

[26] More technically, the steeper the graph of the strictly concave prioritarian function at low levels of welfare, and the more it flattens out at high levels (see Figure 9.13), the fewer individuals are required in B.

should be accepted because, while in some ways counterintuitive, it is at least less counterintuitive than the alternative views. If so, the wide person-affecting version of prioritarianism I have developed here may not be a bad candidate.

Second, we may give up the aim of providing a general account of population ethics and limit our distributive principles to same number comparisons. This would involve 'quarantining' different number choices, as Parfit (2004b: 257) puts it, in the application of our distributive principles. That move is, of course, also available for prioritarians, who will then avoid the commitment to the Repugnant and the Super-repugnant Conclusions. Furthermore, it does give us a *partial* theory of population ethics, because it allows us to compare different populations as long as they do not differ in their size. Nevertheless, it is not a very attractive move either, both because, on a theoretical level, it is unsatisfactory, and, on a more practical level, we cannot fully assess moral challenges such as global poverty and global warming unless we know how to compare different number populations. In fact, we cannot even claim that in the Problem of Suffering, it is worse to bring the miserable population about.

Third, we may temporarily limit our distributive principles to same number comparisons while continuing the search for a better account of population ethics. As we have seen, any such account should imply that the welfare of new individuals contributes to the value of outcomes, and in doing so, it should not exclude specific, modal classes of possible future individuals. Furthermore, I believe that it should incorporate the Wide Person-affecting Principle when explaining the value of outcomes. We may even make predictions about some of the implications it *must* have; for example, it must imply that it is worse to bring about the miserable population in the Problem of Suffering. This is in some ways a more attractive choice than the second option, although it is most of all an expression of the hope that a better theory can be found.

Now, it is of course difficult to predict the extent to which such a more developed welfare function in population ethics will be compatible with prioritarianism, but it is worth noting that it may well be compatible in the same sort of way that, as we have seen, a prioritarian can integrate an average function or a Variable Value View in her prioritarian commitments.

9.12 Summary and a Look Ahead

The wide person-affecting approach to prioritarianism I have developed in this chapter implies the Repugnant Conclusion. In fact, it even implies the

Super-repugnant Conclusion. I have therefore considered various ways in which a prioritarian may attempt to avoid these conclusions. She may opt for a non-additive function; an alternative person-affecting approach (one that captures Narveson's Slogan); or a pluralist approach. However, as I have pointed out, none of these alternatives seems particularly promising.

In light of these findings, I have reconsidered the repugnancy of the Repugnant and the Super-repugnant Conclusions. I have discussed the claim that, while perhaps we cannot make their counterintuitiveness go away, maybe we should accept these conclusions. With respect to the Repugnant Conclusion, I have offered three reasons for this. First, there seem to be no viable alternatives that do not imply the Repugnant Conclusion. Second, there is a train of reasoning that leads to this conclusion on the basis of some very plausible premises. And third, our intuitions about the Repugnant Conclusion may be influenced by the Inadequate Comprehension Factor, and if so, they are to some extent unreliable.

With respect to the Super-repugnant Conclusion, I have argued that while the wide person-affecting prioritarian approach I have developed implies this conclusion, it has more plausible implications than, for example, total utilitarianism when it comes to the Negative Repugnant Conclusion, the Weak Asymmetry, and the explanation of why repugnant conclusions are less repugnant at higher levels. Furthermore, I have suggested that there is a sense in which it may be claimed to be more just if extra individuals come into existence. And finally, our intuitions about the Super-repugnant Conclusion may also be influenced by the Inadequate Comprehension Factor.

All this leaves us with three options. Either we adopt a principle of population ethics on the basis that it is the best (or perhaps rather least bad) choice. If so, prioritarianism may not be a bad candidate. Or we simply claim that the Repugnant and the Super-repugnant Conclusions are too counterintuitive to be acceptable and so limit our distributive principle(s)—including prioritarianism—to same number comparisons. Or we combine this last claim with a further search for a plausible account of population ethics, while perhaps predicting and integrating in our current reflections on moral problems some of the implications it must have. Unfortunately, all three alternatives have their drawbacks, and there seems to be room for reasonable disagreement over which to favour.

In the last few chapters I have discussed some issues in distributive justice on the assumption that outcome value is a function only of welfare. However, as I argued in Chapters 3 and 4, self-interest depends not just on welfare but also on Relation M. Therefore, in order for our theory of outcome value to accommodate our self-interests fully, we need an account of the impact of Relation M on outcome value. It is to this task, then, that I turn in Chapter 10.

10

Metaphysics and Justice

10.1 Prudence and Morality

Moral theorists have sometimes suggested that a plausible theory in normative ethics must be built on an account of human nature. For example, Aristotle (1955) held that it is in the nature of human beings to have certain potentials and that insofar as they realize them, they flourish. And Kant (1965) believed that the moral law can be derived from an account of our nature as rational beings. More recently, and less ambitiously, Rawls (1971) argued that a set of principles of justice is justified insofar as this set is what free, equal, and rational people would agree on in a hypothetical choice situation.

In the present chapter, I want to explore some implications of the metaphysics of personal identity and what matters for distributive justice. My aim is not, in any straightforward sense, to try to *derive* any conclusions about justice from metaphysical facts. Rather, what I want to do is to suggest that the significance we attach to certain facts about our survival, in combination with various other normative judgements, indicate some particular views about distributive justice.

More specifically, what I want to do is to consider the implications of my account of self-interest for my account of distributive justice; that is, the implications of the Prudential View for Overall Outcome Welfare Prioritarianism. How is the Prudential View relevant for my account of justice? Remember that according to the Prudential View, an individual has a present self-interest in a future benefit only if she is M-related to the beneficiary, where the strength of her self-interest equals the size of the benefit, appropriately discounted for reductions in Relation M.

In the account of justice I have given so far, I have ignored the fact that self-interest is a function not just of welfare but also of Relation M. I have done so because I did not want to introduce too many complicating factors all at once. However, it is now time to rectify this omission. I shall begin by arguing that if we hold the Prudential View, we should reject the traditional view that moral rules apply only to conflicts of interest between different individuals. Rather, while an individual's future benefits may not be fully accommodated by her present self-interests, they are fully accommodated by morality. Among other things, this means that our distributive principles, including prioritarianism, apply even to single-individual outcomes.

I shall then consider the view, suggested by Parfit, that if we are reductionists with respect to personal identity, we should give less weight to distribution-sensitive principles. Obviously, this claim threatens my defence of prioritarianism. I have endorsed reductionism in Chapter 3 (Section 3.4) and prioritarianism is obviously distribution-sensitive. However, I shall argue that reductionism is in fact quite compatible with distribution-sensitivity.

I then turn to the issue of the temporal unit of distributive concern. Prioritarians claim that we should give priority to the worse off, but we need to know what the temporal scope of this claim is. An individual may be worse off *now* than another is, but not be worse off when we focus on their *entire lives*. Most political philosophers have focused on whole lives and, presumably, this is because they believe that even if an individual is worse off than another at a particular time, if she is better off at other times, this may compensate her. Thus, if an individual now has, say, two more units of welfare than another, and the other will later have two more units than the former, there is no more reason now to benefit one rather than the other.

However, I shall argue that if we accept the Prudential View, we should revise this account of compensation. To assess the sort of compensation taking place within a life, we should sometimes discount the value of benefits, namely to the extent that Relation M holds to a reduced degree. On the basis of this alternative account of compensation, I develop a principle that I call Prudential Prioritarianism. Prudential Prioritarianism provides an account of how to distribute welfare as well as M-relations. Roughly, it claims that the weaker an individual's self-interest at t in the benefits that occur in his life (or rather, M-relation), the greater the value of a further benefit at t and/or an increase in the strength of the M-relation that links him to benefits at other times. Furthermore, I suggest that in various ways this account is more plausible than alternative prioritarian accounts of the temporal unit of distributive concern.

In light of my inconclusive reflections on the prospects for applying prioritarianism to different number comparisons in the last chapter, I shall not attempt to develop a prudential prioritarian account of such comparisons. While this account would have implications that, in some respects, differ from those of Overall Outcome Welfare Prioritarianism, it would also imply the Repugnant and the Super-repugnant Conclusions. Therefore, it would not add further clarity to the issue. Yet, towards the end of the chapter, I shall consider the implications of Prudential Prioritarianism for the issue of abortion and, here, it will make a difference what our view is on population ethics. Therefore, I shall consider the implications of the options with which I ended Chapter 9, including that of applying prioritarianism to different number comparisons. However, for the purposes of this discussion, we need only a rudimentary account of what Prudential Prioritarianism would imply.

Prudential Prioritarianism deviates from the welfarist framework I developed in Chapter 6. There are several reasons for this. It implies that outcome value is a function not just of welfare but also of Relation M. Furthermore, it does not satisfy the Wide Person-affecting Principle. More importantly, it does not satisfy the Strong Wide Person-affecting Principle, which I invoked in my criticism of egalitarianism. Therefore, I develop an alternative principle—the Prudential Person-affecting Principle—and show how this principle can be motivated by my account of self-interest. Importantly, just like the Strong Wide Person-affecting Principle, this principle is hostile to egalitarianism. Finally, I shall point out that while Prudential Prioritarianism is not a welfarist principle, it is compatible with a fairly similar doctrine, namely what I call 'self-interestism'.

10.2 Expanding the Scope of Morality

Sometimes morality is conceived of as a set of rules designed to settle conflicts of interest between different individuals. This conception has several sources, including the idea that moral rules are the constraints rational individuals would impose on themselves and each other to achieve interpersonal cooperation and protection from harm in an attempt to maximize their own expected welfare (Gauthier 1986: 9), and the idea that issues of justice arise only when individuals are cooperating for mutual advantage (Rawls 1971: 84). However, I now want to suggest that the views on prudence and morality I have defended so far imply that morality applies even to outcomes in which there exists only one individual. In such outcomes, of course, there is no inter-personal conflict of interests.

According to the Prudential View, an individual's present self-interest in a future benefit is reduced when Relation M is reduced between her (relevant) present physical and psychological states and her (relevant) physical and psychological states at the time of the benefit. Thus, it may be in her present self-interest to receive a smaller benefit sooner rather than a larger benefit later. This, though, does not imply that *morally* the later benefit matters less. After all, it is in this individual's *future* self-interest that the later rather than the earlier benefit accrues to her. So this individual has different and competing self-interests at different times. The question, then, is how to accommodate these competing self-interests in our (moral) theory of outcomes.

Suppose that I choose to spend all of my income as I earn it and so not to save for my retirement. Let us assume that I thus ensure for myself a high welfare until I retire, but also render myself worse off in my old age than I would have been had I in fact saved. Let us further assume that had I saved for my retirement, my lifetime sum of welfare would have been higher. And let us make the Additive Assumption about Benefits. With these assumptions, the Identity View implies that my choice of spending all of my income rather than saving is prudentially objectionable. It is in my self-interest to save. But this need not be so according to the Prudential View. To see this, let us finally assume that, since Relation M reduces over time, and my old age lies in the further future, the present discounted value of my future had I saved for my retirement is smaller than the present discounted value of my actual future, in which I do not save. It is then in my present self-interest *not* to save for my retirement.

Consider also another example. Suppose that by smoking, I reduce my lifetime sum of welfare because I develop cancer in my old age. According to the Identity View, it is then in my present self-interest to quit smoking. However, again, the Prudential View may suggest otherwise. Since the harm that accrues to me when I develop cancer lies in the further future (we may assume), perhaps its discounted value is outweighed by the discounted value of the pleasure I take in smoking.

However, it still seems that my present choices of not saving for my retirement and smoking are objectionable. And indeed I think they may well be, only the objection should be made in moral rather than in prudential terms. Whereas the Prudential View fails to accommodate fully my future benefits in my present self-interests, these benefits are fully accommodated by morality (Parfit 1984: 319). This requires a bit of explaining.

Morality requires some kind of impartiality (I have considered and endorsed various kinds in Chapter 6, Section 6.6). Usually, a moral requirement of impartiality is applied only to conflicts between different individuals, but the Prudential View provides a case for applying it intra-personally as well. Since my present self-interest does not reflect the full value of a future benefit (because my present self-interest only reflects its *discounted* value), the full value of the benefit should be catered for in moral terms. More precisely, morally we should be impartial concerning my present self-interests and my future self-interests. After all, my present self-interest discounts the value of the future benefit to the extent that, between me now and me at the time of the benefit, Relation M obtains to a reduced degree. And to the extent that this relation obtains to a reduced degree, from my present prudential point of view, it is *as if* the benefit accrued not to me but to someone else. So the case for requiring inter-personal impartiality extends to the intra-personal sphere. Therefore, I suggest that our theory of outcomes should differ from our theory of self-interest in that it is temporally impartial in a sense in which the Prudential View is not.

Here, though, we need to be careful. As I explained in Chapter 4 (Section 4.8), the Prudential View is not time-relative, it is M-relative. It discounts benefits not according to their temporal location but according to their location in the M-relation, so to speak. However, there is also a sense in which the Prudential View is temporally partial, namely that an individual's present self-interests are based on how her *present* physical and psychological states (or those relevant for Relation M) are related to her states at the time of the benefit. Thus, the discount rate applied to benefits varies with physical and psychological deviations from such present states. Our theory of outcomes, on the other hand, should be impartial concerning the prudential perspectives an individual has at different times. With respect to our present moral ranking of outcomes, my future self-interest in having an income after I retire is just as important as my present self-interest in having a larger income now (which is not to say that they should count the same, one reason being they may have different strengths).

If we accept the Prudential View, we should expand the scope of morality such that it covers the territory abandoned by prudence. And since morality thus applies within lives as well as across lives, it should not be conceived of as concerned only with the conflicting interests of distinct individuals.

I shall not elaborate further on the idea that if we hold the Prudential View, impartiality implies that our distributive principles apply intra-personally. But let me briefly suggest that the idea of impartiality invoked here cannot be captured by anonymity, according to which the value of an outcome is not affected by the permutation of benefits over individuals who exist in that outcome. Admittedly, we could extend the scope of this requirement such that it applies within lives as well as between lives. According to this suggestion, the value of an outcome will not be affected by a permutation of an individual's welfare over time. Yet, for reasons that are to be elaborated in a later section, I do not favour this particular way of extending the scope of impartiality. It is in conflict with the idea that a benefit that falls at one time in an individual's life may provide better compensation for her misfortunes than a similar benefit that falls at another time.

Nevertheless, I believe that ultimately we should revise the requirement of anonymity and perhaps the revised requirement *can* be applied to the intra-personal case. Why should the requirement be revised? Assuming the Prudential View, we may hold that it is better if one individual has a particular welfare profile than if another individual has this same profile, simply because their lives differ regarding the sort of physical and psychological unity they exhibit. That is, differences in the M–relations contained in these lives may explain why a permutation of benefits over those individuals in fact would affect the value of an outcome. I shall elaborate on this later.

I have now contended that if we hold the Prudential View, we should claim that morality applies intra-personally. Furthermore, there is another argument for this claim that is implicit in what I have said in previous chapters. I have suggested that, according to prioritarianism, what has intrinsic value is the compound state of affairs that consists in the state that a benefit of a certain size befalls an individual, and the state that the individual is at a particular welfare level. And it may be suggested that since such compound states have intrinsic value, they have it even in outcomes that include only one individual (McKerlie 2001: 284). Of course, even if these states are good for their own sakes, it does not *follow* that they are good whenever they obtain. But unless we can think of a plausible explanation of why they should *cease* to have such value in the relevant sort of settings, it does seem to be a reasonable conclusion to draw. So prioritarianism may provide us with further grounds to hold that single-individual outcomes have not only prudential value, but also moral value.

10.3 Prudence and Priority

I have suggested that the Prudential View drives a wedge between prudence and morality in the sense that, unlike morality, prudence is not impartial between self-interests held at different times. I now want to propose that the other main normative view I have defended in this book, namely prioritarianism, may drive a further wedge between morality and prudence. Again, this requires a bit of explaining.

To specify fully our prioritarian commitments, we need to settle on a temporal unit of distributive concern. That is, we need to specify the temporal part of an individual's life we should focus on when determining the value of a further benefit to her. I have a great deal to say about the temporal unit of distributive concern later in this chapter, but for now let me briefly mention two possible views. The temporal unit usually thought relevant to distributive justice is whole lives (Arneson 1989: 85; Daniels 1996a: 259–64; Dworkin 1981b: 304–5; Nagel 1991: 69; Rawls 1971: 78). And applied to prioritarianism, this gives us:

> *Whole Lives Prioritarianism.* The lower the sum of welfare in a life, the greater the value of a further benefit.

Note that, like the other views about the temporal unit of prioritarian concern I shall consider, this principle does not amount to a fully-fledged prioritarian principle. This is because it does not say anything about how to aggregate the contributions of different individuals to determine the value of an outcome. Rather, what this principle does is to specify how exactly the moral value of a benefit to an individual depends on *that* individual's welfare. Nevertheless, as is specified in Overall Outcome Welfare Prioritarianism, individual contributions are to be summed up to reach an overall assessment of an outcome's value.

Whole Lives Prioritarianism implies that there is a difference between the sum of welfare in a life and this life's prioritarian value. When assessing its prioritarian value, benefits are *weighted*. Now, let us for a moment assume the Identity View, according to which a present self-interest in a benefit depends only on the benefit's size. And let us make the Additive Assumption about Benefits. These assumptions are not necessary to make the points I want to make, but they simplify the discussion. Thus, the larger a sum of benefits an individual has in an outcome, the stronger his self-interest is in this outcome. Therefore, because prioritarianism weights benefits and the Identity View does not, there is a difference between an individual's self-interest in an outcome and this outcome's prioritarian value, even if he is the only individual who exists in the outcome.

Nevertheless, Whole Lives Prioritarianism also implies that in an ordering of outcomes that includes only one and the same individual (henceforth, 'same-individual outcomes'), one outcome is better than is another if and only if it has a higher total of welfare. This is because, according to Whole Lives Prioritarianism, an extra benefit to an individual always improves the value of a same-individual outcome (although the size of the improvement varies). So the prioritarian ordinal ordering of same-individual outcomes coincides with the prudential ordinal ordering.

But now consider:

> *Time-slice Prioritarianism.* The lower the sum of welfare in a life at a particular point in time t, the greater the value of a further benefit at t.

Unlike Whole Lives Prioritarianism, Time-slice Prioritarianism does not generate an ordinal ordering of same-individual outcomes equal to that generated simply by summing up welfare. Suppose that we can either provide a smaller benefit for an individual at a time at which she is worse off, or a greater benefit for her at a time at which she is better off. Since the latter benefit is greater in size, it contributes more total welfare. However, the smaller benefit would fall at a lower level, and so according to Time-slice Prioritarianism, it may well have a higher moral value. Therefore, Time-slice Prioritarianism may favour the slighter benefit, whereas prudence favours the larger. And so again prudence and morality may diverge, even in same-individual outcomes.[1]

10.4 Metaphysics and Distribution-sensitivity

Having now explored some differences between prudence and morality, I want to turn to the suggestion that my account of the former poses a problem for my account of the latter. Thus, in *Reasons and Persons*, Parfit argues that if we are reductionists with respect to personal identity, this indicates that we should revise our distributive principles in two respects. Insofar as our principles are distribution-sensitive, they should have a greater scope (Parfit 1984: 332–4). So if we are egalitarians, we should be concerned about inequalities *within* lives as well as between lives. I have conceded this point. I have argued that if we accept the Prudential View, we should apply the moral requirement of impartiality both inter- and intra-personally. Thus, we should be concerned not just with how an individual fares over his entire life, but also with how he fares at particular times in his life. And there may be a case for redistribution not just between lives but also within lives. I shall elaborate further on this point in the following sections.

The second revision Parfit (1984: 334–45) proposes is that our distribution-sensitive principles should have less weight. It is sometimes complained that utilitarianism implies that there is no moral difference between decreasing an individual's welfare at one time to increase her welfare at another time, and decreasing one individual's welfare to increase another individual's welfare. This is the crux of Rawls's (1971: 27) complaint that utilitarianism does not take seriously the distinction between persons. The moral difference between these two kinds of redistribution is claimed to be that while an increase in an

---

[1] Furthermore, when applied to uncertain prospects, prioritarianism is a source of a further wedge between prudence and morality; see Rabinowicz (2002: 15–17).

individual's welfare can compensate her for a decrease that occurs to her at a different time, she cannot be compensated by an increase in *someone else's* welfare. Compensation presupposes personal identity.

What Parfit suggests is that if we are reductionists, we consider the fact of personal identity less deep than if we are non-reductionists. And since this fact is presupposed by compensation, we may regard compensation as less important (Parfit 1984: 338). Imagine an individual now suffers a decrease in his welfare. If the relation in virtue of which he is identical over time is less deep, a future increase may offer less by way of compensation. Therefore, it may be less important that it is *he* who is compensated. And if compensation matters less, the objection that utilitarianism is insensitive to it may have less weight (Parfit 1984: 342). More precisely, this objection has less weight than it would have if non-reductionism were true.

Now consider distribution-sensitive principles such as egalitarianism or prioritarianism. Suppose we can help one of two individuals. We can provide a larger increase in the first individual's welfare, but it is the second individual who has suffered most in the past. As egalitarians or prioritarians, we may believe that it would be better to help the second individual. However, if we are reductionists, we may be less inclined to hold this belief. We may give less weight to compensation and so to the thought that if we help the second individual, we compensate him for his past misery. And so we may give less weight to distribution-sensitive principles (again, less weight than we would if we held a non-reductionist theory of personal identity).

Obviously, these claims about the virtues of utilitarianism and the vices of distribution-sensitive principles threaten my defence of prioritarianism. This is especially true since I have myself endorsed a reductionist account of personal identity.

Before I address this problem for prioritarianism, it may be helpful to distinguish between two kinds of compensation: compensation *at a time*, and compensation *over time*. Compensation at a time occurs if some increase in welfare compensates me for a simultaneous decrease in welfare (say, if an unpleasant cold sensation in my one hand is compensated by a pleasant warm sensation in my other hand). Compensation over time occurs if an increase in welfare at one time compensates me for a decrease in welfare at a different time. Both kinds of compensation may be thought to be threatened by reductionism. Consider compensation at a time. The unity between different simultaneous mental states may be claimed to be deeper if, say, these states somehow 'are had' by an immaterial soul, than if they merely are tied together by various physical and psychological relations that obtain between them. However, the greatest threat seems to be not to compensation at a time, but to compensation over time. After all, between times, there are various discontinuities even in a single mind. Memories fade, plans change, and brain cells are replaced. Therefore, if I can argue that it is possible to compensate over time, the possibility of compensation at a time will seem to follow. And this is what I shall argue.

Note that Parfit's case for utilitarianism consists in arguing that there is a particular *objection* to this view that may be less weighty than some of us have assumed, namely the objection that utilitarianism considers compensation irrelevant to distribution. But of course, to claim that a particular objection has less weight does not suffice to establish utilitarianism. Compensation may nevertheless have *enough* weight. And even if we were successfully to argue that the objection has no force at all, utilitarianism does not follow. As Broome (1991: 50) remarks, we need to know why utilitarianism should be the natural 'fall back' position, once weight is removed from compensation and distribution-sensitive principles.

Let me elaborate on the point about compensation. As various commentators have been eager to point out, Parfit's claims about the 'depth' of personal identity do not rule out that, even assuming reductionism, our lives contain enough unity over time to make compensation possible and distribution-sensitivity desirable (Daniels 1996b: 124; Korsgaard 1989: 128–9; Scheffler 1982b: 238; Schultz 1986: 732). Thus, the claim that compensation and distribution-sensitivity have less weight, means that they have less weight than if a non-reductionist account of personal identity had been true. And as Parfit (1984: 342) emphasizes, this is compatible with their having *some* weight.

Furthermore, Parfit's argument is compatible with our holding a distribution-sensitive principle such as prioritarianism as a full-blown theory of outcomes. This may seem paradoxical. If our distribution-sensitive principles should have *less* weight, how can such a principle be our only principle? But in fact there is no paradox. Prioritarianism may be less plausible than if a non-reductionist account of personal identity had been true. But it may still be the only principle that has enough credibility to be acceptable.

Finally, and most importantly, a version of prioritarianism may be devised that fully accommodates the limits reductionism imposes on compensation, as I shall argue in Section 10.6.

Having made these somewhat general points, it is worth pausing to consider the particular relation that provides a life with the sort of unity necessary for prudential significance. I have argued that this relation is Relation M, the continuous physical realization of core and distinctive psychology. Is this relation compatible with compensation over time? According to the Prudential View for which I have argued, it clearly is. This view claims that present self-interest is a function of discounted benefits, where benefits are discounted to the extent that, between the bearer of the self-interest and the recipient, Relation M holds to a reduced degree. Admittedly, the Prudential View may imply that a present reduction in an individual's welfare is not compensated by a later increase of the same size, namely insofar as Relation M obtains to a reduced degree. Nevertheless, if only the future benefit is large enough, its discounted value will equal the size of the present decrease. And since the discounted value of the increase equals the value of the decrease, in terms of this individual's present self-interests, it makes up for it. In other words, compensation is possible.

Interestingly, the Prudential View implies that the weaker the M-relation, the more difficult it is to compensate. That is, the weaker the M-relation, the larger a later increase in welfare would have to be to compensate a present decrease. Thus, it will be more difficult to compensate individuals who exhibit less continuity of distinctive psychology. For example, it will be more difficult to compensate most non-human animals than most humans. I shall return to this issue later.

Besides the claims discussed thus far, Parfit (1984: 342–5) also considers the stronger claim that reductionism altogether *demolishes* the possibility of compensation. Thus, he examines the proposal that compensation presupposes not only personal identity, but also what personal identity consists in if non-reductionism is true; for example, the continued existence of a soul. With this suggestion, we should altogether abandon our distribution-sensitive principles.

In *Reasons and Persons*, Parfit takes both the claim that we should give less (but some) weight to distribution-sensitive principles, and the claim that we should abandon them to be defensible. However, in a later article, he contends that the stronger claim about the implications of reductionism is not only defensible but also true (1986a: 837–43). He asks us to consider a branch-line version of the case of teletransportation. A computer here on earth records the exact states of all your cells and transmits this information to a computer on Mars, where a replica of you is assembled. Unlike in the original case of teletransportation, you are not destroyed here on earth. Now suppose that as you enter the teletransporter, you receive quite a strong electrical shock. The scientist in charge tells you that he is terribly sorry but that, unfortunately, this sometimes happens. However, he assures you that you will be compensated for your pain. In fact, he has already sent a message to Mars, informing the Mars-division to pay a large sum of money to your replica. Presumably, you will protest that *you* should have the money. In fact, most of us believe that the cheque received by your replica does not compensate *you*.

Now, according to reductionism, the reason you are not identical to your replica is that the causal relations between the two of you are abnormal. This is because there is no (or little) physical continuity, which is relevant according to some criteria of personal identity, and because there is a better candidate for being you. Nevertheless, Parfit suggests that when we believe that you are not compensated, this is not because the causal relations are abnormal but because you are not *identical* to your replica. What this shows is that we do not believe in reductionism. We assume that identity consists in something other than physical and psychological continuities. More importantly, since we believe that the reason you are not compensated is that identity does not obtain, we must consider this further fact that we take identity to consist in necessary for compensation. Or so Parfit argues (1986a: 842).

Even if we thus reject the possibility of compensation over time, we may still apply distribution-sensitive principles to the welfare of individuals at particular points in time. Parfit (1984: 344) suggests that if we do so, these principles will roughly coincide with negative utilitarianism; that is, with the view that an outcome is better, the smaller the sum of negative welfare it contains. However, this is not quite right. Consider Time-slice Prioritarianism. According to this principle, the lower the sum of welfare in a life at a particular point in time, the greater the value of a further benefit at that time. In this principle's most plausible version, it does not claim that it is always more important to reduce negative welfare than to increase positive. While it is more important to increase the welfare of individuals at times where they have overall negative welfare, if we can provide greater increases for individuals at times where they have overall positive welfare, the fact that the increase is larger for the latter individuals may outweigh the fact that it falls at a higher level.

However, since I believe that it is possible to compensate over time, I shall not dwell on this issue. Parfit's strongest argument for the impossibility of inter-temporal compensation appeals to the branch-line version of the case of teletransportation. He argues that the reason we believe that it does not allow for compensation is that we consider that compensation requires personal identity in the non-reductionist sense. I now want to offer a different reason why benefits to your replica do not compensate you. I have argued that the relation that prudentially matters is Relation M. And since there is not much, if any, physical continuity between you and your replica, there is no continuous physical realization of relevant psychology. Therefore, Relation M does not obtain between your replica and you. And since Relation M does not obtain, according to the Prudential View, you have no self-interest in his benefits. This is why benefits to him do not compensate you.

If, on the other hand, we consider a case of brain division in which each of your cerebral hemispheres receive a new body, the Prudential View implies that compensation is possible. After all, Relation M obtains between you and each of your continuers. Now suppose that before the transplant, you receive an electrical shock but you are also informed that, after the transplant, one of your continuers will receive a large sum of money. Are you thus compensated? I believe that you are (at least if the sum is large enough compared to the pain). In fact, I have already argued that this sort of compensation is possible. When considering various cases of brain division in Chapter 4 (Section 4.3), I suggested that we would be willing to go through some amount of displeasure to ensure a favoured distribution of benefits and harms among our continuers, and that we would be willing to do so for purely prudential reasons. This is because we believe that we are compensated for our initial burden.

Therefore, I believe that we are justified in thinking that reductionism is compatible with both compensation and distribution-sensitivity. Furthermore, the proposal that it is not compatible is a very radical one and it would force us to change many of our deepest beliefs about how we should live our lives. For example, every day, we all make sacrifices to ensure future benefits for ourselves and it would be deeply surprising if these acts could not be justified in prudential terms. In conclusion, it seems to me that we have not been given a good reason to think compensation impossible. Therefore, we have not been given a good reason to abandon our prioritarian commitments.

10.5 The Compensation Argument

I have suggested that distribution-sensitivity relies on compensation. And I have just argued that the Prudential View allows for the possibility of compensation, both at a time and over time. Therefore, we are not restricted to a principle that allows only for compensation *at a time*, such as Time-slice Prioritarianism. However, this conclusion does not entail any particular account of the temporal unit of distributive concern. That is, it does not answer the question of what temporal part of an individual's life we should focus on when determining the value of a further benefit to her.

Nevertheless, when answering this question, my discussion of compensation may turn out to be highly relevant. Thus, the idea that distribution-sensitivity relies on compensation over time has been used to motivate whole lives as the appropriate temporal unit of distributive concern (see, for example, Nagel 1979b: 120). Consider the outcome represented in Table 10.1.

Table 10.1.

A	T_1	T_2	Total
a	2	4	6
b	4	2	6

Let me explain how this table should be read. It represents an outcome in which the welfare of two individuals is distributed on temporal segments. Thus, A consists of two temporal segments, T_1 and T_2. Unless otherwise indicated, I shall assume that the segments in tables such as this are equally long and that the welfare of each individual in each segment is evenly spread within that segment. Thus, in segment T_1, a has the same level of welfare at all times and it sums up to two welfare units.

Now, in T_1, a is worse off than b. For that reason, we might decide to improve a's welfare in this segment, such that she reaches b's level. However, simply to increase a's welfare in this way would be to ignore the fact that she has a higher welfare in T_2. There is a sense in which her higher level in T_2 *compensates* her for her lower level in T_1. Her higher level in T_2 renders her lower level in T_1 more acceptable to her than it otherwise would have been. And so if we simply ignore the fact that she is better off in T_2, we ignore this element of compensation.

In fact, a's *relative* disadvantage in T_1 is fully compensated by her *relative* advantage in T_2. The extent to which a is worse off than b is in T_1 equals the extent to which b is worse off than a is in T_2. Of course, if we are prioritarians, we are concerned with absolute advantages, not relative ones. However, the claim about relative advantages can be cashed out in prioritarian terms. Thus, a is to some extent compensated for her lower level of welfare in T_1 by her higher level of welfare in T_2. Likewise, b is to some extent compensated for her lower level of welfare in T_2 by her higher level of welfare in T_1. And as prioritarians, we need to compare the extent to which a and b are compensated in particular outcomes to determine the value of these outcomes.

In this sense, then, compensation is not relative to the welfare levels of other individuals. An individual may be compensated, not for being worse off than others, but simply for not being better off than she is. Furthermore, this sort of compensation can take place at all welfare levels. So even an individual who is in fact very well off in a certain part of her life can be compensated for not being better off in that part of her life. But, of course, prioritarianism implies that it is more urgent to compensate individuals who are worse off than she is.

What these considerations suggest is that if we are prioritarians, we should not just look at the welfare levels of a and b in T_1 when distributing further benefits in this segment. We should also look at the extent to which their low or high welfare in this segment is compensated by or compensates their high or low welfare at other times. Thus, we should give priority to individuals who are worse off at times or in segments to the extent they are *not* compensated by being better off at other times. Let us call this the 'Compensation Argument', according to which our distributive principles should accommodate the inter-temporal compensation going on in a life.

It may seem that, applied to prioritarianism, the Compensation Argument simply implies Whole Lives Prioritarianism. After all, compensation seems to be possible over an entire life. However, the implications of the Compensation Argument will depend on the particular theory about self-interest assumed. This is because different theories about self-interest give rise to different theories about compensation. As we have seen, Parfit suggests that compensation presupposes identity. But I want to put forward, rather, that it presupposes prudential concern. And different theories of self-interest assume different accounts of such concern.

Consider again the common-sense idea that a benefit may compensate for a harm. Thus, the benefit of avoiding a future toothache may compensate me for the pain I experience at the dentist at an earlier time. This idea is related to the notion I contemplated above, of being compensated for 'not being better off', in the following way. Suppose, as seems plausible, it will take a benefit of a certain size to compensate me for the pain I experience at the dentist. The pain and the benefit simply cancel each other out. The benefit then compensates me for not being better off when at the dentist and, more specifically, compensates me for the difference between my welfare when at the dentist and the level I would have had at that same time, had I not gone to the dentist. Note also that, as I suggested above, such compensation can take place at all welfare levels. No matter how well off I am, the pain I experience at the dentist can be compensated by a later increase in my welfare.

Suppose now that we hold the Identity View. An individual's self-interest in a benefit will then simply depend on the size of the benefit. Therefore, a present decrease in an individual's welfare is exactly compensated by a later increase of the same numerical size. So if we hold the Identity View, we should also hold:

> *The Identity View of Compensation.* A decrease in P_1's welfare at t_1 is exactly compensated by an increase in P_2's welfare at t_2, if and only if (a) P_1 at t_1 is numerically identical to P_2 at t_2, and (b) the decrease and the increase in welfare have equal numerical value.

When I say that the increase and the decrease have 'equal numerical value', what this means is that if there is an increase of, for example, two units of welfare, there is also a decrease of two units of welfare. And when I say that the increase 'exactly compensates' the decrease, what this means is that the combination of the increase and the decrease is equal in value to the absence of both. Thus, an *exact* compensation neither under- nor overcompensates.

Suppose also that we hold the Additive Assumption about Benefits. An individual's self-interest in a temporal segment of her life is then equivalent to the sum of welfare contained in it. And so a decrease in the sum in a certain segment is exactly compensated by a numerically equal increase in the sum in another segment. This implies that it simply does not matter from an individual's prudential point of view how the welfare is distributed over her life; all that matters is the total sum. Since this is so, as prioritarians we should not seek to compensate individuals on the basis of how badly they are off in particular segments or time-slices. After all, they may be better off in other segments or slices and to the extent that they are, they *are* already compensated (which, of course, does not rule out that they can be further compensated). Since what prudentially matters is the total sum of welfare in a life, this is also what matters with respect to our prioritarian concerns. The lower the sum of welfare in an individual's life, the more reason we have to compensate her. And this claim, of course, amounts to Whole Lives Prioritarianism.

But now suppose that instead of the Identity View we hold the Prudential View, as I have argued that we should. We should then reject both (a) and (b) in the Identity View of Compensation. We should reject (a) because the unit within which compensation is possible is not lives, but Relation M. In fact, I have already argued this. Consider again the case of symmetrical brain division. A person, *a*, stands in the relation that prudentially matters to both of his continuers, *b* and *c*. However, his life and their lives are distinct. Nevertheless, I have argued that it can be in *a*'s self-interest to endure some hardship to secure benefits for them. For example, it may be in his self-interest to divide and so (presumably) reduce the sum of welfare in *his* life, thus securing for them lives with welfare. In other words, *their* welfare compensates *him* for *his* hardship. What makes such compensation possible is that *b* and *c* fall within the scope of *a*'s prudential concern.

Furthermore, we should reject (b) because compensation should not be assessed in terms of the *sum* of welfare contained in a life (or even in an M-relation). Suppose that I can ensure for myself a future benefit by presently undergoing a certain hardship. Assuming that Relation M holds to a reduced degree between me now and at the time of the benefit, the increase in welfare at this later time will have to have a greater numerical size than the present decrease in order for it exactly to compensate me from my present prudential perspective. Since this is so, compensation cannot be assessed simply in terms of sums of benefits. Rather, it is to be assessed in terms of sums of *discounted benefits*, where benefits are discounted to the extent that Relation M holds to a reduced degree.

Also, the Prudential View suggests that welfare is not the only dimension in which an individual can be compensated. After all, it implies that an individual's prudential concern for a future benefit is not just a function of the size of the benefit, but also of the extent to which she is M-related to the beneficiary. And what this suggests is that we can compensate her for a certain hardship she now endures, not just by providing her with future benefits, but also by increasing the strength of the M-relation that prudentially 'ties' her to such benefits. By intensifying the strength of the M-relation, we will be enhancing the importance of these benefits from her present prudential perspective. Metaphorically speaking, it will be as if, to a greater extent, these benefits actually accrue to *her* rather than to someone else.

What the Prudential View suggests, then, is this:

> *The Prudential View of Compensation.* Assessed at t_1, a decrease in P_1's welfare at t_1 is exactly compensated by an increase in P_2's welfare at t_2, or by a strengthening of the M-relation that holds between P_1 at t_1 and P_2 at t_2, or some combination thereof, if and only if (1) there is an increase in P_2's welfare at t_2, where (a) P_1 at t_1 is M-related to P_2 at t_2, and (b) the numerical value of the decrease in welfare equals the discounted numerical value of the increase; or (2) there is a strengthening of the M-relation that holds between P_1 at t_1 and P_2 at t_2, where the numerical value of the decrease in welfare equals the increase in the discounted numerical value of the benefits that occur in the M-relation due to the strengthening of Relation M; or (3) there is an appropriate combination of an increase in P_2's welfare at t_2 and a strengthening of the M-relation that holds between P_1 at t_1 and P_2 at t_2. Assessed at t_2, a decrease in P_1's welfare at t_1 is exactly compensated by an increase in P_2's welfare at t_2, or by a strengthening of the M-relation that holds between P_1 at t_1 and P_2 at t_2, or some combination thereof, if and only if (1) there is an increase in P_2's welfare at t_2, where (a) P_1 at t_1 is M-related to P_2 at t_2, and (b) the numerical value of the increase in welfare equals the discounted numerical value of the decrease; or (2) there is a strengthening of the M-relation that holds between P_1 at t_1 and P_2 at t_2, where the increase in the discounted numerical value of the benefits that occur in the M-relation due to the strengthening of the M-relation equals the decrease in the discounted numerical value of the benefits that accrue to P_1 at t_1 due to the decrease in benefits; or (3) there is an appropriate combination of a benefit to P_2 at t_2 and a strengthening of the M-relation that holds between P_1 at t_1 and P_2 at t_2.

The reason the Prudential View of Compensation is divided into two temporal perspectives is that the Prudential View implies that self-interests vary over time. For example, the size of an increase in welfare necessary at t_2 in order to exactly compensate for a reduction at t_1 depends on whether we assess it from P_1's perspective at t_1, or from P_2's perspective at t_2 (or from some other temporal position, for that matter). From P_1's perspective at t_1, the value of the increase at t_2 is its discounted value at t_1. So in order for P_1 to be exactly compensated in terms of her present self-interests at t_1, the numerical value of the increase will have to exceed the numerical value of the decrease. However, from P_2's perspective at t_2, it is the *decrease* that should be discounted. So in order for P_2 to be exactly compensated in terms of her self-interests at t_2, it is the numerical value of the decrease that must exceed the numerical value of the increase.

Actually, the Prudential View of Compensation is incomplete in the form it is stated above. Just as an individual can be compensated for a decrease in her welfare, she can also be compensated for a reduction in the M-relation she realizes over a given temporal interval. Thus, if the strength of an individual's M-relation is reduced over such an interval, her future benefits will matter less to her from her present prudential perspective. It will be as if, to a larger extent, these benefits will befall someone else. Yet, from her present perspective, she can be compensated for her 'loss', either by gaining additional benefits or by having the strength of her M-relation increased over some other part of her life, such that her present self-interest in the benefits that accrue to her in *that* part of her life is increased. But I shall not elaborate further on this form of compensation here.

There is another reason why the Prudential View of Compensation is incomplete; it does not address negative levels of welfare, or at least it does not address them adequately. Thus, suppose that my life contains nothing but negative welfare, and that now a further burden is imposed on me. Clearly, I cannot be compensated by an increase in the strength of the M-relation that I realize, because this will only make the misery that I experience in the other parts of my life matter *more* from my present perspective. Rather, in order to be compensated by a change in the strength of Relation M, this relation must be *weakened*.

Another complicating factor, that the Prudential View of Compensation does not reflect, is that both the harms that may be compensated, and the compensating benefits, may accrue to *several* distinct individuals. For instance, suppose that a harm occurs to *a* prior to his division. This harm may be compensated by benefits to *each* of *b* and *c*. That is, even from *a*'s present perspective (prior to his division), it may be compensated by benefits to his numerically distinct continuers. Likewise, it may be compensated by an increase in the strength of the M-relation that obtains between *a* and each of *b* and *c*. Now, the possibility of (prudential) compensation across individuals may seem of limited significance in a world in which brain transplants and the like do not occur. However, as I have argued elsewhere (2009) and briefly touch upon in Chapter 3 (Section 3.6), some theories of personal identity imply that we are not identical to, for example, the conscious foetuses from which we developed, and yet the Prudential View implies that we may have self-interests with respect to the benefits and harms that accrue to them, and vice versa. Thus, it is possible that an individual's present high welfare to some extent compensates the numerically distinct foetus from which she developed for its low welfare.

Unlike the Identity View of Compensation, the Prudential View of Compensation provides no support for a whole lives version of prioritarianism. This is because, according to the Prudential View of Compensation, it *does* matter how a certain sum of welfare is distributed over a life (or rather, over an M-relation). Thus, in terms of an individual's present prudential perspective, a present decrease in welfare will typically *not* be exactly compensated by a later increase of an equal numerical value. Nor, for that matter, will the numerically equal later increase exactly compensate the individual from her prudential perspective at this later time (rather, it will overcompensate her). Since there is thus no basis for saying that it is simply the sum of welfare in her life that matters from an individual's prudential point of view, there is no basis for saying that we should give priority to individuals who are worse off in their lives as wholes. Rather, as I shall now argue, the Prudential View of Compensation and the Compensation Argument support a different distributive principle.

10.6 Prudential Prioritarianism

According to the Prudential View of Compensation, the relation that renders compensation possible is Relation M rather than identity. And we have seen that when assessing whether an increase in welfare at one time compensates a decrease at another, these increases and decreases should be discounted to the extent that Relation M holds to a reduced degree. Furthermore, we have seen that welfare is not the only possible mode of compensation. Relation M is another. Therefore, any distributive principle to which the Prudential View of Compensation and the Compensation Argument give rise must accommodate these points.

According to the Compensation Argument, as presented in the last section, we should not simply compensate individuals to the extent that they are worse off at particular times, but to the extent they are worse off at times and are *not* compensated by being better off at other times. I now need to revise slightly this formulation. We should compensate individuals to the extent they are worse off at times and are not compensated by *individuals to whom they are M-related* being better off at other times.

This is the account of compensation we should feed into the Compensation Argument. We should compensate individuals to the extent they are worse off at times and are not compensated by appropriately discounted benefits accruing to individuals to whom they are M-related, or by increases in the strength of the M-relations that generate their prudential concern for benefits that occur at other times. Combining these claims, we should compensate individuals to the extent that their self-interests at times in the benefits that occur in their M-relations are weak. Thus, on the basis of the Prudential View of Compensation, the Compensation Argument, and the ideal of giving priority to the worse off, the following principle may be proposed:

> *Prudential Prioritarianism.* The weaker S's self-interest at *t* in the benefits that occur in the M-relation realized by S (and appropriate predecessors and continuers), the greater the value of a further benefit to S at *t* and/or an increase in the strength of the M-relation that obtains between S at *t*, and at other times at which positive welfare accrues to S (and appropriate predecessors and continuers) and/or a reduction in the strength of the M-relation that obtains between S at *t*, and at other times at which negative welfare accrues to S (and appropriate predecessors and continuers).

The name 'Prudential Prioritarianism', of course, is chosen so as to reveal this principle's affiliation with the Prudential View. This does not mean that it is a principle of prudence. Rather, it is a principle of morality or, more precisely, justice. It implies that an individual's level of priority at a particular point in time is a function of how many benefits occur in the M-relation that she realizes and how strong this relation is between her at that time and at the times the benefits accrue to her (or between her at that time and her predecessors and continuers at the times benefits accrue to them). It also implies that the unit to be distributed—self-interest fulfilment—has two dimensions, namely benefits and Relation M. Variations in either of these dimensions, in the relevant respect, can improve (or worsen) things from her prudential perspective at particular times.

While this does not transpire from Prudential Prioritarianism as defined above, I shall take outcome value to be an additive function of the individual contributions described in this definition. Likewise, I shall take an individual's contribution to be an additive function of the contributions she makes at particular times.

As anticipated in Section 10.2, Prudential Prioritarianism is impartial between the self-interests we hold at different times. Therefore, unlike the Prudential View, it implies that a certain benefit does not matter less if it is located in the future than if it is located in the present. The value of a benefit at t depends only on the beneficiaries' self-interest at t in the (other) benefits that occur in her life (or M-relation), and this is so, irrespective of whether t is past, present, or future. So, assuming an equal level of self-interest now and some time in the future, a benefit of a fixed size will matter no less if it accrues to me at that future time as if it accrues to me now, everything else being equal. And this is so whether we are assessing the moral value of the benefit now or in the future.

Nevertheless, Prudential Prioritarianism still reflects the insight of the Prudential View, according to which the (prudential) importance of benefits to individuals depends on the extent to which they are M-related to the beneficiaries. This is why, according to Prudential Prioritarianism, the value of a benefit to an individual at t depends on the *discounted* value of benefits that accrue to her at other times.

Let us now look more closely at the implications of Prudential Prioritarianism with respect to inter-personal distribution. This principle gives priority to individuals with weaker self-interests at times over individuals with stronger self-interests at times. First, this means that it is better to benefit an individual who has fewer benefits in her life (or M-relation), than an individual who has more benefits in her life (or M-relation), everything else being equal. To illustrate, consider Tables 10.2 and 10.3.

Table 10.2.

A	T_1	T_2	Total	M-relation
a	4	4	8	0.5
b	2	2	4	0.5

Table 10.3.

B	T_1	T_2	Total	M-relation
a	4	2	6	0.5
b	2	4	6	0.5

These two outcomes may represent a choice situation in which we can either confer two extra benefits on a or on b in T_2. Furthermore, a has been better off than b in the past. Also, a and b do not differ with respect to the strengths of the M-relations that they realize. And let us finally assume, for simplicity, that T_1 and T_2 are consecutive time-slices.

Prudential Prioritarianism implies that B is better than A. After all, consider the levels of self-interest at which the two additional units may fall in T_2, depending on whether they go to a or b. Thus, a's and b's self-interests in T_2 are functions of the benefits that accrue to them here, and of the discounted benefits that accrue to them in T_1. And while, in T_2, a and b have an equal self-interest in the two units that they are guaranteed in this time-slice, b has a weaker self-interest in the units that accrue to her in T_1 than a has in the units that accrue to *her* in T_1. Therefore, the additional two units fall at a lower level of self-interest in T_2 if they accrue to b than if they accrue to a and so, according to Prudential Prioritarianism, give rise to a larger increase in moral value in T_2 if they accrue to b.

The issue of whether the two additional units accrue to a or b will have an impact not only on the value realized in T_2, but also in T_1. The more welfare units that accrue to an individual in T_2, the lower the moral value of the welfare units that accrue to her in T_1, everything else being equal. And the two additional units in T_2 will imply a larger reduction in moral value in T_1 if they accrue to a than if they accrue to b, simply because a has more welfare in T_1 (and so more welfare units that will lose in moral value). Thus, B is better than A in both T_1 and T_2, and so better all told. More generally, Prudential Prioritarianism implies that, all things being equal, it is better to give a benefit to an individual who has fewer benefits in her life than to an individual who has more.

Second, since Prudential Prioritarianism gives priority to individuals with weaker self-interests at times, it implies that it is better to benefit an individual who realizes a weaker M-relation than an individual who realizes a stronger M-relation (assuming positive welfare levels), everything else being equal. To illustrate, consider Tables 10.4 and 10.5.

Table 10.4.

C	T_1	T_2	Total	M-relation
a	2	4	6	1
b	2	2	4	0.5

Table 10.5.

D	T_1	T_2	Total	M-relation
a	2	2	4	1
b	2	4	6	0.5

These outcomes may represent a choice situation in which two additional units may either be bestowed on a or on b in T_2, where a and b are similarly situated except for the fact that a realizes the stronger M-relation. In T_2, it is once again b who has the weakest self-interest in the four units that both are guaranteed. This is because in T_2, the M-relation that relates b to her two units in T_1 is weaker than is the M-relation that relates a to *her* two units in T_1. And since the additional units in T_2 thus fall at a lower level of self-interest if they accrue to b, T_2 is better in D than in C. Furthermore, the additional two units that may accrue to either a or b in T_2 will imply a larger reduction in the value of T_1 if they accrue to a than if they accrue to b. This is because it is a who in T_1 has the strongest self-interest in these additional units. Therefore, they will have a higher discounted value in T_1 if they accrue to a and so imply a larger reduction in the moral value of the welfare units that occur in T_1. Thus, D is also better than C in T_1, and so better all told.

Third, Prudential Prioritarianism implies that, everything else being equal and assuming positive welfare levels, it is better to strengthen the M-relation of an individual who is worse off (has a lower welfare) than to strengthen the M-relation of an individual who is better off (has a higher welfare). To illustrate, consider Tables 10.6 and 10.7.

Table 10.6.

E	T_1	T_2	Total	M-relation
a	4	4	8	1
b	2	2	4	0.5

Table 10.7.

F	T_1	T_2	Total	M-relation
a	4	4	8	0.5
b	2	2	4	1

These two outcomes represent a choice situation in which we may either increase the strength of the M-relation that obtains between a at T_1 and T_2 from 0.5 to 1, or implement a similar increase for b. Since b is worse off in both T_1 and T_2 than a is, in both these time-slices b has the weakest self-interest in her benefits. And so it is more urgent to compensate her, which we can do by increasing the strength of her M-relation. By doing this, we render the two welfare units that accrue to her in T_2 prudentially more important from her perspective at T_1, and vice versa. Therefore, Prudential Prioritarianism implies that F is better than E.

Finally, Prudential Prioritarianism implies that, everything else being equal, it is better to strengthen the M-relation of an individual who realizes a weaker such relation, than an individual who realizes a stronger such relation. Consider Tables 10.8 and 10.9.

Table 10.8.

G	T_1	T_2	Total	M-relation
a	2	2	4	0.75
b	2	2	4	0.25

Table 10.9.

H	T_1	T_2	Total	M-relation
a	2	2	4	0.5
b	2	2	4	0.5

These two outcomes may represent a choice situation in which we may either increase a's M-relation from 0.5 to 0.75 or b's such relation from 0.25 to 0.5, where a and b are otherwise similarly situated. Let us assume that these two increases give rise to equal increases in self-interest at times (since each increases the strength of the relation by 0.25). Prudential Prioritarianism implies that it is more urgent to increase b's M-relation, since it is b who has the weakest self-interest at times in her benefits. Thus, H is better than G.

Of course, there may sometimes be an intra- or inter-personal conflict between increases in benefits and in Relation M. That is, there may be cases in which an individual can either receive an increase in her benefits or in the strength of her M-relation, and cases in which one individual can receive an increase in his benefits or another individual can receive an increase in his M-relation. To settle such cases, Prudential Prioritarianism would need to settle the relative weights of these two types of improvements. However, like the task of settling the priority weights in prioritarianism, this is obviously a difficult task, and not one I shall undertake here.

There are also other respects in which Prudential Prioritarianism would need to be further specified. Thus, with respect to intra-personal distribution, Prudential Prioritarianism should imply that, everything else being equal, it is better if a certain sum of welfare is more evenly spread within an M-relation (assuming, realistically, that this relation weakens over time). Thus, everything else being equal, it is better if an individual holds a level of two in both halves of his life than if he holds a level of four in the first half and a level of zero in the second. This is because an even distribution will give an individual better compensation over time. Likewise, everything else being equal and for the same reason, it is better if the M-relation realized by an individual holds the same strength over a life than if the same average strength is unevenly spread. There are various ways in which Prudential Prioritarianism can be further specified that would have these implications, but we do not need this degree of specificity here. I shall simply assume that Prudential Prioritarianism has these implications.

Furthermore, holding everything else constant, including Relation M, Prudential Prioritarianism should imply that it always improves an outcome to add further benefits. More precisely, for fixed M-relations, Prudential Prioritarianism should satisfy the Pareto Principle. This means that an increase in an individual's welfare at t will outweigh decreases in the moral value of (fixed) benefits that occur at times other than t, where these decreases are due to the fact that, because of the increase in welfare at t, the individual will experience an increase in her self-interests at these other times. There are various ways in which Prudential Prioritarianism could be thus specified. One would be simply to devise a prudential prioritarian function that weights increases in welfare at t higher than the decreases in moral value at other times to which they may give rise. Another would be to impose a Pareto Principle for fixed M-relations as a separate restriction on the ordering of outcomes (and so one that trumps violations to which the function may otherwise give rise).

Likewise, holding everything else constant, including benefits, Prudential Prioritarianism should imply that it always improves an outcome to strengthen Relation M (assuming that what Relation M unites is overall positive welfare levels; given negative levels, it will improve an outcome to weaken this relation). Combining this claim and a Pareto Principle for fixed M-relations, everything else being equal, it always improves an outcome to increase an individual's self-interest in it. I shall consider this a constraint on any further specification of Prudential Prioritarianism.

Finally, Prudential Prioritarianism should imply that while benefits at lower levels of self-interest matter more than equal benefits at higher levels, larger benefits at higher levels, if sufficient in size, will outweigh smaller increases at lower levels. Likewise, while increases in Relation M matter more at lower levels of self-interest than at higher levels, larger increases at higher levels, if sufficient in size, will outweigh smaller increases at lower levels. This is analogous to my claim in Chapter 8 (Section 8.2) that Overall Outcome Welfare Prioritarianism is an aggregative principle in the sense that, for any finite sum of benefits that fall at a lower level, it can be outweighed by a sufficiently large sum of benefits that falls at a—indeed any—higher level.

I now want to contrast Prudential Prioritarianism with an account that has been developed by Dennis McKerlie. Like me, McKerlie considers the implications of personal identity and what matters for prioritarianism. He claims that since the psychological relations relevant for personal identity and what matters hold to a higher degree at a time than over time, compensation at a time has special significance (McKerlie 1997: 299). And since Time-slice Prioritarianism relies only on compensation at a time, this principle is supported by a plausible account of personal identity and what matters (1997: 300).[2]

So far, McKerlie's account is similar to Parfit's. But McKerlie also stresses the importance of the unity in a life taken as a whole. And he takes the distributive aspects of this unity to be captured by Whole Lives Prioritarianism. So what he is suggesting is that we combine (appropriate *ceteris paribus* versions of) Time-slice Prioritarianism and Whole Lives Prioritarianism in our account of the temporal unit of prioritarian concern (1997: 296–302).

However, this account seems to me to suffer from various drawbacks. First, the fact that an individual is usually more psychologically united at a time than over time does not really seem to provide any kind of support for Time-slice Prioritarianism. Psychological unity is a matter of degree. Suppose that an individual suffers and that we can either benefit him at the time of his suffering, or immediately after. From his prudential perspective at the time of the suffering, the former option may provide a better compensation, but the latter option may provide a compensation that is *almost* as good, namely if a high degree of unity is preserved from the time of the suffering to the time of the benefit. So we need a principle that accommodates the fact that compensation gradually decreases as the sort of unity relevant for

---

[2] In a later article, however, McKerlie downplays the importance of personal identity for distributive justice, see McKerlie (2006: sect. 4).

prudential concern also decreases. Time-slice Prioritarianism does not do this since it allows only for compensation at a time. And so this principle cannot really be said to deal plausibly with the metaphysical and prudential facts.

Nor, for that matter, does the suggested combined principle deal convincingly with these facts. Imagine that an individual now suffers terribly and that we can benefit him either in two minutes or in two years. Clearly, from his present prudential perspective, it is better to benefit him in two minutes. However, neither Time-slice Prioritarianism nor Whole Lives Prioritarianism captures this point. Since the benefit and the suffering are not simultaneous, everything else being equal, Time-slice Prioritarianism implies indifference, and since the lifetime sum is not affected, so does Whole Lives Prioritarianism. Prudential Prioritarianism, on the other hand, implies that, everything else being equal, the benefit should fall sooner rather than later. After all, the suffering has a higher discounted disvalue two minutes from now than two years from now. Therefore, the benefit falls at a lower level of self-interest if it falls in two minutes.

At one point, McKerlie (1997: 300–1) does consider the possibility of revising Whole Lives Prioritarianism to accommodate the point that the relations that prudentially matter *gradually* weaken over time. And this, of course, is just what Prudential Prioritarianism does. Yet, it seems to me that this move does not really square with McKerlie's aim of supporting Time-slice Prioritarianism. Rather, since Prudential Prioritarianism already accommodates the relevant metaphysical and prudential facts, such a move renders Time-slice Prioritarianism superfluous.

10.7 The Temporal Unit of Distributive Concern

I have now argued that the Prudential View and the Compensation Argument can be invoked to support Prudential Prioritarianism. I have also called attention to various properties this principle has. To assess further Prudential Prioritarianism, it will be instructive to compare its implications to those of some alternative principles.

As I have pointed out, most theorists have assumed that distributive principles should focus on whole lives. However, several egalitarians have objected to this idea. In a classic paper, McKerlie argues that it suffers from at least two problems. It gives too much importance to inequalities in the distant past. And it does not see any disvalue in inequalities that obtain between different lives at particular times, as long as these inequalities do not obtain between whole lives (McKerlie 1989: 477–80). While these objections rely on the value of equality, they are also highly relevant for prioritarianism. So let us consider them in turn. First, consider Tables 10.10 and 10.11.

Table 10.10.

A	T_1	T_2	T_3	Total
a	4	8	4	16
b	8	8	4	20

Table 10.11.

B	T_1	T_2	T_3	Total
a	4	8	6	18
b	8	8	2	18

A and B can be taken to represent a case in which a doctor can help one of two patients who will both experience pain in the third segment, T_3, unless they are treated. If b is treated, A will result, whereas if a is treated, B will result. Further, b's pain is stronger than is a's, which is why b has a lower level of welfare in B than a does in A. But it is a who has been worst off in the past (namely in T_1). The increase in welfare that can be provided for a and b is the same (two units).

According to what we may call Whole Lives Egalitarianism, it is best to treat a and so to bring about B. In B, there is perfect equality between whole lives. The reason it is better to give a more and b less in T_3 is that a has been worse off than b in T_1. However, suppose that T_1 and thus a's past misfortunes lie in the *distant* past. Suppose also that these misfortunes have no impact on a's present life. We may even presume that she no longer remembers them. McKerlie (1989: 478) suggests that with assumptions such as these, it is unreasonable to prefer a highly inegalitarian distribution *now*; that is, in T_3.

McKerlie's other objection can be illustrated by the outcomes represented in Tables 10.12–10.14.

Table 10.12.

C	T_1	T_2	Total
a	6	2	8
b	2	6	8
Inequality	4	4	0

Table 10.13.

D	T_1	T_2	Total
a	6	2	8
b	6	2	8
Inequality	0	0	0

Table 10.14.

E	T_1	T_2	Total
a	4	4	8
b	4	4	8
Inequality	0	0	0

In C, *a* is better off than is *b* in T_1, but then their roles are reversed such that in T_2, *b* is better off than is *a*. Since their roles are simply reversed, *a* and *b* have equal total sums of welfare over their whole lives. Likewise, they have equal whole life shares in D. Thus, according to Whole Lives Egalitarianism, C is as good as D, although *a* and *b* are equally well off even within each temporal segment in D. Likewise, C is equal in value to E, although there is neither inequality within or between segments in the latter outcome. However, McKerlie thinks that D (and E) is (are) clearly better than C. The inequalities that obtain in a given segment in a feudal system would not become unobjectionable just because peasants and nobles change places halfway through their lives (McKerlie 1989: 479; for a similar objection to Whole Lives Egalitarianism, see Temkin 1993a: 235–8).

As I said, McKerlie's objections to Whole Lives Egalitarianism are rather interesting in the present context. This is because very similar objections apply to some versions of prioritarianism. Consider again A and B. Like Whole Lives Egalitarianism, Whole Lives Prioritarianism implies that B is best. The two welfare units that *a* receives in T_3 when we move from A to B matter more than the two units *b* loses because the former fall at a lower lifetime welfare level. So past misfortunes are relevant for the present distribution of welfare, even if they lie in the *distant* past. Now consider

C, D, and E. Since there are equal lifetime sums of welfare in these three outcomes, Whole Lives Prioritarianism implies that they are equally good. And so to the extent this is counterintuitive, Whole Lives Prioritarianism is threatened.

Unlike Whole Lives Prioritarianism, Prudential Prioritarianism to some extent does accommodate McKerlie's first objection. Prudential Prioritarianism implies that to the extent Relation M holds to a reduced degree between an individual at the time of some misfortune and at the time of some benefit, the misfortune counts for less when determining the moral value of this benefit. So suppose that, in T_3 in A and B, the discounted value of the welfare units that fall in T_1 is one-fourth of their original value. In T_3, the discounted value of a's welfare in T_1 is then one, and the discounted value of b's welfare is two. Thus, the difference in a's and b's discounted welfare is much less than the welfare difference itself. This means that when assessing the value benefits that occur in T_3 contribute to the outcome at this time, it matters less that a is much worse off than is b in T_1 than it does with, for example, Whole Lives Prioritarianism. So, by discounting for reductions in Relation M, Prudential Prioritarianism downplays the importance of past misfortunes for present distribution. And, assuming that Relation M weakens gradually over time, the further into the past a certain misfortune lies, the less important it presently is.

However, Prudential Prioritarianism is as vulnerable to McKerlie's second objection as is Whole Lives Prioritarianism. Thus, it implies that C and D are equally good. After all, D differs from C only in that the temporal order of b's welfare units is reversed such that she enjoys six units in T_1 and two units in T_2, rather than the other way around. But it is not so clear that this should be considered an embarrassment for the proponent of Prudential Prioritarianism. The reason McKerlie considers D better than C, is that in D there is no inequality between simultaneous temporal segments of lives. But a prioritarian will not worry about such an (or any) inequality and there seems to be no other reason to consider D better than C.[3] So it seems to me that Prudential Prioritarianism deals nicely with both of McKerlie's objections to Whole Lives Egalitarianism.

Note also that Prudential Prioritarianism implies that E is better than both C and D. As I pointed out in the last section, everything else being equal, Prudential Prioritarianism should favour an equal distribution to an unequal

---

[3] Strictly speaking, this is not quite right. Some egalitarians claim that inequalities between *corresponding* segments are intrinsically bad (see below). But since a prioritarian will not care about this sort of inequality either, I need not consider this option any further here.

distribution of welfare over a life. An equal distribution will better compensate an individual where he is most in need of compensation. I believe that all this gives Prudential Prioritarianism an edge over Whole Lives Prioritarianism.

Now, in order to assess the relative strength of Prudential Prioritarianism, we must compare this principle's implications with respect to McKerlie's two objections to alternative ways of dealing with them. One way of rendering the further past irrelevant for present distribution would be by adopting a temporally partial view, according to which only present and future welfare matters for present distribution. In this view, when comparing A and B, it would be irrelevant that a was worse off in T_1. Only the welfare levels in T_3 would matter, and so it would be better to bring about A. After all, T_3 is better in A than in B in both egalitarian and prioritarian terms.

However, this kind of temporal partiality is hardly very plausible. Suppose that a's misfortunes were not in the distant past but in the immediate past. In fact, assume that a has suffered terribly for a long time and continues to do so. We can now either relieve his pain or relieve b's slightly greater, but much more recent, pain. Surely it matters that a has been much worse off in the past. Of course, we may instead claim that it is only the *distant* past that is irrelevant to present distribution, but unless we can provide an explanation of what is so special about the *distant* past, this would be entirely arbitrary.

McKerlie's own preferred solution to the problems generated by Whole Lives Egalitarianism is to replace or at least complement it with another egalitarian principle, namely Simultaneous Segments Egalitarianism.[4] According to this latter principle, what has intrinsic disvalue is inequality between individuals in simultaneous temporal segments. Consider again outcomes A and B. The inequality in segment T_1 lies in the past and so cannot now be avoided, but the inequality in T_3 can, if A is brought about. According to Simultaneous Segments Egalitarianism, B would merely add further inequality to that which already exists in T_1. Therefore, inequalities that lie in the distant past are not relevant for present distribution.

Now consider outcomes C, D, and E. In C, where a and b change places halfway through their lives, there is considerable inequality in each segment. In D and E, on the other hand, there is no such inequality. Therefore, according to

---

[4] In his earlier writings, McKerlie (1989: 491) seems to hold that Simultaneous Segments Egalitarianism should *replace* Whole Lives Egalitarianism, but in later writings he seriously considers the option of combining these two principles (McKerlie 2001: 276). Temkin (1993a: 240–2) also seems to find both versions of egalitarianism in some ways attractive, as he does a third principle, also considered by McKerlie, namely Corresponding Segments Egalitarianism. According to Corresponding Segments Egalitarianism, it is inequality between corresponding segments of different individuals that has intrinsic disvalue. For instance, it is bad if one individual in her youth is worse off than another individual is in *her* youth.

Simultaneous Segments Egalitarianism, D and E are equally good and are better than C is. Thus, this principle avoids a feature that McKerlie finds objectionable in Whole Lives Egalitarianism, namely that inequalities within segments do not matter, as long as they do not give rise to inequalities between whole lives.

Yet, I doubt that Simultaneous Segments Egalitarianism is the solution to the problems McKerlie considers. First, it has some rather counterintuitive implications of its own. Consider Tables 10.15 and 10.16.

Table 10.15.

F	T_1	T_2	Total
a	2	4	6
b	4	2	6
Inequality	2	2	0

Table 10.16.

G	T_1	T_2	Total
a	2	2	4
b	4	4	8
Inequality	2	2	4

Since both F and G hold an inequality of two welfare units in each temporal segment, Simultaneous Segments Egalitarianism implies that F and G are equally good. However, intuitively, F seems much better than G. After all, in G, a is worse off than is b in *both* temporal segments. Surely it is better if, halfway through their lives, a and b change places. Note, incidentally, that the egalitarian cannot solve this problem by invoking some version of utilitarianism as a supplementary principle. After all, F and G contain equal sums of welfare. However, another solution rather naturally suggests itself. If we combine appropriate *ceteris paribus* versions of Simultaneous Segments Egalitarianism and Whole Lives Egalitarianism, we can explain why F is better. F and G are equally good with respect to simultaneous segments, but F is better with respect to whole lives. Therefore, F is better all told.

A more serious problem is that it is difficult to see how one can divide lives into temporal segments in a principled manner that is supportive of Simultaneous Segments Egalitarianism. Suppose that, on the favoured division of segments, a short episode of excruciating pain falls at the very end of what is now the previous segment. As far as Simultaneous Segments Egalitarianism is concerned, this pain is then not relevant to present distribution. But now imagine instead that the pain falls at the very beginning of the present segment. Now the pain is suddenly relevant, although the difference in when it occurs may be minute. This seems strange. And note that here it will not help to combine *ceteris paribus* versions of Simultaneous Segments Egalitarianism and Whole Lives Egalitarianism, because the sum of welfare in a life is not affected by the mere fact that a certain pain occurs later rather than sooner.

There is also another problem that threatens the ambition of dividing up lives in a principled manner, supportive of Simultaneous Segments Egalitarianism. Consider again outcome E (Table 10.14). And suppose that each segment consists of forty years. In each of these forty-year segments, there is perfect equality. Yet, presume also that the welfare in each of these segments is not spread out evenly over the entire segment, but rather in twenty-year segments in the manner illustrated in Table 10.17.

Table 10.17.

E	T_{11}	T_{12}	T_{21}	T_{22}	Total
a	4	0	4	0	8
b	0	4	0	4	8
Inequality	4	4	4	4	0

What we have then is a case in which, if we assume one division of temporal segments, there is perfect equality, whereas if we assume another, there is substantial inequality. So which particular segments should we assume? If we choose forty-year segments, we are vulnerable to the following objection. Since we are so concerned about inequalities between forty-year segments, why are we not at all concerned about inequalities between twenty-year segments? What is so special about the former? If, on the other hand, we choose twenty-year segments, we may have to face the same problem as if we choose forty-year segments. There can be cases in which there is no inequality between twenty-year segments, but substantial inequality between ten-year segments.[5]

It may seem that the solution is to settle on the shortest possible time segments. I have called such segments 'time-slices'. The point is that time-slices

---

[5] McKerlie (1989: 483–4) briefly considers some of the problems in determining appropriate segment lengths, but suggests that these problems do not constitute a decisive objection to Simultaneous Segments Egalitarianism. However, he does not say anything about how they are to be solved.

cannot be further subdivided, and so if there is equality between time-slices, there cannot turn out to be inequalities within these slices. Let us call the resulting egalitarian principle Time-slice Egalitarianism.

Obviously, this principle is the egalitarian equivalent of Time-slice Prioritarianism. And, indeed, just as Time-slice Egalitarianism seems to be the only stable temporal alternative to Whole Lives Egalitarianism, Time-slice Prioritarianism appears to be the only stable temporal alternative to Whole Lives Prioritarianism (and Prudential Prioritarianism). Any timespan shorter than whole lives but longer than time-slices will leave us wondering why, if an individual is worse off *within* such a segment, although not worse off over the segment taken as a whole, she is not entitled to priority. Again, this can be illustrated by outcome E. Assuming the forty-year segments represented in Table 10.14, there is no basis for redistribution. But assuming the twenty-year segments represented in Table 10.17, one individual is worse off than the other is in each segment, and so it would be better if the welfare were more evenly distributed between times.

In fact, as McKerlie points out, the claim that time-slices are the appropriate temporal units of distributive concern is much more plausible in the case of prioritarianism than in the case of egalitarianism. According to Time-slice Egalitarianism, it will be important that two individuals go to the dentist for a painful treatment at the exact same time, rather than, say, five minutes apart (McKerlie 1989: 483). But this seems pedantic. Time-slice Prioritarianism, on the other hand, has no such implication. This is because it attaches no importance to simultaneity in benefits to different individuals (McKerlie 2001: 279). It merely states that benefits to individuals at times where they are worse off have greater moral value than benefits to individuals at times where they are better off. Whether these welfare states are simultaneous or not makes no difference.

Furthermore, McKerlie suggests that with respect to the outcome represented in Table 10.18, our intuitions seem to be better explained by Time-slice Prioritarianism than by Time-slice Egalitarianism.

Table 10.18.

H	T_1	T_2	Total
a	1	6	7
b	1	5	6
Inequality	0	1	1

Suppose that the welfare is evenly spread for both individuals within each of these segments. Presume also that we can give b a gain of one unit of welfare in either T_1 or in T_2, and that this extra unit will be spread evenly in the segment in which it falls. Intuitively, it would seem better to give the benefit to b in T_1 where he is much worse off than in T_2. And, indeed, Time-slice Prioritarianism implies that this is when it is best to give it to him. The benefit will then fall at a lower level. Time-slice Egalitarianism, on the other hand, implies that it is better to give b the benefit in T_2 (McKerlie 2001: 279). There will then be perfect equality in each and every time-slice. Note that it will not help the time-slice egalitarian to invoke *ceteris paribus* versions of Whole Lives Egalitarianism or Total Outcome Utilitarianism. This is because, whether the extra benefit falls in T_1 or T_2, the sum of benefits in b's life is the same.

Of course, the case for providing b with an additional unit of welfare in T_1 rather than in T_2 does not automatically support Time-slice Prioritarianism. This is because Prudential Prioritarianism also favours placing the additional unit in T_1. After all, Prudential Prioritarianism favours even distributions of welfare over M-relations.

I have now considered different possible temporal units of distributive concern. A simultaneous segments view seems to be an unstable compromise between whole lives and time-slices. So leaving out Prudential Prioritarianism, it seems that if we are prioritarians, we should opt either for Whole Lives Prioritarianism or Time-slice Prioritarianism. The former principle, however, suffers from at least one problem: it implies that past misfortunes are *just* as important for present distribution if they lie in the *distant* past as if they happened yesterday. Time-slice Prioritarianism, on the other hand, suffers from the opposite problem: it implies that past misfortunes are entirely irrelevant to present distribution. Consider again outcomes F and G (Tables 10.15 and 10.16). And assume that the welfare of each of a and b is evenly spread over the segment in which it occurs. The fact that a is worse off in T_1 is irrelevant with respect to whom should have the higher welfare level in T_2. Either a has four units and b has two units in T_2, or a has two units and b has four units, and Time-slice Prioritarianism does not give us reason to prefer one or the other.

It may seem that the answer to these problems is simply to combine appropriate *ceteris paribus* versions of Whole Lives Prioritarianism and Time-slice Prioritarianism. As we have already seen, McKerlie (1997: 296–302) suggests that if we are prioritarians, we should accept such a combined principle.[6] This will enable us to give the best explanation of our intuitions about cases. So whereas the reductionist argument for Time-slice Prioritarianism fails, perhaps

---

[6] For a more recent statement of this view, see McKerlie (2001: 280).

a *ceteris paribus* version of this principle receives support from our intuitions. It allows us to explain why, in H, *b* should have the extra benefit in T_1. At the same time, the *ceteris paribus* version of Whole Lives Prioritarianism enables us to explain why F is better than G.

Yet, when it comes to the problem of past misfortunes, the combined view does not quite solve the problem. Admittedly, since it takes past (and future) welfare to be irrelevant to present distribution, Time-slice Prioritarianism will to some extent downplay the importance Whole Lives Prioritarianism attaches to misfortunes in the distant past. But the problem is that it will equally downplay the importance of misfortunes that lie in the *immediate* past. Therefore, the combined view implies that past misfortunes are *just* as important for present distribution if they lie in the distant past as if they happened yesterday.

It seems, then, that Prudential Prioritarianism has two advantages compared to the combined prioritarian principle. In that it receives support from the Prudential View and the Compensation Argument, it can be said to respond to the metaphysical and prudential points about reductions in Relation M. And it plausibly implies that past misfortunes *gradually* matter less for present distribution, the further into the past they lie.

10.8 Psychological Differences

I now want to consider further the implications of Prudential Prioritarianism with respect to whether it is better to distribute benefits on strong or weak M-relations. As I pointed out in Section 10.6, this principle implies that it is better to benefit an individual who realizes a weaker M-relation than an individual who realizes a stronger M-relation (assuming positive welfare levels), everything else being equal. Assuming negative welfare levels, on the other hand, it is better to benefit an individual who realizes a stronger M-relation than an individual who realizes a weaker M-relation, everything else being equal.

More particularly, I want to consider an objection that has been raised by Klemens Kappel in a brief comment on a principle relevantly similar to Prudential Prioritarianism. Kappel objects that 'it seems difficult to accept that it could be more important to help one person rather than another merely because this person has richer psychological relations to some past or future hardship that both endured or must endure' (1997: 220). After all, it seems difficult to believe that one person should be benefited rather than another '*merely* because one person more vividly remembers some past hardship they both had to endure' (1997: 220).

I shall assume that the hardship in question rendered these two people's lives (temporarily) worth *not* living. After all, if these people had lives worth living at the time, it is unclear why it should be considered a disadvantage for one of them to be more strongly M-related to himself at the time of the misfortune. Suppose also, for simplicity, that no other units of welfare (positive or negative) occur in the M-relations realized by these two individuals. On these assumptions, Prudential Prioritarianism implies that it is better if the individual realizing the stronger M-relation receives the benefit. After all, this individual is most in need of compensation as he presently has the weakest (or the strongest *negative*) self-interest in the misfortune that once occurred.

Kappel's objection does not convince me. If one individual has a more vivid memory of some past misfortune than does another, what this amounts to is a *very* minimal psychological difference. In the overall pattern of psychological relations that hold over time in the life of a normal person, it is almost *nothing*. And so, according to Prudential Prioritarianism, it cannot carry much weight when assessing possible present distributions. This, of course, is compatible with the claim that *if everything else is equal*, the individual who remembers his past misfortune more vividly should be benefited, rather than the individual who remembers it less vividly. But my point is that since the psychological difference between these two individuals is minute, the extra value that is realized by benefiting the individual with the better memory will be very slight indeed. And, therefore, we should not be surprised if our prudential prioritarian intuitions reveal to us little moral difference between these two outcomes.

More importantly, I have already provided a rationale for the view that reductions in the relation that prudentially matters leads to a reduction in the importance of past misfortunes for present distribution. An individual has a greater prudential concern for past welfare to the extent that the M-relation is stronger. A past misfortune simply *matters* more from his present prudential point of view, the stronger this relation is. Therefore, if this relation is strong, he is more in need of compensation for the misfortune. Furthermore, if it is strong, the benefit provides a better compensation from his perspective at the time of the misfortune.

Another implication of Prudential Prioritarianism that may be considered disturbing is apparent from the outcomes represented in Tables 10.19 and 10.20.

Table 10.19.

A	T_1	T_2	Total
a	4	4	8
b	4	4	8

Table 10.20.

B	T_1	T_2	Total
a	4	3	7
b	4	5	9

A seems to be better than B. However, if the M-relations realized in the lives of a and b are not equally strong, A need not be better. Suppose that the M-relation is much stronger in the life of a than in the life of b. Because the relation is less strong in the life of b, his self-interest at T_2 in the benefits that accrue to him in T_1 is less strong than a's similar self-interest. Let us assume that, for this reason, Prudential Prioritarianism implies that B is better than A. Thus, Prudential Prioritarianism favours an unequal rather than an equal distribution of a fixed sum.

However, there are two points that should be borne in mind here. First, A exhibits the nice feature that a and b are equal, even within each temporal segment. But for a prioritarian, of course, this is an entirely irrelevant feature of the outcome. Second, while in B, a is worse off in T_2 than is b, b is in much greater need of compensation than a is. Since the M-relation is much weaker in the life of b, the four units he received in T_1 matter much less from his prudential point of view in T_2 than a's four units in T_1 matter from *his* prudential point of view in T_2. Therefore, the conclusion, on the assumptions made, that B may be better than A, does not strike me as very troubling.

Importantly, the sensitivity of Prudential Prioritarianism to psychological differences does not have just theoretical interest, it has real-life implications. Consider individuals who realize relatively weak M-relations; for example, (some) people with severe cognitive disabilities, (conscious) foetuses, and many non-human animals. Suppose that one such individual has experienced a certain misfortune in the past, which nevertheless did not reduce her to the level where life ceases to be worth living. Compared to a (normal) human being who realizes a stronger M-relation and has suffered a similar misfortune (at the same time), this individual will be more in need of compensation.

Note that, as transpired from my discussion of moral standing in Chapter 8 (Section 8.9), there is a built-in tendency in Overall Outcome Welfare Prioritarianism to favour non-human over human animals, because non-human animals will typically realize less welfare in their lives. And since non-human animals will typically also realize less welfare in their M-relations, this is a factor that will tend to favour non-human animals according to Prudential Prioritarianism as well. On top of this, there is the factor mentioned in the passage above, namely that, everything else being equal, an individual who realizes a weak M-relation is more in need of compensation than is a(n) (otherwise) similarly situated individual who realizes a strong such relation. Thus, there are two distinct factors that tend to make Prudential Prioritarianism favour non-human animals (and other individuals who realize weak M-relations). And it may seem as if Prudential Prioritarianism is becoming all too accommodating to the needs of such individuals at the expense of others.

However, I believe that in at least some cases, there is a certain intuitive and theoretical plausibility to the claim that a weaker M-relation may in itself generate a stronger claim for welfare. For example, consider people with Alzheimer's disease. Presumably, this disease causes a significant reduction in their welfare, and for this reason they are entitled to higher levels of priority than most other humans. Furthermore, the loss of memory and other psychological changes implies that people with this disease experience a significant weakening of the M-relation linking them to their past and future welfare. According to Prudential Prioritarianism, this may be a reason why we should give them further priority. And this seems to me exactly right. Normally, if a person now has a low level of welfare but has experienced a reasonably high level in the past, her past high welfare to some extent will compensate her for her present low welfare. But if a person with Alzheimer's disease (or an advanced stage of this disease) is in a similar situation, her past welfare will provide less by way of compensation. To a larger extent, it will be as if these past benefits accrued to someone else.

Second, even if, everything else being equal, an individual who realizes a weak M-relation is more in need of compensation than a(n) (otherwise) similarly situated individual who realizes a strong such relation, everything else need not be equal. As I also pointed out in Chapter 8 (Section 8.9), some theories of welfare imply that individuals capable of, for example, knowledge and autonomy, are also capable of realizing greater welfare levels than are individuals who do not have such rich psychologies. Therefore, it may often be the case that we can provide greater benefits for typical mature human beings than for, say, most non-human animals. And so the fact that average mature human beings are capable of greater benefits may in many cases counterbalance the fact that most non-human animals are in greater need of compensation.

Third, the point that weaker M-relations have priority is only partly correct, even according to Prudential Prioritarianism. In fact, with respect to negative levels of welfare, this principle will favour individuals with stronger M-relations, as I have already mentioned. Thus, if (say) a non-human animal with a weak M-relation and human with a strong M-relation have both experienced a period of negative welfare in the past, it is the human who is now most in need of compensation (as it is she who is now most strongly related to her suffering), everything else being equal.

For these reasons, I do not find the implications of Prudential Prioritarianism, with respect to distributions between M-relations of different strengths, excessive, or at least not clearly so. In other words, I am inclined to accept the implications of Prudential Prioritarianism in this regard.

10.9 Psychological Changes

I have argued that Prudential Prioritarianism is plausible enough when applied to cases that involve psychological differences, but what about cases that involve psychological *changes*? Here, Prudential Prioritarianism tends to favour the existence of strong over weak M-relations. Consider the outcomes represented in Tables 10.21 and 10.22.

Table 10.21.

A	T_1	T_2	Total	M-relation
a	2	2	4	1

Table 10.22.

B	T_1	T_2	Total	M-relation
a	2	2	4	0.5

A and B are identical, except that the M-relation realized by a from T_1 to T_2 has full strength in A but it is reduced to half in B. Prudential Prioritarianism implies that A is better than B. This simply follows from the restriction I have imposed on Prudential Prioritarianism, according to which,

holding everything else constant, it always improves an outcome to strength-
en Relation M (assuming that what Relation M unites is positive welfare
levels).

Prudential Prioritarianism, then, favours the existence of strong M-relations.
This is of course no surprise, since an individual who realizes a stronger
M-relation is more psychologically and/or physically unified—and so is better
compensated—over time (again, assuming positive welfare). And, indeed, this
result seems plausible enough. Consider an individual who always enjoys a
positive level of welfare and is strongly M-related to himself over time. Now
suppose that we significantly weaken the strength of the M-relation he realizes
(say, by clubbing him hard on the head, thus causing severe memory loss and
permanently rendering his cognitive abilities no more advanced than those
of a seven-year-old child). Imagine also that, surprisingly, we do not thereby
reduce his welfare, even in the long run. In fact, his welfare level does not at
any time differ from what it otherwise would have been. Plausibly, Prudential
Prioritarianism implies that we have made a change for the worse. Likewise,
this principle implies that we make a change for the worse if we fail to develop
a seven-year-old child's cognitive capacities, even if we do not thereby affect
her welfare. Again, this seems plausible enough.

10.10 Prudential Prioritarianism and the Badness of Death

Consider again the issue of the badness of death. Just as my account of prudence
has implications for the badness of death, my account of justice has implications
for which deaths it would be best to prevent. But while my account of justice
in part reflects my account of prudence, it differs in that it does not allow value
to vary over time. Thus, an outcome will not differ in moral value, depending
on the temporal perspective from which it is assessed. This is because, while
Prudential Prioritarianism reflects the distinct perspectives individuals have at
different times with respect to their self-interests, it does so by being impartial
between these temporal perspectives.

Prudential Prioritarianism implies that, everything else being equal, it is
better (or less bad) if an older individual dies, than if a younger individual dies.
Everything else being equal, if an individual dies at the age of, say, sixty, this
is better than if an individual dies at the age of, say, twenty. By ensuring the
survival of the twenty-year-old rather than the sixty-year-old, we guarantee
the existence of more benefits, as well as of more benefits weighted according

to the levels of self-interest at which they fall. The death of the sixty-year-old thus causes a smaller *loss* of value, and is in that sense better, or less bad.

However, now compare the death of a twenty-year old and the death of an infant (or, for that matter, a (sentient) foetus). As we have seen, the Prudential View may well imply that the twenty-year-old has the strongest present self-interest in surviving, because the M-relation that links him to his future benefits is stronger. And this seems plausible. However, Prudential Prioritarianism implies that, while the twenty-year-old has the strongest present self-interest in surviving, everything else being equal, it is better if the infant survives. This is because outcome value is a function not just of their *present* self-interests, but of *all* of their self-interests in the relevant outcomes. It may be suggested that this is implausible. Nevertheless, I believe that Prudential Prioritarianism has the right implications, even for cases like this. As I have argued in this chapter, we should *morally* be impartial concerning the self-interests individuals have at different times. And so we should not focus only on the *present* self-interests of the twenty-year-old and the infant.

Interestingly, Jeff McMahan has recently argued for the opposite view, and from a view of prudence that is quite similar to mine. McMahan believes that, everything else being equal, it is morally worse if the twenty-year-old dies than if an infant or foetus dies. This is part of the reason why it is (almost always) wrong to kill a twenty-year old, but usually not wrong to perform an abortion (even of a sentient foetus). Indeed, McMahan seems to have the more intuitive view here.

As I pointed out in Chapter 4 (Section 4.6), McMahan's account relies in part on his account of the badness of death, which again in part relies on the Time-relative Interest Account. Like the Prudential Account of the badness of death, the Time-relative Interest Account implies that the future benefits death deprives an individual of should be discounted for reductions in relevant psychological relations when assessing the badness of her death. With respect to killing beings that do not have a psychology comprehensive enough to be worthy of respect—where such worth is based on the capacity for autonomy—the wrongness of killing them consists in the frustration of time-relative interests. And according to McMahan, an individual's time-relative self-interest in not being killed is her self-interest, at the time of her death, in the appropriately discounted benefits that would otherwise have occurred in her future.

More generally, the Time-relative Interest Account suggests that a self-interest is relevant for the moral assessment of an act, insofar as it is an actual self-interest and is affected (satisfied or frustrated) by the act (McMahan 2002: 283). Thus, not just present but also (actual) future self-interests may be relevant for assessing the moral status of present acts. Furthermore, as a result of this, McMahan's account of the wrongness of killing is time-relative in the sense that it is an individual's self-interest at the time of her death in her future that should be taken into account when explaining the wrongness of killing her (as well as when explaining the badness, to her, of dying then). After all, if an individual is killed, her future self-interests are not actual, and so they are not relevant to the moral value of the killing.

In terms of beings that are worthy of respect, McMahan argues that the wrongness of killing them consists not only in frustrating their time-relative interests, but also in violating the requirement of respect. Nevertheless, it is *equally* wrong to kill two persons who are worthy of respect, no matter how much their time-relative interests in survival differ (assuming that they both do have an interest in survival). Thus, McMahan (2002: ch. 3) proposes a 'two-tiered' account of the wrongness of killing, that relies on both time-relative interests and respect for autonomous persons.

According to McMahan, then, there are two reasons why, everything else being equal, it is worse to kill the twenty-year-old than to kill the infant. It is worse because only the twenty-year-old is a being worthy of respect (which, of course, does not mean that there are no direct moral reasons not to kill the infant). And it is worse to kill the twenty-year-old because he has a stronger present self-interest in his future than does the infant.

However, I have a number of reservations with respect to McMahan's account. First, it does not quite seem to have the implications with respect to killing a twenty-year-old and killing an infant that McMahan seems to want. Suppose we will either kill a twenty-year-old or an infant (perhaps we cannot avoid hitting one of them with our car, but by turning the wheel we can determine who will be killed). Presume also that, as a matter of fact, we kill the twenty-year-old. Clearly, the twenty-year-old has a strong actual self-interest in surviving, namely the self-interest he has at the time of the killing. But the infant also has such a self-interest. Since he is not killed, the infant has a strong actual *future* self-interest in surviving. Furthermore, this is a self-interest that will exist and be fulfilled because we steer the car towards the twenty-year-old. So it is by no means clear why a concern for the actual self-interests of the infant and of the twenty-year-old should render our act of killing the twenty-year-old wrong. Of course, McMahan's second reason for why it is worse to kill the twenty-year-old, namely that only he is worthy of respect, is still in play, but that is a different matter.

Additionally, as I also pointed out in Chapter 2 (Section 2.5), I have certain reservations about the modal partiality with respect to self-interests inherent in McMahan's account. I shall not repeat my discussion here, but simply note the general problem that there are certain benefits that seem relevant for our moral assessments that have no weight in this account. Moreover, this is coupled with a curious feature of an actualist account of the rightness of acts, namely that the moral status of the act of bringing an outcome about may depend on whether or not one brings the outcome about. Thus, one can make an act—that would otherwise have been wrong—right simply by performing it. This is because, by performing it, one can affect the actuality of the self-interests on the basis of which the act should be assessed.

Having now considered McMahan's alternative account, let me return to Prudential Prioritarianism. Consider again briefly the implication that, everything else being equal, an outcome in which a twenty-year-old is killed is better, or less bad, than an outcome in which an infant or a foetus is killed. As I said, I think this is as it should be. But it is also worth pointing out that this implication is of course compatible with a deontological constraint against killing the twenty-year-old, for example, because only he is an autonomous person. Thus, one of the reasons why McMahan claims it is morally worse to kill a twenty-year-old than to kill an infant or a foetus is equally available to prudential prioritarians.

Let me also examine briefly the implications of Prudential Prioritarianism for the issue of abortion. Here, it will make a difference what assumptions we make about population ethics. Suppose first we adopt the stance, to which I referred towards the end of the last chapter, according to which our distributive principles apply only to same number comparisons. In that case I believe we should say that Prudential Prioritarianism does not apply to the abortion of foetuses that do not yet realize Relation M. I have argued that what matters, prudentially, is not when we begin to exist but when we start to realize this relation. Assuming the restriction to same number comparisons, we should then claim that since assessing the abortion of an unconscious foetus will involve comparing an outcome in which an M-related individual exists, and an outcome in which it does not exist, this is a different number comparison. Therefore, Prudential Prioritarianism does not imply that it is bad to perform such an abortion (nor, of course, does it imply that it is good).

When considering the abortion of a conscious foetus, on the other hand, we will be comparing same number outcomes. And since we should be morally impartial between the self-interests individuals realize at different times, we cannot rule out such a foetus's self-interests merely because they are temporally located in the future. Of course, if a foetus is aborted, her 'future' self-interests will not be actual but merely possible. However, as I have argued, we should not restrict ourselves to self-interests that are actual; merely possible self-interests matter too. And once we factor in not only present self-interests but also possible future self-interests, the case against aborting a conscious foetus becomes much stronger.

Suppose, instead, that we apply our prioritarian principle to different number comparisons, which is one of the other options I listed at the end of the last chapter. In that case, Prudential Prioritarianism implies that the future self-interests of not only conscious foetuses, but also non-conscious foetuses, have moral significance. And since Prudential Prioritarianism implies that we should be impartial between self-interests held at different times, the case against aborting non-conscious foetuses becomes (at least roughly) equivalent to the case against aborting conscious foetuses, everything else being equal.

However, even assuming that we apply Prudential Prioritarianism to different number comparisons, it does not follow that abortion cannot be justified. In light of my discussion of the Disturbing Conclusion, and in light of the existing rate of population growth, it seems plausible that there are limits to how much further population growth we can justify, even adopting a prioritarian principle. Assuming, then, that what can be justified is at most a limited increase, it is not so clear that this is best accomplished, or partially accomplished, by a ban on abortion. There are several reasons for this.

First, if women are forced to go through with their pregnancies, this is likely to have severe psychological costs for many women and couples. Second, there are other possible policies that may increase population size where and when most needed, including of course the provision of various (positive) incentives. Third, a ban on abortion is likely in many cases to cause parents to have children at a time when they are less inclined to have them for social, emotional, or other reasons, and then not to have children at a later time when they would in fact be more inclined and better equipped to do so (Hare 1975: 221). For example, a couple may be prepared to have only two children, and may come to have them at a very young age if they do not have access to abortion. Fourth, it is well known that a ban on abortion does not prevent (although it may reduce the number of) abortions, but it does significantly lower the safety of this procedure. And finally, in developed nations, a ban on abortion will increase the workforce and so reduce the need for labour migration from developing nations, where such migration tends to significantly increase the standard of living of migrants and of people in the countries from which they migrate (due to large remittances; Pritchett 2006; World Bank 2006). Clearly, the value of such migration may be substantial in prioritarian terms.

10.11 Prudential Prioritarianism and Impersonal Values

I now need to consider how well my account of justice in this chapter accommodates my aim of developing a person-affecting account of outcome value. In fact, my account violates both the Wide Person-affecting Principle and the Strong Wide Person-affecting Principle. And as you may remember, the former principle is included in my favoured welfarist doctrine, and the latter principle partly motivates my criticism of egalitarianism. I shall return to the issue of whether my account is compatible with welfarism in the next section. In this section, I shall consider the implications with respect to the Strong Wide Person-affecting Principle.

There are in fact two types of situations in which my account may seem incompatible with the Strong Wide Person-affecting Principle. In Section 10.6, I pointed out that Prudential Prioritarianism is not indifferent with respect to how a certain sum of welfare is distributed on a particular life. Thus, everything else being equal, it is better if a fixed sum of welfare is equally distributed over an individual's life. However, even if we go from an unequal to an equal distribution of welfare over a life, this does not seem to be better for the individual leading this life in any respect. And so the claim that the equal distribution is better seems to contradict the Strong Wide Person-affecting Principle.

This principle is in fact under-described in terms of its temporal focus. When it is said that in order for an outcome to be better (or worse) than another, the former outcome must be better (or worse) for someone, or the latter outcome worse (or better) for someone, it is not clear *when* these outcomes must be better or worse for these individuals. The natural reading, which is also the one I have implicitly assumed so far, is that an outcome must be better or worse for someone in a temporally neutral sense. Yet, this is not the only possible reading. Instead, it may be suggested that an outcome need only be better or worse for someone *at some particular point in time*. With such a 'time-slice' interpretation, the claim that an equal distribution over a life is better than an unequal distribution is in fact compatible with the Strong Wide Person-affecting Principle. After all, when we go from an unequal to an equal distribution of a fixed sum, we must increase the share of benefits in some part of this life. And this interpretation is of course available to the prudential prioritarian.

The other type of case in which my account seems to violate the Strong Wide Person-affecting Principle cannot be dealt with in this manner. Consider two outcomes that include a particular individual (and no one else). These two outcomes do not differ with respect to welfare; in fact, the welfare this individual enjoys at any particular time in one outcome equals the welfare she enjoys at that very time in the other outcome. However, she realizes a stronger M-relation in the former outcome than in the latter. And Prudential Prioritarianism favours the existence of stronger M-relations over weaker ones. And so, according to this principle, the outcome in which the individual realizes the stronger M-relation is better. But, this judgement contradicts the Strong Wide Person-affecting Principle. After all, these two outcomes do not differ with respect to this individual's welfare.

As I said, the strategy I mentioned in connection with the first type of case is not available here. The two outcomes differ neither with respect to this individual's lifetime level of welfare, nor with respect to the timing of the welfare units. Therefore, it will not help to embrace a 'time-slice' interpretation of the Strong Wide Person-affecting Principle, because there is *no* time at which this individual is better off in one outcome than in the other.

Rather, my account implies the rejection of the Strong Wide Person-affecting Principle. Obviously, this raises some important issues. First, how does it affect my objections to egalitarianism? In Chapter 7 (Section 7.4) I argued that egalitarianism is threatened by the Levelling Down Objection. And when explaining the force of this objection, I appealed to the Strong Wide Person-affecting Principle. Roughly, levelling down cannot improve the value of an outcome in any respect because no one is affected for the better. In other words, the link between improvements in equality and improvements in welfare is entirely contingent. But as it turns out, my account of justice implies that the link between improvements in outcome value and improvements in welfare is also contingent. We can have the former even in the absence of the latter.

However, I now want to suggest that, ultimately, the Strong Wide Person-affecting Principle should be replaced with:

> *The Prudential Person-affecting Principle.* An outcome, O_1, cannot be *in any respect* better (or worse) than another outcome, O_2, if there is no one who, were O_1 to obtain, would at some time have a stronger (or weaker) self-interest in O_1 than in O_2, and no one who, were O_2 to obtain, would at some time have a weaker (or stronger) self-interest in O_2 than in O_1.

Before I explain why, let me point out how this principle is in fact compatible with the claim that we can improve the value of an outcome simply by increasing the strength of an M-relation. Consider again the two outcomes that differ only in that an individual realizes a stronger M-relation in one than in the other. In the outcome in which she realizes the stronger relation, at each point in time, she is more strongly related to herself at other times at which she enjoys benefits than she is in the other outcome. Therefore, clearly there are times at which she has a stronger self-interest in the outcome in which she realizes the stronger relation. And so the Prudential Person-affecting Principle is compatible with the claim that this outcome is better.

How can the Prudential Person-affecting Principle be motivated? It differs from the Strong Wide Person-affecting Principle in two respects. First, it explicitly claims that what is required, in order for an outcome to be better than another, is only that at least one individual has a stronger self-interest in the former outcome at *some* point in time (or alternatively, were the latter outcome to obtain, at some point in time has a weaker self-interest in this outcome). It this respect, it responds to my claim that self-interests may vary over time. Since self-interests can vary over time, even if an individual has a stronger self-interest in one outcome than in another at one time, she need not have a stronger self-interest in the former outcome at a different time. And it would be unreasonable to require that there must be an individual who has a stronger self-interest in one outcome at all times in order for this outcome to be better.

The other respect in which the Prudential Person-affecting Principle differs from the Strong Wide Person-affecting Principle is the following. The Prudential Person-affecting Principle expands the Strong Wide Person-affecting Principle in the sense that it links outcome value to self-interest, not just to welfare. As I have argued, self-interests rely on both welfare and Relation M. And when we realize that an individual's self-interests depend also on Relation M, we can see how outcome value can depend on this relation. For example, by increasing the strength of the M-relation an individual realizes over time, we can increase her present prudential concern for her future benefits. In a sense, we are thus giving her more to look forward to. And if she is now undergoing some hardship that will enable her to reap certain benefits in the future, by strengthening her M-relation we may ensure that, from her present point of view, these future benefits more fully *compensate* her for her present hardships. Thus, it is something that we may have reason to do *for her sake*.

Of course, it can be objected that if we may revise the Strong Wide Person-affecting Principle such as to accommodate the importance of Relation M for outcome value, surely there is no principled reason why we may not also revise it such as to embrace the importance of other factors, say, the value of equality. And obviously, this would be unfortunate for me in light of my criticism of egalitarianism. But before I address this point, let me indicate why, just like the Strong Wide Person-affecting Principle, the Prudential Person-affecting Principle rules out egalitarianism.

Consider an outcome in which there is perfect equality and an outcome in which we add a number of positive welfare units such that everyone is always better off than in the former outcome, but unequally so. Suppose also that these two outcomes do not differ with respect to the strengths of the M-relations that are realized in them. With these assumptions, at each point in time, everyone will have a stronger self-interest in the unequal outcome. After all, these outcomes differ only with respect to welfare, and in this respect the unequal outcome is better for everyone at all times. Therefore, the Prudential Person-affecting Principle is incompatible with egalitarianism, and so by substituting this principle for the Strong Wide Person-affecting Principle I do not open the door for egalitarianism.

Nevertheless, as I have just mentioned, an egalitarian may ask why we *cannot* allow deviations from the Strong Wide Person-affecting Principle to accommodate changes in inequality if we *can* allow deviations to accommodate changes in Relation M. Of course, as is clear from my discussion of egalitarianism in Chapter 7, I have no conclusive argument for why we cannot include equality in our theory of outcomes, and so none for why we cannot allow deviations from the Strong Wide Person-affecting Principle to accommodate this value. However, let me just point out that the Prudential Person-affecting Principle is similar to the Strong Wide Person-affecting Principle in a way that any principle compatible with the value of equality could not be. Usually, self-interests are taken to depend only on welfare. But I have argued that they also depend on Relation M. Thus, the Prudential Person-affecting Principle may be claimed to be the natural extension of the Strong Wide Person-affecting Principle once we realize that self-interests rely on both of these factors. Equality, on the other hand, is a value that can be realized quite independently of any increase in self-interest fulfilment. It is a quite different kind of value.

10.12 Prudential Prioritarianism and Welfarism

How does the account of justice I have developed in this chapter relate to welfarism? As you may remember, I have defined Person-affecting Outcome Welfarism as the view that the value of an outcome is an increasing person-affecting function only of the individual benefits it contains. There are three respects in which Prudential Prioritarianism does not satisfy this welfarist doctrine.

First, as we have just seen, Prudential Prioritarianism does not satisfy the Strong Wide Person-affecting Principle (and for the same reason, it does not satisfy the Wide Person-affecting Principle). Second, it implies that outcome value is a function *not* only of benefits, but also of Relation M. And third, it does not satisfy the Pareto Principle. After all, two identical welfare distributions need not have the same value, and while an increase in welfare will always contribute to the value of an outcome, this increase may be outweighed by changes in the strength of the M-relations realized in it.

Thus, the argument presented in this chapter provides a reason to reject Person-affecting Outcome Welfarism (or indeed, any purely welfarist framework). But, of course, the changes one would have to make to this framework to accommodate the argument would not be drastic. One such change would be to replace the Wide Person-affecting Principle with something like the Prudential Person-affecting Principle. Another would be to claim that outcome value is a function not (only) of individual benefits but more generally of self-interests. And a third would be to revise the Pareto Principle in terms of such interests. Thus, as I have pointed out, we could propose a Pareto Principle for fixed M-relations. More generally, we could claim that if two outcomes do not differ with respect to either welfare or M-relations, or with respect to the timing of these values, they are equally good. And if at least one individual at some point in time has a stronger self-interest in one outcome than in another, and no individual at any time has a stronger self-interest in the latter, the former outcome is better. While the resulting doctrine would not be a welfarist one, it would of course be closely related to welfarism. It would be a doctrine of 'self-interestism'.

10.13 Summary

I have argued that if we hold the Prudential View we should deny that moral rules apply only to conflicts of interest between different individuals. Rather, our distributive principles apply even to single-individual outcomes. Thus, just as we have a moral reason to be impartial concerning the interests of different individuals, we have a moral reason to be impartial concerning the interests a single individual has at different times, even in cases where this individual does not have a present prudential reason to be indifferent between them.

I have also considered Parfit's claim, according to which a reductionist account of personal identity implies that we should give less weight to our distribution-sensitive principles. Against this I have argued that a reductionist account is in fact quite compatible with distribution-sensitivity. And so we may continue to endorse prioritarianism.

However, as prioritarians, we need an account of the temporal unit of distributive concern. I have suggested that many political philosophers are attracted to a 'whole lives' account because they take it to follow from the Compensation Argument. But I have argued that if we accept the Prudential View, what the Compensation Argument suggests is not Whole Lives Prioritarianism but Prudential Prioritarianism. And I have contended that this principle is in various respects more plausible than are alternative prioritarian accounts of justice. It tends to favour (a) an equal over an unequal distribution of welfare over a life, (b) strengthening the M-relation of the worse off rather than of the better off (assuming positive welfare levels), (c) the strengthening of weak M-relations over the strengthening of strong ones, (d) the existence of strong M-relations over weak ones, and (e) a benefit that falls sooner rather than later to compensate for a past or present misfortune. Furthermore, it tends to downplay the importance of misfortunes for present distribution, the further into the past they lie.

As we have seen, Prudential Prioritarianism is not fully welfarist. But it is, of course, fairly similar. It implies that outcome value is a function only of self-interests. Importantly, nor does Prudential Prioritarianism satisfy the Strong Wide Person-affecting Principle on which I partly relied in my criticism of egalitarianism. However, I have argued that this principle should be replaced with something like the Prudential Person-affecting Principle—a principle that is equally hostile to the (alleged) value of equality.

Bibliography

Aristotle (1955), *The Nicomachean Ethics* (Harmondsworth: Penguin Books).

Armstrong, D. M. (1978), *A Theory of Universals* (Cambridge: Cambridge University Press).

—— (1997), *A World of States of Affairs* (Cambridge: Cambridge University Press).

Arneson, R. J. (1989), 'Equality and Equal Opportunity for Welfare', *Philosophical Studies*, 56/1: 77–93.

—— (2000), 'Luck Egalitarianism and Prioritarianism', *Ethics*, 110/2: 339–49.

—— (2006), 'Desert and Equality', in N. Holtug and K. Lippert-Rasmussen (eds), *Egalitarianism. New Essays on the Nature and Value of Equality* (Oxford: Clarendon Press), 262–93.

Arrhenius, G. (2000), 'Future Generations: A Challenge for Moral Theory', dissertation (Uppsala University).

Attfield, R. (1995), 'Population and the Total View', in R. Attfield, *Value, Obligation, and Meta-ethics* (Amsterdam: Rodopi), 149–73.

Audi, R. (1996), 'Intuitionism, Pluralism, and the Foundations of Ethics', in W. Sinnott-Armstrong and M. Timmons (eds), *Moral Knowledge* (New York: Oxford University Press), 101–36.

Barry, B. (1989a), *Theories of Justice* (London: Harvester-Wheatsheaf).

—— (1989b), 'Utilitarianism and Preference Change', *Utilitas*, 1/2: 278–82.

Bayles, M. D. (1975–6), 'Harm to the Unconceived', *Philosophy and Public Affairs*, 5/2: 292–304.

Benbaji, Y. (2005), 'The Doctrine of Sufficiency: A Defence', *Utilitas*, 17/3: 310–32.

Berscheid, E. and Gangestad. S. (1982), 'The Social Psychological Implications of Facial Physical Attractiveness', *Clinics in Plastic Surgery*, 9/3: 289–96.

Bigelow, J. and Pargetter, R. (1988), 'Morality, Potential Persons and Abortion', *American Philosophical Quarterly*, 25/2: 173–81.

Blackburn, S. (1984), *Spreading the Word* (Oxford: Clarendon Press).

Blackorby, C., Bossert, W., and Donaldson, D. (1997), 'Critical Level Utilitarianism and the Population-ethics Dilemma', *Economics and Philosophy*, 13/2: 197–230.

Blackorby, C., Donaldson, D., and Weymark, J. A. (1984), 'Social Choice with Interpersonal Utility Comparisons: A Diagrammatic Introduction', *International Economic Review*, 25/2: 327–56.

Bodanszky, E. (1987), 'Parfit on Selves and Their Interests', *Analysis*, 47/1: 47–50.

Brandt, R. (1979), *A Theory of the Good and the Right* (Oxford: Clarendon Press).

Brennan, A. (1988), *Conditions of Identity* (Oxford: Clarendon Press).

Brickman, P., Coates, D., and Janoff-Bulman, R. (1978), 'Lottery Winners and Accident Victims: Is Happiness Relative?', *Journal of Personality and Social Psychology*, 36/8: 917–27.

Brink, D. O. (1989), *Moral Realism and the Foundations of Ethics* (Cambridge: Cambridge University Press).

—— (1997), 'Rational Egoism and the Separateness of Persons', in J. Dancy (ed.), *Reading Parfit* (Oxford: Blackwell Publishers), 96–134.

Broome, J. (1991), *Weighing Goods* (Oxford: Basil Blackwell).

—— (1992), *Counting the Cost of Global Warming* (Cambridge: White Horse Press).

—— (1993), 'Goodness is Reducible to Betterness: The Evil of Death is the Value of Life', in P. Koslowski and Y. Shionoya (eds), *The Good and the Economical* (Berlin: Springer-Verlag), 70–84.

—— (2004), *Weighing Lives* (Oxford: Oxford University Press).

—— (forthcoming), 'Equality versus Priority: A Useful Distinction', in D. Wikler and C. J. L. Murray (eds), *'Goodness' and 'Fairness': Ethical Issues in Health Resource Allocation* (World Health Organization).

Bykvist, K. (1996), 'Utilitarian Deontologies? On Preference Utilitarianism and Agent-Relative Value', *Theoria*, 62/1–2: 124–43.

—— (1998), 'Changing Preferences: A Study in Preferentialism', dissertation (Uppsala University).

Carlson, E. (1994), *Some Basic Problems of Consequentialism* (Uppsala: Uppsala University).

—— (1998), 'Mere Addition and Two Trilemmas of Population Ethics', *Economics and Philosophy*, 14/2: 283–306.

Carter, W. R. (1982), 'Do Zygotes Become People?', *Mind*, 91/1: 77–95.

Cristiano, T. (2006), 'A Foundation for Egalitarianism', in N. Holtug and K. Lippert-Rasmussen (eds), *Egalitarianism. New Essays on the Nature and Value of Equality* (Oxford: Clarendon Press), 41–82.

Cohen, G. A. (1989), 'On the Currency of Egalitarian Justice', *Ethics*, 99/4: 906.

—— (2000), 'The Pareto Argument for Inequality', in M. Clayton and A. Williams (eds), *The Ideal of Equality* (London: Macmillan; originally published in *Social Philosophy and Policy*, 12, 1995), 162–81.

Copp, D. (1993), 'Reasons and Needs', in L. G. Frey and C. W. Morris (eds), *Value, Welfare and Morality* (Cambridge: Cambridge University Press), 112–37.

Cowen, T. and Parfit, D. (1992), 'Against the Social Discount Rate', in P. Laslett and J. S. Fishkin (eds), *Justice Between Age Groups and Generations* (New Haven: Yale University Press), 144–61.

Crisp, R. (1992), 'Utilitarianism and the Life of Virtue', *Philosophical Quarterly*, 42/167: 139–60.

—— (2003), 'Equality, Priority, and Compassion', *Ethics*, 113/4: 745–63.

—— (2006), *Reasons and the Good* (Oxford: Clarendon Press).

Dancy, J. (1993), *Moral Reasons* (Oxford: Blackwell).

Daniels, N. (1979), 'Wide Reflective Equilibrium and Theory Acceptance in Ethics', *Journal of Philosophy*, 76/4: 256–82.

—— (1996a), 'The Prudential Life-span Account of Justice Across Generations', in N. Daniels, *Justice and Justification: Reflective Equilibrium in Theory and Practice* (Cambridge: Cambridge University Press), 257–83.

——(1996b), 'Moral Theory and the Plasticity of Persons', in N. Daniels, *Justice and Justification: Reflective Equilibrium in Theory and Practice* (Cambridge: Cambridge University Press), 120–43.

Davis, N. A. (1991), 'Contemporary Deontology', in P. Singer (ed.), *A Companion to Ethics* (Oxford: Basil Blackwell), 205–18.

Doran, B. (2001), 'Reconsidering the Levelling Down Objection against Egalitarianism', *Utilitas*, 13/1: 65–85.

Dworkin, R. (1981a), 'What is Equality? Part 1: Equality of Welfare', *Philosophy and Public Affairs*, 10/3: 185–246.

——(1981b), 'What is Equality? Part 2: Equality of Resources', *Philosophy and Public Affairs*, 10/4: 283–345.

——(1984), 'Rights as Trumps', in J. Waldron (ed.), *Theories of Rights* (Oxford: Oxford University Press), 153–67.

Elliot, R. (1993), 'Identity and the Ethics of Gene Therapy', *Bioethics*, 7/1: 27–40.

——(1997), 'Contingency, Community and Intergenerational Justice', in N. Fotion and J. C. Heller (eds), *Contingent Future Persons* (Dordrecht: Kluwer Academic Publishers), 157–70.

Engelhardt, H. T., Jr., (1986), *The Foundations of Bioethics* (New York: Oxford University Press).

Epicurus, (1940), 'Letter to Menoeceus', in W. J. Oates (ed.), *The Stoic and Epicurean Philosophers* (New York: Modern Library), 30–34.

Fehige, C. (1998), 'A Pareto Principle for Possible People', in C. Fehige and U. Wessels (eds), *Preferences* (Berlin: Walter de Gruyter), 508–43.

——and Wessels, U. (1998), 'Preferences—An Introduction', in C. Fehige and U. Wessels (eds), *Preferences* (Berlin: Walter de Gruyter), xx–xliii.

Feinberg, J. (1980), 'The Rights of Animals and Unborn Generations', in J. Feinberg, *Rights, Justice, and the Bounds of Liberty* (Princeton: Princeton University Press), 159–84.

——(1984), *Harm to Others* (Oxford: Oxford University Press).

Feldman, F. (1992), *Confrontations with the Reaper* (New York: Oxford University Press).

——(2004), *Pleasure and the Good Life: Concerning the Nature, Varieties, and Plausibility of Hedonism* (Oxford: Clarendon Press).

Fleurbaey, M. (forthcoming), 'Equality versus Priority: How Relevant is the Distinction?', in D. Wickler and C. J. L. Murray (eds), *'Goodness' and 'Fairness': Ethical Issues in Health Resource Allocation* (World Health Organization).

Frankfurt, H. (1987), 'Equality as a Moral Ideal', *Ethics*, 98/1: 21–43.

Garrett, B. (1990), 'Personal Identity and Extrinsicness', *Danish Yearbook of Philosophy*, 25: 23–40.

——(1998), *Personal Identity and Self-Consciousness* (London: Routledge).

Gauthier, D. (1986), *Morals by Agreement* (Oxford: Clarendon Press).

Glover, J. (1977), *Causing Death and Saving Lives* (London: Penguin Books).

——(1992), 'Future People, Disability, and Screening', in P. Laslett and J. S. Fishkin (eds), *Justice Between Age Groups and Generations* (New Haven: Yale University Press), 127–43.

Goodin, R. E. (1987), 'Egalitarianism, Fetishistic and Otherwise', *Ethics*, 98/1: 44–9.

—— (1991a), 'Utility and the Good', in P. Singer (ed.), *A Companion to Ethics* (Oxford: Basil Blackwell), 241–8.

—— (1991b), 'Actual Preferences, Actual People', *Utilitas*, 3/1: 113–19.

Green, M. B. and D. Wickler, (1980), 'Brain Death and Personal Identity', *Philosophy and Public Affairs*, 9/2: 105–33.

Griffin, J. (1986), *Well-Being* (Oxford: Clarendon Press).

Hanser, M. (1990), 'Harming Future People', *Philosophy and Public Affairs*, 19/1: 47–70.

Hare, R. M. (1963), *Freedom and Reason* (Oxford: Clarendon Press).

—— (1975), 'Abortion and the Golden Rule', *Philosophy & Public Affairs*, 4/3: 201–22.

—— (1981), *Moral Thinking* (Oxford: Clarendon Press).

—— (1988), 'When Does Potentiality Count? A Comment on Lockwood', *Bioethics*, 2/3: 214–26.

—— (1989), 'Rawls's Theory of Justice', in R. M. Hare, *Essays in Ethical Theory* (Oxford: Clarendon Press; originally published in *Philosophical Quarterly*, 23, 1973), 145–74.

—— (1991), 'Moral Reasoning About the Environment', in B. Almond and D. Hill (eds), *Applied Philosophy* (London: Routledge).

—— (1993), 'Possible People', in R. M. Hare, *Essays on Bioethics* (Oxford: Clarendon Press), 67–83.

—— (1998), 'Preferences of Possible People', in C. Fehige and U. Wessels (eds), *Preferences* (Berlin: Walter de Gruyter), 399–405.

Harris, J. (1985), *The Value of Life* (London: Routledge).

Harsanyi, J. C. (1982), 'Morality and the Theory of Rational Behaviour', in A. Sen and B. Williams (eds), *Utilitarianism and Beyond* (Cambridge: Cambridge University Press), 39–62.

Hausman, D. M. (forthcoming), 'Equality Versus Priority: How Relevant is the Distinction?', in D. Wikler and C. J. L. Murray (eds), *'Goodness' and 'Fairness': Ethical Issues in Health Resource Allocation* (World Health Organization).

Heyd, D. (1992), *Genethics: Moral Issues in the Creation of People* (Berkeley: University of California Press).

Holtug, N. (1996a), 'Is Welfare All That Matters in Our Moral Obligations to Animals?', *Acta Agriculturae Scandinavica*, section A, suppl. 27: 16–21.

—— (1996b), 'In Defence of the Slogan', in W. Rabinowicz (ed.), *Preference and Value: Preferentialism in Ethics*, Studies in Philosophy (Lund: Department of Philosophy, Lund University), 64–89.

—— (1998), 'Egalitarianism and the Levelling Down Objection', *Analysis*, 58/2: 166–74.

—— (1999), 'Utility, Priority and Possible People', *Utilitas*, 11/1: 16–36.

—— (2000), 'Against Deontology', *Sats—Nordic Journal of Philosophy*, 1/2: 125–41.

—— (2001), 'On the Value of Coming into Existence', *Journal of Ethics*, 5/4: 361–84.

—— (2002) 'Review of Torbjörn Tännsjö's *Hedonistic Utilitarianism*', manuscript.

—— (2003a), 'Good for Whom?', *Theoria*, 69/1–2: 4–20.

—— (2003b), 'Welfarism—the Very Idea', *Utilitas*, 15/2: 151–74.

—— (2004), 'Person-affecting Moralities', in J. Ryberg and T. Tännsjö (eds), *The Repugnant Conclusion: Essays on Population Ethics* (Dordrecht: Kluwer Academic Publishers), 129–61.

—— (2005), 'Equality, Priority and Levelling Down', in A. G. Parkis (ed.), *Contemporary Ethical Issues* (New York: Nova Science Publishers), 97–112.

—— (2006a), 'Prioritarianism', in N. Holtug and K. Lippert-Rasmussen (eds), *Egalitarianism. New Essays on the Nature and Value of Equality* (Oxford: Clarendon Press), 129–56.

—— (2006b), 'Personal Identity, Self-interest and Preferences', in L. V. Siegal (ed.), *Philosophy and Ethics* (New York: Nova Science Publishers), 59–114.

—— (2007a), 'A Note on Conditional Egalitarianism', *Economics and Philosophy*, 23/1: 45–63.

—— (2007b), 'Animals: Equality for Animals', in J. Ryberg, T. S. Petersen and C. Wolf (eds), *New Waves in Applied Ethics* (Basingstoke: Palgrave Macmillan), 1–24.

—— (2009), 'Who Cares About Identity?', in M. A. Roberts and D. T. Wasserman (eds), *Harming Future Persons. Ethics, Genetics and the Nonidentity Problem* (Dordrecht: Springer), 71–92.

Holtug, N. and Lippert-Rasmussen, K. (2006), 'An Introduction to Contemporary Egalitarianism', in N. Holtug and K. Lippert-Rasmussen (eds), *Egalitarianism. New Essays on the Nature and Value of Equality* (Oxford: Clarendon Press), 1–37.

Holtug, N. and Sandøe, P. (1996), 'Who Benefits? Why Personal Identity Does Not Matter in a Moral Evaluation of Germ-line Gene Therapy', *Journal of Applied Philosophy*, 13/2: 157–66.

Hooker, B. (2000), *Ideal Code, Real World* (Oxford: Clarendon Press).

Hurka, T. (1983), 'Value and Population Size', *Ethics*, 93/3: 496.

Jackson, F. (1991), 'Decision-theoretic Consequentialism and the Nearest and Dearest Objection', *Ethics*, 101/3: 461–82.

—— (1998), *From Metaphysics to Ethics: A Defence of Conceptual Analysis* (Oxford: Clarendon Press).

Jensen, K. K. (2003), 'What is the Difference between (Moderate) Egalitarianism and Prioritarianism?', *Economics and Philosophy*, 19/1: 89–109.

Johansson, J. (2005), *Mortal Beings: On the Metaphysics and Value of Death* (Stockholm: Almqvist & Wiksell International).

Johnston, M. (1997), 'Human Concerns without Superlative Selves', in J. Dancy (ed.), *Reading Parfit* (Oxford: Blackwell Publishers), 149–79.

Kagan, S. (1988), 'The Additive Fallacy', *Ethics*, 99/1: 5–31.

—— (1989), *The Limits of Morality* (Oxford: Clarendon Press).

—— (1998), *Normative Ethics* (Boulder, CO: Westview Press).

Kant, I. (1965), *Grundlegung zur Metaphysik der Sitten* (Hamburg: Felix Meiner Verlag).

Kappel, K. (1997), 'Equality, Priority, and Time', *Utilitas*, 9/2: 203–25.

Kavka, G. S. (1982), 'The Paradox of Future Individuals', *Philosophy and Public Affairs*, 11/2: 93–112.

Kim, J. (1996), *Philosophy of Mind* (Boulder, CO: Westview Press).

Kirkham, R. (1997), *Theories of Truth* (Cambridge, MA: The MIT Press).

Kitcher, P. (2000), 'Parfit's Puzzle', *Noûs*, 34/4: 550–77.

Korsgaard, C. M. (1983), 'Two Distinctions in Goodness', *The Philosophical Review*, 92/2: 169–95.

—— (1989), 'Personal Identity and the Unity of Agency: A Kantian Response to Parfit', *Philosophy & Public Affairs*, 18/2: 103–31.

Kripke, S. (1980), *Naming and Necessity* (Oxford: Basil Blackwell).

Kuhse, H. (1987), *The Sanctity-of-Life Doctrine in Medicine* (Oxford: Clarendon Press).

Kuhse, H. and Singer, P. (1985), *Should the Baby Live?* (Oxford: Oxford University Press).

Kymlicka, W. (1990), *Contemporary Political Philosophy* (Oxford: Clarendon Press).

Lewis, D. (1976), 'Survival and Identity', in A. Rorty (ed.), *The Identities of Persons* (Berkeley: University of California Press), 17–70.

—— (1986), *On the Plurality of Worlds* (Oxford: Blackwell Publishers).

Lippert-Rasmussen, K. (2006), 'The Insignificance of the Distinction between Telic and Deontic Egalitarianism', in N. Holtug and K. Lippert-Rasmussen (eds), *Egalitarianism. New Essays on the Nature and Value of Equality* (Oxford: Clarendon Press), 101–24.

Lockwood, M. (1979), 'Killing and the Preference for Life', *Inquiry*, 22: 157–70.

—— (1985), 'When Does a Life Begin?', in M. Lockwood (ed.), *Moral Dilemmas in Modern Medicine* (Oxford: Oxford University Press), 9–31.

—— (1994), 'Identity Matters', in K. W. M. Fulford, G. Gillett and J. M. Soskice (eds), *Medicine and Moral Reasoning* (Cambridge: Cambridge University Press), 60–74.

Lowe, E. J. (2002), *A Survey of Metaphysics* (Oxford: Oxford University Press).

Lucretius, (1940), *On the Nature of Things*, in W. J. Oates (ed.), *The Stoic and Epicurean Philosophers* (New York: The Modern Library), 69–219.

Mackie, J. (1976), *Problems From Locke* (Oxford: Clarendon Press).

—— (1985), 'The Combination of Partially-ordered Preferences', in J. Mackie, *Persons and Values*, vol. 2 (Oxford: Clarendon Press), 249–53.

Mackie, P. (1994), 'Sortal Concepts and Essential Properties', *The Philosophical Quarterly*, 44/176: 311–33.

Madell, G. (1985), 'Derek Parfit and Greta Garbo', *Analysis*, 45/1: 105–9.

Marquis, D. (1989), 'Why Abortion is Immoral', *The Journal of Philosophy*, 86/4: 183–202.

Mason, A. (2001), 'Egalitarianism and the Levelling Down Objection', *Analysis*, 61/3: 246–54.

McKerlie, D. (1989), 'Equality and Time', *Ethics*, 99/3: 475.

—— (1994), 'Equality and Priority', *Utilitas*, 6/1: 25–42.

—— (1996), 'Equality', *Ethics*, 106/2: 274–96.

—— (1997), 'Priority and Time', *Canadian Journal of Philosophy*, 27/3: 287–309.

—— (2001), 'Dimensions of Equality', *Utilitas*, 13/3: 263–88.

—— (2006), 'Egalitarianism and the Difference between Interpersonal and Intrapersonal Judgments', in N. Holtug and K. Lippert-Rasmussen (eds), *Egalitarianism: New Essays on the Nature and Value of Equality* (Oxford: Clarendon Press), 157–73.

McKie, J. (2001), 'Thinking About Possible People: A Comment on Tooley and Rachels', *Bioethics*, 15/2: 146–56.

McMahan, J. (1981), 'Problems of Population Theory', *Ethics*, 92/1: 96–127.

—— (1988), 'Death and the Value of Life', *Ethics*, 99/1: 32–61.

—— (1995), 'The Metaphysics of Brain Death', *Bioethics*, 9/2: 91–126.

—— (1998), 'Preferences, Death, and the Ethics of Killing', in C. Fehige and U. Wessels (eds), *Preferences* (Berlin: Walter de Gruyter), 471–502.

—— (2002), *The Ethics of Killing: Problems at the Margins of Life* (New York: Oxford University Press).

Mellor, D. H., (1981), *Real Time* (Cambridge: Cambridge University Press).

Moore, A. and Crisp, R. (1996), 'Welfarism in Moral Theory', *Australasian Journal of Philosophy*, 74/4: 598–613.

Nagel, T. (1979a), 'Death', in T. Nagel, *Mortal Questions* (Cambridge: Cambridge University Press), 1–10.

—— (1979b), 'Equality', in T. Nagel, *Mortal Questions* (Cambridge: Cambridge University Press), 106–27.

—— (1986), *The View From Nowhere* (New York: Oxford University Press).

—— (1991), *Equality and Priority* (New York: Oxford University Press).

Narveson, J. (1967), 'Utilitarianism and New Generations', *Mind*, 76/301: 62–72.

—— (1976), 'Moral Problems of Population', in M. D. Bayles (ed.), *Ethics and Population* (Cambridge, MA: Schenkman), 59–80.

—— (1978), 'Future People and Us', in R. I. Sikora and B. Barry (eds), *Obligations to Future Generations* (Philadelphia: Temple University Press), 38–60.

Ng, Y.-K. (1990), 'Welfarism and Utilitarianism: A Rehabilitation', *Utilitas*, 2/2: 171–93.

Noonan, H. (1989), *Personal Identity* (London: Routledge).

Norcross, A. (1997), 'Comparing Harms: Headaches and Human Lives', *Philosophy and Public Affairs*, 26/2: 135–67.

Norman, R. (1998), 'The Social Basis of Equality', in Andrew Mason (ed.), *Ideals of Equality* (Oxford: Blackwell Publishers), 37–51.

Nozick, R. (1974), *Anarchy, State, and Utopia* (New York: Basic Books).

—— (1981), *Philosophical Explanations* (Oxford: Clarendon Press).

Oderberg, D. (1997), 'Modal Properties, Moral Status and Identity', *Philosophy and Public Affairs*, 26/3: 259–76.

Olson, E. T. (1997), *The Human Animal. Personal Identity without Psychology* (New York: Oxford University Press).

Parfit, D. (1971), 'Personal Identity', *The Philosophical Review*, 80/1: 3–27.

—— (1976), 'On Doing the Best for Our Children', in M. D. Bayles (ed.), *Ethics and Population* (Cambridge, MA: Schenkman), 100–15.

Parfit, D. (1982), 'Future Generations: Further Problems', *Philosophy and Public Affairs*, 11/2: 113–72.

—— (1984), *Reasons and Persons* (Oxford: Clarendon Press).

—— (1986a), 'Comments', *Ethics*, 96/4: 832–72.

—— (1986b), 'Overpopulation and the Quality of Life', in P. Singer (ed.), *Applied Ethics* (Oxford: Oxford University Press), 145–64.

—— (1991), *Equality or Priority?*, The Lindley Lecture, University of Kansas (reprinted in M. Clayton and A. Williams (eds), *The Ideal of Equality* (Basingstoke: Macmillan Press Ltd. 2000).

—— (1995), 'The Unimportance of Identity', in H. Harris (ed.), *Identity* (Oxford: Clarendon Press), 13–45.

—— (2004a), 'Justifiability to Each Person', in P. Stratton-Lake (ed.), *On What We Owe to Each Other* (Oxford: Blackwell Publishing), 67–89.

—— (2004b), 'Postscript', in J. Ryberg and T. Tännsjö (eds), *The Repugnant Conclusion: Essays on Population Ethics* (Dordrecht: Kluwer Academic Publishers), 257.

Paul, E. F., Miller, F. D. Jr. and Paul, P. (eds) (1997), *Self-interest* (Cambridge: Cambridge University Press).

Perry, J. (1975), 'Personal Identity, Memory, and the Problem of Circularity', in J. Perry (ed.), *Personal Identity* (Berkeley: University of California Press), 135–55.

—— (1976), 'The Importance of Being Identical', in A. Rorty (ed.), *The Identities of Persons* (Berkeley: University of California Press), 67–90.

Persson, I. (1985), 'The Universal Basis of Egoism', *Theoria*, 51/3: 137–58.

—— (1995), 'Genetic Therapy, Identity and Person-Regarding Reasons', *Bioethics*, 9/1: 16–31.

—— (1997), 'Person-affecting Principles and Beyond', in N. Fotion & J. C. Heller (eds), *Contingent Future Persons* (Dordrecht: Kluwer Academic Publishers), 41–56.

—— (2001), 'Equality, Priority and Person-affecting Value', *Ethical Theory and Moral Practice*, 4/1: 23–39.

—— (2003), 'The Badness of Unjust Inequality', *Theoria*, 69/1–2: 109–24.

—— (2004), 'The Root of the Repugnant Conclusion and its Rebuttal', in J. Ryberg and T. Tännsjö (eds), *The Repugnant Conclusion: Essays on Population Ethics* (Dordrecht: Kluwer Academic Publishers), 187–99.

—— (2006), *The Retreat of Reason: A Dilemma in the Philosophy of Life* (Oxford: Clarendon Press).

—— (2008), 'Why Levelling Down could be Worse for Prioritarianism than for Egalitarianism', *Ethical Theory and Moral Practice*, 11/3: 295–303.

Petersen, T. S., (2001), 'Generocentrism: A Critical Discussion of David Heyd', *Philosophia*, 28/1–4: 411–23.

Pettit, P. (1997), 'The Consequentialist Perspective', in M. W. Baron, P. Pettit and M. Slote (eds), *Three Methods of Ethics* (Oxford: Blackwell Publishers), 92–174.

Plantinga, A. (1979), 'Actualism and Possible Worlds', in M. J. Loux (ed.), *The Possible and the Actual* (Ithaca: Cornell University Press), 253–73.

Plato (1963), 'The Republic', in E. Hamilton and H. Cairns (eds), *The Collected Dialogues of Plato* (Princeton: Princeton University Press), 575–844.

Pritchett, L. (2006), *Let Their People Come: Breaking the Gridlock on International Labor Mobility* (Washington, DC: Center for Global Development).

Quine, W. V. O. (1961a), 'Two Dogmas of Empiricism', in W. V. O. Quine, *From a Logical Point of View*, 2nd edn (Cambridge, MA: Harvard University Press), 20–46.

—— (1961b), 'Identity, Ostension, and Hypostasis', in W. V. O. Quine, *From a Logical Point of View*, 2nd edn (Cambridge, MA: Harvard University Press), 65–79.

Quinn, W. (1993), 'Abortion: Identity and Loss', in W. Quinn, *Morality and Action* (Cambridge: Cambridge University Press), 24–54.

Rabinowicz, W. (2002), 'Prioritarianism for Prospects', *Utilitas*, 14/1: 2–21.

—— (2003), 'The Size of Inequality and Its Badness. Some Reflections Around Temkin's Inequality', *Theoria*, 69/1–2: 60–84.

Rabinowicz, W. and Österberg, J. (1996), 'Value Based on Preferences: Two Interpretations of Preference Utilitarianism', *Economics and Philosophy*, 12/1: 1–27.

Rachels, J. (1993), *The Elements of Moral Philosophy*, 2nd. edn (New York: McGraw-Hill).

Rachels, S. (1998), 'Counterexamples to the Transitivity of *Better Than*', *Australasian Journal of Philosophy*, 76/1: 71–83.

—— (2001), 'A Set of Solutions to Parfit's Problems', *Noûs*, 35/2: 214–38.

—— (2004), 'Repugnance or Intransitivity: A Repugnant but Forced Choice', in J. Ryberg and T. Tännsjö (eds), *The Repugnant Conclusion: Essays on Population Ethics* (Dordrecht: Kluwer Academic Publishers), 163–86.

Rawls, J. (1971), *A Theory of Justice* (Oxford: Oxford University Press).

Raz, J. (1986), *The Morality of Freedom* (Oxford: Clarendon Press).

Regan, T. (1984), *The Case for Animal Rights* (London: Routledge).

Roberts, M. A. (1998), *Child versus Childmaker: Future Persons and Present Duties in Ethics and the Law* (Lanham, MD: Rowman & Littlefield).

—— (2002), 'A New Way of Doing the Best That We Can: Person-based Consequentialism and the Equality Problem', *Ethics*, 112/2: 315–50.

—— (2004), 'Person-based Consequentialism and the Procreation Obligation', in J. Ryberg and T. Tännsjö (eds), *The Repugnant Conclusion: Essays on Population Ethics* (Dordrecht: Kluwer Academic Publishers), 99–128.

Roberts, M. A. and Wasserman, D. T. (eds), (2009), *Harming Future Persons: Ethics, Genetics and the Nonidentity Problem* (Dordrecht: Springer).

Rosenberg, A. (1995), 'Equality, Sufficiency, and Opportunity in the Just Society', *Social Philosophy and Policy*, 12/2: 54–71.

Ryberg, J. (1996), 'Is the Repugnant Conclusion Repugnant?', *Philosophical Papers*, 25: 161–77.

—— (2004), 'The Repugnant Conclusion and Worthwhile Living', in J. Ryberg and T. Tännsjö (eds), *The Repugnant Conclusion: Essays on Population Ethics* (Dordrecht: Kluwer Academic Publishers), 239–55.

Savage, L. J., (1992), *The Foundations of Statistics* (New York: Dover Publications).

Scanlon, T. M., (1975), 'Preference and Urgency', *The Journal of Philosophy*, 72/19: 655–69.

—— (1982), 'Contractualism and Utilitarianism', in A. Sen and B. Williams (eds), *Utilitarianism and Beyond* (Cambridge: Cambridge University Press), 103–28.

—— (1988), 'Rights, Goals, and Fairness', in S. Scheffler (ed.), *Consequentialism and Its Critics* (Oxford: Oxford University Press), 74–92.

—— (1998), *What We Owe to Each Other* (Cambridge, MA: The Belknap Press of Harvard University Press).

—— (2004), 'Replies', in P. Stratton-Lake (ed.), *On What We Owe to Each Other* (Oxford: Blackwell Publishing), 123–38.

Scheffler, S. (1982a), *The Rejection of Consequentialism* (Oxford: Clarendon Press).

—— (1982b), 'Ethics, Personal Identity, and Ideals of the Person', *Canadian Journal of Philosophy*, 12/2: 229–46.

Schultz, B. (1986), 'Persons, Selves, and Utilitarianism', *Ethics*, 96/4: 721–45.

Sen, A. (1979), 'Utilitarianism and Welfarism', *Journal of Philosophy*, 76/9: 463–89.

—— (1980), 'Equality of What?', in S. McMurrin (ed.), *Tanner Lectures on Human Values* (Cambridge: Cambridge University Press), 197–220.

—— (1987), *On Ethics and Economics* (Oxford: Blackwell).

—— (1994), 'Population: Delusions and Reality', *The New York Review*, 22 September.

—— (1997), *On Economic Inequality*, 2nd edn (Oxford: Clarendon Press).

Shoemaker, S. (1963), *Self-Knowledge and Self-Identity* (New York: Ithaca).

—— (1984), 'Personal Identity: A Materialist's Account', in S. Shoemaker and R. Swinburne, *Personal Identity* (Oxford: Basil Blackwell), 67–132.

Sidgwick, H. (1907), *The Methods of Ethics* (London: Macmillan).

Sikora, R. I. (1978), 'Is It Wrong to Prevent the Existence of Future Generations?', in R. I. Sikora and B. Barry (eds), *Obligations to Future Generations* (Philadelphia: The White Horse Press), 112–66.

Singer, P. (1974), 'Sidgwick and Reflective Equilibrium', *The Monist*, 58: 420–48.

—— (1993), *Practical Ethics* (Cambridge: Cambridge University Press).

Smith, M. (1994), *The Moral Problem* (Oxford: Blackwell).

Snowdon, P. F. (1990), 'Persons, Animals, and Ourselves', in C. Gill (ed.), *The Person and the Human Mind* (Oxford: Clarendon Press), 83–107.

Sosa, D. (1993), 'Consequences of Consequentialism', *Mind*, 102/405: 101–22.

Sosa, E. (1990), 'Surviving Matters', *Noûs*, 24/2: 297–322.

Sprigge, T. L. S. (1968), 'Professor Narveson's Utilitarianism', *Inquiry*, 11/1: 332–46.

Stalnaker, R. C. (1979), 'Possible Worlds', in M. J. Loux (ed.), *The Possible and the Actual* (Ithaca: Cornell University Press), 225–34.

Steinbock, B. (1992), *Life Before Birth* (Oxford: Oxford University Press).

Stretton, D. (2004), 'The Deprivation Argument Against Abortion', *Bioethics*, 18/2: 144–80.

Sumner, L. W. (1996), *Welfare, Happiness, and Ethics* (Oxford: Clarendon Press).

Swinburne, R. (1984), 'Personal Identity: The Dualist Theory', in S. Shoemaker and R. Swinburne, *Personal Identity* (Oxford: Basil Blackwell), 1–66.

—— (1987), 'The Structure of the Soul', in A. Peacocke and G. Gillett (eds), *Persons and Personality* (Oxford: Basil Blackwell), 33–55.

Tännsjö, T. (1998), *Hedonistic Utilitarianism* (Edinburgh: Edinburgh University Press).

—— (2002), 'Why We Ought to Accept the Repugnant Conclusion', *Utilitas*, 14/3: 339–59.

Temkin, L. (1987), 'Intransitivity and the Mere Addition Paradox', *Philosophy and Public Affairs*, 16/2: 138–87.

—— (1993a), *Inequality* (New York: Oxford University Press).

—— (1993b), 'Harmful Goods, Harmless Bads', in R.G. Frey and C. W. Morris (eds), *Value, Welfare, and Morality* (Cambridge: Cambridge University Press), 290–325.

—— (1996), 'A Continuum Argument for Intransitivity', *Philosophy and Public Affairs*, 25/3: 175–210.

—— (2000), 'Equality, Priority, and the Levelling Down Objection', in M. Clayton and A. Williams (eds), *The Ideal of Equality* (London: Macmillan), 126–61.

—— (2003a), 'Personal versus Impersonal Principles: Reconsidering the Slogan', *Theoria*, 69/1–2: 21–31.

—— (2003b), 'Equality, Priority, or What?', *Economics and Philosophy*, 19/1: 61–87.

Tersman, F. (1993), *Reflective Equilibrium: An Essay in Moral Epistemology* (Stockholm: Almqvist & Wiksell International).

Thomson, J. J. (1997), 'People and their Bodies', in J. Dancy (ed.), *Reading Parfit* (Oxford: Blackwell Publishers), 202–29.

Tooley, M. (1983), *Abortion and Infanticide* (Oxford: Clarendon Press).

Tungodden, B. (2003), 'The Value of Equality', *Economics and Philosophy*, 19/1: 1–44.

—— and Vallentyne, P. (2005), 'On the Possibility of Paretian Egalitarianism', *Journal of Philosophy*, 102: 126–54.

—— and Vallentyne, P. (2006), 'Who Are the Least Advantaged?', in N. Holtug and K. Lippert-Rasmussen (eds), *Egalitarianism: New Essays on the Nature and Value of Equality* (Oxford: Clarendon Press), 174–95.

Unger, P. (1990), *Identity, Consciousness and Value* (New York: Oxford University Press).

Vallentyne, P. (1987a), 'The Teleological/Deontological Distinction', *Journal of Value Inquiry*, 21/1: 21–32.

—— (1987b), 'Utilitarianism and the Outcomes of Actions', *Pacific Philosophical Quarterly*, 68: 57–70.

—— (2000a), 'Equality, Efficiency, and the Priority of the Worse-off', *Economics and Philosophy*, 16/1: 1–19.

—— (2000b), 'Roberts's *Child versus Childmaker: Future Persons and Present Duties in Ethics and the Law*', *Noûs*, 34/4: 634–47.

—— (2002), 'Brute Luck, Option Luck, and Equality of Initial Opportunities', *Ethics*, 112/3: 529–57.

Vallentyne, P. (2006), 'Of Mice and Men: Equality and Animals', in N. Holtug and K. Lippert-Rasmussen (eds), *Egalitarianism: New Essays on the Nature and Value of Equality* (Oxford: Clarendon Press), 211–37.

van Inwagen, P. (1990), *Material Beings* (Ithaca: Cornell University Press).

Velleman, J. D. (1991), 'Well-being and Time', *Pacific Philosophical Quarterly*, 72: 48–77.

von Wright, G. H. (1971), *The Logic of Preference* (Edinburgh: Edinburgh University Press).

Voorhoeve, A. and Binmore, K. (2003), 'Defending Transitivity against Zeno's Paradox', *Philosophy & Public Affairs*, 31/3: 272–79.

Warren, M. A. (1978), 'Do Potential People Have Moral Rights?', in R. I. Sikora and B. Barry (eds), *Obligations to Future Generations* (Philadelphia: Temple University Press), 14–30.

—— (1997), *Moral Status* (Oxford: Oxford University Press).

Wheale, A. (1980), 'The Impossibility of Liberal Egalitarianism', *Analysis*, 40/1: 13–19.

Wilkes, K. V. (1988), *Real People: Personal Identity without Thought Experiments* (Oxford: Clarendon Press).

Williams, A. (1995), 'The Revisionist Difference Principle', *Canadian Journal of Philosophy*, 25/2: 257–82.

Williams, B. (1973a), 'The Self and the Future', in B. Williams, *Problems of the Self* (Cambridge: Cambridge University Press), 46–63.

—— (1973b), 'The Makropulos Case: Reflections on the Tedium of Immortality', in B. Williams, *Problems of the Self* (Cambridge: Cambridge University Press), 82–100.

—— (1973c), 'A Critique of Utilitarianism', in J. J. C. Smart and B. Williams, *Utilitarianism: For and Against* (Cambridge: Cambridge University Press), 77–150.

—— (1990), 'Who Might I Have Been?', Ciba Foundation Symposium 149, *Human Genetic Information: Science, Law and Ethics* (Chichester: John Wiley), 167–73.

Williams, C. J. F., (1981), *What is Existence?* (Oxford: Clarendon Press).

Wolf, C. (1997), 'Person-affecting Utilitarianism and Population Policy; Or, Sissy Jupe's Theory of Social Choice', in N. Fotion and J. C. Heller (eds), *Contingent Future Persons* (Dordrecht: Kluwer Academic), 99–122.

Wolff, J. (2001), 'Levelling Down', in K. Dowding, J. Hughes and H. Margetts (eds), *Challenges to Democracy* (Hampshire: Palgrave), 18–32.

Woodward, J. (1986), 'The Non-Identity Problem', *Ethics*, 96/3: 804–31.

World Bank, (2006), *Global Economic Prospects: Economic Implications of Remittances and Migration* (Washington DC: World Bank).

Wright, C. (1988), 'Realism, Anti-realism, Irrealism, Quasi-realism', *Midwest Studies in Philosophy*, 12/1: 25–49.

Zimmerman, M. J., (2001), *The Nature of Intrinsic Value* (Lanham: Rowman and Littlefield Publishers).

Zohar, N. J. (1991), 'Prospects for 'Genetic Therapy'—Can a Person Benefit From Being Altered?', *Bioethics*, 5/4: 275–88.

Index